MICROSOFT
EXCHANGE
SERVER
IN A NUTSHELL

A Desktop Quick Reference

MICROSOFT EXCHANGE SERVER

IN A NUTSHELL

A Desktop Quick Reference

Mitch Tulloch

O'REILLY®

Beijing · *Cambridge* · *Farnham* · *Köln* · *Paris* · *Sebastopol* · *Taipei* · *Tokyo*

Microsoft Exchange Server in a Nutshell: A Desktop Quick Reference

by Mitch Tulloch

Copyright © 1999 O'Reilly & Associates, Inc. All rights reserved.
Printed in the United States of America.

Published by O'Reilly & Associates, Inc., 101 Morris Street, Sebastopol, CA 95472.

Editor: Robert Denn

Production Editor: Jane Ellin

Printing History:

April 1999:   First Edition.

This book is printed on acid-free paper with 85% recycled content, 15% post-consumer waste. O'Reilly & Associates is committed to using paper with the highest recycled content available consistent with high quality.

ISBN: 1-56592-601-3   [7/99]

Table of Contents

Preface

Microsoft Exchange Server is arguably the most successful product in Microsoft's history. In less than three years, Exchange:

- Has sold more than 20 million seats
- Is now outselling Lotus Notes on a seats/quarter basis
- Has become the messaging standard for the majority of Fortune 500 companies

There are many good books available on Exchange, but most of them are of a step-by-step tutorial nature that help you get Exchange up and running quickly but are difficult to use if you are looking for specific information about some aspect of Exchange.

This book attempts to fill that gap by providing a quick desktop reference to all of the Exchange 5.5 components and directory objects, GUI and command-line tools, services, and directories.

I haven't documented every single setting on each dialog box or property sheet; there are simply too many of them. Instead I've tried to omit what is obvious and focus instead on what is not self-evident from the user interface itself. I've also included a lot of useful information about the history, clients, architecture, and operation of Exchange.

The intended readership of this book is primarily network administrators and system integrators who have or plan to implement Exchange for their companies or clients. However, as a Microsoft Certified Trainer, I think this book may also be of use to students pursuing their MCSE designation who need to learn the ins and outs of Exchange tools, services, and the Exchange directory hierarchy.

Organization of the Book

This book consists of three parts.

Part I, The Big Picture

This part of the book consists of two chapters:

Chapter 1, *Using Exchange*, starts with an historical overview of Microsoft client- and server-side messaging products, culminating in Exchange 5.5 and Outlook 98. Interoperability of Exchange with Microsoft and non-Microsoft clients is discussed, along with a brief comparison between Exchange and the Unix SMTP mail transport program Sendmail. The chapter concludes with a brief look at the typical steps involved in a rollout of Exchange.

Chapter 2, *Architecture and Operation*, takes a detailed look at how Exchange components and services interact to provide messaging functionality. A series of increasingly complex diagrams show component communication and message flow in single-server, multiserver, and multi-site Exchange implementations.

Part II, Alphabetical Reference

This part forms the core of the book and organizes every Exchange component or directory object, GUI tool, and command-line utility in alphabetical order. It is divided into three chapters:

Chapter 3, *Directory*, provides a detailed reference section for each object in the Exchange directory database. Exchange is administered by configuring these directory objects using the graphical Exchange Administrator program.

Chapter 4, *GUI Tools*, looks at the various tools for graphically administering an Exchange organization, with particular focus on the most important of these, the Exchange Administrator program. Also covered are enhancements to certain Windows NT 4.0 administrative tools that are provided by installing Exchange.

Chapter 5, *Command-Line Tools*, looks at the troubleshooting and maintenance utilities included with Exchange and also details the optional switches for running Exchange GUI tools from the command line.

Part III, Appendixes

This section includes supplemental background information and various handy quick reference lists:

Appendix A, *X.400*, deals with the X.400 messaging standards of the International Telecommunications Union (ITU), upon which much of the Exchange architecture and operation is based.

Appendix B, *X.500*, provides background on the X.500 recommendations and how they relate to the Exchange directory service and database.

Appendix C, *Raw Mode*, looks at running the Exchange Administrator program in raw mode to expose all the schema attributes of the Exchange directory hierarchy.

Appendix D, *Services*, lists the various Exchange services and their dependencies, executables, command-line equivalents, and Event Source identifiers.

Appendix E, *Directories*, describes the function of the various directories and subdirectories that are created when Exchange is installed on a machine.

Appendix F, *Share Points*, summarizes the shared folders within the Exchange directory structure and their default permissions.

Appendix G, *Ports*, examines TCP port numbers of significance when Exchange is installed behind a firewall.

Appendix H, *Service Packs*, summarizes the various enhancement provided by Service Packs 1 and 2 for Exchange 5.5.

Appendix I, *Links*, contains useful web sites, Usenet newsgroups, and Listservers for the Exchange administrator.

Appendix J, *BORK*, contains a brief summary of some of the more important Exchange utilities in Microsoft's BackOffice Resource Kit (BORK).

There is also a *Glossary* of common Exchange terminology at the end of the book.

Conventions Used in This Book

The following typographical conventions are used in this book:

`Constant width`
> Is used to indicate command-line computer output and text files such as those produced by the Directory Export command, and to indicate keyboard keys, commands, command options, and anything to be typed literally.

`Constant width italic`
> Is used to indicate variables or user-defined elements in examples.

`Constant width bold`
> Is used to indicate user input in examples.

Italic
> Is used to introduce new terms and to indicate URLs, variables or user-defined files and directories, file extensions, filenames, directory or folder names, and UNC pathnames.

Path Notation

Instead of listing the steps involved in performing a task using a GUI tool, I use a shorthand path notation to summarize these steps. For example, instead of saying "Click the File menu, select New Other to open an expanding submenu, and then choose X.400 Connector from the submenu," I simply say:

> File → New Other → X.400 Connector

The owl indicates a note or tip relating to the nearby text.

The turkey indicates a warning, something that you should pay close attention to.

We'd Like to Hear from You

I've tested and verified all the information in this book to the best of my ability, but you may find mistakes or omissions. Please let O'Reilly know about any errors you find by writing:

> O'Reilly & Associates, Inc.
> 101 Morris Street
> Sebastopol, CA 95472
> 800-998-9938 (in U.S. or Canada)
> 707-829-0515 (international/local)
> 707-829-0104 (fax)

You can also send O'Reilly messages via email. To request a catalog or be put on the O'Reilly mailing list, send email to:

> *nuts@oreilly.com*

To ask O'Reilly technical questions or comment on this book, send email to:

> *bookquestions@oreilly.com*

You can also contact me (the author, Mitch Tulloch) directly by sending email to:

> *info@mtit.com*

Acknowledgments

Thanks to my wife, Ingrid, not only for her patience and encouragement, but also for her research, proofreading, and other technical help she has provided as my Editorial and Research Assistant. I could never do the things I do without you, Schatz. May the Bears go marching on.

To David L. Rogelberg, my agent from Studio B Productions (*http://www.studiob.com*). Thanks for encouraging me to take on this project. Live long and prosper, friend.

To Robert Denn, my editor at O'Reilly, for his attention to detail and for helping me keep on track during this project. Thanks, Robert.

To Tim O'Reilly, who repeatedly pushed me further by asking deep questions I should have thought of myself. How do you do it?

To those who took the time out from their busy jobs to do a technical review of all or portions of my manuscript in order to weed out errors and provide additional helpful information, namely:

Charles Festel, Systems Engineer, Softnet Systems Inc.
Chris Scharff, Email Administrator, Black & Veatch LLP
Doug Hampshire, System Administrator, CCN
Ed Crowley, Senior Consultant, NCR Corporation
Eric Allman, Sendmail Inc.
Missy Koslosky, U.S. Department of Labor
Paul Robichaux, Independent Consultant

Thanks for your patience and many helpful suggestions. Any errors or omissions still present in this work are solely my responsibility.

To Jeremy and Melissa of GrabbaJava, whose coffee kept me going during this project.

Finally, a plug for my personal web site, *http://www.mtit.com,* where readers of this book can find updates and errata for this book and the other books I have written. Feel free to drop by sometime and submit an error, make a suggestion, or recommend a resource that other readers of *Exchange in a Nutshell* might find useful. Thanks also to Escape Communications (*http://www.escape.ca*), who have graciously provided me with Internet hosting and mail services.

—Mitch Tulloch, MCT, MCSE
Winnipeg, Canada

PART I

The Big Picture

CHAPTER 1

Using Exchange

Let us begin our look at Exchange with a brief survey of the evolution of Microsoft server-side messaging products, starting from Neanderthal times until the latest and most highly evolved representative of the species, Exchange Server 5.5 (see Figure 1-1). Included is a parallel look at the evolution of Microsoft client-side messaging products and how they interoperate with each other and with Exchange. Finally, we will conclude this chapter with an imaginary journey that takes the reader through planning and implementing an enterprise-level rollout of Exchange. While this book is not intended as a tutorial on Exchange, the imaginary journey will provide readers new to Exchange with the big picture on how to implement and administer Exchange, and should assist you in getting Exchange up and running quickly.

This chapter and the next one go hand-in-hand to provide an overview of what Exchange is and how it works. Specifically:

- This chapter provides the background on Exchange and what a typical Exchange rollout might look like.

- Chapter 2, *Architecture and Operation*, examines in detail how Exchange works and how various messaging clients interact with it.

Server-Side Genealogy

To understand Exchange, it helps to understand the version history of the product and how it relates to earlier Microsoft server-side messaging products. This section contains two brief surveys:

- A look at Microsoft server-side messaging products, starting with Microsoft Mail for PC Networks

- A look at Microsoft client-side messaging products, starting with the Microsoft Mail Client program

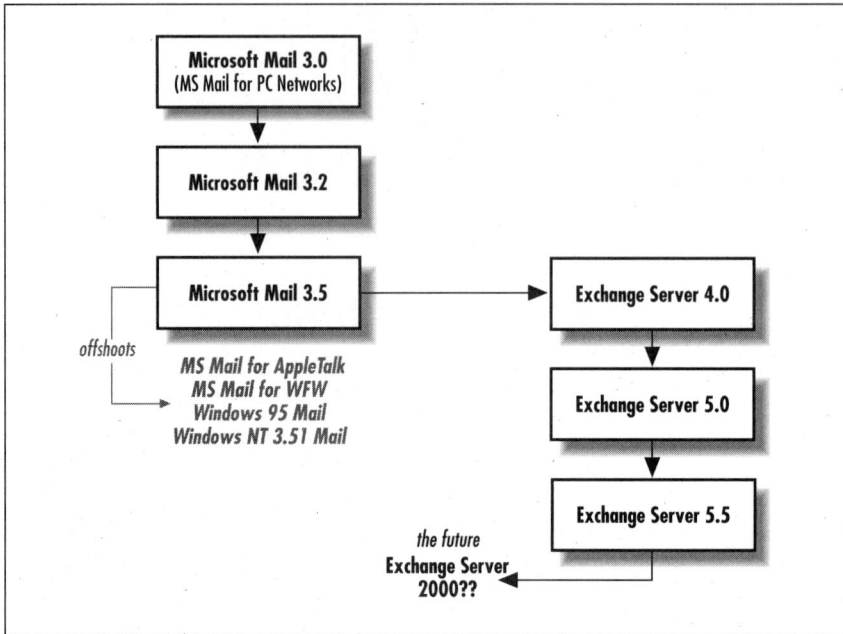

Figure 1-1: Genealogy of Microsoft messaging server products, culminating in Exchange Server 5.5

Microsoft Mail for PC Networks

MS Mail derives from an earlier messaging product, Network Courier, which was developed in the late 1980s by Consumer Software, Inc. Microsoft purchased Network Courier Version 2.0 in 1991 shortly after rival Lotus Corp. acquired cc:Mail, and Microsoft renamed Network Courier as Microsoft Mail Version 2.0. Microsoft and Lotus soon became the heavy hitters in the LAN messaging arena, and the battle is still raging today between them.

The design of Network Courier (and hence MS Mail) was based on the X.400 messaging standards of the CCITT (Consultative Committee for International Telephony and Telegraphy), which was absorbed in 1993 into the ITU (International Telecommunications Union). MS Mail was designed to use the file copy capability of MS-DOS–compatible network operating systems such as Microsoft LAN Manager 2.1 and Novell NetWare 2.x to enable messaging communication between users on a network.

MS Mail was essentially a workgroup mail system consisting of a passive central message store with a shared file system on a network server. MS Mail is usually described as a *store-and-forward mail system.* In other words, the sending client program creates a mail message and copies it as a file to a folder in the Postoffice on the MS Mail server. The server then moves the message file to another folder in that same Postoffice or to another Postoffice either on the same or on a different server. When the message file reaches its destination folder, it waits there until the receiving client program connects to the destination Postoffice to retrieve its mail. MS Mail Postoffices are limited to several hundred users per Postoffice, but implementations with multiple Postoffices can be scaled upwards to thousands of users, though administration becomes a headache at that point. (Microsoft Exchange is far better at managing thousands of users due to its single seat administration.)

MS Mail included gateways that repackage messages for transmission through LAN or WAN links to other mail systems, including the Internet's SMTP mail system, foreign X.400 mail systems over X.25 links, IBM's mainframe SNA Distribution Services (SNADS) message transport systems, IBM Professional Office System (PROFS) mail system, Novell's Message Handling Service (MHS), and other third-party mail systems, many of which have fallen (like MS Mail itself) into eclipse. This system of gateways raised MS Mail in stature somewhat from a strict small-scale workgroup messaging product to an aspiring all-in-one enterprise-level messaging solution, but the reality was that until the mid-90s most large-scale organizations used a variety of messaging systems integrated together using various gateways into a complex and difficult-to-administer heterogeneous messaging system. Even today, it is not uncommon to find large companies that still support mainframe-based mail, Unix-based SMTP mail, cc:Mail networks, LAN-based MS Mail, and other legacy messaging systems all held together with bits of tape and thread. Microsoft Exchange, however, is now making some inroads in these organizations as an all-in-one messaging solution.

Much of the terminology of Exchange derives from MS Mail and from the X.400 messaging standards on which MS Mail and Exchange are based. (See Appendix A, *X.400*, for a brief overview of X.400 messaging terminology.) Table 1-1 lists a brief comparison of MS Mail and Exchange terms. Many of these parallels are not exact equivalents because of the differences in architecture and operation between MS Mail and Exchange.

Table 1-1: Comparison Between MS Mail and Exchange Terminology

MS Mail Term	Exchange Parallel or Equivalent
Administrator Program	Exchange Administrator Program
External Program (MMTA)	Message Transfer Agent (MTA) or MS Mail Connector MTA
Multitasking MTA	Message Transfer Agent (MTA)
Postoffice	Information Store
Gateway	Connector
SMTP Gateway	Internet Mail Service
User	Recipient
Postoffice Group	Distribution List
Postoffice Address List	Global Address List
Group Folder	Public Folder
Shared Folder, Group Folder	Public Folder
Custom Message	Form
Directory Synchronization	Directory Synchronization/Directory Replication

Table 1-1: Comparison Between MS Mail and Exchange Terminology (continued)

MS Mail Term	Exchange Parallel or Equivalent
Directory Synchronization Server	Directory Bridgehead Server
Import.exe	Directory Import and Export
Mail Message File (MMF)	Personal Folders (PST)

The original MS Mail 2.0 product (Network Courier) was revised first to Version 2.1 and then to Version 3.0 in 1992. MS Mail 3.0 added some essential features such as directory synchronization across MS Mail networks and with external mail systems, better administration tools, enhancements to gateways for third-party mail systems, and clients for Windows and OS/2 Presentation Manager. These features made MS Mail 3.0 a workable and popular product. Microsoft's main marketing strategy at that time seemed to be to target users of IBM's host-based PROFS and Office Vision messaging systems by providing a cheap and easy migration path from these systems to workgroup-based MS Mail.

MS Mail 3.2 added an X.400 gateway that worked over various transports, including the TP0/X.25 and TP4/CLNP transport protocols based on the OSI model and implemented in parts of Europe. It also included a number of other enhancements such as the Move User utility, Batch User-Create utility, a Multitasking MTA, and AT&T Easylink Gateway to improve scalability and connectivity with other mail systems.

MS Mail 3.5 was the evolutionary endpoint of the product and included client support for Windows NT and Windows 95. MS Mail 3.5 was also available for the Microsoft Windows NT Server 3.5x operating system as part of the Microsoft Back-Office family of server products.

Microsoft Mail for AppleTalk Networks

MS Mail for AppleTalk Networks was a parallel version of MS Mail developed for the Apple Macintosh computer and is sometimes referred to as QuarterDeck Mail. Like Microsoft Mail for PC Networks, this is now considered a legacy product.

Microsoft Windows for Workgroups Mail

Microsoft Windows for Workgroups Mail was a watered-down or workgroup version of MS Mail for PC Networks that was included as a freebie with Windows for Workgroups 3.11 (WFW). MS Mail for WFW let users set up a single Workgroup Postoffice (WGPO) on a network to send and receive rich-text format (RTF) LAN mail using the GUI-based WFW Mail client program.

MS WFW Mail was limited to only one Postoffice, did not support connections to MS Mail Postoffices, did not support messaging gateways, and could not be administered by the Administrator program of MS Mail. MS WFW Mail was therefore really more of a toy than a tool, or perhaps an advertising gimmick. However, the basic directory structure of MS Mail for WFW was the same as for MS Mail for PC Networks, and therefore the upgrade path was simple. A product called the Microsoft Mail and Schedule+ Extensions for Windows for Workgroups was available for upgrading MS WFW Mail to MS Mail for PC Networks functionality.

Microsoft Windows NT 3.51 Mail

MS Windows NT 3.51 Mail was a workgroup-level product, similar to MS WFW Mail, that came with Windows NT Workstation 3.51 and supported only one Workgroup Postoffice (WGPO) and provided no connectivity or gateway functionality. It included a GUI-based client called Mail.

Microsoft Windows 95 Mail

Microsoft Windows 95 Mail was another workgroup-level product similar to MS WFW Mail that came with Windows 95 and supported only one Workgroup Postoffice (WGPO) and provided no connectivity or gateway functionality. It included a GUI-based client called Microsoft Exchange, which was later renamed Windows Messaging in the OSR2 release of Windows 95, probably so that people who bought Windows 95 didn't think they had gotten Exchange Server as well as the Exchange client. (Exchange Server was still in the beta-testing stage when Windows 95 was commercially released.) The Exchange client, however, became the standard client for Exchange Server 4.0, described next. The Microsoft Exchange client included with the original version of Windows 95 was also enhanced with Internet SMTP-based mail capability in the Microsoft Plus 95! Pack of add-ons to Windows 95.

The MS Mail for Windows 95 product could be upgraded to full Microsoft Mail for PC Networks functionality using a product called the Microsoft Mail Post Office Upgrade for Windows 95.

Microsoft Exchange Server 4.0

Exchange Server 4.0 was the first release of a new genealogical line of Microsoft messaging products. What happened to Exchange 1.0, 2.0, and 3.0? Microsoft probably jumped directly to 4.0 to emphasize that Exchange was meant to supersede and eventually replace Microsoft Mail 3.5 for PC Networks. After all, who would buy Exchange 1.0 if they could still get the obviously more advanced MS Mail 3.5? The numbers tell the story....

Released in 1996, Microsoft Exchange Server 4.0 (or simply Exchange 4.0) represented a departure from the LAN-based shared-file messaging systems of Microsoft Mail for PC Networks and its various offshoots. MS Mail used a passive Postoffice file-server architecture in which the mail clients did all the processing. Additional programs were needed to enable communication between different Postoffice servers and between Postoffices and gateways to other mail systems. Each client required read/write permission on the entire file structure of the Postoffice, and clients either had to manually initiate contact with the Postoffice to download new mail or had to poll the Postoffice repeatedly for new mail, which added to network traffic linearly with the number of clients.

In contrast to this, Exchange 4.0 enabled true client/server messaging environments, in which the processing of messages was split between the mail client at the frontend and Exchange at the backend. The Exchange Server and Exchange Client programs communicated using Remote Procedure Calls (RPCs), which allowed servers to notify logged-on clients the moment new mail arrived and reduced network traffic by eliminating polling. Clients no longer required read/ write permission on the entire Postoffice directory structure, which made the Exchange messaging environment more secure than previous MS Mail networks. Server messaging functions were integrated together and implemented as *services* (the NT equivalent of Unix *daemons*) on the Windows NT Server 3.51 network operating system environment and provided extensibility for additional gateways implemented as new services. Much of Exchange's new security and administration features are based on and derive from those of the Windows NT Server 3.51 operating system.

Exchange 4.0 supported the existing messaging, scheduling, and forms technologies of MS Mail and included new support for public folders to enable workgroup collaboration between users. Centralized administration could be performed using a GUI-based Exchange Administrator program that provided a hierarchical view of the Exchange directory of sites, servers, folders, and recipients. Connectivity with existing MS Mail networks was fully supported; in fact, Microsoft claimed that Exchange 4.0 could manage existing MS Mail networks better than they could manage themselves. Originally, Microsoft touted Exchange's seamless integration with MS Mail networks using Exchange's Microsoft Mail Connector as a big selling feature, but later, they began to push more on migrating away from MS Mail to Exchange when the MS Mail product line died out with Version 3.5.

Exchange 4.0 operation and architecture is also tied closely to the X.400 messaging standards of the International Telecommunications Union (ITU). The Message Transfer Agent (MTA) service is responsible for all communication between servers and servers and between servers and gateways. Messaging gateways are referred to as *connectors*, and Exchange 4.0 provided connectors for many foreign mail systems, including MS Mail, Internet SMTP mail, X.400 foreign mail systems, and host-based mail systems such as IBM PROFS and SNADS. The main message store is called the Information Store, which replaced the MS Mail hierarchy of folders with a database-like structure for improved efficiency and scalability. Other new features included an X.500-based directory database, symmetric multiprocessing (SMP) support, easy Windows-based setup and installation, a hierarchical organization/site/server topology, automatic directory synchronization within a site, message tracking, multithreaded routing, SMTP support (but not POP3), SSL encryption and digital signature support, public folder replication, link and server monitoring, integration with Office 95, primitive access to mail via HTTP through the Exchange Web Connector, and built-in migration tools.

Exchange 4.0 was taken seriously by Microsoft's competitors in the arena of enterprise messaging and groupware products, and with good reason—Microsoft Exchange was gearing up to roll right over their products. The new Connector for cc:Mail probably made Lotus shake in its boots and see signs of the impending battle. Migration tools were included to facilitate switching from Novell GroupWise and Netscape Collabra to Exchange—though many of those users would "rather fight than switch." About the only thing negative about Exchange 4.0 was a series of bugs that had to be fixed, for which Microsoft released a total of five Service Packs over about 24 months.

Microsoft Exchange Server 5.0

Released in 1997, Exchange 5.0 increased the stability and power of Exchange through a number of new features and enhancements. Support for Lightweight Directory Access Protocol (LDAP) gave Internet clients the ability to access attributes of recipients stored in the Exchange directory. Exchange 5.0 included a wizard-based Internet Mail Service (IMS), which replaced the less functional Internet Mail Connector (IMC) that had to be purchased as a separate add-on to Exchange 4.0. Support for POP3 and NNTP increased the functionality of Exchange as a competitor for Unix-based SMTP mail and NNTP news systems. Exchange Active Server components integrated with Microsoft Internet Information Server (IIS) to provide users with access to their private mailboxes, public folders, and the Global Address List through a standard web browser using the Active Server Pages (ASP)-based application called Outlook WebView. A new integrated MAPI client, Microsoft Outlook 97, replaced the older Exchange Client and Schedule+ programs, making Exchange a real competitor for collaboration and messaging systems such as Lotus Notes.

Of course, there were bugs; so far two Service Packs have been released for Exchange 5.0.

Microsoft Exchange Server 5.5

Which brings us to the present. Released later in 1997, Exchange 5.5 is an incremental upgrade to Version 5.0 that includes enhancements to its connectivity with Lotus Notes, SNADS and PROFS mail systems, support for the additional Internet protocols IMAP4 and LDAPrev3, a deleted item recovery feature, the Outlook 97 client (which has now been superseded by Outlook 98), support for S/MIME and SSL over SMTP, integrated Key Manager (KM) Server setup, enhanced Outlook Web Access for user access to mail through HTTP, an optional IRC chat service, support for Microsoft NetMeeting ILS lookups, and separate Standard and Enterprise Editions. The Enterprise Edition supports failover clustering using Microsoft Windows NT Server 4.0 Enterprise Edition and has a virtually unlimited message store capacity.

There are currently two Service Packs available for this product, which are discussed in Appendix H, *Service Packs*.

That's what this book is all about: Exchange 5.5, the culmination of Microsoft's evolutionary track of server-side messaging products. Exchange is arguably the most successful product in Microsoft's history, with more than 20 million seats sold as of the time of writing of this book. The Exchange/Outlook combination is now outselling Lotus Notes as the world's most popular groupware product, having already left Novell GroupWise and Netscape SuiteSpot in the dust.

Client-Side Genealogy

Having looked at the evolution of Microsoft Exchange from the earlier product Microsoft Mail, let's look now at the bewildering genealogy of Microsoft's various client-side mail programs, shown in Figure 1-2.

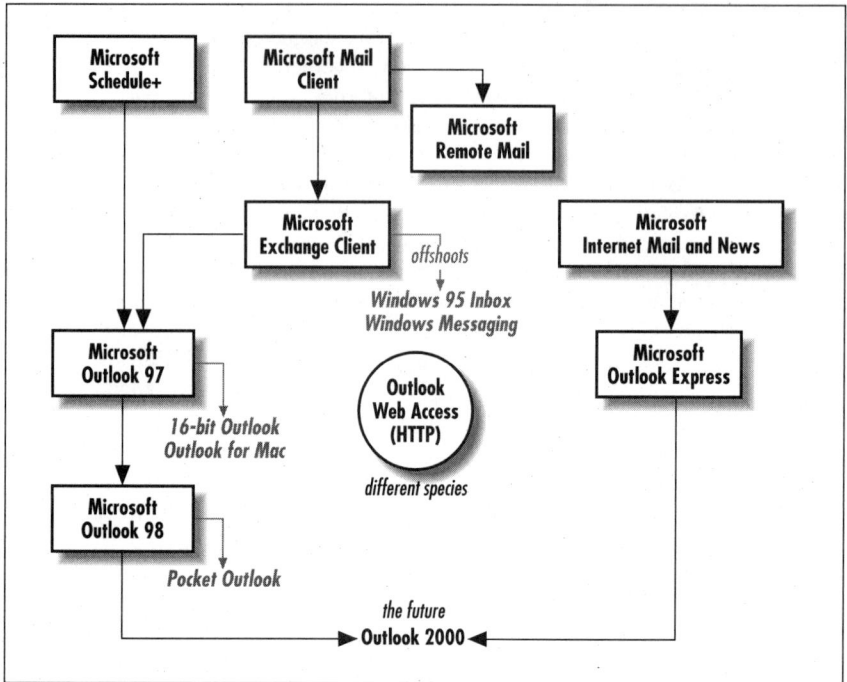

Figure 1-2: Genealogy of Microsoft client messaging products, leading to the future
Outlook 2000

Microsoft Mail Client

Microsoft Mail for PC Networks 3.x included mail clients (simply called Mail) for
the MS-DOS, Windows 3.x, OS/2 Presentation Manager, and Macintosh platforms.
Functionality differed with the platform used, with the Windows for Workgroups
3.11 client being the most sophisticated and providing automatic word-wrap and
tabbing, embedded objects through OLE 1.0, document attachments, address
books with name lookup (you typed someone's name and Mail replaced it with
the email address of the person from the address book), a customizable folder
filing system with search tools for storing and organizing your messages, and
support for both online and offline use.

The functionality of Mail for Windows 3.x was based upon Version 1.0 of
Microsoft's Messaging Application Programming Interface (MAPI) standard, which
enabled Mail to integrate with programs such as Word and Excel from Microsoft's
Office 4.2 suite of client applications. For example, you could send a Word document through Mail as an attachment by opening the document in Word and
selecting File → Send To from the Word menu.

Microsoft Mail Remote Client

Microsoft Mail Remote Client was a version of the Mail Client program for the MS-
DOS and Windows 3.x platforms that allowed users to access MS Mail 3.x servers

remotely using a modem. This was Microsoft's first remote messaging client and had most of the functionality that the LAN-based Mail Client program had.

Microsoft Schedule+

Schedule+ 1.0 was a personal scheduling tool included with Microsoft Mail 3.x that let users keep track of appointments, view other users' availability (called free/busy information) and book meetings with them, set reminders of meetings and calendar events using Terminate and Stay Resident programs (TSRs), create and manage a task list, and delegate scheduling responsibilities to an assistant (another Schedule+ user). Schedule+ could even interoperate with IBM's host-based PROFS and OfficeVision scheduling products, a major selling point of the product at the time it was released.

Schedule+ was ultimately available for the Windows 3.x, Windows 95, Windows NT, and Macintosh platforms. The version of Schedule+ that was included with Windows for Workgroups 3.11 lacked some of the functionality of the separately available commercial version; this seems to be a common and confusing practice of Microsoft. The Schedule+ program for Windows 95 included with Microsoft Exchange 4.0 and as part of the Office 95 suite of productivity tools was the last incarnation of the product and had the most advanced functionality. This product was called Schedule+ 7.0. As far as can be determined, there was never any Schedule+ 2.0, 3.0, 4.0, 5.0, or 6.0!

Schedule+ 1.0 could function both in online or offline mode, though viewing other users' available times obviously required being connected to a MS Mail 3.x server. To support these two modes of operation, Schedule+ 1.0 stored a user's appointments and tasks in two calendar (*.cal*) files, one on the client machine and one on the MS Mail server. Polling caused the calendar file on the server to be copied every few minutes to the client machine. A special MS Mail program called the Schedule Distribution Program copied this information between different Post-offices on an MS Mail network to allow enterprise-level booking of meetings. A special Schedule+ Admin program included with MS Mail enabled administrators to configure and manage Schedule+ operation.

Schedule+ 7.0 functioned similarly but much better by requiring and being integrated with Exchange Server 4.0 instead of the earlier MS Mail 3.x product. In Schedule+ 7.0, the format for storing schedule information was altered, and the information was stored in the user's mailbox on the Exchange server and saved with the file extension *.scd*. A hidden public folder on the Exchange server was used to store users' free/busy information, and this information was automatically replicated to all other Exchange servers.

The biggest problem with Schedule+ is that it was a separate product from the Exchange Client messaging program. However, Microsoft later integrated the functionality of these two clients into a new product called Microsoft Outlook that is described later. Schedule+ was a relatively advanced program, but I can't remember how many times I had to try to fix corrupt *.scd* files for my boss at one place I worked.

Schedule+ 1.0 used an older technology that was a precursor to MAPI called Microsoft Mail File Format API, or MS Mail FFAPI. That acronym seems to be around no more, with good reason.

Microsoft Exchange Client

MS Exchange Client is the MAPI messaging client that was included with Exchange Server 4.0. Exchange Client was intended as a kind of universal inbox for all forms of user communication, a goal it never quite realized. Nevertheless, Exchange Client introduced a rich set of new features and messaging enhancements including rich-text format (RTF) messaging and OLE support, remote mail and offline folder synchronization, support for MIME, support for digital certificates, an Inbox Assistant for filtering incoming mail, an Out of Office Assistant for handling incoming mail when on vacation or otherwise unavailable, a configurable folder hierarchy, and rule-based searching for messages stored in folders.

Versions of Exchange Client were created for the MS-DOS, Windows 3.x, Windows 95, Windows NT, and Macintosh platforms. The greatest functionality was provided by the 32-bit version for Windows 95/NT. Exchange Client also interoperated to a degree with the earlier Microsoft Mail server product.

Microsoft Windows 95 Inbox

The familiar icon on the Windows 95 desktop, Microsoft Windows 95 Inbox is actually a watered-down version of the Microsoft Exchange Client that lacks some of the functionality of the true Exchange Client. Microsoft later supplied the missing functionality through the Microsoft Plus 95! optional package of add-ons for Windows 95, which also included support for Internet SMTP mail not included in the original Exchange Client. This functionality was later directly provided for users purchasing new computers through the OEM update Windows 95 OSR2 release.

Microsoft Windows Messaging

Microsoft Windows Messaging was the new name for Inbox on the Windows 95 OSR2 and Windows NT 4.0 Workstation platforms.

Microsoft Exchange Forms Designer

MS Exchange Forms Designer was not an email client, but rather an Exchange 4.0 client-side tool that let users create custom electronic forms for simplifying the posting of information to Exchange public folders. The functionality of this tool was later rolled into the Microsoft Outlook client.

Microsoft Internet Mail and News

Sometimes referred to as IMN, Internet Mail and News is the SMTP/NNTP client program included with Internet Explorer 3.0 as a direct competitor for the Netscape Navigator 3.0 component called Netscape Mail and News. IMN was intended by Microsoft as a "lightweight" email client for SMTP/POP3 Internet mail and Usenet newsgroup access.

IMN did not support MAPI, but it could be used in conjunction with Exchange Server 4.0 running the Internet Mail Connector (IMC), or Exchange Server 5.0 running the Internet Mail Service (IMS), or with any Unix-based SMTP mail host.

Microsoft Outlook Express

The successor to Internet Mail and News, Outlook Express is part of the Microsoft Internet Explorer 4.0 suite of Internet tools and provides both SMTP mail and Usenet newsgroup access. Outlook Express supports both the POP3 and IMAP4 Internet mail access protocols and allows messages to be sent and received in HTML format (something people with older SMTP mail clients really hate!). Outlook Express also supports access to X.500-based directories using the LDAP protocol. This lets you look for information about people on the Internet using services such as Four11 and Bigfoot.

Outlook Express has the look and feel of Microsoft Outlook, with a variety of views including an Outlook bar, hierarchical folder list, and drop-down folder selection. Mail and newsgroups are integrated together into one window, which is nice. Filters can be used to filter downloaded messages and Usenet postings. Attachments can be sent in MIME, Uuencode, or BinHex. Offline mail access is supported through the IMAP4 protocol. A lot of other features make this a strong competitor for other free email clients such as Eudora Light and Netscape Messenger.

Outlook Express does not support MAPI, but it can be used in conjunction with Exchange Server 5.x running the Internet Mail Service (IMS). Outlook Express is in fact included together with Exchange Server 5.x as the default Usenet news reader.

The current version of Outlook Express at the time of writing is Version 4.01, the same as for Internet Explorer.

Microsoft Exchange Web Client

Released in early 1997, Microsoft Exchange Web Client was not really a separate client program but rather a set of Active Server Page (ASP) components that run on Microsoft Internet Information Server (IIS) 3.0 to provide users with access to their mailboxes, address lists, and public folders on an Exchange 5.0 server through a standard web browser such as Internet Explorer 3.0 or Netscape Navigator 3.0. The main advantage here was that the client web browser could run on any Windows or non-Windows platform and allow users to access their mail from these platforms from anywhere in the world.

Microsoft Outlook Web Access

The successor to the Microsoft Exchange Web Client, Outlook Web Access is also not a client program but a set of Active Server Page (ASP) components that runs on Microsoft Internet Information Server (IIS) 3.0 or higher and provides users with access to their mailboxes, address lists, calendar information, and public folders on an Exchange 5.5 server through a standard web browser. This lets users access the mail from anywhere using a standard web browser running on either a Windows or non-Windows platform. Note that the functionality which Outlook

Web Access provides depends on the version of Exchange Server and the applied Exchange service packs.

Microsoft Outlook 97

Designed as the primary client for Exchange Server 5.0 and included as part of the Microsoft Office 97 suite of tools (but actually shipping in late 1996), Outlook 97 (or Outlook Version 8.03) combines the messaging functionality of Exchange Client with the workgroup scheduling capability of Schedule+ into one convenient Personal Information Management (PIM) software package. Microsoft Outlook provides users with email, calendar, group scheduling, contact and task management, and to-do lists. Outlook also provides users with access to the Exchange Global Address List (GAL), custom address book views, and public folder replicas. Although primarily a MAPI client, Outlook 97 also supports SMTP and POP3 protocols for sending and receiving Internet mail.

Outlook interoperates to a fair degree with the earlier Exchange Client program as far as messaging capability is concerned and with the earlier Schedule+ 1.0 and 7.0 clients for appointment management, but you are better off upgrading all your client machines to Outlook than leaving a mixed Exchange Client/Schedule+/ Outlook configuration in place. This is because Outlook includes many new features that Schedule+ does not support, including integrated mail, journalling, updated contact management, additional views, enhanced task delegation capability, message recall, customizable voting buttons, and new printing options.

Exchange 5.5 also includes a limited-functionality 16-bit Outlook client for Windows 3.x platforms and an Outlook client for the Macintosh.

There are some third-party MAPI clients becoming available for administrators who want an alternative to Outlook. One example is Shark!mail available from LANshark (*www.lanshark.com*). Third-party clients such as Shark!mail may appeal to administrators looking for an alternative to Outlook that has similar functionality but a different user interface.

Microsoft Outlook 98

This is the latest version of Microsoft Outlook and is now the client of choice for Exchange organizations. Outlook 98 (or Outlook Version 8.5) includes full support for a broad range of recognized and proposed Internet standards, including POP3, IMAP4, S/MIME, NNTP, LDAP, vCard, vCalendar, and iCalendar. Outlook 98 supports both rich-text format (RTF) and HTML mail. Outlook 98 makes the pure Internet client Outlook Express gratuitous, except for the fact that Outlook Express is free and Outlook 98 isn't.

Other enhancements of this new version include a new Rules Wizard for easy rules-based processing of incoming messages, message flagging and auto-preview,

---

customizable voting buttons for scheduling meetings, message recall (works only with Exchange Server), a Meeting Planner, and a Contact Manager.

Outlook 98 is included as a component of Exchange 5.5 Service Pack 1, which is described in Appendix H.

If you have implemented Office 97 in Run from Network Server (RNS) mode in your company, you may be surprised to find out that Outlook 98 does not support this mode. Outlook 98 cannot be installed on clients if Office 97 is installed in RNS mode. This is due to dependencies between Outlook 98 and Internet Explorer 4.0, which must also be installed before installing Outlook 98. This could be a big issue in some corporate environments determining whether or not to upgrade to Outlook 98. Microsoft is reconsidering this for the next version of Outlook; see *Microsoft Knowledge Base* article Q812633 for more information.

Microsoft Pocket Outlook

We can't forget Microsoft Pocket Outlook, the version of Outlook for Windows CE-based hand-held computers! This is a limited-feature version of Outlook that can synchronize its information with Outlook 98 running on a desktop PC. It is evolving rapidly, sort of like the way bacteria do.

Microsoft Outlook 2000

Still on the horizon is the next generation of the ever-evolving Microsoft Outlook client. If only the human race could evolve as fast as Outlook does! Outlook 2000 will apparently include built-in support for other backend messaging systems such as Lotus Notes and cc:Mail, Hewlett-Packard OpenMail, and who knows what else. In this respect, Outlook seems to be like the human race: it evolves at the expense of all other species!

Outlook 2000 will function in three modes:

- As a standalone Personal Information Management (PIM) tool
- As an Internet-only mail and scheduling client
- As a LAN server-based MAPI client for Microsoft Exchange, Microsoft Mail, or other messaging servers

In other words, Outlook 2000 will be everything for everybody. Look out for Outlook.

Client Interoperability

If you are upgrading the backend of your mail system to Exchange 5.5, the issue of client program interoperability is an important one. Must all your users upgrade to Outlook 98? What functionality will be supported for users with earlier client programs? What about Unix users with non-Microsoft clients such as Eudora or Netscape Messenger? Let's deal briefly with some of these issues here.

Unix Users and Non-Microsoft Clients

Third-party clients such as Eudora Light, Eudora Pro, and Netscape Messenger compare favorably with Microsoft Outlook Express in a head-to-head features comparison. In other words, wherever you would use Outlook Express, you can usually use any of these other clients, with various overlap in features. For example, if users need multiple POP3 accounts, they can use either Eudora Pro or Outlook Express. If they need access to LDAP servers, they can use either Netscape Messenger or Outlook Express. It's difficult to do an exact features comparison, because all of these products are constantly evolving.

The main thing to note is that all of these Internet clients (Eudora Light, Eudora Pro, Netscape Messenger, and Microsoft Outlook Express) are only Internet mail and news clients; they don't support the personal calendar and scheduling, contact and task management, and journalling features of Microsoft Outlook. So if access to SMTP mail and Usenet newsgroups is all your users need, any third-party Internet client will probably suffice.

However, if some of your company's users run Unix workstations, there is a way for them to access their email, schedule meetings, manage contacts, and do many of the things that full Outlook client users do: they can use a web browser such as Netscape Navigator on the client-side, together with the optional Outlook Web Access feature of Exchange on the server-side. Outlook Web Access is an Active Server Pages (ASP) application that runs on Microsoft Internet Information Server (IIS) Version 3.0 and higher and allows users to access their mail, calendar, contacts, task list, and journal using a standard web browser. At present, this is the only way for Unix users to interoperate with Outlook users in an Exchange implementation.

Outlook Web Access is also the best solution for users who require roaming, remote access to these features. Outlook Web Access supports less functionality than the true Outlook client, but this is improving as upgrades to this product are being released. Service Pack 1 for Exchange 5.5 in particular upgrades the functionality of Outlook Web Access.

For Readers with a Unix Background

For readers from a Unix Sendmail background, Exchange may seem rather strange at first. Table 1-2 briefly highlights some of the differences between Exchange and Sendmail-based messaging systems. For more information on the architecture and operation of Exchange, see Chapter 2 in this book, and for information about Sendmail, see the book *sendmail, 2nd Edition,* by Bryan Costales and Eric Allman, published by O'Reilly & Associates.

Table 1-2: Comparison of Exchange and Sendmail

Feature	Sendmail	Exchange
Created by	Eric Allman; developed and enhanced by Lennart Lovstrand, Neil Rickert, Paul Pomes, Paul Vixie, and many others.	Microsoft Corporation
Current version	Sendmail V8.9.3	Exchange Server 5.5 Standard and Enterprise editions, plus Exchange Server 5.5 Service Pack 2
Intended purpose	General purpose SMTP mail-routing program	Corporate email and integrated groupware mail-routing and delivery program
Programming architecture	Open (for Open Source version, available from *http://www.sendmail.org*); Sendmail Pro includes the source code; the NT version does not	Proprietary (MAPI) (see Chapter 2)
Messaging architecture	RFC-compliant Internet SMTP-based messaging	ITU X.400-based messaging
Service architecture	Unix daemon	Windows NT services (see Chapter 2)
Cost items	Software only; Open Source version free (*http://www.sendmail.org*), commercial version now available from Sendmail Inc. (*http://www.sendmail.com*)	Software plus a client access license (CAL) for each mail client connecting to server, regardless of client program
Availability	Comes bundled with most Unix operating systems; commercial version now available from Sendmail Inc.	Must be separately purchased from Windows NT Server operating system
Implementation topology	Arbitrary net	Hierarchical: organization contains sites, sites contain servers (MTAs)
Email types supported	SMTP is built-in, but Sendmail supports UUCP, DECnet, and most other email types with the aid of helper apps	X.400, SMTP, MS Mail, cc:Mail, PROFS, SNADS, etc.
Platforms supported	Over 50 flavors of Unix; Windows NT version now available from Sendmail Inc.	Exchange: Windows NT only Outlook: All flavors of Windows; Mac
Network protocols supported	TCP/IP (you can also compile in support for XNS if desired)	TCP/IP, NWLink, NetBEUI, TP4/TP0, X.25
Integrated MUA/client	None, but all Unix operating systems come bundled with MUAs	Outlook email, scheduling, contact and task management client; Outlook Express news client

Table 1-2: Comparison of Exchange and Sendmail (continued)

Feature	Sendmail	Exchange
Clients supported	Any Internet mail client such as Elm, Pine, Eudora, Messenger, Outlook Express, etc.	Any proprietary MAPI client such as Outlook, Schedule+, Inbox, etc.; any Internet mail client
Message storage locations	Files (using *mail.local*), directories (using *procmail*), or almost anything you want by installing the appropriate local mailer	The Information Store (IS), using proprietary JET97 database files (**.edb*)
Message queue locations	Directories	The Information Store priv. edb and pub.edb files plus other proprietary binary *db*.dat* files
Message format	Plain text and MIME	Microsoft Database Exchange Format (MDBEF), a proprietary binary format
Configuration files	Plain text (*sendmail.cf*)	Proprietary (Windows NT Registry)
Administration tools	Command line, text editor, m4 macros; the Sendmail Pro GUI tool allows access to all Sendmail configuration options	The GUI tool Exchange Administrator (Chapter 4, *GUI Tools*) gives access to most configuration settings through hundreds of property sheets (Chapter 3, *Directory*); very few command-line tools available (Chapter 5, *Command-Line Tools*)
Troubleshooting tools	Any standard Telnet client; text editor; popular command-line utilities like *checksendmail* by Rob Kolstad; Sendmail also includes a test mode for probing internal operation and extensive debugging flags	*Eseutil, isinteg, mtacheck,* and other cryptic command-line utilities (see Chapter 5)

Outlook Express Versus Internet Mail and News

Outlook Express offers considerably more functionality than Microsoft Internet Mail and News (IMN). When Windows users upgrade from Internet Explorer Version 3.02 to Version 4.01, IMN is automatically upgraded to Outlook Express. In fact, both executables have the same name, *msimn.exe*. There is really no reason for Windows users to remain with IMN, just as there is no real reason for them to remain with IE 3.02. Outlook Express is much easier to use.

Outlook 98 Versus Outlook Express

To upgrade users of the "light" Outlook Express client to the "full" Outlook client, Outlook 98 includes a Setup Wizard that can import existing account, profile information, and personal address book files from Outlook Express into Outlook.

Outlook 98 Versus Outlook 97

Besides the Run from Network Server issue discussed previously, there are very few interoperability issues between these two versions of Microsoft Outlook as far as basic messaging and information management functions are concerned. Both versions use the same file formats, so scheduling meetings, designating delegates, and viewing free/busy times of other users works the same for both versions. Outlook 98 does include support for HTML mail, which Outlook 97 doesn't support; this can be an annoyance for users with the older version.

It's not difficult to manage a mixed environment of Outlook 97/98 clients from an administrator's point of view, since they are both MAPI clients with similar messaging and scheduling functionality. On the other hand, the training and support costs of supporting a mix of these two clients can be enormous. Microsoft has made many changes to the user interface in the new client, and users who are used to using the old client will probably need training in order to learn how to use the newer one. The changes to the Tools → Options menu alone are enough to give you a headache! Furthermore, your support staff will need two machines since you can't install both Outlook clients on a single machine (unless you do a dual-boot). So you're probably better off upgrading all your Outlook 97 clients to 98. The Outlook 98 Setup Wizard makes the upgrade to the new version fast and simple.

Outlook Versus Exchange Client

Users running Exchange Client can easily send and receive messages with Outlook users. A typical scenario would be upgrading a network that has an Exchange 4.0 backend and users running Exchange Client on their workstations. Once the Exchange 4.0 servers are upgraded to Version 5.5, users' machines should also be upgraded to Outlook to provide users with the enhanced features of Outlook.

If a mixture of Outlook and Exchange Client machines are used, basic messaging functions such as rich-text formatting (RTF), embedded hyperlinks, and attachments will work, but other difficulties may arise. For example, extended properties of messages composed using Outlook cannot be viewed by Exchange Client users. This includes things such as voting buttons and message expiration information. Different formats are used by the program for storing saved views of message information. Outlook can send HTML mail, which can be a mess if viewed using Exchange Client. None of these difficulties is serious, but they can cause confusion in a mixed Outlook/Exchange Client environment.

Of course, Exchange Client supports messaging but not the advanced information management functions of calendaring and contact management; that's what Schedule+ was for.

Outlook Versus Schedule+

If you are migrating from a Microsoft Mail 3.x environment, or if you have a mixed Exchange/MS Mail network, you may have to deal with administering a mixed Outlook/Schedule+ environment for users. These two client programs are interoperable at least as far as basic scheduling features are concerned: users can view free/busy information for other users and send meeting request messages. However, Schedule+ users will need a special "Outlook driver" installed to be able to view Outlook users' calendar information.

Other difficulties can arise. For example, users of the older Schedule+ 1.0 client can receive a one-time meeting request from an Outlook user but cannot receive recurring meeting requests since these are sent as attachments. Time blocked out by Outlook users as "tentative" or "out of office" appear as "free" to Schedule+ users viewing the Outlook users' calendars. Outlook users cannot delegate access to their folders to a Schedule+ user and vice versa. Outlook includes richer features for managing tasks and contacts that Schedule+ users do not have.

Interoperability between Outlook and Schedule+ really requires Exchange Server as a backend solution. This is because Outlook users cannot view the free/busy information of Schedule+ users on a MS Mail system.

Bottom line is, you should consider mixed MS Mail/Exchange networks as a temporary solution only and should plan to migrate your MS Mail users to Exchange as soon as possible. Similarly, Schedule+ clients should be upgraded to Outlook as soon as the server migration is complete.

Outlook and Microsoft Mail 3.x

In a mixed MS Mail/Exchange environment, Outlook does work with MS Mail Postoffices, but only in a limited way. For example, when Outlook is run on MS Mail, users cannot access public folders, perform full-text searches, encrypt and sign messages using SSL, set deferred delivery and message expiration options, send messages on behalf of someone else, or grant delegate access on their mail folders to another user. Furthermore, Outlook and MS Mail cannot share the same message store; Outlook users must import information from an MS Mail message store into a format compatible with Outlook.

You really don't want to use Outlook with MS Mail servers. If you are migrating your MS Mail network to an Exchange/Outlook one, migrate the servers first and then the clients.

Compatibility Charts

To summarize what we have discussed, two tables are included, indicating the relative degree of compatibility between various Microsoft messaging clients and servers and between clients and clients. Table 1-3 illustrates the compatibility between different servers and clients, and Table 1-4 indicates the compatibility between different clients when Exchange 5.5 is used as a backend messaging solution. Compatibility ranges from None to Excellent and depends on whether the client can take advantage of the features of the other client or the server product.

Table 1-3: Relative Compatibility Between Microsoft Messaging Servers and Clients

Client-Side Product	Server-Side Product		
	Exchange 5.x	*Exchange 4.0*	*MS Mail 3.x*
MS Mail Client	Poor	Poor	Excellent
Schedule+	Fair	Good[1]	Excellent
Exchange Client	Fair	Good[2]	Good
Internet Mail and News[3]	Fair	Good	Good[4]
Outlook Express[5]	Excellent	Excellent	Fair
Outlook	Excellent	Excellent	Poor
Outlook Web Access	Good	None	none

[1] Schedule+ 7.0 shipped with Exchange 4.0 and was part of Office 95, so the fit was excellent. Schedule+ 1.0 operates only to a fair degree with Exchange 4.0, however; thus (Excellent + Fair)/2 = Good.
[2] Same argument as note 1 above.
[3] Or Eudora Light.
[4] Requires the SMTP Gateway.
[5] Or Eudora Pro or Netscape Messenger.

Table 1-4: Relative Compatibility Between Different Microsoft Messaging Clients When Using Exchange Server 5.5 as a Backend Solution

	Mail	*Sched+*	*Exchange Client*	*IMN[1]*	*OE[2]*	*Outlook*	*OWA*
Mail	Excellent	—	—	—	—	—	—
Sched+	Good[3]	Excellent	—	—	—	—	—
Exchange Client	Fair	Good[4]	Excellent	—	—	—	—
IMN[5]	Poor	None	Fair	Excellent	—	—	—
OE[5]	Poor	None	Fair	Good	Excellent	—	—
Outlook	Poor	Fair	Fair	Fair	Fair	Excellent	—
OWA	Poor	Poor	Fair	Fair	Fair	Good	Excellent

[1] Or Eudora Light.
[2] Or Eudora Pro or Netscape Messenger.
[3] Schedule+ 1.0 was designed to work together with the Mail Client for MS Mail 3.2.
[4] Schedule+ 7.0 was designed to work together with the Exchange Client for Exchange Server 4.0.
[5] MS Mail Client users can send mail via the SMTP Gateway to the Internet.

Y2K compliance is obviously a big issue for administrators, and Service Pack 2 for Exchange Server 5.5 deals with many of these issues. However, be sure to check for Post-SP2 hotfixes for Exchange on the Microsoft web site in case additional Y2K issues are uncovered, and check frequently for more information on Microsoft's Y2K web site at *http://www.microsoft.com/y2k.*

Exchange Magical Mystery Tour

We'll now complete this introductory chapter with an imaginary walkthrough of implementing Exchange Server 5.5 in an enterprise environment. This will provide readers new to Exchange with a brief survey of some of the important concepts and practices involved in rolling out Exchange. This is not intended to be an authoritative guide on implementing Exchange: many steps are left out, and only enough is included to give you the flavor of what needs to be done. Remember, this book is not a tutorial but a quick desktop reference for those implementing or administering Exchange Server or for those who just want to dig deeper into how Exchange works. If you need a step-by-step look at the issues of planning, installing, configuring, maintaining, and troubleshooting an Exchange implementation, see the upcoming book by Paul Robichaux published by O'Reilly called *Managing Microsoft Exchange Server.*

Let's start! For reference, Figure 1-3 shows the final topology of the Exchange rollout.

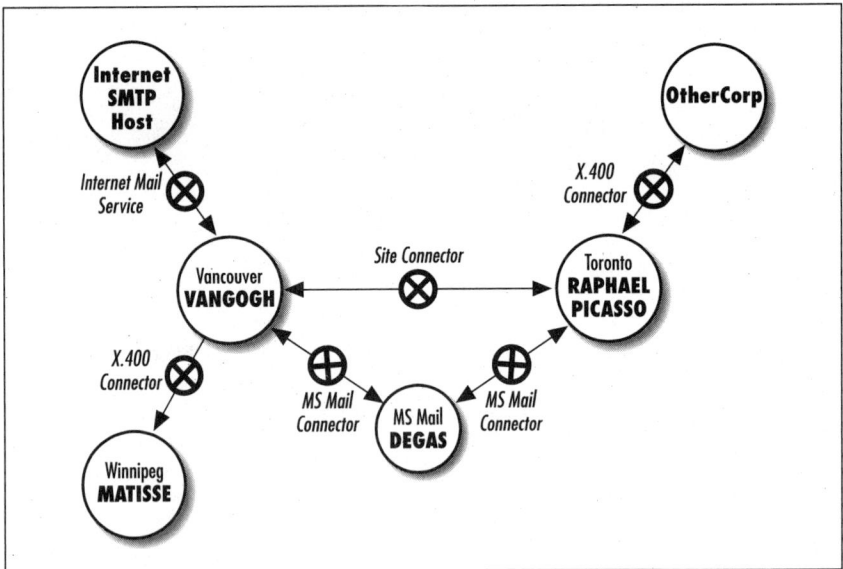

Figure 1-3: Final result of implementing Exchange Server at SampleCorp

1. Company Profile

Our imaginary company is called SampleCorp and consists of 1,200 users located in three Canadian cities, Toronto, Vancouver, and Winnipeg. (Hollywood makes movies in Canadian cities because it's cheaper than doing it in the States, so to keep costs under control in our Exchange rollout, we'll use Canada too.) The company is currently using a legacy Microsoft Mail 3.x network for messaging purposes, but it is showing its age. Only a portion of SampleCorp employees actually have MS Mail accounts, and the majority of these are in Toronto. The plan is to empower employees by giving everyone access to electronic mail and groupware collaboration tools. That way, productivity will increase, profits will rise, and the boss will make a lot of money.

Toronto and Vancouver are connected by a high-speed 1.544Mbps T1 link, while Vancouver and Winnipeg are joined by a dedicated 128Kbps ISDN link. The TCP/IP protocol is used throughout the enterprise as the sole network protocol. Toronto wants to eventually install a dedicated 64Kbps ISDN link to a partner company called OtherCorp; they are currently using a 33.6Kbps modem over a dial-up connection to that company. Since Toronto and Vancouver are the largest offices, the majority of the messaging traffic takes place between these sites.

SampleCorp has recently completed migrating employee desktop computer operating systems from Microsoft Windows for Workgroups 3.11 to Microsoft Windows 95 and plans to upgrade Microsoft Office 4.2 on employee machines to Office 97 in the near future. Administrators have Windows NT 4.0 Workstation on the desktop computers, upgraded to Windows NT 4.0 Service Pack 3.

Should you upgrade Exchange Server 5.5 machines with SP4 for Windows NT 4.0? NT4 SP4 fixes some problems not solved with NT4 SP3 but also creates new problems. For example, some administrators have reported that the Internet protocols POP3 and IMAP4 may fail on the Exchange server after applying NT4 SP4. Also, if you already had SP1 or 2 for Exchange Server 5.5 installed on your machine, make sure you reapply these after you apply NT4 SP4. For more information about applying NT4 SP4 to Exchange servers, see the *Microsoft Knowledge Base* article Q214864 and check out Microsoft's web site for any post-SP4 hotfixes.

SampleCorp also recently migrated its servers from Novell 3.12 to Windows NT 4.0 Server. The company consists of three Windows NT domains that are quite logically named Toronto, Vancouver, and Winnipeg. Trust relationships are configured so that the Vancouver and Winnipeg domains trust the Toronto domain.

LAN backbones in each office have also been upgraded to 100Mbps Fast Ethernet, though most desktop computers still have only 10Mbps network cards.

2. User Needs

SampleCorp employees need more than just messaging; they need software that will enable them to collaborate together on projects, manage contacts and meetings, and organize their daily work. Employees need departmental address books that will enable them to easily address mail to other members of their department instead of scrolling through the entire Global Address List every time they address mail. They also need connectivity to the Internet for sending and receiving SMTP mail, something only a few have at present. Finally, a small number of SampleCorp employees use Unix workstations or Macintosh computers, and management wants to make sure that these employees have similar access to messaging and collaboration facilities as do the majority Windows users.

3. Administrator Needs

Servers are kept locked in wiring closets, so administrators need to be able to administer them from remote workstations. There are administrators in each city, but those in the Toronto headquarters need to be able to administer servers throughout the enterprise as much as possible. Administrators want to be notified automatically when a server is down or a messaging link to another site is not functioning. Administrators would like to be able to eventually chuck their MS Mail system once the new system is in place and fully tested.

4. Management Needs

Managers want to make company policies available to all employees using Public Folders. Managers are concerned that employees are not all that computer literate and want to ensure that users don't accidentally delete important mail. The training budget is zero so unfortunately, simple education is not an option. Managers also want to restrict how much mail users store in their mailboxes. Technical support will be provided through discussion groups posted to public folders; that way, once a problem is solved and a solution is posted, other users can read this information and provide support for themselves. SampleCorp is a very supportive company; it comes from the top down.

5. The Solution

Exchange Server 5.5 for the server-side and Outlook 98 for the client-side. (Install Office 97 on client machines without the Outlook 97 component first.) Apply Service Pack 2 for Exchange Server 5.5 and any post-SP2 hotfixes available to make Exchange Y2K-compliant.

6. The Organization

The largest administrative unit in an Exchange implementation is the Organization. This usually reflects the business name of the enterprise, so SampleCorp is chosen as the Organization name.

7. Sites

A Site is a group of Exchange servers that can communicate using a high-speed, permanent LAN or WAN connection. The logical choice here is to have three sites named Toronto, Vancouver, and Winnipeg. Since Toronto is headquarters, this is planned as the first site to set up.

8. Servers

Two Exchange servers are planned for Toronto, both to handle the higher message volume of headquarters and for fault-tolerance. Administrators considered using Microsoft Cluster Server, a clustering solution included with Windows NT 4.0 Server Enterprise Edition, as an alternative solution that would provide a two-node failover cluster. Management nixed this idea as too expensive. The names proposed for the two servers are *Picasso* and *Raphael*, as the head of MIS is an art enthusiast.

Vancouver will have one server called *Vangogh*, and Winnipeg one server called *Matisse*. The Microsoft Mail server in Toronto is called *Degas*.

9. First Install

The Toronto headquarters decides to make the first Exchange installation the server *Picasso*. A Pentium II system with three SCSI disk drives is readied by installing Windows NT 4.0 Server and then Windows NT 4.0 Service Pack 3 and then being given a static IP address. User Manager for Domains is used to create a new account called Exchange Service in the Toronto domain. This account will be the Exchange service account and will provide a security context for Exchange services to run throughout the organization. Exchange 5.5 is then installed on *Picasso* along with the Exchange Administrator program. The name of the Organization and Site are specified during installation, along with the service account. When setup is finished, the Exchange Performance Optimizer program is run to optimize the placement of Exchange files on the machine. This results in the operating system and pagefile being on drive C, the Exchange transaction log files on drive E, and the rest of the Exchange components on drive D.

10. Administrator Console

For the administrator to manage the new server from his Windows NT 4.0 Workstation desktop computer instead of using the server's console in the wiring closet, the administrator runs the Exchange setup program on his desktop computer in Custom mode and selects the option of installing only the Exchange Administrator program, not Exchange Server itself.

11. Permissions

Once that is done, the administrator then grants permission for all other SampleCorp administrators to use the Exchange Administrator program by modifying the permissions on the Organization, Site, and Configuration containers using the Exchange Administrator program. Other administrators in Toronto then install Exchange Administrator on their Windows NT 4.0 Workstation desktops and try connecting to the *Picasso*.

12. Site Configuration

Next the administrator configures default settings for the new Toronto site. Using the Exchange Administrator program, the administrator finds the Configuration container within the Toronto (Site) container in the Exchange directory hierarchy and then configures the following directory objects by opening their property sheets:

- DS Site Configuration
- MTA Site Configuration
- Information Store Site Configuration
- Site Addressing

> These site-level directory objects are described in detail in Chapter 3, while operation of the Exchange Administrator program is covered in Chapter 4. In fact, almost anything that is capitalized in this section, such as Organization, Site, Server, DS Site Configuration, and so on, represent objects that are part of the Exchange directory hierarchy and can be managed using the Exchange Administrator program.

13. Server Configuration

Next the administrator configures default settings for the new Exchange server *Picasso*. Again using the Exchange Administrator program, the following directory objects within the *Picasso* (Server) container are configured:

- Directory Service
- Message Transfer Agent
- System Attendant
- Private Information Store
- Public Information Store

14. Testing

Administrators create and configure their own mailboxes on *Picasso*. Then they install Office 97 on their workstations, configure Outlook to connect to *Picasso* as their messaging service provider, and have fun mail bombing each other and booking useless meetings. Everything is fine.

15. Second Install

Exchange is installed next on *Raphael*. During installation, *Raphael* is configured to join the existing Toronto site using the same service account used by *Picasso*. When setup is finished, *Raphael* is configured using the Exchange Administrator program, and directory synchronization starts and automatically copies the directory information on *Picasso* to *Raphael*.

16. Vancouver Site

Exchange is then installed on the server *Vangogh* in Vancouver, creating a new site called Vancouver in the process. The Exchange Service account in the Toronto domain is used as the service account for the Vancouver site; this is possible because of the configured trust relationships. Administrators in Vancouver install Exchange Administrator on their workstations. The Vancouver site and its server *Vangogh* are both configured.

17. Site Connector

To establish messaging connectivity between Toronto and Vancouver, the Site Connector is chosen to take advantage of its simplicity and the high-speed permanent T1 link joining these locations. The Toronto administrator configures both ends of the Site Connector from his location. The messaging link is tested by having administrators in Toronto spam administrators in Vancouver. Administrators in Vancouver are shown to have an underdeveloped sense of humor.

18. Directory Replication Connector

To establish directory replication of addressing and other information between Toronto and Vancouver, the Directory Replication Connector is installed and configured in both sites. Initial replication is manually forced, while automatic replication is scheduled to take place every six hours. Administrators in both sites use the Exchange Administrator program to verify that directory replication has indeed taken place.

19. Winnipeg Site

Exchange is now installed on the server *Matisse* in Winnipeg, creating a new site called Winnipeg in the process. The Exchange Service account in the Toronto domain is used as the service account for this new site. Winnipeg administrators install Exchange Administrator on their workstations. The Winnipeg site and its server *Matisse* are both configured.

20. X.400 Connector

Due to the low bandwidth of the Winnipeg/Vancouver WAN link, administrators want to have more control over messaging traffic between these two sites. They would like to be able to schedule messaging traffic and prohibit messages over a certain size limit. The choice is made to use an X.400 Connector to join these two sites, since the X.400 Connector has these capabilities while the Site Connector doesn't. Administrators now spend a sleepless week trying to understand what X. 400 messaging standards are all about. Finally they install the connector, installing first an MTA Transport Stack for TCP/IP. Believe it or not, it works!

21. MS Mail Connector

Consideration is now given to integration with the existing Microsoft Mail 3.x network. The MS Mail Connector is installed and configured to provide messaging connectivity between the Toronto and Vancouver Exchange sites and the MS Mail server *Degas*. Dirsync Requestors are installed on Exchange servers in the two sites, and the Directory Synchronization object is configured also; these enable replication of addressing information between the Exchange organization and the MS Mail system.

Connectors eat up a lot of processing power and memory resources, so don't put too many connectors on a single Exchange server unless it is functioning in the role of a dedicated connection server. Make sure you run Performance Optimizer (see Chapter 4) after installing connectors on your server.

22. Creating Mailboxes

At this point, it's time to get the rest of the employees up and running. The Exchange Administrator program is used to extract Windows NT account lists from domain controllers in the three NT domains and export this information to a comma-delimited text file. This information is then edited appropriately and imported into Exchange using the Directory Import function of Exchange Administrator, a batch process that creates a series of mailboxes homed on the various Exchange servers.

23. Address Book Views

Address Book Views are created for each department so that employees can have customized address books showing only those employees in their own department, as well as have access to the master list of all employees, the Global Address List.

24. Private Information Store

Mailbox storage limits are configured for all employees using the Private Information Store object in the directory hierarchy displayed in Exchange Administrator. Deleted item retention time is specified so that if users delete a message, they still have a chance to recover it.

25. Outlook Web Access

Outlook Web Access is installed on a Microsoft Internet Information Server (IIS) machine to provide non-Windows users access to their mail and scheduling functions using a standard web browser.

26. Microsoft Outlook

Setup files for Microsoft Outlook are preconfigured as much as possible, and Microsoft Office 97 is rolled out to users. Many weeks of technical support calls ensue, and administrators get no sleep during this period. Bit by bit, users report success at sending and receiving mail. If only SampleCorp had a training budget!

27. Internet Mail Service

The Vancouver site is chosen as the gateway for SMTP mail for the organization because things are so cheap there and because the weather is better than Toronto. A fractional T1 line is installed to a local ISP and the Internet Mail Service is installed and configured on server *Vangogh* to relay SMTP between SampleCorp and the ISP's Unix-based SMTP host. The Protocol containers are configured at both the site and server levels. Since users have already automatically had SMTP email addresses generated for them by Exchange when their mailboxes were created, they are ready to go. Soon spam is flowing freely throughout the organization.

28. Message Tracking

Message Tracking is enabled on core Exchange components, and the Message Tracking Center in Exchange Administrator is used to track the flow of spam throughout the organization. Administrators find themselves spending all their free time killing spam, but through this activity and by reading Chapter 2, they learn a lot about how messages are routed and flow through the components of an Exchange organization.

29. Custom Recipients

Custom Recipients are created with SMTP addresses for external Internet users that SampleCorp employees will frequently need to send email to.

30. OtherCorp

A Dynamic RAS Connector is installed on one of the Toronto servers to provide dial-up connectivity through the 33.6 modem to the partner company OtherCorp's Exchange server. Unfortunately administrators can't get this to work and then realize that the Dynamic RAS Connector only works between sites in the same Exchange organization. The connector is removed, the modem is ditched, and a 64Kbps dedicated ISDN connection is established with OtherCorp at a reasonable cost. An X.400 Connector is then installed to provide messaging connectivity between SampleCorp and OtherCorp.

31. Public Folders

Administrators configure public folders for management and tech support to use at Toronto. This includes configuring both the Public Information Store on selected servers and the properties of the Public Folder objects within the Exchange directory hierarchy. These public folders are replicated to Winnipeg so users in that city won't have to access them over their slow WAN link. Polices and procedures start to flow out of Toronto.

32. Distribution Lists

Distribution Lists (DLs) are created to enable managers to easily send important bulletins throughout the organization.

33. Backup

Tape backup hardware is installed and procedures for regular backups are established. (This should have been done earlier!) Circular logging is disabled to make sure transaction logs are complete; this enables critical information to be restored in the event of a catastrophe. Windows NT Backup is the tool to be used for backing up the Exchange servers. The new backup system is not tested; why bother?

34. Server Monitor

Server Monitors are created to allow administrators to monitor the health of their Exchange servers. These are configured to automatically alert administrators using both email messages and Windows NT alerts should an Exchange service stop or a server become unresponsive.

35. Link Monitor

Link Monitors are created to monitor the health of the various messaging links between the Exchange sites and the link to OtherCorp.

36. Diagnostic Logging

Diagnostic logging is configured on a number of Exchange components. Administrators have little time to analyze these logs but discover a problem with the message transfer agent (MTA) on one server and run the command line utility *mtacheck* to fix it. Command-line utilities are covered in Chapter 5.

37. Message Journalling and Service Packs

Big brother insists on keeping copies of all messages sent and received by employees of SampleCorp. Administrators apply Exchange Server 5.5 Service Pack 1 and enable the Message Journalling feature. Feeling they are on a roll, they then apply Service Pack 2 only to discover that POP3 clients can no longer connect to the Internet Mail Service and retrieve their messages. Fortunately for them, the company's subscription to Microsoft TechNet saves the day (again).

> A good alternative to using the Message Journalling feature of SP1 is a third-party software product called MimeSweeper (*http://www. mimesweeper.com*).

---

38. Migration

After some period of time, administrators use the Migration Wizard to migrate existing MS Mail accounts and mailboxes to Exchange, and the server *Degas* is recommissioned as a Quake XVII server for lunch-time stress release for administrators.

39. The Future

Administrators now twiddle their thumbs as they wait for the next Exchange 5.5 Service Pack to arrive.

We're now finished our imaginary journey. In the next chapter, we will examine how Exchange works by considering its architecture and operation.

CHAPTER 2

Architecture and Operation

Let's look now at the architecture and operation of Exchange. By *architecture* I mean the fundamental components that make up an Exchange messaging system. By *operation* I mean how these components all work together to provide messaging functionality for users. We'll begin by reviewing some of the architecture and operation of the Windows NT Server network operating system on which Exchange runs. Then we'll look at the various components of Exchange and how they work together to provide messaging services to users for progressively more complex mail systems. And along the way, various Exchange concepts are explained as they relate to addressing and routing of messages.

Readers with a Unix background will find much of how Exchange works strange at first. This is probably because Exchange did not evolve from a Unix SMTP environment, but instead is based on the abstract and complex X.400 specifications developed by the International Telecommunications Union (ITU). These specifications define the architecture and operation of a generalized messaging system that is broadly implemented in Europe but relatively new to North America. To the American mind, X.400 may seem to have the flavor of the highly bureaucratic civil service that has pervaded Europe for centuries, with layer upon layer of organization and responsibility. Perhaps Microsoft chose the X.400 model for Exchange because they gave serious consideration to international standards in the area of messaging. More likely it chose the model to advance its marketing inroads in Europe.

In any case, Exchange is quite unlike Unix-based SMTP mail. One could even make the claim today that SMTP and related Internet protocols such as POP3 and IMAP4 have a better claim to being a global messaging standard than does X.400. (Europeans will probably disagree.) But SMTP mail is only one small part of Exchange; it is implemented as an optional component called the Internet Mail Service (IMS) that can be installed to provide an SMTP gateway between your Exchange organization and the Internet. Nevertheless, some consideration will be given in this chapter on how SMTP is implemented in Exchange from an architectural and operational point of view.

Although Exchange is based upon and fundamentally works like an X.400 messaging system, I've relegated an overview of basic X.400 concepts to Appendix A, *X.400*, so as not to burden the reader with abstract (and unnecessary) terminology in this chapter. Instead, I've chosen to focus on the more familiar Windows terminology such as Windows NT services, Remote Procedure Calls (RPCs), and Microsoft's Messaging Application Programming Interface (MAPI) to explain the function and communication of Exchange components and to highlight the communication between different messaging components using a series of simple flowcharts.

Exchange and Windows NT

The Exchange architecture builds upon the extensible, component-based architecture of the Windows NT network operating system. Windows NT networking is *component-based* because it consists of a number of core and optional services that can be loaded and unloaded. It is *extensible* because third-party companies can write their own services to the specifications of the Windows NT application programming interface.

Examples of *core* Windows NT services include the Alerter Service, Eventlog Service, RPC Locator, and RPC Service. Most Windows NT Server computers will have these services running at all times. To see what services (both core and optional) are currently installed on an NT server, and to start, stop, or pause these services, use the Services utility in the Control Panel. Various dependencies exist between these services so that if you stop one service others may be affected as well.

Examples of *optional* Windows NT services include networking services such as the Server Service, Workstation Service, DHCP Server Service, and Remote Access Service. These optional services can be installed, removed, and configured using the Network utility in the Control Panel. Some of these services, like the Server and Workstation Services, are installed by default during installation. Others, like the DHCP Server Service, must be manually installed by administrators when they are required.

Windows NT also has additional services called *Executive Services* that are not displayed using the Services utility in the Control Panel. These Executive Services include the I/O Manager, Process Manager, Local Procedure Call Facility, and Virtual Memory Manager. Executive Services are essential to the operation of the Windows NT operating system and cannot be stopped, started, or paused. Well, that's not entirely true; if you use the Windows NT Task Manager; you can view all running processes on your servers, including processes running in the Windows NT Executive. You can use Task Manager to kill any process that is running, but if this is done indiscriminately you will likely kill your operating system entirely and be forced to reboot.

Windows NT *services* are essentially the Microsoft counterpart of *daemons* in the Unix world. In other words, they are processes that run continually in the background waiting for an application to connect to them and request their services.

To dig a little deeper, the relationship between an application running on an NT server and the underlying services is essentially a client/server one. The application functions as the client and passes its requests to the appropriate *subsystem,* which acts in a server role toward the application and handles its request. Windows NT includes subsystems for 32-bit Windows, 16-bit Windows, POSIX, and OS/2 applications. These subsystems are components of something called the *Windows NT Executive,* which is essentially an overarching structure that includes all Windows NT operating system components.

RPCs and LPCs

Messages are passed between applications and Executive components using various *interprocess communications* (IPC) mechanisms. For example, the Windows NT Executive includes a message-handling component known as the *Local Procedure Call* (LPC) facility that enables applications running on an NT server to communicate with Windows NT Executive components on that server. Messages called Local Procedure Calls (LPCs) are exchanged between client and server components on the same machine.

To enable communication between Windows NT Executive components on different machines, a similar IPC mechanism called *Remote Procedure Calls* (RPCs) is used. RPC messages are handled by two Windows NT networking services called the RPC Locator Service and RPC Server Service. These two services make possible distributed applications that run on multiple Windows NT computers and communicate using RPCs.

The original work on RPC facilities was done by Sun Microsystems, and Microsoft's implementation of its RPC facilities is compatible with (but not compliant with, since its code base is different) the Distributed Computing Environment (DCE) standard of the Open Software Foundation (OSF). RPCs enable Microsoft NT-based clients and servers to communicate over the network with DCE-compliant Unix servers such as AIX, Digital Unix, HP-UX, Solaris, and others. Microsoft's RPC facilities can use several different mechanisms for making API function calls and transferring data between two Windows NT machines, including named pipes, NetBIOS, and Windows Sockets.

Let's look a little further into RPCs, since this particular IPC mechanism plays an important role in the operation of Exchange. The idea behind RPCs is the same as the one behind structured programming, in which code can be separated into the program's logic (like a backbone) and various component procedures (like ribs attached to the backbone). Microsoft programming uses dynamic-link libraries (DLLs) to separate the procedures from the backbone code. This way a programmer can upgrade his application by providing users with updated DLLs without the need to modify the backbone portion of the program. With RPCs the backbone and the ribs of an application can be on different machines on the network. To support such a distributed application, the operating system must include components that enable one portion of an application to locate where on the network other components are located, how messages will be passed between components, and so on. The Windows NT RPC Locator and RPC Server services provide these necessary functions.

Essentially, the server portion of a distributed application registers itself with the RPC Locator service. The client portion then queries the RPC Locator service to locate the desired server portion. Once located, the Remote Procedure Stub process packages the function call into an RPC and then uses the RPC Run Time process to send it to the remote machine along with any necessary parameters. At the remote machine, the Application Stub process receives the request, unpackages it, and makes the appropriate function call to the remote procedure, which returns its results using the same mechanisms. As far as the client portion of the application is concerned, it thinks it is making a function call to a local procedure on the same machine.

Figure 2-1 shows a Microsoft Network Monitor capture of network traffic between two Exchange servers in the same site during directory synchronization. The protocol for the selected frame is MSRPC for Microsoft Remote Procedure Call. Notice in the middle portion of the window that RPCs use connection-oriented TCP packets for reliable network communications. The actual data in an RPC packet is often binary and here appears as gobbledygook when converted to ASCII in the bottom-right corner of the window.

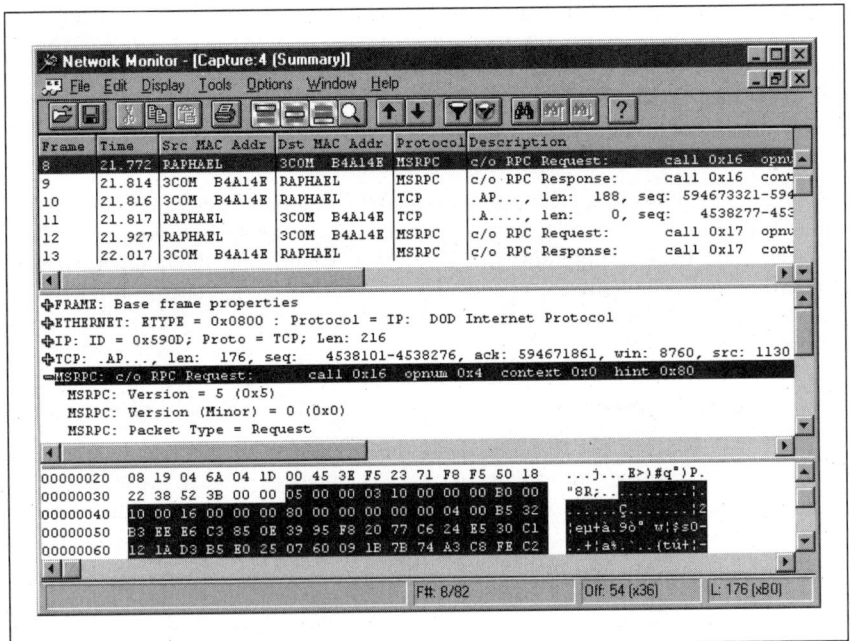

Figure 2-1: Network Monitor capture of RPC packets during directory synchronization

MAPI

RPCs might be thought of more like envelopes than messages. The actual contents of the envelope are the specific API function calls being performed by the RPC, which in the case of Exchange involve calls to the *Messaging Application Programming Interface* (MAPI) subsystem. MAPI is a Microsoft Windows technology that provides a layer of programming functionality between messaging applications such as Exchange on the server side or Microsoft Outlook on the client side and an underlying messaging subsystem common to all Windows platforms. MAPI acts like a broker between an application and the Windows messaging subsystem. For example, a client application such as Outlook can use RPCs to pass MAPI function calls to a server application such as Exchange, which returns information the same way (see Figure 2-2).

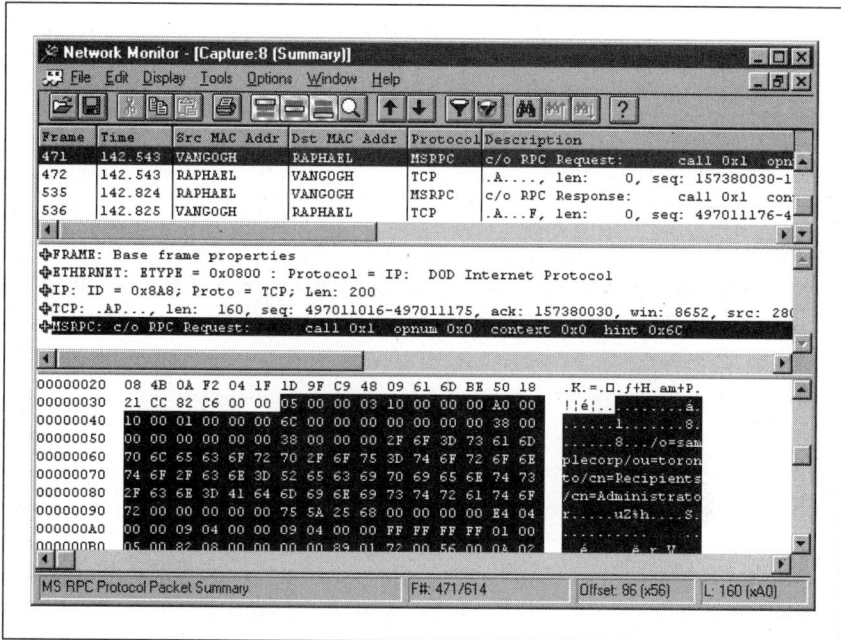

Figure 2-2: Another Network Monitor capture, this time of the MAPI client Microsoft Outlook using RPCs to access the Administrator's mailbox on the Exchange server Raphael. The client passes the Distinguished Name (DN) of the recipient (Administrator) to the server as clear text (see bottom-right corner).

MAPI defines a set of common messaging APIs that developers can use to write frontend or backend messaging applications that will interoperate with each other. MAPI is the foundation of how Exchange works and provides the rich set of programming features that allow Exchange to support complex desktop information management programs like Microsoft Outlook. Outlook is more than just an email client; it also provides a calendar, contacts list, journal, and task organizer. Outlook uses MAPI to provide this broad functionality.

MAPI is more than a set of APIs for messaging; it also defines a messaging subsystem and dynamic link library (*mapi.dll*) that is part of the Windows operating system for all current Windows platforms. MAPI provides:

- A common user interface for sending, receiving, reading, saving, and deleting messages
- Support for attachments and object linking and embedding (OLE)
- Management of different messaging transports
- Session and memory management functions
- Functionality for managing message stores (folders) and address books
- Outbox functionality for offline storage of sent messages
- Notification services for mail delivery

The key thing to note here is that if you want to get the most out of implementing Exchange, your messaging client should be a MAPI-aware client like Microsoft Outlook. POP3 clients like Eudora don't use MAPI and hence lack much of the functionality that can be provided by MAPI-based clients. In for a penny, in for a pound!

RPC Connection Order

One rarely understood issue is the fact that RPC connectivity between MAPI clients and Exchange servers has some configurability. This is because RPCs support a number of different connection methods, as shown in Table 2-1.

Table 2-1: RPC Connection Methods Between MAPI Clients and Exchange Server

RPC Connection Method	How a MAPI Client Communicates with Exchange Server
LPC	Used only when MAPI client is on same machine that Exchange Server is installed on
TCP/IP	Uses Windows Sockets (WinSock over TCP/IP) interface
SPX	Uses Windows Sockets (WinSock over SPX) interface
Named Pipes	Uses named pipes
NetBIOS	Uses NetBIOS over the underlying network protocol (TCP/IP, IPX, or NetBEUI)
VINES IP	Uses VINES IP

For Windows NT or Windows 95/98 clients, the order in which these RPC connections are attempted is as shown in Table 2-1. The order is slightly different for older clients such as Outlook for Windows 3.x or the MS-DOS-based Exchange Client program. The key here is that the RPC connection attempt order can be configured to improve the responsiveness with which the client connects to Exchange. For example, if your server runs only IPX/SPX for its network protocol, while remote clients on your network run both TCP/IP and IPX/SPX, your clients will first try to connect to the server using TCP/IP and will wait until this times out before trying IPX/SPX.

The RPC connection order can significantly impact client connection speeds, and you should be aware that you can configure the RPC connection attempt sequence in two ways:

- By modifying the *Outlook.stf* file, which is used during the setup of Microsoft Outlook

- By editing the Registry after Outlook has been installed on client machines

Exchange Architecture

As mentioned earlier, Exchange has a component-based architecture. The components of Exchange are all implemented as Windows NT services. Exchange components can be classified into two types: core components and optional components.

Core Components

There are four core components to every Exchange server. These components supply services for managing the Exchange directory, storing and forwarding messages, and other essential functions. These core components are:

Directory Service (DS)
> Maintains the Exchange directory database (*dir.edb*), an X.500-compliant database that contains the attributes and configuration settings of recipients, sites, servers, connectors, and gateways. By default, this *dir.edb* file is located in the \dsadata directory, along with its transaction logs, checkpoint file, reserved log files, and temporary file. See the section "Directory Database" at the beginning of Chapter 3, *Directory*, for an explanation of these various terms, and refer to Appendix E, *Directories*, for the directory structure of Exchange.

> Every directory object in the Exchange directory database has attributes and stores these attributes in the directory database. For example, personal information concerning a recipient's address, phone number, and company name are stored as attributes of the recipient's mailbox object in the directory. You can access an object's attributes by opening the object's property sheet using the Exchange Administrator program described in Chapter 4, *GUI Tools*. The various objects in the Exchange directory database are covered alphabetically in Chapter 3.

> The Directory Service is also responsible for automatically replicating the directory database to all Exchange servers in a site. Every Exchange server in an organization maintains a complete copy of the Exchange directory database. This is unlike true X.500 directories, in which the directory information can be distributed among multiple directory servers.

> The Directory Service also maintains the Global Address List (GAL), which contains information about all the recipients in the Exchange organization. Clients can access the GAL using Microsoft's Messaging Application Programming Interface (MAPI), Lightweight Directory Access Protocol (LDAP), and through Outlook Web Access using HTTP, depending on how Exchange is configured. MAPI is the default method.

Information Store (IS)

Maintains two databases called the Private Information Store (*priv.edb*) and the Public Information Store (*pub.edb*). These are located by default in the *mdbdata* directory, along with their transaction logs, checkpoint files, reserved log files, and temporary file. See "Directory Database" at the beginning of Chapter 3 for an explanation of these various terms, and refer to Appendix E for the directory structure of Exchange.

The Private Information Store holds the messages and attachments for users whose mailboxes are homed on the Exchange server. The Public Information Store holds the contents of public folder replicas homed on the server. An Exchange server can have one Private Information Store, one Public Information Store, or one of each kind of store.

The Information Store is also involved in transporting messages, as is explained later in this chapter.

Clients can access the Information Store using Microsoft's MAPI or the Internet protocols POP3, IMAP4, and NNTP, depending on how Exchange is configured. MAPI is again the default method.

Message Transfer Agent (MTA)

An X.400-compliant message transfer agent responsible for routing messages and for converting them from the native *Microsoft Database Exchange Format* (MDBEF) to X.400 format. MDBEF is the format in which messages and attachments are stored in the Information Store. The MTA is involved together with the Information Store in transporting messages. The MTA can route messages to other Exchange MTAs, to MTAs of foreign X.400 mail systems, or to Microsoft Mail Connectors.

System Attendant (SA)

A manager that performs watchdog services for other components. The System Attendant must be running for any other Exchange services to run. Stopping the System Attendant will stop all Exchange services on a machine. Activities of the System Attendant include auto-generation of email addresses when new recipients are created, maintaining the Exchange message routing table (the GWART), maintaining the message tracking logs, and other maintenance and supervisory functions.

Optional Components

There are a number of optional components that can be installed on Exchange servers. These optional components, which are also implemented as Windows NT services, provide support for enterprise-level Exchange implementations, advanced security, legacy mail systems, and connectivity with foreign mail systems. Listed here are some of these additional components with a brief description of their functions. Further information on these components can be found in Chapter 3.

Site Connector and Directory Replication Connector

Connects Exchange sites together into an enterprise-level messaging system

Dynamic RAS Connector

Connects Exchange sites together using an asynchronous dial-up connection

---

Internet Mail Service
> Connects Exchange sites together using the Internet's SMTP mail system as a backbone or connects Exchange organizations to the Internet's SMTP mail system itself

Internet News Service
> Connects Exchange to the Internet's Usenet news system using the NNTP Internet protocol

MS Mail Connector and Directory Synchronization
> Provides messaging and directory synchronization with legacy Microsoft Mail 3.x mail systems

Microsoft Schedule+ Free/Busy Connector
> Provides scheduling capability for legacy Microsoft Schedule+ clients

X.400 Connector
> Connects Exchange sites together over dedicated low-bandwidth connections or connects Exchange sites to X.400-based foreign mail systems

Connector for cc:Mail
> Connects Exchange sites to Lotus cc:Mail foreign mail systems

Exchange Operation

By Exchange operation, I am referring here to several things:

- How Exchange stores, transfers, and routes messages in an electronic messaging environment

- How Exchange supports messaging with foreign mail systems

- How different kinds of mail clients interact with various Exchange components

- How the Exchange Administrator program interacts with various Exchange components

To simplify things, we will start with a simple messaging system involving one Exchange server and various clients and then enlarge this to include more complexity.

Single-Server Scenario

When you have only one Exchange server deployed, communication between Exchange core components on that server are performed using Local Procedure Calls (LPCs). Communication with Exchange clients such as Microsoft Outlook on different machines is accomplished using Remote Procedure Calls (RPCs).

The communications between the Exchange core components on a single server are illustrated in Figure 2-3.

Here is the description of these various interactions between core components, keyed to the numbers in Figure 2-3. Note that these numbers simply identify the

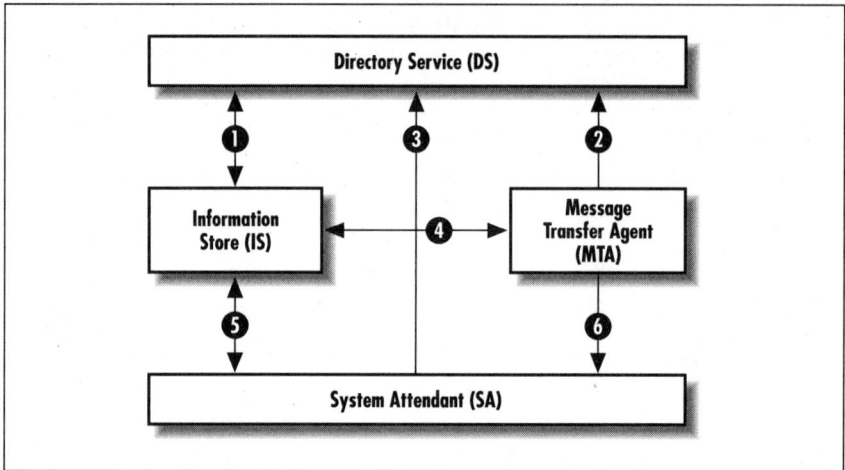

Figure 2-3: Communication between core Exchange components in a single-server scenario

various interactions, and in this diagram they do *not* indicate a series of sequential steps. The abbreviations used are:

DS = Directory Service
IS = Information Store
MTA = Message Transfer Agent
SA = System Attendant

1. DS ↔ IS

   The DS initiates communication with the IS during directory replication with other sites. Directory replication between sites is performed using email messages; directory synchronization within a site is accomplished using RPCs.

   The IS initiates communication with the DS to:

   – Look up addresses in the Global Address List (GAL)

   – Obtain recipient information from the directory database

   – Update entries in public folders

2. MTA → DS

   The MTA initiates communication with the DS to look up addresses in the GAL.

3. SA → DS

   The SA initiates communication with the DS to:

   – Look up addresses in the GAL

   – Automatically generate email addresses when a new recipient is created

   – Verify directory replication information

   – Build the Exchange message routing table (GWART) for routing of messages

4. IS ↔ MTA

The IS initiates communication with the MTA to:

– Expand messages addressed to distribution lists (DLs)

– Submit messages to the MTA for delivery to a remote server or mail system through a connector

The MTA initiates communication with the IS to:

– Deliver a messages from a remote server or mail system that arrived through a connector

– Resolve the email address of a connector or gateway

5. IS ↔ SA

The IS initiates communication with the SA to create log entries when message tracking is enabled on the IS.

The SA initiates communication with the IS to send or receive notifications for Link Monitors that are running.

6. MTA → SA

The MTA initiates communication with the SA to create log-file entries when message tracking is enabled on the MTA.

Single-Server with Connectors

If connectors or gateways are installed on a lone Exchange server to provide messaging interoperability with foreign mail systems, the communication between components becomes slightly more interesting (see Figure 2-4).

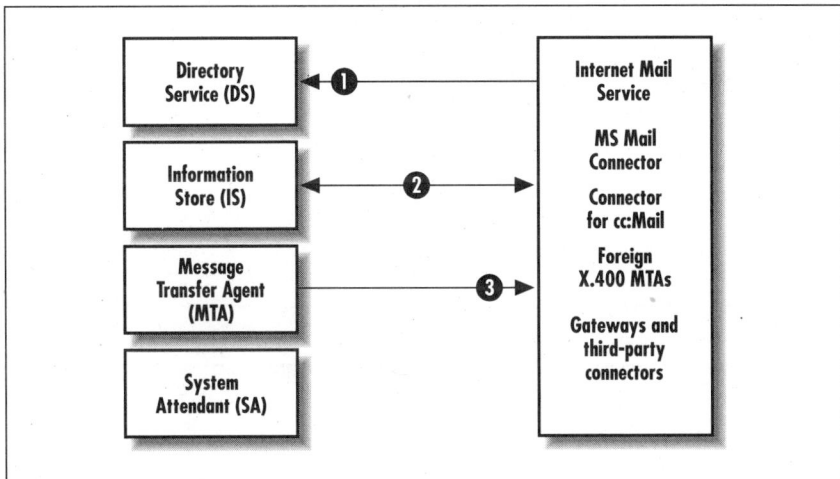

Figure 2-4: Communication between core Exchange components and a connector or gateway in a single-server scenario

Here is the description of the additional interactions occurring between components, keyed to the numbers in Figure 2-4. Note that these numbers simply identify the various interactions, and in this diagram they do *not* indicate a series of sequential steps:

1. Connector → DS

   Connectors initiate communication with the DS to look up addresses in the GAL. For example, the Internet Mail System communicates with the DS to look up the SMTP address of a message addressed to a Custom Recipient on the Internet. Custom Recipients are recipients in the GAL who do not match any users in your organization, but instead match users on external mail systems such as the Internet's global SMTP mail system. You create Custom Recipients in your GAL for external users whom your own users frequently send mail to.

2. Connector ↔ IS

   The IS initiates communication with the connector to announce that there is a message waiting to be routed through the connector to the foreign mail system.

   Connectors initiate communication with the IS to process and deliver messages send from foreign mail systems to recipients on your Exchange server (or to other Exchange sites within your organization).

3. MTA → Connector

   The MTA initiates communication with the connector to deliver a message to the connector for routing to the foreign mail system.

Exchange Server and the Exchange Administrator Program

If the Exchange Administrator program is installed on an Exchange server to enable management of that server, the program communicates with the Exchange components using LPCs. If the Administrator program is installed on a different machine, it communicates with the server using RPCs. Figure 2-5 shows the interaction between the Exchange Administrator program and the core Exchange components.

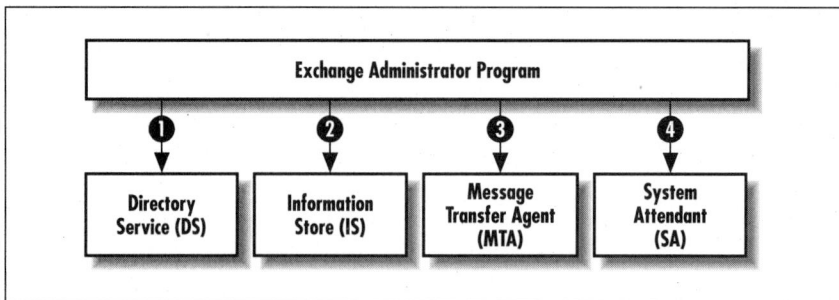

Figure 2-5: Communication between the Exchange Administrator program and core Exchange components

Here is the description of the interactions occurring between the Administrator program and the core Exchange components, keyed to the numbers in Figure 2-5. Note that these numbers simply identify the various interactions, and in this diagram they do *not* indicate a series of sequential steps:

1. Exchange Administrator → DS

   The Exchange Administrator program initiates communication with the DS to:

   – Display the Exchange directory hierarchy in the Administrator program window

   – Create, delete, and modify the attributes of directory objects

2. Exchange Administrator → IS

   The Exchange Administrator program initiates communication with the IS to:

   – Obtain and display statistics on logons, connections, and resources being used

   – Configure mailboxes and public folders

   – Manage public folder replication

   – Delete mailboxes when the corresponding Windows NT account is deleted

3. Exchange Administrator → MTA

   The Exchange Administrator program initiates communication with the MTA to view, re-order, and delete messages in MTA queues.

4. Exchange Administrator → SA

   The Exchange Administrator program initiates communication with the SA to:

   – Create, configure, start, and stop Server Monitors and Link Monitors

   – Recalculate and display the Exchange message routing table (GWART)

   – Configure auto-generation of email addresses for new recipients

Exchange Server and Client Programs

Exchange supports six kinds of messaging clients:

- MAPI-based clients such as Microsoft Outlook and the older Windows Messaging, Schedule+, and Exchange client programs. Use these clients if you want to take advantage of Exchange's capability to be used as a groupware server for managing mail, contacts, journals, and schedules. Microsoft Outlook is the preferred MAPI client since it is the latest version of this evolutionary line of clients. The older Exchange Client/Schedule+ combination of clients support more limited groupware functionality.

- POP3 clients such as Microsoft Outlook Express, Microsoft Outlook 97 or 98, and third-party programs such as Eudora, Pegasus Mail, and Netscape Communicator. These clients use Post Office Protocol Version 3 (POP3), a standard Internet protocol for accessing SMTP mail on a POP3 server.

- IMAP4 clients such as Microsoft Outlook Express, Microsoft Outlook 98 (but not 97), Eudora Pro, and Netscape Communicator. These clients use the

Internet Message Access Protocol Version 4 (IMAP4), a standard Internet protocol for accessing SMTP mail on an IMAP4 server. IMAP4 has additional features not supported by POP3, including personal and public folders, reviewing headers before downloading messages, and searching for messages on the server.

- LDAP clients such as Microsoft Outlook Express and Netscape Communicator. These clients use the Lightweight Directory Access Protocol (LDAP) to view attributes of recipients within the Exchange directory (or any other directory based on the X.500 recommendations). LDAP clients can also modify attributes of recipients if they have the appropriate permissions. (Outlook Express does not have this capability.)

- HTTP clients such as Microsoft Internet Explorer and Netscape Communicator. These web browsers use HTTP to access information on web servers such as Microsoft Internet Information Server (IIS). Exchange includes an optional component called Outlook Web Access that enables Exchange to integrate with an IIS server running Active Server Pages (ASPs) to let users access their mail, address books, and public folders using a standard Web browser.

- NTTP clients like Microsoft Outlook Express, which use the NNTP protocol for accessing Usenet-style newsgroups on an Exchange server.

The communication between the core components on an Exchange server and each kind of client is illustrated in Figure 2-6.

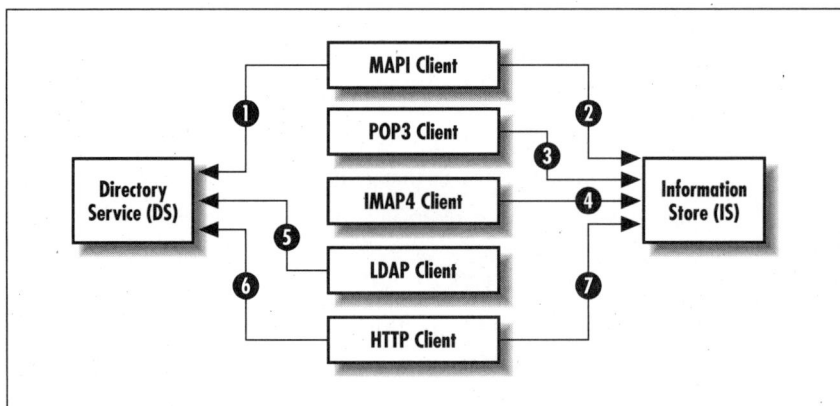

Figure 2-6: Communication between Exchange core components and various clients

Here is the description of the interaction between the core Exchange components and various kinds of client programs, keyed to the numbers in Figure 2-6. Note that these numbers simply identify the various interactions, and in this diagram they do *not* indicate a series of sequential steps:

1. MAPI client → DS

   MAPI clients initiate communication with the DS to:

   – Display the contents of the Address Book

   – Display the attributes of recipients in the Address Book

- Resolve email addresses of recipients when sending messages
- Modify the membership of a distribution list owned by the user

2. MAPI client → IS

MAPI clients initiate communication with the IS to:
- Submit a message to the IS for delivery
- Create, delete, and move folders
- Modify the properties and contents of folders

3. POP3 client → IS

POP3 clients initiate communication with the IS to:
- Submit a message to the IS for delivery
- Modify properties and contents of folders

4. IMAP4 client → IS

IMAP4 clients initiate communication with the IS to:
- Submit a message to the IS for delivery
- Create, delete, and move folders
- Modify the properties and contents of folders

5. LDAP client → DS

LDAP clients initiate communication with the DS to:
- Display the contents of the Address Book
- Display the attributes of recipients in the Address Book
- Resolve email addresses of recipients when sending messages
- Modify the membership of a distribution list owned by the user

6. HTTP client → DS

HTTP clients initiate communication with the DS to:
- Display the contents of the Address Book
- Display the attributes of recipients in the Address Book
- Resolve email addresses of recipients when sending messages
- Modify the membership of a distribution list owned by the user

7. HTTP client → IS

HTTP clients initiate communication with the IS to:
- Submit a message to the IS for delivery
- Create, delete, and move folders
- Modify the properties and contents of folders

Single-Server MAPI Message Flow

If you only have one Exchange server, both the recipient sending a message and the recipient receiving it are homed on the same server. By homed we mean that this server is their *home server*. A recipient's home server is the Exchange server in whose Information Store database the recipient's messages and attachments are stored.

Figure 2-7 shows the interaction between clients and a lone Exchange server when a message is sent. Note that the MTA is not involved in this process; the MTA *is* used when moving messages between servers, however.

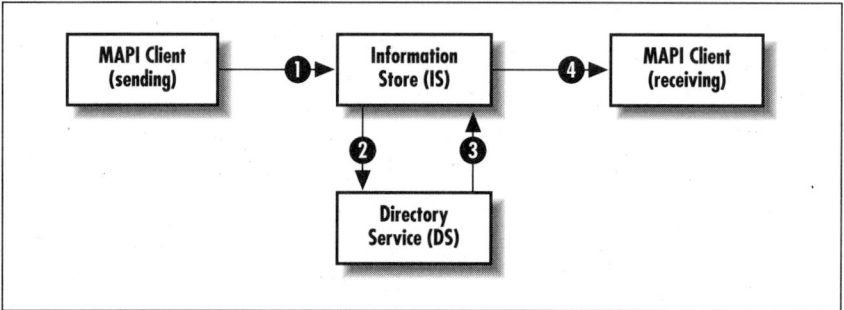

Figure 2-7: Message flow between a client and a single Exchange server

Here is the description of the interaction between the core Exchange components and a MAPI client such as Microsoft Outlook, keyed to the numbers in Figure 2-7. Note that in this diagram, the numbers *do* refer to a series of sequential steps that take place as the various components interact:

1. MAPI client (sending) → IS

   The MAPI client sending the message initiates communication with the IS and submits the message to the IS. In this case, the distinguished name (DN) of the destination recipient is used to route the message.

2. IS → DS

   The IS initiates communication with the DS to locate the home server of the message recipient.

3. DS → IS

   The DS responds to the request from the IS by indicating that the message recipient is on this Exchange server (since we are considering a single-server scenario here).

4. IS → MAPI client (receiving)

   If the message recipient has his MAPI client running, the IS initiates a connection with the receiving MAPI client and notifies the client that a new message has arrived. If the message recipient does not have his MAPI client running, the IS will initiate a connection as soon as the receiving client is started.

Distinguished name (DN) is the native addressing format for Exchange recipients. Every object in the Exchange directory database is identified by a unique DN, including recipients such as Mailboxes, Distribution Lists, and Custom Recipients. DNs are part of the X.500 directory recommendation and consist of a hierarchical set of attributes starting with the name of the organization, then the name of the organizational unit (site), then names of any containers, and finally the internal name of the directory object itself. For example, the recipient *Bob Smith* with mailbox *BobS* homed on a server in the site *Toronto* in the organization *SampleCorp* would have the distinguished name:

   o=SampleCorp/ou=Toronto/cn=recipients/cn=BobS

Here we have:

— *o* for Organization

— *ou* for Organizational Unit (site)

— *cn* for Common Name (anything else)

Exchange recipients also have other addresses besides DNs. These are discussed later in this chapter.

Single-Server SMTP Message Flow

This scenario expands on the previous one by considering single-server message flow when the Internet Mail Service is installed on the server to provide a gateway to other SMTP hosts on the Internet. Figure 2-8 outlines the process involved when an Exchange recipient uses a MAPI client such as Outlook to send an SMTP message to someone on the Internet.

Another note on terminology. What others might consider a *gateway*, Exchange refers to as a *connector*. The Internet Mail Service is an example of an Exchange connector because it provides messaging connectivity with SMTP hosts on the Internet. But it can also be thought of as a gateway between the Exchange mail system and the Internet SMTP mail system. Unfortunately Exchange uses the term "gateway" to refer to a connector from a third-party company, which causes some confusion.

Here is the description of the interaction between the sending MAPI client, the core Exchange components, and the Internet Mail Service (IMS), keyed to the numbers in Figure 2-8. Note that in this diagram, the numbers *do* refer to a series of sequential steps that take place as the various components interact:

1. MAPI client (sending) → IS

    The sending MAPI client initiates communication with the IS and submits the message to the IS.

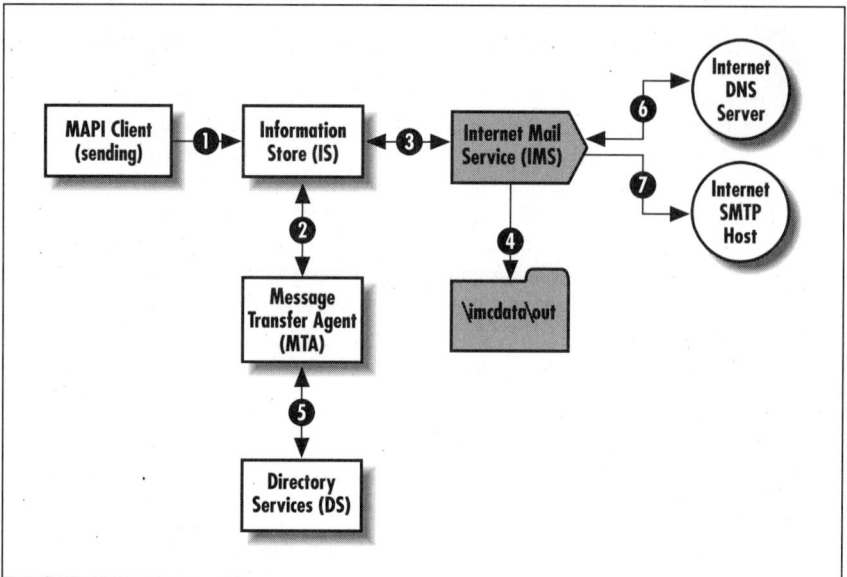

Figure 2-8: Message flow between a MAPI client and an Internet SMTP recipient in a single-server scenario

2. IS ↔ MTA

The IS recognizes that the message is not addressed to a user on the Exchange server (actually, by communicating with the DS), so it initiates communication with the MTA. The MTA is notified whenever a message is addressed to a recipient that is not homed on the sender's home server. The MTA recognizes the destination address as being of type SMTP, determines from the Exchange message routing table (GWART) that there is only one IMS and that it is on the same server, and checks the *address space* of the IMS to see if it is capable of routing the message to its destination. If it can't route the message, it returns a non-delivery receipt (NDR) to the sender, since there is only one connector to try. If it can route the message, it places the message in the folder MTS-OUT. This folder is not a physical folder you can find using Windows Explorer; it is a virtual folder within the Private Information Store on the Exchange server where outgoing messages are queued until the MTA can process them.

3. IS ↔ IMS

The IS then initiates communication with the IMS to inform it of the queued message. The IMS then requests that the IS convert the message format to SMTP and retrieves the message from the MTS-OUT queue in the IS.

4. IMS → *imcdata**out*

The IMS then places the retrieved message in another queue, this time a physical folder with the path *imcdata**out* representing the outgoing queue for the Internet Mail Service.

An *address space* is a collection of partial addresses for a connector that specifies which destination addresses the connector is capable of routing. In practical terms, what this means is that a connector's address space specifies the possible messaging paths through the connector or the possible destination addresses that the connector can handle. The address space of a connector must be specified when the connector is installed and is usually a partial email address that identifies the possible range of destinations the connector can route messages to. For the Internet Mail Service, which uses SMTP addresses, some examples of possible address spaces might be:

— "*" which means that the connector can be used to route any SMTP mail (the asterisk is a wildcard). This is the usual choice for SMTP messaging to provide full connectivity with the Internet.

— ".com" which means that the connector can route messages to any *.com* domain. In other words, if a message is addressed to *user@somecorp.edu,* then the Internet Mail Service would not be able to route this message to its destination.

— "anycorp.com" which means that the connector can only be used to route SMTP messages addressed to any recipient in the SMTP domain *anycorp.com.* In other words, it can route a message to *user@anycorp.com* but cannot be used to send mail to *user@anothercorp.com.*

5. MTA ↔ DS

Meanwhile, the MTA initiates communication with the DS to get the SMTP address of the destination recipient. If the destination recipient is a Custom Recipient within the Exchange directory, the SMTP address of this custom address is obtained. For example, if the message is addressed to BobS, a Custom Recipient on the server that has an SMTP address of *bobs@othercorp.com,* then this step of the process resolves BobS into *bobs@othercorp.com.* If the SMTP address of the destination recipient was manually typed into the "To:" field on the client program, the DS cannot resolve the destination and encapsulates it as an SMTP address.

6. IMS ↔ Internet DNS server

The message is now ready to be routed to the Internet, but first the IMS queries a DNS server for an MX record to obtain the IP address of the destination SMTP host.

7. IMS → Internet SMTP Host

The IMS now uses TCP/IP to establish a connection with the destination SMTP host (or a relay host if this is configured) and delivers the message.

The single-server SMTP message flow for a message coming from the Internet to a recipient homed on an Exchange server is the reverse process, with MTS-IN substituted for MTS-OUT and \imcdata\in for \imcdata\out.

POP3 and IMAP4 clients such as Microsoft Outlook Express, Eudora Pro, and Netscape Communicator interact with Exchange in essentially the same way that MAPI clients do as described. Microsoft has integrated POP3 and IMAP4 functionality directly into the Information Store at an API level similar to MAPI. This allows POP3 and IMAP4 clients to use the same security features that MAPI clients use. For example, POP3 and IMAP4 clients can use Windows NT Challenge/Response (NTLM) for secure authentication, if they support it.

The sole difference is that when a POP3 or IMAP4 client retrieves a message from the Information Store, the Information Store converts it to an appropriate format for that client. MAPI clients can access messages in the native format in which they are stored in the Information Store, namely the Message Database Encapsulated Format (MDBEF). POP3 and IMAP4 clients cannot understand this format, so the Information Store must convert it to an appropriate format for that client, such as MIME, Uuencode, or BinHex.

To send messages, POP3 and IMAP4 clients use SMTP to connect to the Internet Mail Service (IMS) on port 25, and the IMS forwards the message to the Information Store after which it is processed just as in Figure 2-8 starting with step 6.

Single-Site Scenario

Let's now look at the situation where several Exchange servers are installed to form a single site. Exchange servers within the same site communicate with each other using Remote Procedure Calls (RPCs). It is therefore essential that servers in the same site have RPC connectivity. In practice this means having a LAN or dedicated, high-bandwidth, permanent WAN connection between all servers in the site and running an RPC-supporting protocol such as TCP/IP or NWLink IPS/SPX Compatible Protocol. The network connectivity between servers in the same site requires high bandwidth because every server in a site opens an RPC connection to every other server in the site. This makes bandwidth increase rapidly with each new added server. (Actually, it increases as n(n+1) where n is the number of servers in the site.)

Since all recipients in the single-site scenario are contained within the Exchange directory, the distinguished name of the destination recipient is used to route the message.

The communications between the Exchange core components on two servers in the same site are illustrated in Figure 2-9.

For simplicity, let's consider a site consisting of only two servers. This scales easily with no significant changes to larger numbers of servers. Here is the description of these various interactions between core components on the two servers, keyed to the numbers in Figure 2-9. Note that these numbers simply identify the various

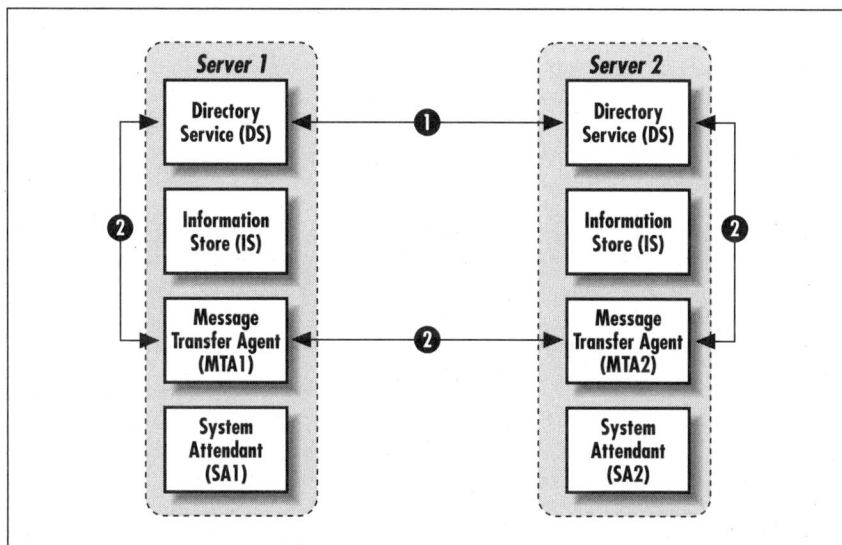

Figure 2-9: Communication between core Exchange components in a single-site scenario

interactions, and in this diagram they do *not* indicate a series of sequential steps. The abbreviations used are:

DS1 and DS2 = Directory Service on servers 1 and 2
IS1 and IS2 = Information Store on servers 1 and 2
MTA1 and MTA2 = Message Transfer Agent on servers 1 and 2
SA1 and SA2 = System Attendant on servers 1 and 2

1. DS1 ↔ DS2

   The DS on one server communicates with the DS on the other server to perform *directory replication*. This allows all Exchange servers in the site to have a full copy of the directory database, which provides fault-tolerance and reduces network traffic during directory lookups. The process works as follows:

   Let's say a change is made to the DS1 directory, such as adding or deleting a directory object or modifying the attributes of an object. DS1 then waits 300 seconds (the replication latency interval) in case additional changes are made; this allows changes to be batched if possible. After the replication latency interval expires, DS1 sends a notification to DS2. If there were other servers, DS1 would pause 30 seconds before notifying the next server. DS2 receives the notification and checks its *update sequence number* (USN) to see when it last received a directory update. USNs are used by the Directory Server to prevent duplication of updates. DS2 then responds to DS1 by requesting (pulling) any updates that DS1 has. DS1 connects to DS2 using RPCs and transfers the updates, and DS2 then processes the updates to ensure its directory database is complete and current.

When you create a new recipient (mailbox, custom recipient, distribution list, or even a public folder), Exchange automatically creates
several different kinds of *addresses* for that recipient. These include:

— Distinguished Name (DN), also known as type EX, the native,
internal address of the recipient in the Exchange X.500 directory system.

— An X.400 Originator/Recipient (O/R) address, also known as
type X400, which serves as a backup address type in case the
DN is corrupt or unavailable. X400 addresses are also used for
connectivity with foreign X.400 mail systems, which are common in Europe.

— An Internet or type SMTP address, used for connectivity with
the Internet system of SMTP hosts.

— A Microsoft Mail 3.x address, known as type MS, used for connectivity with legacy Microsoft Mail networks.

— Other types of addresses may also be generated when a recipient is created. For example, if the Connector for cc:Mail is
installed in a site, new recipients will also have a type "CCMAIL"
address created for them.

These various types of addresses are covered in more detail in
Chapter 3 in the context of directory objects where they are relevant.

2. MTA1 ↔ MTA2

All other communication between two Exchange servers in the same site (and
messages destined for a connector on another server) take place through the
MTAs on the initiating and receiving servers. While the DSs exchange directory replication information in direct binary form, the MTAs always exchange
information in the form of email messages using the *distinguished name* (DN)
or *Originator/Recipient* (O/R) *address* of the destination recipient or service
for addressing purposes. The kinds of messages exchanged between MTAs
can be:

– Regular email messages addressed to recipients homed on another server

– Notification and alert messages generated by Exchange services

– System messages generated by the System Attendant

– Directory replication messages to other sites

and so on. Messages can be submitted to an MTA by a user, a connector, a
service, or another MTA. The general process by which the MTA on one
server communicates with the MTA on another server in the same site is as
follows:

If the data handed to MTA1 for delivery is not in the form of an email
message, MTA1 converts it to this form. MTA1 then looks up the destination
recipient or service in DS1 to find out how to route the message to its destina-

tion. Let's say that it determines that the destination recipient or service is on server 2. MTA1 then opens an RPC connection (called an association) to MTA2 using the site service account as the security context. More than one association can be opened if there are a large number of messages to be delivered. MTA1 then delivers the message to MTA2 using RPCs. MTA1 keeps the association open for 300 seconds in case more messages need to be delivered either way. MTA2 consults DS2 to see if the message is to be delivered to a recipient or service on server 2 or routed to another site or foreign mail system and then delivers the message accordingly.

> By default, 50 messages must be queued in the MTA before it opens a second association for sending messages. If your network connection is poor or you are having RPC connection problems, try lowering the association threshold value on the Messaging Defaults tab of the MTA Site Configuration property sheet.
>
> The MTA can deliver messages to both recipients and services because both recipients and Exchange services have unique email addresses. For example, a message addressed to the Directory Service on server *Raphael* in site Toronto of organization SampleCorp would be, in SMTP format:
>
> *RAPHAEL-DSA@toronto.samplecorp.com*
>
> The System Attendant has a hidden mailbox called RAPHAEL-DSA within the Private Information Store on server *Raphael* for receiving messages from other services on the Exchange server and from Exchange components on other servers in the organization. Some of the services that use the MTA for delivering messages include the Information Store, the System Attendant, the MS Mail Directory Synchronization object, and various Exchange connectors.

Let's look some more at the MTA routing process. When a message is submitted to MTA1, it communicates with DS1 and goes through the following steps:

1. It checks the DN or O/R address or the destination recipient or service to see if the site portion of the address is the local site. If this is not the case, it uses the Exchange message routing table (GWART) to route the message to the appropriate connector. This is described later in this chapter.

2. Since the site portion of the address is the local site, it checks whether the address is a valid one. If invalid, an NDR is returned to the originating recipient or service.

3. If the address is valid and it is the recipient is a distribution list (DL), it expands the DL and then delivers the message to each member of the DL.

4. If the address is a custom recipient, it obtains the DN of the destination recipient from DS1 and starts the routing process over again.

5. If the address is on the local server (the home server of the sending recipient), it delivers the message directly to IS1.

6. Otherwise, the destination recipient or service is on another server in the site (e.g., server 2), so MTA1 uses the process previously described to transfer the message to MTA2. If this can't be done (perhaps server 2 is down), the MTA retries at intervals until it succeeds or times out. The default timeout is 24 hours.

Single-Site Message Flow

Figure 2-10 shows the interaction between two Exchange servers in the same site when a message is sent from a recipient homed on server 1 to a recipient homed on server 2. This should be fairly obvious by now.

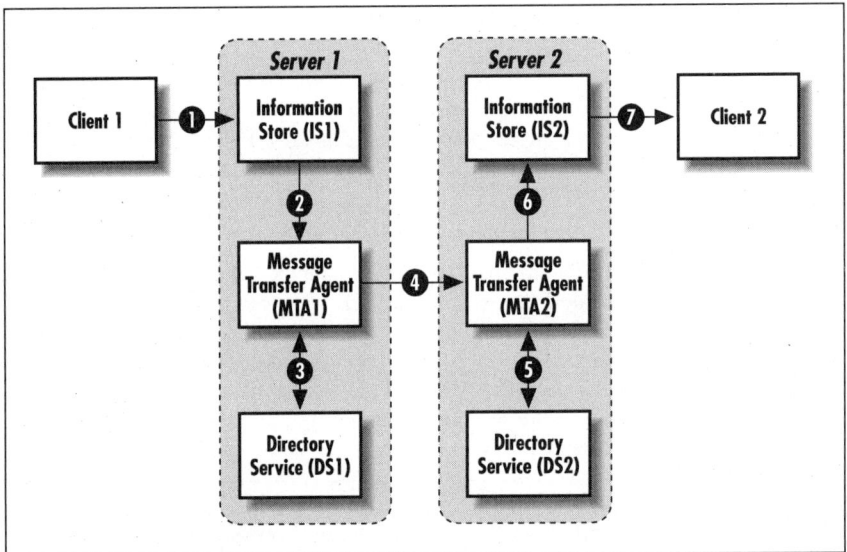

Figure 2-10: Message flow between two Exchange servers in the same site

Here is the description of the interaction between the core Exchange components on the two servers, keyed to the numbers in Figure 2-10. Note that in this diagram, the numbers *do* refer to a series of sequential steps that take place as the various components interact:

1. Client 1 → IS1

   Client 1 initiates communication with IS1 and submits the message to IS1.

2. IS1 → MTA1

   IS1 recognizes that the message is not addressed to a user on the Exchange server (actually, by communicating with DS1), so it initiates communication with MTA1.

3. MTA1 ↔ DS1

MTA1 consults DS1 to determine whether the message is destined for the local site or a remote site. Since it is the local site, it checks the validity of the destination address. If the address is invalid, an NDR is returned.

4. MTA1 → MTA2

MTA1 opens an association with MTA2 using RPCs, if there is currently no association open between them. MTA1 transfers the message to MTA2.

5. MTA2 ↔ DS2

MTA2 consults DS2 to see if the message is addressed to the local server or to another server.

6. MTA2 → IS2

MTA2 puts the message into the incoming queue and notifies IS2 of its arrival. IS2 then retrieves the message from MTA2 and places it in the MTS-IN virtual queue in the Private Information Store on server 2.

7. IS2 → Client 2

If client 2 is currently logged on (has Outlook running), IS2 notifies client 2 of the arrival of a new message.

Summary of Single-Site Communications

Table 2-2 shows the various kinds of data that are typically transferred between Exchange servers in the same site and the Exchange services responsible for generating the data. Between two Exchange servers in the same site, all data is actually transferred by either the Directory Service (directory synchronization traffic only) or the Message Transfer Agent (all other forms of messaging traffic, whether initiated by users or Exchange services).

Table 2-2: Types of Exchange Inter-Server Traffic and Services Responsible

Service Generating Data	Kind of Data
Directory Service	Directory replication information
Information Store (private)	Mail messages sent by users
Information Store (public)	Public folder hierarchy information
	Public folder contents

Table 2-3 presents a rather more complex look at how services on different servers in the same site communicate with each other. Dirsync refers to directory replication between an Exchange site and a legacy Microsoft Mail 3.x network. All communications between two services on different servers take place through the two servers' MTAs, except for communication between their Directory Services which takes place directly using RPCs. Again, DS1 refers to the Directory Service on server 1, DS2 for server 2, and so on.

Table 2-3: Amplification of Detail in Table 2-2

Initiating Service	Receiving Service	Type of Communication
DS1	DS2	Directory synchronization updates
IS1priv	IS2priv	User-initiated messages
	IS2pub	User-initiated messages
	connector	User-initiated messages
IS1pub	IS2priv	User-initiated messages
	IS2pub	Public folder replication
	connector	User-initiated messages
SA1	IS2priv	User-initiated messages
	IS2pub	User-initiated messages
	SA2	Link Monitor (between two sites)
Dirsync	MS Mail system	Directory synchronization updates

Multi-Site Scenario

There are various reasons for setting up multiple sites in an Exchange organization:

- Available network bandwidth and transport modes may dictate that servers on either sides of slow, costly WAN links should be in different sites.

- Geography may be the deciding factor for enterprises that span countries or continents.

- Administrative considerations may dictate that branch offices or subsidiaries be responsible for managing their own Exchange sites.

Whatever the reasons, having multiple sites in your Exchange organization raises issues about site connectivity, message delivery, and routing. Exchange uses connectors to provide messaging connectivity between different sites. There are two kinds of connectors that can be installed:

Messaging connectors
These connectors enable email messages to be moved from one site to another. The four kinds of messaging connectors that can be used to provide message transfer capabilities between Exchange sites are:

- *Site Connector*; The simplest way of connecting two sites together that have a permanent, high-bandwidth network connection.

- *X.400 Connector*: An alternate to the Site Connector, the X.400 Connector gives more control over the schedule and amount of information transferred between sites, but is considerably more complex to configure. The X.400 Connector can also make use of an existing X.400 backbone network (such as those common in Europe) to connect geographically separated Exchange sites together.

- *Dynamic RAS Connector*: For sites that don't have a permanent network connection, the Dynamic RAS Connector uses Windows NT Remote

Access Service (RAS) to provide dial-on-demand or scheduled message transfer between sites.

– *Internet Mail Service*: This connector can provide both dedicated and dial-up messaging connectivity between geographically separated Exchange sites using the Internet as a backbone network.

Directory replication connector

This connector is responsible for exchanging directory updates between Exchange sites and requires that messaging connectivity be established first using one of the four messaging connectors described here.

The X.400 Connector and Internet Mail Service (why didn't they call it the SMTP Connector?) can both be used for a different function, to provide a messaging *gateway* between your Exchange organization and external mail systems such as the Internet or a foreign X.400 mail system. There are also other connectors that can perform gateway functions but cannot be used for linking together Exchange sites. These include:

— MS Mail Connector (also PROFS and SNADS)

— Connectors for cc:Mail and Lotus Notes

As far as message delivery and routing is concerned, Exchange servers in different sites communicate in much the same way as servers in the same site do, with one exception: all transfers of information between servers in different sites, including directory updates, take place in the form of email messages and are handled by the message transfer agent (MTA). The role of the MTA in message transport, routing, and connector selection is crucial in understanding a multi-site Exchange scenario. The MTA can route messages to:

• The MTA on another Exchange server in the same site

• The MTA on another Exchange server in another site using a messaging connector

• A remote X.400 MTA belonging to a foreign X.400-based mail system

• An external connector such as the Microsoft Mail Connector or Internet Mail Service that acts as a messaging gateway to an MS Mail system or SMTP hosts on the Internet

The MTA holds the central position in delivering messages between servers in a multi-site scenario. The MTA makes its decision about which connector to route a message through based upon several factors, including:

Address space

The MTA compares the destination address of the message with the list of all possible address spaces. Each connector installed in an Exchange organization has one or more address spaces defined for it, which are possible messaging paths along which the connector can route messages. By comparing these address spaces with the destination address, the MTA can determine which connectors are capable of routing the message to its destination and which are not.

Note that when we refer here to the MTA of a site, we really mean the MTAs of the servers in that site. For simplicity, you can think of each site consisting of only one Exchange server for the remainder of this chapter, since we are now focusing on inter-site traffic rather than intra-site traffic.

Routing cost

Each address space for a connector has a *cost value* assigned to it by the administrator using the connector's Address Space property page. The cost value can range from 1 to 100, with preference being given to paths with lower cost. If two connectors can provide message routing to a given site, messages are always sent over the connector whose address space has the lowest cost. Routing costs are cumulative, so that if several connectors must be traversed to reach a given destination, the cost values of each connector along the way must be added together to determine the routing cost for each possible routing pathway.

To confuse things, there is another kind of cost value associated with Exchange: *connected site cost.* This kind of cost only applies to a connector when it is being used to connect Exchange sites together, and is configured using the Connected Sites property page of that connector. The X.400 Connector, for example, uses this cost value to select between different bridgehead servers if more than one is available. The connected site cost can range between 1 to 100.

Even more confusing, the online documentation for the X.400 Connector indicates that routing costs can range from 0 to 100 instead of from 1 to 100. A routing cost of zero is said to indicate that the selected route will always be tried and other routes will only be attempted if this route fails. However, this clashes with the concept of cumulative routing costs described earlier. The inconsistency is with the documentation.

Figure 2-11 shows an example of an organization consisting of three sites. Site A is connected to Sites B and C using Site Connectors over T1 lines. Sites B and C are connected using a Dynamic RAS Connector over a dial-up ISDN connection. If a recipient in site A wants to send a message to a recipient in site B, the MTA in site A first looks at the possible address spaces to see which connectors it can use to route the message. The Site Connector and Dynamic RAS Connector can use either a recipient's distinguished name (DN) or O/R address to route messages, and we'll assume that address spaces for all connectors are configured to allow routing of messages anywhere within the organization. The MTA in site A next looks at the total cost of the messaging paths to site B. These costs are:

- Direct AB path: Cost = 1
- Indirect ACB path: Cost = 1 + 5 = 6

Since the direct path has the lower cost, messages sent from A to B will always be routed through the Site Connector joining sites A and B.

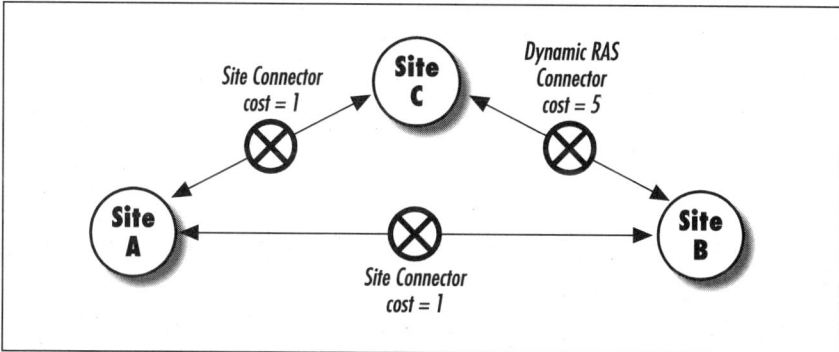

Figure 2-11: Routing costs in a multi-site scenario

Note that if a recipient in site B sends a message to a recipient in site C, the indirect route BAC will be used instead of the direct route BC because of its lower cost. In that case, why install the Dynamic RAS Connector at all if it isn't used for message routing? The obvious reason is to provide a backup messaging path in case the T1 line between sites A and B goes down. In complex scenarios, cost values need to be chosen carefully with consideration given to organization topology and WAN link bandwidth to ensure that messages are routed as efficiently as possible and to provide fault-tolerance to your messaging system.

Cost values can also provide load balancing of messaging traffic. If two connectors are used to join two sites together and these connectors both have the same cost, Exchange will randomly choose between them each time they are used to route messages.

Scope

Sometimes you may want to prevent messages from being routed to a specific connector. In Figure 2-12 we have two sites, A and B, connected by a Site Connector over a high-speed permanent WAN link. Each site is also connected to the Internet using the Internet Mail Service (IMS) because users in the organization frequently need to communicate with external users on the Internet using SMTP mail. The administrator in site A wants to ensure that when a recipient in site A sends SMTP mail it will be routed directly to the Internet using the IMS A connector and not indirectly via the Site Connector followed by IMS B connector. Cost values can assist in accomplishing this, but another method is to restrict the scope of the address space for the IMS A connector to users belonging only to site A. This is accomplished by specifying an *address space restriction* for the connector. The MTA checks the originator of each SMTP message sent by users in site A and only allows messages originating with users in this site to be routed through the IMS A connector. SMTP messages sent by users in site B are not permitted to be routed through IMS A.

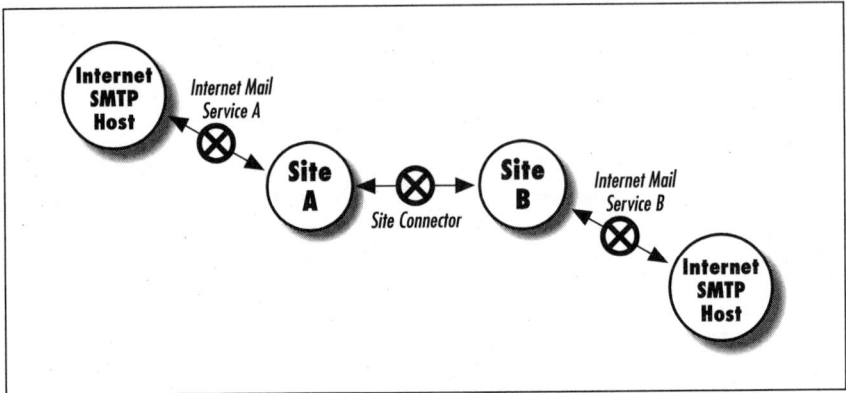

Figure 2-12: Defining address space restrictions can prevent messages from being routed to specific connectors

The possible address space restrictions that can be applied to an address space are:

Organization
> Messages sent from anyone in the Exchange organization can be routed through this connector.

This Site
> Only messages originating from recipients in this site can be routed through this connector.

This Location
> Only messages originating from recipients homed on servers in this location can be routed through this connector.

> *Locations* are a method of grouping one or more servers together within a site, that is, forming "subsites." Locations can be used in message routing as described later in this chapter. The location of a server can be specified as:
>
> — "<None>" which is the default value (i.e., no locations are defined in the site)
> — A specific text string such as "Headquarters" or "Downtown"
> — "*" which enables servers in this location to have access to and be accessed from all servers in all locations

---

Re-Routing

Because large Exchange organizations can have quite complex site topologies, some mechanism must be provided to prevent messages from endlessly looping.

Furthermore, if a connector or gateway stops functioning, there must be some way of re-routing messages to use alternate paths if available. To this end, the MTA tracks which connectors a message uses in trying to reach its destination.

As an example, consider Figure 2-11 again. A message is sent from a recipient in site B to a recipient in site C. Since the indirect route BAC has a lower cost than the direct route BC, the MTA in site B will route the message through the Site Connector to the MTA in site A. Now suppose the MTA in site A receives the message destined for site C and determines that the Site Connector between A and C is down. The MTA in site A then determines that the next lowest cost route to its destination site C is back through site B and then using the Dynamic RAS Connector to site C. So the MTA in site A re-routes the message back to the MTA in site B. The MTA in site B determines that the indirect route through A has already been attempted; if it didn't recognize this, it might send the message back to site A and have it endlessly loop. Having determined this, the MTA in site B then re-routes the message directly to site C.

Multi-Site Message Flow

The process by which the MTA determines which connector or gateway to route a given message through is really a two-step process called Routing and Selection:

Routing Process
> MTA determines which connectors *can be used* to route the message.

Selection Process
> MTA determines which connector *should be attempted* to route the message when the Routing Process gives more than one possibility.

In the final two sections of this chapter, we will examine the details of these processes and bring to a conclusion our look at the operation of Exchange.

Routing

The first thing the MTA must do when it is handed a message by the Information Store, Directory Services, System Attendant, or another MTA is determine whether the message is destined for the MTA's local server, a server in the local site, a server in a different site, or a foreign mail system such as the Internet. We will consider here only the last two options, since we have already dealt with local delivery earlier.

The MTA receives a message; this message needs to be forwarded to the appropriate connector. The routing process is the determination of which connectors can route the message towards its destination. The key here is address spaces, discussed earlier. Each connector in an organization has one or more address spaces, that is, paths over which it is capable of routing messages. Address space information is replicated between all servers in an organization by directory synchronization (within a site) and directory replication (between sites). The System Attendant and the MTA on each server use this information to create a local message routing table called the *Gateway Address Routing Table* or GWART. Each server keeps a copy of the GWART in its directory and updates it as connectors are installed, removed, or reconfigured in the organization.

Besides the address spaces of connectors in the GWART, the MTA also considers address space restrictions and server locations in determining which connectors can route the message. Combining these three possible values for locations with the three possible scopes for address space restrictions lets administrators have a great deal of control over how messages are routed. Table 2-4 shows the "equivalent restriction" of combining a location with an address space restriction.

Table 2-4: The "Equivalent Restriction" Formed by Combining Locations with Address Space Restrictions

| | Address Space Restriction | | |
Location	Organization	Site	Location
<None>	Organization	Site	Site
Specific Location	Organization	Site	Specific Location
*	Organization	Site	Site

Exchange also maintains a text-file version of the GWART in the *mtadata* folder with the filename *Gwart0.mta*. Whenever the GWART is updated, the old version is renamed *Gwart1.mta* and the new GWART is saved as *Gwart0.mta*. You can print these files for reference or troubleshooting purposes. This text-file version of the GWART is not used in the routing process.

Figure 2-13 shows a sample GWART for the organization SampleCorp, whose current messaging topology is displayed in Figure 2-14. (Figure 2-14 is the same as Figure 1-3 from the Magical Mystery Tour in Chapter 1, *Using Exchange*.)

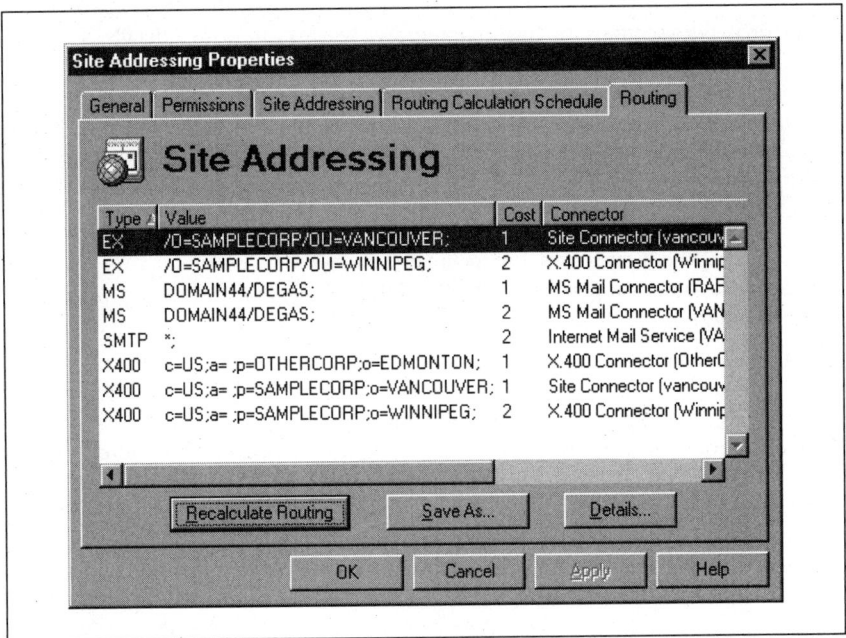

Figure 2-13: The GWART for SampleCorp, as displayed using the Site Addressing object for the Toronto site

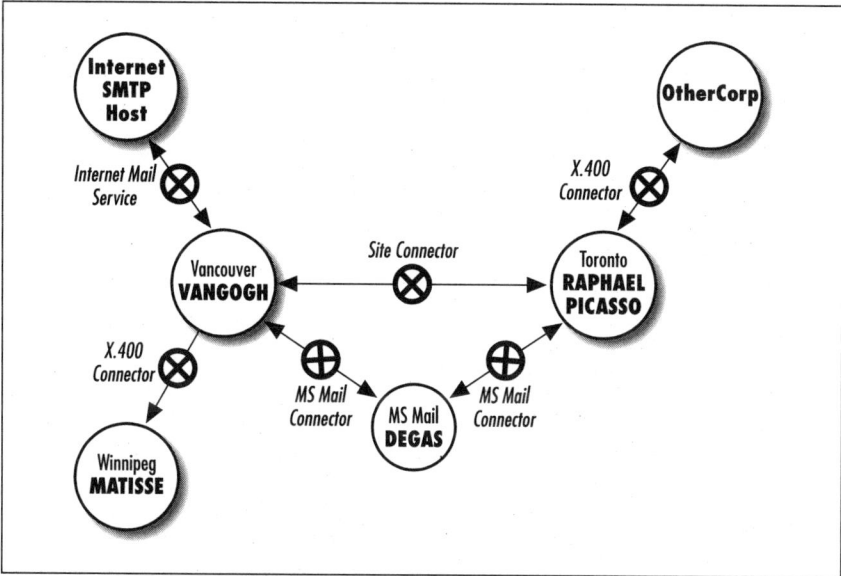

Figure 2-14: The messaging topology for SampleCorp when the GWART for Figure 2-13 was displayed

From Figure 2-14 we see that:

- SampleCorp has three sites: Toronto, Vancouver, and Winnipeg. Toronto has two servers, *Raphael* and *Picasso*, while the other two sites each have one server.

- Toronto and Vancouver are connected using a Site Connector, while Vancouver and Winnipeg are joined with an X.400 Connector.

- The Vancouver site has the Internet Mail Service (IMS) to provide an SMTP gateway to the Internet.

- The Vancouver and Toronto sites have MS Mail Connectors for joining with a legacy Microsoft Mail server *Degas*.

- The Toronto site uses an X.400 Connector to provide messaging connectivity with a foreign X.400 mail system belonging to OtherCorp.

The GWART is divided into three sections:

1. Distinguished Name (DN)

   Address spaces of type EX use the native Exchange addressing format, Distinguished Names.

2. Domain Defined Attribute (DDA)

   These are address spaces used for Custom Recipients, that is, recipients defined in the Exchange directory that represent users of external mail systems. Exchange automatically generates MS Mail (type MS) and Internet (type SMTP) addresses for each recipient you create, but other DDA addresses can be created using third-party gateways.

3. Originator/Recipient (O/R)

Address spaces of type X400 use the native X.400 addressing format.

Each line in the GWART represents a messaging path that can be used by the MTA for routing messages within the organization and to foreign mail systems. The Details button provides additional information for each address space, including the associated connectors used by that address space.

The GWART will look a little different depending on the site in which it is being viewed. This is because the Site Addressing object in Figure 2-13 displays how the GWART can be used to route messages from the local site (Toronto) to other sites and foreign mail systems.

If we look at this GWART line by line, it says the following concerning the MTAs in the Toronto site:

EX /O=SAMPLECORP/OU=VANCOUVER; 1 Site Connector (Vancouver)
Messages can be routed directly to the Vancouver site using the Site Connector (Vancouver). The distinguished name of the destination recipient can be used to route the message. The cost of this routing path is 1.

EX /O=SAMPLECORP/OU=WINNIPEG; 2 X.400 Connector (Winnipeg)
Messages can be routed indirectly to the Winnipeg site using the X.400 Connector (Winnipeg). The distinguished name of the destination recipient can be used to route the message. The cost of this routing path is 2 because the message would have to first traverse the Site Connector (Vancouver) to the Vancouver site and then traverse the X.400 Connector (Winnipeg) to the Winnipeg site. Note that routing costs are cumulative costs.

MS DOMAIN44/DEGAS; 1 MS Mail Connector (RAPHAEL)
Messages can be routed directly to the legacy Microsoft Mail server *Degas* using the MS Mail Connector *(Raphael)*. The MS Mail address of the destination recipient can be used to route the message. The cost of this routing path is 1.

MS DOMAIN44/DEGAS; 2 MS Mail Connector (VANGOGH)
Messages can be routed indirectly to the legacy Microsoft Mail server *Degas* using the MS Mail Connector *(Vangogh)*. The MS Mail address of the destination recipient can be used to route the message. The cost of this routing path is 2 because the message would have to first traverse the Site Connector (Vancouver) to the Vancouver site and then traverse the MS Mail Connector *(Vangogh)* to server *Degas*.

SMTP *; 2 Internet Mail Service (VANGOGH)
Messages can be routed indirectly to the Internet using the Internet Mail Service *(Vangogh)*. The SMTP address of the destination recipient can be used to route the message. The "*" indicates that SMTP mail can be sent to any

---

recipient on the Internet, that is, to any SMTP domain. The cost of this routing path is 2 because the message would have to first traverse the Site Connector (Vancouver) to the Vancouver site, and then traverse the Internet Mail Service *(Vangogh)* to an SMTP host on the Internet.

X400 c=US;a= ;p=OTHERCORP;o=EDMONTON; 1 X.400 Connector (OtherCorp)
Messages can be routed directly to the remote X.400 MTA of OtherCorp using the X.400 Connector (OtherCorp). The O/R address of the destination recipient can be used to route the message. The cost of this routing path is 1.

In this example, OtherCorp is another Exchange organization and has the same country code and Administrative Management Domain (ADMD) in its O/R Address. If OtherCorp were a foreign X.400 mail system, then its O/R Address might read something like:

C=US;a=ATT;p=OTHERCORP;o=EDMONTON;

where American Telephone and Telegraph (AT&T) is the ADMD for the Private Management Domain (PRMD) OtherCorp. For more information on ADMDs and PRMDs see the entry "X.400 Connector" in Chapter 3.

X400 c=US;a= ;p=SAMPLECORP;o=VANCOUVER; 1 Site Connector (Vancouver)
Messages can be routed directly to the Vancouver site using the Site Connector (Vancouver). The O/R address of the destination recipient can be used to route the message. The cost of this routing path is 1.

X400 c=US;a= ;p=SAMPLECORP;o=WINNIPEG; 2 X.400 Connector (Winnipeg)
Messages can be routed indirectly to the Winnipeg site using the X.400 Connector (Winnipeg). The O/R address of the destination recipient can be used to route the message. The cost of this routing path is 2 because the message would have to first traverse the Site Connector (Vancouver) to the Vancouver site and then traverse the X.400 Connector (Winnipeg) to the Winnipeg site.

Two things to note here:

There are two address spaces for the Site Connector (Vancouver) and the X.400 Connector (Winnipeg), a distinguished name (DN) address space of type EX, and an Originator/Recipient (O/R) address space of type X400. These connectors may use either address space for routing messages.

The O/R addresses specify the country attribute as *c=US*, even though all of SampleCorp's sites are located in Canadian cities. Perhaps this indicates that SampleCorp has been acquired by a U.S. conglomerate!

Selection

Once the MTA has used the GWART to determine all possible routing paths that can be used to route the message, the next step for the MTA is to determine which is the best route to use. This process differs depending on which of these scenarios is true:

- The local MTA is communicating directly with another Exchange server MTA using a Site Connector, X.400 Connector, or Dynamic RAS Connector. This case is quite complicated and is described later in this section.

- The local MTA is communicating with a foreign mail system through the Internet Mail Service, an X.400 Connector, a Connector for cc:Mail, MS Mail Connector, or some third-party gateway. This case is relatively straightforward: the MTA uses address spaces and routing costs from the GWART, as described previously, to route the message to the foreign mail system.

When the local MTA wants to connect to a remote MTA in another site through an available connector, there are 10 different criteria the MTA uses to determine the most efficient routing path to select. The MTA processes these criteria sequentially; each connector that passes one criterion is tested for the next criterion, until at the end a single connector is selected. Here are the steps followed by the MTA for selecting a connector to deliver a message, making the selection from the list of possible connectors that resulted from the earlier Routing process:

1. Was the message previously delivered to the local MTA by any connectors? If so, eliminate those connectors from consideration; otherwise, the message may loop endlessly.

2. Do any connectors have Retry Count equal to Max Open Retries? Retry Count is included with each message and indicates how many attempts the MTA has made to route the message through the connector. Max Open Retries can be configured specifically for an X.400 Connector or Dynamic RAS Connector or globally for all connectors using the Site MTA Configuration object.

3. Do any connectors have delivery restrictions or message size limits that apply to this message? If so, eliminate those connectors. This does not apply to messages containing directory replication updates.

4. Try active connectors first. If that fails, try scheduled connectors, and if that fails, try remote initiated connectors. Some connectors, such as the Site Connector, Internet Mail Service, and Microsoft Mail Connector, are always on (active). Other connectors, such as the X.400 Connector and Dynamic RAS Connector, have several possible activation states as shown in Table 2-5.

Table 2-5: Possible Activation States for Connectors

Activation State	Description
Always	This connector is currently active.
Schedule Time	This connector is scheduled to become active at some future time.
Remote Initiated	This connector is activated only when its remote partner contacts it.
Never	This connector is turned off.

5. Which connectors have the lowest Retry Counts? These will be given preference in routing attempts.

6. Which connectors are currently in a Retry State and are attempting to retry delivery? Eliminate these. This step applies only to connectors on the local server.

7. Which connectors have the lowest cost values? These will be given preference in routing attempts.

8. Which connectors are local and which are remote? A local connector is capable of sending a message directly to the destination site. For example, a connector on a messaging bridgehead server would be considered local. To use a remote connector, the MTA must first send the message to a messaging bridgehead server where the connector is installed. Local connectors are given preference.

9. If there is still more than one possible connector selected after all these steps, a connector is selected randomly to load balance the connection.

10. If, however, all possible connectors are in a Retry State, the connector with the lowest Retry Counter value is selected so that the message can be routed as soon as possible.

Re-Routing

Finally, if the local MTA routes a message over a connector and the message cannot reach its destination, the MTA tries to reroute the message by a different connector. By default, it does this by going through the entire Selection process all over again. You may also choose to disable this behavior by restricting the MTA to use *least-cost routing* to route messages. This has to be done for each server by configuring the Message Transfer Agent for that server object accordingly. This streamlines the routing process by eliminating steps 5, 6, and 10 from the Selection process, and by performing step 2 after step 9 instead of near the beginning.

If the MTA has delivered a message to a connector with an activation state of Remote Initiated, it waits until the connector is activated before it considers whether to reroute a message that cannot be delivered.

If the MTA attempts to deliver a message to a foreign mail system such as the Internet through a connector or gateway such as the Internet Mail Service, there is no re-routing possible. As far as the MTA is concerned, once the message has been turned over to the connector, it has reached its destination. It will be the responsibility of the foreign mail system to issue a non-delivery receipt (NDR) to indicate to the message originator that the message failed to reach its intended destination.

PART II

Alphabetical Reference

CHAPTER 3

Directory

This chapter and the next two compose the main body of this quick desktop reference. Specifically:

- This chapter provides an *alphabetical directory reference* to each of the 70-odd different types of directory objects, covering their function and configuration. Also included is an overview of the Exchange *directory database*, a summary of how *permissions* flow within the directory hierarchy, and background information as needed on Exchange concepts and terminology.

- Chapter 4, *GUI Tools*, covers the main *GUI tools* used to administer Exchange, focusing primarily on the most important of these tools, the *Exchange Administrator* program, which is the central tool for administering the directory space of an Exchange organization.

- Chapter 5, *Command-Line Tools*, covers the various *command-line tools* that are used to administer specific aspects of Exchange. These tools have limited functionality but are important for performing specific Exchange-related tasks.

Directory Hierarchy

The job of administering servers within an Exchange organization is essentially the job of creating and configuring objects within the organization's abstract hierarchy of directory objects called the Exchange *directory hierarchy*. The organization of this hierarchy is based on the International Telecommunications Union (ITU) X.500 directory specification. The directory hierarchy includes objects representing the Exchange organization, sites, servers, mailboxes, Distribution Lists, connectors, protocols, monitors, messaging agents, system attendants, information stores, address book views, and a host of other types of objects. The overall functioning and administration of an Exchange organization depends on how these various objects are defined and configured by the administrator using the Exchange Administrator program and how they are managed and replicated by the Exchange *directory service*.

71

Exchange directory objects belong to one of two different categories:

Container objects

These objects can contain other directory objects, both container and leaf types, and are primarily used to organize directory objects into a hierarchical directory space. These are often referred to simply as *containers*.

Leaf objects

These objects are end-nodes of the directory space and cannot contain other objects. They may represent anything from an individual user's mailbox to a control operation such as directory replication among Exchange sites.

Figure 3-1 shows a view of the directory hierarchy for a typical Exchange organization.

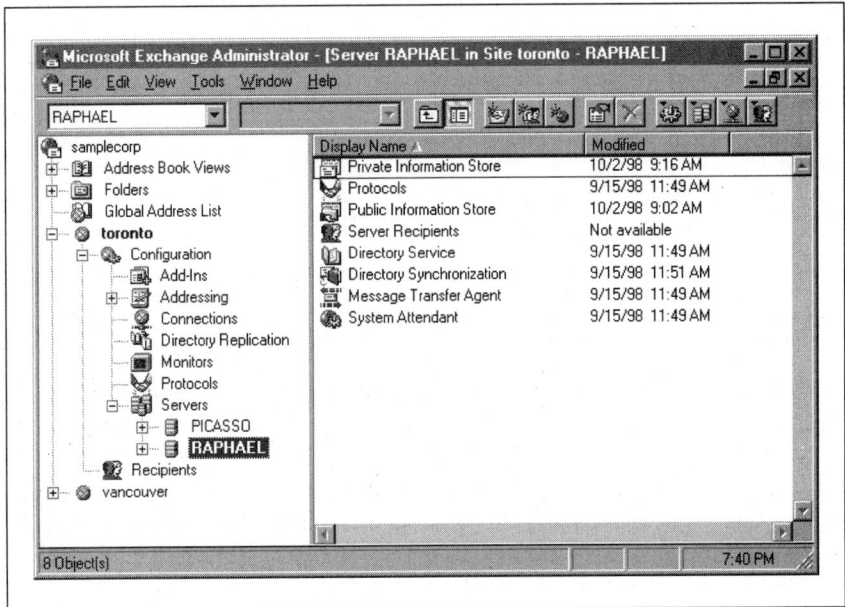

Figure 3-1: A view of the directory hierarchy for a typical Exchange organization

The view in the figure is displayed using the main GUI tool for administering an Exchange organization, the Exchange Administrator program. The actual directory hierarchy is displayed in the left window pane and shows an Organization container SampleCorp, which contains two Site containers, Toronto and Vancouver. The Toronto site container itself contains two exchange Server containers, *Picasso* and *Raphael*. The server container *Raphael* is currently selected, and the various directory objects contained within it are displayed in the right window pane.

The Exchange directory hierarchy can be collapsed and expanded using the plus and minus signs, allowing a complex organization consisting of many sites and servers to be displayed within one window. The directory hierarchy flows from container to container, with the root or highest level of the hierarchy being the organization container.

Figure 3-2 shows a complete, expanded view of the Exchange directory hierarchy, starting from the root container Organization. Note that the directory hierarchy of your own Exchange organization will probably only contain a subset of these objects, depending on what connectors and other items you have defined and created within your organization. Also, some objects will be defined multiple times within your organization's directory hierarchy, such as multiple sites and servers.

The information contained in the Exchange directory automatically replicates to all Exchange servers in a given Exchange site; no further configuration is required. The Exchange directory services can be configured to replicate between Exchange sites by creating and configuring a Directory Replication Connector leaf object.

All Recipient objects (that is, objects that can receive messages, e.g., Mailboxes, Distribution Lists, Custom Recipients, Public Folders, and Mailbox Agents) are collected together into the Global Address List container. This Global Address List functions like a telephone directory, allowing you to select recipients for sending messages.

For information on the purpose, function, and configuration of specific directory objects such as Organization, Site and Server containers, Directory Replication Connectors, Mailboxes, and any other Exchange directory objects, see each object's individual entry in this chapter. For more information on using the Exchange Administrator program to administer the Exchange directory space, see Chapter 4.

Directory Database

The actual location of the directory space information for an Exchange organization is a series of files that form the Exchange *directory database*. A copy of this database exists on each Exchange server in the organization, and these copies are identical if directory replication is configured properly between sites in the organization.

The location of the directory database files depends on the physical components of the server's disk subsystem, such as the number of hard drives, the partitioning scheme, whether RAID is used, and so on. If Exchange is installed without running Performance Optimizer, the directory database files are located by default in the folder *C:\Dsadata* and comprise the following:

dir.edb
> Contains the actual directory database, although the actual directory information at any given moment consists of a combination of the *dir.edb* file and uncommitted transactions within the *edb.log* file. The *dir.edb* file uses the Microsoft ESE97 Joint Engine Technology (JET) database engine technology.

edb.log
> A *transaction log file* that accepts and tracks all changes that are made to the directory database. When a change is made to a directory object, that change is simultaneously written to the *edb.log* and to a cache in memory. The cached information is later flushed to the *dir.edb* file, and the flushed transaction is marked as committed in the *edb.chk* file.

```
Organization (C)
    Address Book Views (C)
        Address Book Views (L)
    Folders (C)
        Public Folders (C)
            Public Folders (L)
        System Folders (C)
            EFORMS Registry (C)
                Organization Forms Library (L)
            Events Root (C)
                EventConfig_SERVER (L)
            Offline Address Book (C)
                Offline Address Book (L)
            Schedule+ Free Busy (C)
                Schedule+ Free Busy Information (L)
    Global Address List (L)
    Site (C)
        Configuration (C)
            Add-Ins (C)
                Extension (L)
            Addressing (C)
                Details Templates (C)
                E-Mail Address Generators (C)
                One-Off Address Templates (C)
            Connections (C)
                Site Connector (L)
                Dynamic RAS Connector (L)
                X.400 Connector (L)
                MS Mail Connector (L)
                Connector for cc:Mail (L)
                Internet Mail Service (L)
                Newsfeed (L)
                DirSync Server (C)
                    Remote DirSync Requestor (L)
                DirSync Requestor (L)
            Directory Replication (C)
                Directory Replication Connector (L)
            Monitors (C)
                Link Monitor (L)
                Server Monitor (L)
            Protocols (C)
                HTTP (Web) Site Settings (L)
                IMAP4 (Mail) Site Defaults (L)
                LDAP (Directory) Site Defaults (L)
                NNTP (News) Site Defaults (L)
                POP3 (Mail) Site Defaults (L)
```

—Continued—

Figure 3-2: The hierarchical structure of the Exchange directory space, where C stands for Container and L stands for Leaf object

```
                    Servers (C)
                        Server (C)
                            Server Recipients (C)
                                    Custom Recipient (L)
                                    Distribution List (L)
                                    Mailbox (L)
                                    Public Folder (L)
                                    Mailbox Agent (L)
                                Directory Service (L)
                                Directory Synchronization (L)
                                Message Transfer Agent (L)
                                Private Information Store (L)
                                Protocols (C)
                                        IMAP4 (Mail) Settings (L)
                                        LDAP (Directory) Settings (L)
                                        NNTP (News) Settings (L)
                                        POP3 (Mail) Settings (L)
                                Public Information Store (L)
                                System Attendant (L)
                                MTA Transport Stack (L)
                        DS Site Configuration (L)
                        Gateway (L)
                        Information Store Site Configuration (L)
                        MTA Site Configuration (L)
                        Site Addressing (L)
                        Certificate Authority CA (L)
                        Site Encryption Configuration (L)
                Recipients (C)
                        Custom Recipient (L)
                        Distribution List (L)
                        Mailbox (L)
                        Public Folder (L)
                        Mailbox Agent (L)
                        Microsoft Schedule+ Free/Busy Connector (L)
```

*Figure 3-2: The hierarchical structure of the Exchange directory space, where C
stands for Container and L stands for Leaf object (continued)*

Transaction files help to improve performance of write operations to the
directory database and help to ensure the recoverability and integrity of the
directory database in case of system failures such as power outages, which
can cause memory cache information to be lost. Transaction log files are
always exactly 5MB in size and there may be several of them at any given
time. Committed transactions are purged when a backup of the directory database files is performed or when the server is rebooted.

edb.chk
A *checkpoint file* that keeps track of which transactions have been committed
in the *edb.log* file and which are still uncommitted.

res1.log and res2.log
> *Reserved log files* used only in low disk-space situations to ensure the integrity of the *dir.edb* and *edb.log* files.

temp.edb
> A temporary file that stores transactions in progress.

The information store database files located in *mdbdata* use the same JET database technology as the directory database files and have a similar file structure

---

The sizes of these database files as displayed in Windows Explorer may not be accurate; Exchange directory database files are locked open while Exchange services are running, and the NTFS file system cannot access their properties. To accurately determine the size of the database files, stop all Exchange services and view the file size information in Windows Explorer.

The Exchange directory database files can be checked, defragmented, and repaired using the command-line tool *eseutil* described in Chapter 5.

Property Sheets

Directory objects are created or defined using the menus and toolbar of the Exchange Administrator program. During the creation of a directory object, certain essential configuration settings must be specified using property sheets, dialog boxes, or wizards. Once an object has been created, however, its reconfiguration is accomplished entirely through property sheets.

A *property sheet* is a GUI element with a series of tabs and controls for specifying the attributes of a directory object. Figure 3-3 shows a property sheet for a *mailbox*, a leaf object mapped to a user's Windows NT account that represents a receptacle for storing messages that user receives from other users.

One of the greatest hurdles to learning how to administer Exchange is the vast number of property sheets that need to be configured, some having as many as a dozen or more tabs. This chapter deals with the significant features of each directory object's property sheet tabs, focusing on those settings that are important for administrators to know.

Common Properties

The General and Permissions tabs are common to almost all property sheets of Exchange directory objects, so it will simplify things if we consider these tabs here.

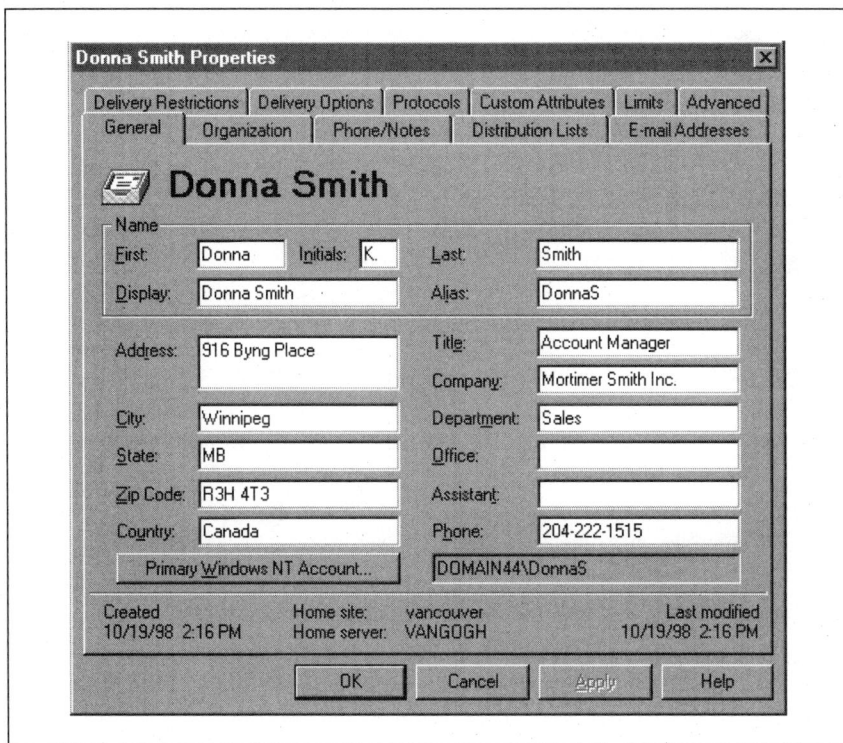

Figure 3-3: An example of a property sheet for a mailbox object showing the General tab

General (Figure 3-3)

For many (but not all) property sheets, the General tab contains two pieces of essential information that must be specified when creating the associated directory object:

- *Display name.* This is the name that is displayed beside the object in the Exchange Administrator program window. It can be up to 256 characters in length and can include spaces and special characters. This must be specified when you create the object, but you can modify it later if desired.

- *Directory name.* This is the internal name for the object within the Exchange directory. It can be up to 64 characters in length and can include spaces and special characters. This must also be specified when you create the object, and it *cannot* be modified afterwards. Note that for the Mailbox object shown in Figure 3-3, the directory name is the same as the Alias. You could later change the Alias on the property sheet from DonnaS to DSmith, but this does not change the underlying directory name—it remains DonnaS (the original Alias) as long as the Mailbox object remains in the directory.

Other information may also be displayed or can be configured using the General tab, but this differs for different types of directory objects.

Directory names are the more important of the two types of names. The directory name of an Exchange directory object is combined together with the directory names of the object's parent containers to form a unique identifier called the *distinguished name* (DN) of the object. The distinguished name uniquely identifies each directory object within the Exchange directory database and is used for routing messages within your organization.

For example, consider a mailbox object belonging to user DonnaS who resides in the site Toronto of the organization SampleCorp:

- The directory name of the mailbox is DonnaS.
- The directory name of the container in which the mailbox resides is Recipients.
- The directory name of the site in which the recipients container resides is Toronto.
- The directory name of the organization in which the site resides is SampleCorp.

From this information, the distinguished name of the user's mailbox, which uniquely identifies this object within the organization's Exchange directory database, would be specified as:

o=SampleCorp/ou=Toronto/cn=recipients/cn=DonnaS

For more on distinguished names, see the associated note in "Single-Server MAPI Message Flow" in Chapter 2, *Architecture and Operation*.

Not just recipients but every container or leaf object in the directory hierarchy of an Exchange organization has a distinguished name (DN). You can view the distinguished name of a directory object by running the Exchange Administrator program in *raw mode*. See Appendix C, *Raw Mode*, for more information.

Permissions (Figure 3-4)

The Permissions tab is normally hidden but can be exposed using Tools → Options from the Exchange Administrator program's menu. Portions of the Permissions tab can be hidden or displayed also, depending on how the Options menu item is configured.

The Permissions tab can be used to:

- View Windows NT accounts that have inherited permissions on the selected directory object
- Grant permissions to Windows NT accounts by assigning them predefined roles
- Grant permissions to Windows NT accounts by creating a custom role

The topic of Exchange permissions and roles is important enough that we will now deal with it in detail.

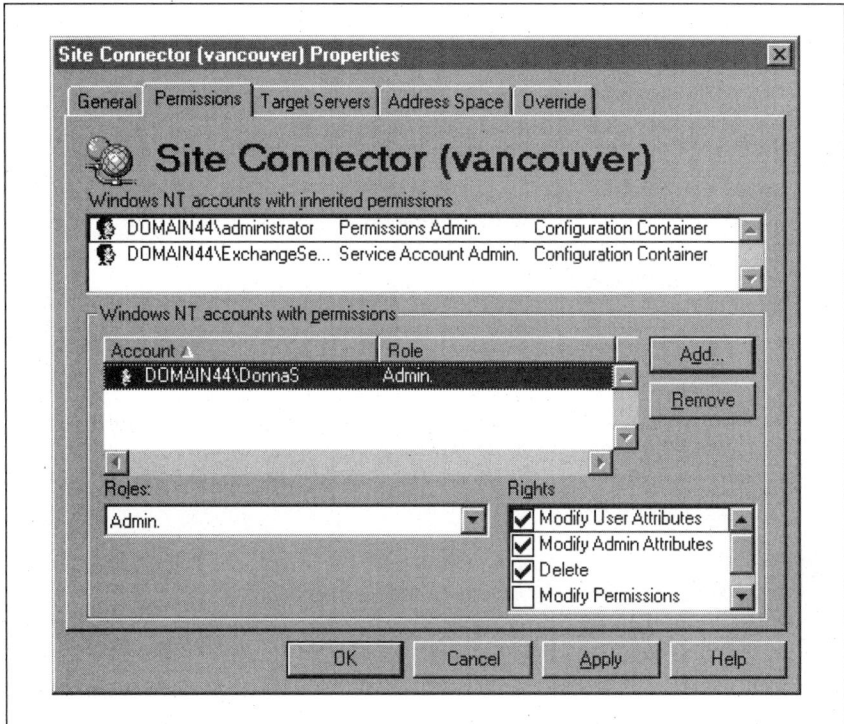

Figure 3-4: An example of a property sheet showing the Permissions tab

Permissions and Roles

Permissions control the kinds of actions users can perform on different directory objects. Exchange permissions are not the same as Windows NT (NTFS) permissions, as we shall see later. Permissions do not need to be assigned to every object in the directory hierarchy, since permissions assigned to a container object automatically flow down the hierarchy of objects inside a container. This is referred to as *inherited permissions*.

There are two exceptions to this concept of inherited permissions:

- Permissions assigned to the Organization container are not inherited by any other objects inside the container. The only thing accomplished by assigning a user permissions on the Organization container is to give that user the right to change the display name of the container (i.e., the name of the container as displayed in the Exchange Administrator window).

- Permissions assigned to a Site container are inherited by:

    - The Recipients container for the site and all recipients within this container

- The Address Book View container and everything within it
- All Public Folders whose home site is the selected Site container

Note that permissions assigned to a Site container are *not* inherited by the site's Configuration container or any site configuration objects within this container.

Permissions are generally assigned to allow users to manage aspects of certain portions of an Exchange organization or have access to certain objects within the organization. The aspects that can be managed will depend on the level of permissions assigned. Examples of how you would assign permissions might include:

- Assign permissions to the Configuration container of a site to grant users rights for managing site-specific aspects of the selected site and all Exchange servers within the site.

- Assign permissions to the Servers container of a site to grant users rights for managing server-specific aspects of all Exchange servers within the site. The user will not be able to manage any site-specific aspects of the site, however.

- Assign permissions to a particular Server container within a site to grant users rights for managing aspects of that server. The user will not be able to manage any other servers within the site or any site-specific aspects of the site.

Watch out for users who seem to have "super user rights" in Exchange. This may inadvertently happen if Exchange permissions are assigned to a group that the user is a member of. This may be further complicated by permissions inheritance.

The individual *rights* that can be assigned to Windows NT users and groups for granting them permissions on directory objects are described in Table 3-1. Note that not all rights can be assigned to a given directory object; the list of rights listed on the Permissions tab of the object's property sheet vary with the type of object selected.

Table 3-1: Individual Exchange Rights That Can Be Granted to Windows NT Users and Groups

Rights	Users with This Right Can...
Add Child	Create objects within the selected container.
Modify User Attributes	Modify user-level properties of the selected object (e.g., add members to a Distribution List).
Modify Admin Attributes	Modify administrator-level properties of the selected object (e.g., the Display Name property).
Modify Permissions	Modify the permissions on existing directory objects.
Delete	Delete an object.
Send As	Send messages using the sender's return address for the selected mailbox object. Users have this permission on their mailboxes by default.
Mailbox Owner	Read and delete messages in the selected mailbox object.

Rights	Users with This Right Can...
Logon Rights	Use the Exchange Administrator program to access the directory. Exchange services also need this permission.
Replication	Replicate directory updates to other servers. Needed by the Exchange service account.
Search	View the contents of a container. Used especially for controlling access to Address Book View containers.

For administrative convenience, the individual rights listed in Table 3-1 are grouped into predefined sets of permissions called *roles*. The rights for each of the specific roles are listed in Table 3-2. Note that not all roles can be assigned to a given directory object; the list of roles listed on the Permissions tab of the object's property sheet vary with the type of object selected.

Table 3-2: Exchange Roles and the Rights They Specify

Roles	RIGHTS									
	Add Child	Modify User	Modify Admin	Delete	Logon Rights	Modify Permissions	Replication	Mailbox Owner	Send As	Search
Admin.	✓	✓	✓	✓	✓					
Permissions Admin.	✓	✓	✓	✓	✓	✓				
Service Account Admin.	✓	✓	✓	✓	✓	✓	✓	✓	✓	
View Only Admin.					✓					
User		✓						✓	✓	
Send As									✓	
Search		✓								✓

In addition, a Custom role can be assigned to an account by choosing an existing role for the account and then selecting or deselecting individual rights to customize the role. To do this you must first have selected Display Rights For Roles using Tools → Options → Permissions from the Exchange Administrator menu.

When you first install an Exchange server to create a new site, two existing Windows NT accounts are assigned predefined roles:

Administrator Account

The administrator-level account you were logged on as when you installed an Exchange server in your site is assigned the Permissions Admin role on the Organization, Site, and Site Configuration containers (and is inherited by other objects as described previously). To grant another user full administrative powers on your site, assign the Permissions Admin role to these three containers.

Directory

Service Account

The site *service account* you created prior to installing the first Exchange server in your site is assigned the following roles:

– Service Account Admin role on the Site and its Configuration container.

– A custom role on the Organization container granting all necessary rights for that container.

Finally, although Exchange Administrator is the main tool for assigning permissions to users, permissions to access public folders can also be granted using clients such as Microsoft Outlook. Permissions and roles for accessing public folders are called *client permissions* and are different from the directory permissions we have discussed in this section. Permissions for client access to Outlook mailbox folders such as the Contacts or Tasks folder can also be assigned using Outlook itself. See the entry "Public Folder" in this chapter for more information on client permissions.

Alphabetical Reference of Directory Objects

The rest of this chapter is an alphabetical reference of Exchange directory objects. Not all these objects may be installed in your Exchange organization, depending upon its size and scope. For each object, the following information is provided:

• A brief synopsis of its purpose or function.

• The icon used in Exchange Administrator to represent the type of object in the directory.

• The object's type: container or leaf object.

• The directory path to the object from the root Organization container.

• If the object is a container, a list of other objects it can contain.

• A detailed description of the object. This varies from brief to fairly extensive when new Exchange concepts have to be introduced.

• An overview of significant settings on the object's property sheet tabs.

• Additional notes, usually tips or warnings of a practical nature.

• Occasional screenshots are provided when they help to illustrate a concept or procedure.

Add-Ins

Contains third-party extensions if installed.

Type

Container

Path

Organization\Site\Configuration\Add-Ins

Can Contain

Extension

Description

This container is provided for extensions (services) supplied by other companies. There is nothing of importance to configure on this object's property sheet.

Properties

General

Shows the display name, directory name, an Administrative note up to 1,024 characters, Home Site to which the container belongs, date that home site was created, and most recent date when the object was modified.

Permissions

See the section "Permissions and Roles" at the beginning of this chapter.

Notes

For more information, see the entry "Extension" in this book.

Address Book Views

Lets you organize recipients into address lists.

Type

Container or Leaf object.

Path

```
Organization\Address Book Views[\Address Book View[\Address
Book View...]]
```

Can Contain

Address Book View

Description

An Address Book View is a subset of the Global Address List and consists of Mailboxes and Custom Recipients grouped together by some common attribute or attributes. These Views can then be made available to client software such as Microsoft Outlook, enabling users to more easily access frequently used types of addresses.

For example, you might want to group recipients in your organization according to the department they belong to. To do this, you would create a new Address Book View object by selecting File → New Other → Address Book View from the Exchange Administrator program menu and then specify Department as the grouping attribute. This might create a series of new Address Book Views called Management, Sales, Accounting, and Tech Support, depending on the various departments you have defined on recipient property sheets. The result might be a hierarchy of new directory objects as shown in Figure 3-5.

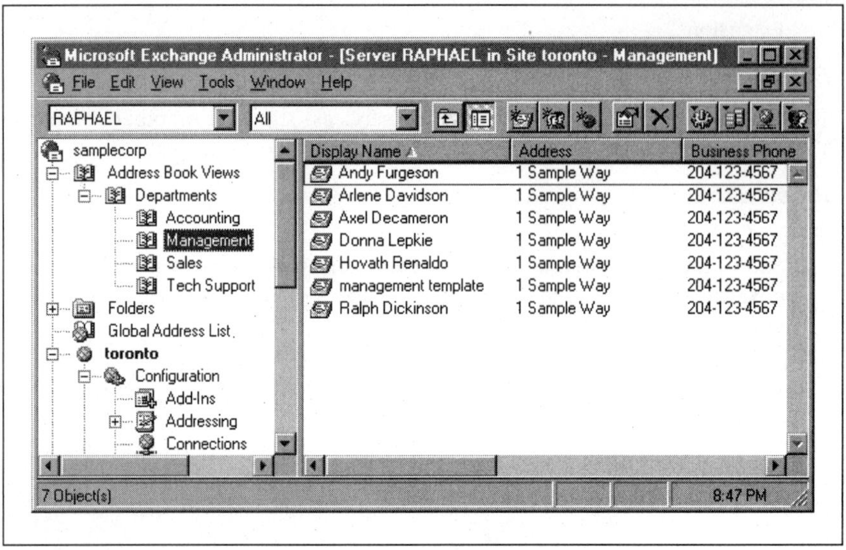

Figure 3-5: Address Book Views based on Department attribute

The hierarchy in the figure consists of the following objects:

Address Book Views container
> This container holds all Address Book Views created for the organization. This is a bit confusing, because although it has the display name Address Book Views, it is not itself an Address Book View, but instead a container for organizing and grouping together all Address Book Views. The property sheet for this container has a General tab, displaying the directory name and allowing you to change the display name, and a Permissions tab.

Departments container
> This is the Address Book View container that defines the grouping of recipients by Department. Its property sheet is described in the next section under Properties.

Accounting, Management, Sales, and Tech Support objects
> These are the Address Book View subcontainers that actually contain the recipients. They appear in the directory hierarchy as leaf objects but can be reconfigured as containers of further Address Book View subcontainers. In other words, under Accounting you could have additional subcontainers to group recipients by some other attribute like location or seniority. The property sheet for these subcontainers are the same as for their parent Departments container and are described below under "Properties."

The hierarchy of Address Book Views created appear in the address book of Microsoft Outlook. Users or groups of users can be granted or denied the ability of seeing specific Address Book Views by accessing the Permissions property page for that View and granting or removing the Search permission from that user or group of users.

The property sheet for an Address Book View container or subcontainer lets you:

- Specify attributes for grouping recipients
- Enable Address Book Views to be visible from clients

Properties

General
Lets you specify the display name and an administrative note. Also lets you view the directory name.

Group By
Lets you create up to four levels of Address Book View subcontainers by specifying the attributes by which recipients will be grouped. You must specify at least one Group By attribute when you create a new Address Book View, and you can specify as many as four different attributes for grouping. Possible attributes include site, home server, personal attributes such as phone number or address, and custom attributes defined using the DS Site Configuration object.

Permissions
See the section "Permissions and Roles" at the beginning of this chapter. To give a Windows NT user or group permission to see an Address Book View in their Outlook client, assign the Search permission to that user or group. To allow all users to see an Address Book View, assign the Search permission to the Windows NT built-in system group Everyone.

Note that once you grant explicit Search permission for an Address Book View to a specific user or group, you automatically deny access to that Address Book View to all other users and groups. In other words, you must assign explicit Search permissions to all users and groups that you want to have access to that Address Book View.

Advanced
Lets you remove empty containers, allow the Address Book View to appear in the address book of the Outlook client program, and specify whether recipients should also be visible parent Address Book View containers. Note that this tab is only present on the parent Address Book View container, for example the Departments container in Figure 3-5, and not on subcontainers such as the Accounting or Management containers.

Notes

- When you create a new Address Book View, you can specify up to four Group By attributes. These attributes are applied hierarchically when creating the Address Book View. For example, you might create a two-level address book view called Location where the first attribute is State and the second is City. In this case, your Address Book View might have a structure like:

```
Location
    California
        San Francisco
        Los Angeles
    Colorado
        Denver
```

- If you have a multi-level Address Book View like the preceding one, you can use the Promote option on the Advanced tab to enable the names or recipients to be visible in both the State subcontainers and the City sub-subcontainers. If this option is not selected, recipients will only be found in the lowest level containers (i.e., City).

- If you add a recipient to an Address Book View using Tools → Add to Address Book View, the recipient acquires whatever attributes were used to define that Address Book View. For example, if Bob Smith is in the Managers department and you add his mailbox to the Accounting subcontainer of the Department Address Book View, the Department attribute on Bob Smith's mailbox property sheet automatically changes from Managers to Accounting.

  Similarly, if you changed Bob Smith's department from Managers to Accounting directly by accessing his mailbox property sheet, Exchange would update the Department Address Book View automatically to reflect this change. In other words, Address Book Views are automatically updated.

- Empty Address Book View containers and subcontainers are not automatically deleted; use the Advanced tab to delete them all, or use the Delete button on the toolbar to deleted selected subcontainers.

- You can allow anonymous users to access an Address Book View by assigning the Search role to the anonymous account you specified on the DS Site Configuration object's property sheet.

- If you have a large number (roughly a hundred or more) of Address Book Views defined, then 16-bit Outlook and Exchange mail clients may bomb.

Addressing

Contains objects for customizing dialog boxes and auto-generation of email addresses.

Type

Container

Path

Organization\Site\Configuration\Addressing

Can Contain

Details Templates
E-Mail Address Generators
One-Off Address Templates

Virtual Organizations

If you plan to use your Exchange organization to provide messaging services for several different companies, you can use Address Book Views to create "virtual organizations" within your actual Exchange organization. The idea is that each company's recipients should only be able to see their own recipients in the Global Address List, not recipients from other companies hosted by your Exchange organization. To implement a virtual organization, perform the following steps:

1. Create a Windows NT account using User Manager for Domains and specify it as the anonymous account in the DS Site Configuration property sheet.

2. Create a separate global group for each company using User Manager for Domains and add each company's user accounts to its global group.

3. Create an Address Book View and specify Company in the Group By field. You could give your Address Book View the name "By Company."

4. Select the new Address Book View in the Container pane of the Exchange Administrator program so that each company's Address Book View subcontainer is visible in the contents pane. Open the Permissions property page of each subcontainer and assign the Search role to the global group for its company.

5. Open the Permissions property page of the Organization container and add the Search right to the permissions for the Exchange service account.

Now when a user logs on to his mailbox with Microsoft Outlook and views the Global Address List, they will only see recipients from his own company.

Note: Since you are changing the permissions of the Exchange service account in this procedure, as a precaution you should make sure first that there is at least one other Windows NT account with the Permissions Admin Role on the Organization container. For more information, see the *Microsoft Knowledge Base* article Q182902.

Description

The Addressing container is used to logically group together various Exchange objects relating to auto-generation of email addresses and address templates. There is nothing of importance to configure on the property sheet for this object.

Properties

General

Shows the display name, directory name, an Administrative note up to 1,024 characters, Home Site to which the container belongs, date that home site was created, and most recent date the object was modified.

Permissions

See the section "Permissions and Roles" at the beginning of this chapter.

Notes

For more information, see the entries on "Details Templates," "E-Mail Address Generators," and "One-Off Address Templates" in this chapter.

Certificate Authority (CA)

Lets you configure advanced security for users in your organization.

Type

Leaf object

Path

`Organization\Site\Configuration\CA`

Description

The Certificate Authority or CA object is used to enable advanced security features on Exchange, such as digital certificates and SSL encryption. To enable these features, you need to first install Key Management Server (KMS) from the Exchange 5.5 compact disk by using the Complete/Custom option. You also need a Windows NT server running Internet Information Server (IIS) 4.0 with the Microsoft Certificate Server installed and configured. And finally, you must install the Exchange Policy Module on the IIS computer from the Exchange compact disc. Most of this is beyond the scope of this work, so for more information you will need to refer to the documentation for IIS 4.0 and to the online documentation for Exchange, or see the forthcoming O'Reilly book *Managing the Exchange Server* by Paul Robichaux.

Once you have everything set up and configure the properties of the CA object, you should next configure the Site Encryption Configuration object to configure advanced security for your site.

The CA property sheet can be used to:

- Specify KM server administrators and passwords
- Set password policies
- Enroll users in advanced security and issue digital certificates
- View certificate information for users

Properties

General

Lets you specify the display name. Also lets you view the directory name, name of the computer running Microsoft Certificate Server, home site, date the Key Management Server was installed, and date the object was last modified.

Permissions

See the section "Permissions and Roles" at the beginning of this chapter.

Administrators

Lets you view, delegate, and change the password for Windows NT accounts that can administer the KM server. When you try to access this tab, you will be prompted by a dialog box to enter one or more passwords for accessing the KM server through this CA object. Once you enter the passwords, you can access this property page.

Passwords

Lets you specify a password policy for the KM server. Specify the number of KM Server administrator passwords that must be entered to perform administrative tasks on the KM Server such as:

- Adding or removing administrators

- Recovering users' keys

- Revoking users' keys

- Importing or untrusting the certificate of another Certificate Authority

Enrollment

Lets you specify policies for temporary keys and bulk enrollment of users. Temporary keys can be given to users through email or in person on a floppy disk. If sent by email, a welcome message can be specified. Bulk enrollment generates keys for all users in a selected Recipients container, but keys still have to be either emailed or delivered in person to each user.

You can also specify which version of X.509 digital certificates will be used. Refer to the documentation on Microsoft Certificate Server for more information.

Certificate Trust List

Lets you establish certificate trust relationships with other organizations to allow message verification by digital certificates. You need to import the certificate of the other organization in order to establish a trust relationship with it. You can also import certificate revocation lists, which contain a list of those digital certificates that no longer hold valid keys. You can view the details of certificates you import also.

Notes

- The default password for a new KM Server administrator is *password*. This should be changed immediately the first time the administrator accesses the KM server through the CA object.

- Exchange Server 5.5 Service Pack 1 has hotfixes for the Outlook 98 client to enable it to use S/MIME using KM Server. Also included in SP 1 is a new version of KM Server and extensive instructions on how to configure and use it in the included *readme* file.

One important tip: If you install KM Server, be sure to make a backup diskette of the KM Server passwords. If these passwords are lost, all mail that was created using the private key of the KM Server is lost forever!

Configuration

Contains objects for configuring a site.

Type

Container

Path

Organization\Site\Configuration

Can Contain

Add-Ins
Addressing
Connections
Directory Replication
Monitors
Protocols
Servers
DS Site Configuration
Gateway
Information Store Site Configuration
MTA Site Configuration
Site Addressing
Certificate Authority (CA)
Site Encryption

Description

The Configuration container is used to logically group together directory objects that are used to configure site-level properties of Exchange sites and how they connect to each other in your organization.

The Configuration property sheet lets you specify the password for the Exchange *service account.*

Properties

General

Shows the display name, directory name, an Administrative note up to 1,024 characters, Home Site to which the container belongs, date that home site was created, and most recent date the object was modified.

Permissions

See the section "Permissions and Roles" at the beginning of this chapter.

Service Account Password

Lets you enter a new password for the site *service account.* This is the account created prior to installing the first Exchange server in a site and used as a context for Exchange services to run within. The service account is also used to validate whether other servers in the site will be allowed to use the messaging services of your Exchange server. The service account is granted the following Windows NT rights by the first Exchange server installed in your site:

- — Act as part of the operating system
- — Log on as a service
- — Restore files and directories

Note that entering a new password on the Configuration object's property sheet does *not* actually change the password of the service account for your site; you need to also do that using User Manager for Domains. Finally, once you have changed the password in both User Manager and the Configuration container, you need to stop and restart the Exchange services on all servers in your site.

Notes

- • Updating the password of the service account on one Exchange server should automatically update it on all Exchange servers in a site. Check the Application Log in Event Viewer if any problems result from changing the service password.

- • If the same service account is used for multiple sites, you must update it on one server in each site.

- • Do not modify the rights of the service account as this may cause Exchange services to fail.

Connections

Contains all Exchange components related to connectivity with other sites, remote organizations, and foreign mail systems.

Type

Container

Path

Organization\Site\Configuration\Connections

Can Contain

DirSync Requestor
DirSync Server
Dynamic RAS Connector
Connector for cc:Mail
Internet Mail Service
MS Mail Connector
Newsfeed
Site Connector
X.400 Connector

Description

The Connections container is used to logically group together various Exchange objects enabling messaging connectivity outside the local Exchange site. This includes *connectors* and *services* that function as gateways to enable messages to be sent outside and received from outside the site. These components comprise four overlapping groups, as shown in Table 3-3.

Table 3-3: Exchange Connectors and Their Functions

Used to Connect to...	Component
Other sites within your organization	Site Connector X.400 Connector Dynamic RAS Connector Internet Mail Service
Foreign mail systems	X.400 Connector Internet Mail Service MS Mail Connector (PC or AppleTalk Networks) Connector for cc:Mail
Usenet news servers	Newsfeed
MS Mail directory server	DirSync Requestor DirSync Server

These connectors and services create paths for sending messages outside your site to other sites, organizations, or mail systems. These paths are called *address spaces*, and every connector must have one or more address spaces defined. A connector then uses its address spaces to determine which types of messages it is able to route. Table 3-4 lists the various types of address spaces can be created for Exchange connectors.

Table 3-4: Possible Address Space Types for Connectors

Address Space Type	Abbreviation	For More Information, See in This Chapter...
X.400 address space	X.400	"X.400 Connector"
Microsoft Mail address space	MS	"MS Mail Connector"
Internet (SMTP) address space	SMTP	"Internet Mail Service"
Unspecified	Other	—

For more on address spaces, see the entries in this chapter on individual connectors and also the last few sections of Chapter 2. Otherwise, there is nothing of importance to configure on the property sheet for this object.

Properties

General

Shows the display name, directory name, an Administrative note up to 1,024 characters, Home Site to which the container belongs, date that home site was created, and most recent date the object was modified.

Permissions

See the section "Permissions and Roles" at the beginning of this chapter.

Notes

For more information on using any of the preceding components for messaging connectivity, see the individual entries on each connector in this book.

Connector for cc:Mail

Lets you connect your organization to Lotus cc:Mail systems.

Type

Leaf object

Path

```
Organization\Site\Configuration\Connections\Connector for
cc:Mail
```

Description

The Connector for cc:Mail is a Windows NT service that lets you connect your Exchange organization to a Lotus cc:Mail foreign mail system for both messaging and directory synchronization. Directory synchronization between an Exchange organization and a Lotus cc:Mail system works both ways: Exchange recipients are created on the connected cc:Mail Postoffice and replicated to other cc:Mail Postoffices, and cc:Mail recipients are created on the Exchange server running the Connector for cc:Mail and replicated throughout the Exchange organization by intra-site directory synchronization and inter-site directory replication.

Prior to installing the connector on a server in your organization, you must:

- Ensure that the cc:Mail system is running either of the following software configurations:

  - Lotus cc:Mail Postoffice Database Version 6, cc:Mail Import Version 5.15, and cc:Mail Export Version 5.14.

  - Lotus cc:Mail Postoffice Database Version 8 and cc:Mail Import/Export Version 6.0.

- Ensure that the Exchange server on which you plan to create the connector has licensed copies of the Lotus cc:Mail Import and Export programs installed within the system path.

- Have LAN or dedicated WAN connectivity to an available cc:Mail Postoffice.

If you are connecting to a cc:Mail Postoffice of Version DB8, you *must* also have the *ie.ri* file in your system path, in addition to *import.exe* and *export.exe*.

There must be a one-to-one correspondence between Connector for cc:Mail connectors in your organization and Lotus cc:Mail Postoffices you are connecting to. Furthermore, each Exchange server may run only one instance of the Connector for cc:Mail.

The Connector for cc:Mail property sheet lets you:

- Configure a cc:Mail Postoffice and local administrator mailbox
- Configure, schedule, and force directory replication of address lists between your organization and the cc:Mail system directory database
- Specify address spaces for load-balancing routing through multiple connectors
- Enable diagnostic logging for troubleshooting purposes
- View and delete messages in the message queues
- Specify message size limits and other miscellaneous options

Properties

Post Office

Lets you configure the administrator mailbox, cc:Mail Postoffice, Import/ Export version, Postoffice language, message tracking, directory synchronization, and forwarding history. In particular:

Administrator's mailbox

This is where messages will be forwarded if the connector cannot convert them. Create a special mailbox for your local cc:Mail administrator and assign it here.

cc:Mail Postoffice

Lets you specify the cc:Mail Postoffice you want to connect to. The path should be entered in Universal Naming Convention (UNC) form, and is usually of the form *server**share**ccdata*.

Import/Export version

Choose the version you have installed on your Exchange server.

Postoffice language

Lets you select the appropriate code-page for messages transferred through the connector. This should normally be the same as that specified using Regional Settings in the Control Panel.

Message tracking

Lets you enable message tracking for both inbound and outbound messages routed through the connector. Use the Message Tracking Center to view message tracking events (see Chapter 4).

Permit ADE

Automatic Directory Exchange (ADE) may be installed on your directly connected cc:Mail system. If so, select this checkbox to propagate your Global Address List to indirectly connected cc:Mail Postoffices using ADE.

Preserve forwarding history

The forwarding history of a message sent from the cc:Mail system to your organization is attached to the message in the form of a text file called *forward.txt*.

General

Specify message size limits and an administrative note. Also displays the server name, the server's home site, date the connector was installed, and date the connector's configuration was last modified. The message size limit applies to both inbound and outbound messages.

Permissions

See the section "Permissions and Roles" at the beginning of this chapter.

Dirsync Schedule

Lets you schedule when the Connector for cc:Mail will attempt to connect to the remote cc:Mail Postoffice for transferring address list updates. There are three possible settings:

Always

The connector performs directory synchronization every 15 minutes.

Never

Disables directory synchronization but still allows the connector to deliver messages.

Selected times

Use the grid to assign times in 1-hour or 15-minute intervals for directory synchronization.

Address Space

Lets you specify address spaces for the Connector for cc:Mail. An *address space* represents a messaging path through the connector to the remote cc:Mail Postoffice. When an MTA in your local site attempts to route a message through the connector, it checks the list of address spaces to determine whether the connector can route the message, and it load-balances the choice of connectors based on the cost.

An address space for the remote postoffice must be specified when the connector is created. For example, if you wanted to route messages to any possible recipient at server *Post7*, use the wildcard (*) and create the following address space:

Type

CCMAIL

Address

* at POST7

Cost

Routing cost between 0 and 100 for load-balancing across multiple connectors.

Scope

Restrictions on who can use this address space for sending messages through the connector. You can specify users at your location only, your local site only, or users throughout the entire organization.

Delivery Restrictions

Lets you accept or reject outgoing messages, that is, messages from recipients in your organization that are attempting to use the connector as a path to another site, organization, or mail system. Incoming messages are not affected by these settings.

Import Container

Lets you control which cc:Mail addresses are imported from the connected cc:Mail Postoffice and where they are imported to within your directory hierarchy, and lets you manually force directory synchronization.

The import container contains addresses of cc:Mail recipients imported from the cc:Mail Postoffice using directory synchronization. This includes usernames, mailing lists, and bulletin boards. Once a cc:Mail address is imported, it becomes a Custom recipient in the Exchange directory hierarchy. You need to specify:

Container

Lets you select a recipient container for receiving imported cc:Mail addresses. You should probably create a special container for this using File → New Other → Recipients Container from the Exchange Administrator program menu.

Filtering

Lets you specify which addresses to include or reject when importing cc:Mail addresses from the connected cc:Mail Postoffice. You can either import all addresses or import subsets of addresses by creating filters. These filters can use wildcards; for example, `*` at `POST7` would import all cc:Mail recipients from postoffice *Post7*.

Run dir synch now

Lets you manually force directory synchronization between the Exchange server running the Connector for cc:Mail and the connected cc:Mail Postoffice.

When importing cc:Mail addresses, be sure to filter the Exchange addresses from import at the Exchange site or they will be re-imported from cc:Mail. In other words, once the addresses of your Exchange recipients have replicated successfully to the cc:Mail system, you don't want the connector to try to replicate them back to Exchange as new cc:Mail addresses! To prevent this, place a restriction on the import that specifies the connector should not import any address of the form at `ExchangeSite`.

Export Containers

Lets you control which Exchange recipients are exported to the connected cc:Mail Postoffice directory database. You can export any kind of Exchange recipient object to cc:Mail systems. Select the site where the recipient container resides, click Add to move the container into the Export list, and specify a *trust level* for that container. Trust levels are specified on the Advanced tab of a recipient's property sheet. If the recipient's trust level is equal to or lower than the trust level specified here, it will be exported.

The checkbox lets you toggle whether to allow Custom Recipients to be exported.

Queues

Displays the MTS-IN and MTS-OUT message queues and the number of messages in each queue awaiting delivery. In particular:

MTS-IN

These messages have been converted and are inbound through the connector.

MTS-OUT

These messages are waiting to be delivered to the connector.

Select a message in any queue and click Details to display the sender's address, time submitted, size, and other information. If you delete a message from the queue, it is returned to its sender with a non-delivery report (NDR).

Diagnostic Logging

Specify the types and levels of Connector for cc:Mail service events that are logged to the Application Log. Connector for cc:Mail events are logged under the name MSExchangeCCMC in the Application Log and can be viewed using Event Viewer. See the "Properties" section under the entry "Server" for more information about diagnostic logging.

Notes

- Once the Connector for cc:Mail is created and configured, the Connector for cc:Mail Service must be manually started using Services in the Control Panel.

- If you don't know the version of the cc:Mail *import.exe* and *export.exe* programs you have installed on your Exchange server, type `import /?` or `export /?` at the command line to find out.

- If the Lotus cc:Mail Postoffice you want to connect to is on a Novell NetWare network, make sure you have the Windows NT service Gateway Services for NetWare (GSNW) installed on your Exchange server.

- When the Connector for cc:Mail is installed, it automatically generates a cc:Mail email address for all existing Exchange recipients and for any new recipients created thereafter. The address takes the form:

`CCMAIL `*username*` at `*siteproxy*

where *username* is the alias of the user who owns the mailbox, and *siteproxy* is the site containing the user's home server. For example, if BobS has a mailbox homed in site Toronto, then his automatically generated cc:Mail email address would be:

`CCMAIL BobS at Toronto`

- The default address generation method can be modified using Tools → Options → AutoNaming from the Exchange Administrator program menu.

- If you want to use Distribution Lists (DLs) to send messages from your organization to a large number of cc:Mail recipients, create the DLs on the connected cc:Mail Postoffice, not the Exchange server running the Connector for cc:Mail. This is because Exchange expands DLs containing cc:Mail recipients prior to routing through the Connector for cc:Mail.

- Embedded objects in Exchange messages are sent as attachments when routed through the Connector for cc:Mail.

- If you configure Exchange public folders to replicate messages to a cc:Mail bulletin board, do not configure the bulletin board to replicate messages to the Exchange folders or messages may loop endlessly.

Custom Recipient

A type of *recipient* identifying a user outside your Exchange organization.

Type

Leaf object

Path

Organization\Site\Recipients\Custom Recipient

Description

Custom recipients represent users from other Exchange organizations or from foreign mail systems such as cc:Mail. A custom recipient exists in the Exchange directory database but not in the information store. Custom recipients are not normally associated with Windows NT accounts as is the case with *mailboxes*.

Create custom recipients for users who do not belong to your company but to whom your employees will often be sending messages. These custom recipients will appear in the Global Address List, which is accessible from clients such as Microsoft Outlook 98 and will save users from having to create these recipients themselves in their Personal Address Book.

When you create a new custom recipient, you must specify which type of email address (SMTP, MS Mail, X.400, and so on) the custom recipient uses. For example, if you create a custom recipient for someone on the Internet, you would create an SMTP address for that recipient.

The Custom Recipient property sheet lets you:

- Specify personal information about the recipient
- Add the recipient to Distribution Lists
- View and modify the recipient's email addresses
- Configure delivery restrictions for receiving messages
- Specify which Internet protocols the recipient can use
- Define custom attributes for the recipient

Unlike Mailbox objects, Custom Recipients are not homed on any particular Exchange server in your organization. Since Custom Recipients represent recipients that are *outside* your organization, they exist only in the directory database and have no folders for storing messages inside the private information store.

Properties

General

Lets you specify personal information associated with the custom recipient. This includes name, address, company, title, phone number, display name, alias, and email address. Also displays the recipient's home site, the date the recipient was created, and the most recent date the recipient properties were modified.

The email address of a custom recipient is defined when the recipient is created using the Exchange Administrator program. Here you can modify that address (e.g., change the DNS domain of an SMTP address) or replace it with an address of a different type (e.g., an X.400 address).

Organization

Lets you specify whom the custom recipient reports to and who reports to the custom recipient.

Phone/Notes

Lets you specify various phone and fax numbers and any additional notes concerning the custom recipient.

Permissions

See the section "Permissions and Roles" at the beginning of this chapter.

Distribution Lists

Shows the Distribution Lists to which the custom recipient belongs and allows you to add the recipient to other Distribution Lists.

E-mail Addresses

Displays the custom recipient's various email addresses and allows you to modify these addresses or add additional addresses. Email addresses are the means by which Exchange recipients are known, both within your Exchange organization and by outside mail systems. See the entry "Mailbox" in this chapter for more details.

Delivery Restrictions

Lets you control which recipients the custom recipient will accept messages from. If you specify a Distribution List, the members of the list are used (not the list itself) to restrict delivery.

Protocols

Lets you specify which Internet protocols the custom recipient can use when connecting to the Exchange server. Note that SMTP is not listed here since SMTP is enabled by installing the Internet Mail Service through File → New

Other → Internet Mail Service from the Exchange Administrator program menu (see Chapter 4). The configurable protocols include:

- HTTP: Hypertext Transfer Protocol (Web)
- IMAP4rev1: Internet Message Access Protocol Version 4 rev 1 (Mail)
- NNTP: Internet News Transfer Protocol (News)
- LDAP: Lightweight Directory Access Protocol (Directory)

These protocols can be selectively enabled or disabled for individual custom recipients and can have their own configured properties or use the default properties of the Protocols container on their home server. See the entry "Mailbox" in this chapter for more details.

Custom Attributes

Lets you specify the values for custom attributes defined using the DS Site Configuration object for your Exchange site.

Advanced

Miscellaneous settings, including:

- Specify a simple display name for systems that cannot read special characters in the normal display name.

- View the directory name (which is the first Alias Name assigned to the mailbox) and the parent Recipients container of the custom recipient.

- Select a trust level when directory synchronization with MS Mail servers is performed using a MS Mail Connector.

- Specify an ILS server and account if your system uses Microsoft NetMeeting.

- Hide the custom recipient from the address book. Users can still send mail to a hidden recipient if they know its email address, however.

- Allow rich-text format (RTF) messages to be sent to the custom recipient. You must ensure that the recipient's mail system can handle this kind of message format first.

- Specify a message size limit. Set this less than or equal to any message size limits on the outside user's mail system.

- Associate the custom recipient with a Windows NT account on your network. This account will have Owner permissions on the custom recipient object and can use the custom recipient's email address to send and receive messages.

- Provide a descriptive note.

Notes

- An example (from real life) of when you could associate a Windows NT account with a custom recipient is as follows: A company has two mail systems, an Exchange server for internal office mail, contact management, and scheduling, and SMTP mail with their local Internet Service Provider (ISP) for external mail. Most employees use Microsoft Outlook at work to access both kinds of mail, but a few employees work from home and don't have access to the Exchange server directly as the company has not yet installed a Remote Access Server (RAS) or configured a proper firewall. These remote workers only need SMTP mail through the ISP, so the mail administrator creates custom recipients for them with SMTP addresses, allowing employees at the office to send mail to them via the ISP's mail server by sending it to their custom recipients and vice versa.

- When you change the display name and alias of a custom recipient, the recipient's email addresses are not automatically updated. You will have to manually edit each email address to match the name of the recipient.

- Custom recipients take up no space in the *private information store*. Since they do not belong to your organization, they don't store messages on your servers.

It may seem unnecessary for custom recipients to have X.400, MS Mail, and Lotus cc:Mail email addresses when you are only planning on implementing Internet (SMTP) mail services, so you may be tempted to delete these extra addresses for housecleaning purposes. *Don't do this!* Deleting the automatically generated email addresses for a list can cause directory replication to fail and cause other messaging problems. This is especially true of the X.400 address, which is used internally together with a recipient's distinguished name (DN) in order to route messages throughout an Exchange organization. Deleting X.400 addresses of recipients may prevent them from receiving mail, and deleting the X.400 of an Exchange service or connector may prevent that service or connector from functioning.

You use the Site Addressing object to disable generation of the address types you don't need for future recipients you create, but don't disable the generation of X.400 addresses!

Details Templates

Let you customize how information on Exchange recipients is displayed in client address books.

Type
Container or Leaf object

Path
Organization\Site\Configuration\Addressing\Details Templates

Can Contain
Language
Language\Details Template

Description

Details Templates are descriptions of how and what properties are shown when the properties of a recipient are viewed in client address books. For example, when a Microsoft Outlook client accesses the client-side address book and selects a recipient, a dialog box appears showing the recipient's name, address, department, and so on (Figure 3-6). The layout and attributes of this dialog box are defined by a Details Template on the Exchange server.

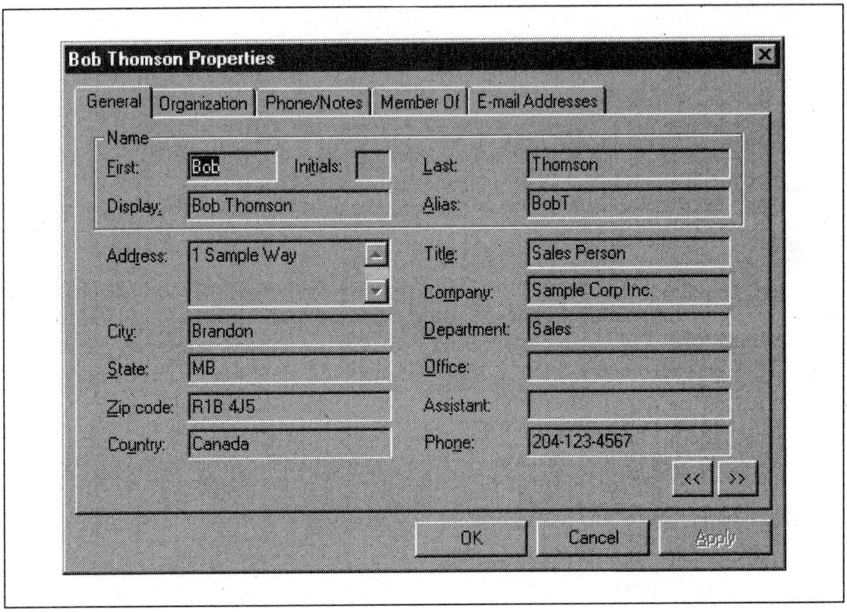

Figure 3-6: The Microsoft Outlook dialog box generated by the Details Template for mailboxes

There are three levels of directory objects that we are dealing with here:

Details Template container
> This container holds Language containers and has a General and Permissions tab with the usual attributes.

Language container
> This container represents the installed language (e.g., English/USA) and has a General and Permissions tab with the usual attributes.

Details Template leaf objects
> These are the objects of interest here. A variety of Details Templates are installed with Exchange defining the appearance of client address book and search dialog boxes. These templates can be modified, for example, to add or remove a textbox or listbox or to rearrange the appearance of controls on a dialog box.

The Details Template property sheet lets you:

- Modify the type, position, and size of controls on the template
- Associate a Help file with the template

Properties

General

Lets you specify the display name, import a custom Help file, and specify an administrative note. Also displays the directory name, date the template was created, and date it was last modified.

The Help file is the file accessed when the client presses F1 while viewing the dialog box associated with the template. Microsoft has software developer's kit (SDK) tools for creating these Help files.

Permissions

See the section "Permissions and Roles" at the beginning of this chapter.

Templates

Lets you modify the type, position, and size of controls on the template. Controls include textboxes, listboxes, and other items.

For example, you might add a new textbox for the custom attribute Employee ID to the Mailbox template. This field will then appear when the client accesses a recipient's address properties. Click the Test button at any time to see what the dialog box created from the template looks like.

Select Original to return to your default template and undo your changes.

MS-DOS Templates

Same as for Templates, except these settings are for the 16-bit MS-DOS Exchange client.

Notes

- Importing a Help file overwrites the existing Help file for the template.
- Additional languages can be installed by importing the *.csv files from the Outlook compact disk. See the readme file for details.

Directory Replication

Contains directory replication connectors if these are installed.

Type

Container

Path

`Organization\Site\Configuration\Directory Replication`

Can Contain

Directory Replication Connector

Description

The Directory Replication container contains any Directory Replication Connectors you have installed on your site. The property sheet for this object has nothing of importance to configure.

Properties

General
> Shows the display name, directory name, an Administrative note up to 1,024 characters, home site to which the container belongs, date that home site was created, and most recent date the object was modified.

Permissions
> See the section "Permissions and Roles" at the beginning of this chapter.

Notes

For more information, see the entry "Directory Replication Connector" in this chapter.

Directory Replication Connector

Replicates directory database updates between two sites.

Type

> Leaf object

Path

> Organization\Site\Configuration\Directory Replication\
> Directory Replication Connector

Description

Directory replication copies directory database information between Exchange servers. This is an important process; if directories get out of sync, messaging can fail. For example, if a new recipient (such as a mailbox) is created on Server A and the recipient directory object fails to replicate to Server B, a user whose home server is Server B will have no reference to the new recipient in his address book and will be unable to send the recipient mail.

There are two kinds of directory replication that can take place with Exchange:

Intrasite Directory Replication
> Within a site, all Exchange servers automatically replicate directory updates to each other using synchronous *remote procedure calls* (RPCs). This occurs within about five minutes after a directory object is created, deleted, or modified on a server. Directory synchronization updates take place like this:
>
> 1. A directory object is modified on a server.
>
> 2. The server notifies another server of the update.
>
> 3. The other servers request the update from the first server.

4. The first server sends the update.

5. Steps 2–4 are repeated for each additional server in the site.

Intersite Directory Replication

Between sites, Exchange servers replicate directory updates to each other using system email messages. This process has to be manually configured, which requires Administrator permissions on both sites (or an administrator in both sites). To configure directory replication between two sites, you must:

1. Designate a bridgehead server for each site. A *bridgehead server* is an Exchange server that functions as a connection endpoint between two sites and is responsible for sending and receiving directory replication update messages between the two sites. When a bridgehead server receives an update message, it distributes the update to all servers in its site using directory synchronization. The bridgehead server in your site is called the *local bridgehead server,* while the one in the remote site is called the *remote bridgehead server* (but from the point of view of the administrator in the other site, these roles are reversed).

2. Make sure all services relating to messaging are started on the bridge-head servers. If you can start the Exchange Administrator program on each server, then you're okay.

3. Configure a messaging connector at each bridgehead server. The connectors must be of the same type and can be any of the following:

   Site Connector
   X.400 Connector
   Dynamic RAS Connector
   Internet Mail Service

4. Test that messaging connectivity has been established between the two sites by sending some test messages. Intersite directory replication uses the *message transfer agents* (MTAs) of the bridgehead servers to request and send directory updates, not remote procedure calls (RPCs).

5. Once messaging connectivity has been verified, configure a Directory Replication Connector at each bridgehead server.

How do you test messaging connectivity when you can't pick the name of a recipient in the remote site from your Global Address List (GAL)? Remember, directory replication has not yet been established with the remote site, so the recipients in the remote site have not yet been replicated to your GAL. The answer is to use a *one-off address,* that is, to contact the administrator of the remote site for a valid recipient address and then manually enter this address into your email client program's To: field. This is called a one-off address because you only want to send one message off to the address. An alternative would be to create a temporary Custom Recipient with the address of a user in the remote site. In either case, make sure you use an address type that is valid for the connector (X.400, SMTP, and so on).

Directory replication now takes place between the sites using the point-to-point connection between the two bridgehead servers, operating according to a schedule that you can configure using the property sheet of the Directory Replication Connector object.

The Directory Replication Connector property sheet lets you:

- Specify local and remote bridgehead servers
- Schedule directory replication between sites
- Specify inbound and outbound sites

Properties

General

Lets you specify the local and remote bridgehead servers. Also shows the display name, directory name, name of the target site whose directory you want to replicate with, an Administrative note up to 1,024 characters, Home Site to which the connector belongs, date that home site was created, and most recent date the connector was modified.

Permissions

See the section "Permissions and Roles" at the beginning of this chapter.

Schedule

Lets you specify how often your local bridgehead server sends requests for directory updates to the remote bridgehead server. Choosing Always causes replication to be initiated every 15 minutes.

Sites

Displays your inbound and outbound sites and lets you manually trigger directory replication.

Inbound sites are those sites from which your site receives directory updates (directly or indirectly), while *outbound sites* are sites to which your bridgehead server sends directory updates (i.e., your own site). This terminology can be confusing; basically, you always replicate your site with inbound sites. Note that you don't have to populate these boxes; they are configured automatically once replication is established and is working.

The list of inbound sites will include:

- The target site you are replicating with
- Other sites that replicate with the target site

The Request Now button sends a notification to selected inbound sites that they should send you updated directory information. When you select Request Now, you can choose between:

- Copying the whole directory database from the selected inbound sites. This can take a long time and is usually used after a restore from tape backup.

- Copying only items that have been modified since the last replication cycle. Choose this if possible.

Notes

- The type of messaging connector you use to connect your sites depends on the type of network connection between them:

  Sites on the same LAN

  Best messaging performance is achieved using a Site Connector. Both Directory Replication Connector objects (the one in your site and the one in the remote site) can be created at once if you have Administrator permissions in both sites; this is the easiest and fastest way of doing things. Use File → New Other → Directory Replication Connector from the Exchange Administrator menu (see Chapter 4).

  Sites on different networks

  Configure an X.400 Connector or the Internet Mail Service to establish messaging connectivity between the sites. You can also use the Dynamic RAS Connector if your sites are connected by asynchronous modems. Then manually create a Directory Replication Connector on each bridgehead server and configure them appropriately using Exchange Administrator as before.

- Another consideration in choosing the right connector is connection speed or bandwidth. If a dedicated networking link between your sites is unreliable or has less than 128Kbps of available bandwidth, consider using an X.400 connector to achieve best messaging performance; otherwise, use a Site Connector. The Site Connector is easier to configure, but the X.400 Connector only uses about one third of the bandwidth of the Site Connector.

- Remember that the remote bridgehead server for your site is the local bridgehead server for the remote site, and vice versa, when you are configuring the Directory Replication Connector!

- You can only create one Directory Replication Connector with a given remote site.

- Your bridgehead server can replicate directory information with more than one site by creating additional Directory Replication Connectors for each remote site, but this is not recommended as the server may become a messaging bottleneck.

- Adjust the replication schedule depending on the frequency with which mailboxes are created, address lists are generated, and other directory objects are modified. Every few hours is usually sufficient.

- If you are using the Dynamic RAS Connector and your sites are only connecting at certain times of the day, schedule your Directory Replication Connector accordingly. Otherwise, update notification messages may pile up and use excessive bandwidth the next time your sites connect.

- Use the Request Now button if:

  - Your server has been down and its directory has become unsynchronized with other servers in the organization

- A large number of changes have just been made to a remote server (e.g., many new mailboxes being created) and you want to update your directory with that information immediately

- Note that the Directory Replication Connector for the *local* site is named Directory Replication Connector (*RemoteSiteName*), and vice versa. It is named after the target site, not the local site!

Directory Service

Configures the directory service (DS) for the server.

Type
Leaf object

Path
Organization\Site\Configuration\Servers\Server\Directory Service

Description

The Exchange directory stores all information about an organization's sites, servers, and recipients. The Microsoft Exchange Directory service is one of the core components of Exchange and is a Windows NT service that maintains the Exchange directory on a server and replicates it throughout the site. See the beginning of this chapter for more information on the Exchange directory space and its hierarchy of objects, and see Appendix D, *Services*, for more on the directory service.

The Directory Service object lets you:

- Configure email addresses for directory replication
- Manually force an update of the Exchange directory within a site
- Configure diagnostic logging for troubleshooting purposes

Properties

General

Lets you force synchronization of directories within a site, check knowledge consistency, and specify an administrative note. Also displays the server's home site, date the server was installed, and date the MTA configuration was last modified.

Synchronization of Exchange directories within a site occurs automatically every five minutes. If you have added new recipients or made other directory changes to other servers in your site and want these changes propagated immediately to other servers, click the Update Now button and choose either to refresh the entire directory or request only updates. Note that this button causes the selected server to request directory updates from other servers in your site, not vice versa.

Checking *knowledge consistency* means looking for new servers in your site and new sites in your organization. This happens automatically every three hours, but if you add a new server or site while your server is offline, your server will have no information about the new server or site when it comes back online. You should then:

1. Select Check Now on this property sheet.

2. Select Update Now to request outstanding directory updates from all other servers in your site.

3. Select Recalculate Routing on the Message Transfer Agent property sheet.

Checking for knowledge consistency by clicking the Check Now button on the General property page of the Directory object to run the Knowledge Consistency Checker (KCC) is not the same as running the DS/IS Consistency Adjuster by using the Advanced property page of the Server object! Running the latter carelessly can have disastrous results; see the warning in the "Server" entry and the sidebar "Re-Homing Public Folders" in the entry "Public Folder," both in this chapter, for further details.

Permissions

See the section "Permissions and Roles" at the beginning of this chapter.

E-mail Addresses

Displays the various email addresses by which the Directory Service is known on your server. These email addresses are used by the Directory Replication Connector object for addressing and routing directory replication messages between sites in your organization. You can modify these addresses or add additional ones if necessary. See the "Mailbox" entry in this chapter for more information about email addresses.

Diagnostic Logging

Specify the types and levels of Directory Service events that are logged to the Application Log. Directory Service events are logged under the name MSExchangeDS in the Application Log and can be viewed using Event Viewer. See the related property for the Server object for more information about diagnostic logging.

Notes

- The email addresses are used for addressing the Directory Replication messages sent between sites. For example, the X.400 address for directory replication messages sent by server *Raphael* that resides in the site Toronto of organization SampleCorp in Canada would be:

  C=US;a= ;p=SampleCorp;o=Toronto;s=Raphael-DSA;

  See the "Mailbox" entry in this chapter for more info on X.400 addresses. The thing to note here is that the surname (s) for this address is of the form **server_name**-DSA that identifies it as a Directory Service Agent (DSA) message relating to directory replication between sites.

  It works something like this: each Exchange directory service in an organization has a unique identifier called an Invocation ID. When a directory object is modified, the Invocation ID attribute for the local directory is stamped against the DSA-Signature attribute of the object. When a directory replication request is made to the server, only information about objects stamped this way are returned via Directory Service messages. The Invocation ID and DSA-Signature are raw attributes that can be viewed by running Exchange Administrator program in *raw mode* (see Appendix C).

Directory Synchronization

Configures directory synchronization with remote MS Mail directory servers.

Type
Leaf object

Path
```
Organization\Site\Configuration\Servers\Server\Directory
Synchronization
```

Description

The Directory Synchronization object is responsible for importing and exporting addressing information to Microsoft Mail directory servers. It is *not* responsible for directory replication between Exchange servers within a site; that process takes place automatically and cannot be configured.

Before you configure this object, you should have created either a Dirsync Server or a Dirsync Requestor on your selected Exchange server. See the related entrys in this chapter for more information on how to configure these objects.

The Directory Synchronization property sheet lets you:

- View and modify the email addresses for the Directory Synchronization object
- Specify delivery restrictions
- Map incoming and outgoing templates
- Enable diagnostic logging for troubleshooting

Properties

General

Lets you specify an administrative note. Also displays the dirsync connection, home server, home site, date the requestor was installed, and date the object's configuration was last modified. The dirsync connection is the name of the Dirsync Server or Dirsync Requestor installed on the selected server.

Permissions

See the section "Permissions and Roles" at the beginning of this chapter.

E-mail Addresses

Displays the various email addresses by which the Directory Synchronization object is known on your server. These email addresses are used by the Directory Synchronization object for addressing and routing directory synchronization messages between Exchange and Microsoft Mail directory servers. You can modify these addresses (don't!) or add additional ones if necessary. See the entry "Mailbox" in this chapter for more information about email addresses.

The Directory Synchronization object uses the email alias DXA to identify itself to Exchange services and components.

Delivery Restrictions

Lets you control which recipients the Dirsync Server will accept messages from. This usually does not have to be configured unless for some reason unwanted messages are being sent to the DXA.

Incoming Templates

MS Mail uses templates for storing extended information like Employee ID or Social Security Number (SSN) of recipients. This property page lets you map incoming template attributes to related attributes of the imported recipient objects. You would do this so that recipient information stored in MS Mail directory servers is stored and displayed in a consistent way within the Exchange directory hierarchy. In other words, if a user's phone number is defined in the MS Mail directory, you want it to appear in the Phone field of the imported Custom Recipient objects in the Exchange directory.

Typically you would map the desired attributes in the MS Mail directory to its related attribute for the imported recipient. If there is no related Exchange attribute, map the MS Mail directory attribute to a custom attribute. (See "Mailbox" for information on custom attributes.)

To map incoming templates, click New, type the template string from the MS Mail Administrator program, and select the desired attribute. See the MS Mail documentation for more details.

Outgoing Templates

Just the reverse of mapping incoming templates. Here you ensure that attributes of an Exchange mailbox are mapped to the appropriate attribute for the exported mailbox in the MS Mail directory database.

Diagnostic Logging

Specify the types and levels of Directory Synchronization events that are logged to the Application Log. Directory Synchronization events are logged under the name MSExchangeDX in the Application Log and can be viewed using Event Viewer. See the related property for the Server object for more information about diagnostic logging.

Notes

- Don't forget to start the Microsoft Exchange Directory Synchronization Service after configuring this object. Use Services in the Control Panel to do this.

- Instead of waiting for directory synchronization to take place as scheduled, you can manually force it to occur from the command prompt. First use Services in the Control Panel to make sure the Microsoft Exchange Directory Synchronization Service is started, and then type:

```
net pause msexchangedx
```

This procedure will generate an error message; just ignore it. And don't ask why you use net pause to force a directory synchronization to occur!

DirSync Requestor

Enables directory synchronization with remote MS Mail directory servers.

Type

Leaf object

Path

`Organization\Site\Configuration\Connections\Dirsync Requestor`

Description

Dirsync stands for Directory Synchronization and refers to the sharing of addressing information between mail systems. While the MS Mail Connector can be used to enable messages to be transferred between an Exchange organization and a remote Microsoft Mail network, other components must be used for exchanging directory information between these systems.

Microsoft Mail makes use of the MS Mail directory synchronization protocol for exchanging address lists between MS Mail Postoffices. Two different components can be created on an Exchange server to enable the exchanging of addressing information between Exchange servers and MS Mail directory servers:

Dirsync Requestor

This component periodically polls the server it is installed on for any changes to the *Global Address List* (GAL). If changes are found, the Dirsync Requestor sends update messages to MS Mail directory servers at scheduled times and requests any updates the MS Mail server may have.

As far as MS Mail servers are concerned, an Exchange server with a Dirsync Requestor acts just like an MS Mail Directory Requestor Postoffice. For example, a possible scenario might be one MS Mail Directory Server Postoffice replicating directory information with two MS Mail Directory Requestor Postoffices and one Exchange server having a Dirsync Requestor installed.

Dirsync Server

Receives updates from MS Mail requestors to update the Exchange recipients list and sends updates of new Exchange recipients to remote dirsync requestors. New MS Mail mailboxes are created as Custom Recipients on the Exchange dirsync server. See the entry "DirSync Server" in this chapter for more information.

As far as MS Mail servers are concerned, an Exchange server with a Dirsync Server acts just like an MS Mail Directory Server Postoffice. For example, a possible scenario might be an Exchange server having a Dirsync Server installed replicating directory information with three MS Mail Directory Requestor Postoffices.

The key thing to keep in mind is that Dirsync Requestors (which can be either Exchange or MS Mail servers) send their updates to Dirsync Servers (which can be either Exchange or MS Mail servers).

For more information on setting up the MS Mail side of directory synchronization, refer to the documentation for MS Mail.

The Dirsync Requestor property sheet lets you:

- Configure import and export containers for directory synchronization with Dirsync Servers
- Specify a schedule for directory synchronization
- Configure other advanced parameters relating to directory synchronization

Properties

General

Lets you specify the display name, dirsync address, type of mail system, requestor language, and other general settings. Also displays the home site, date the requestor was installed, and date the requestor's configuration was last modified. Requiring more explanation are:

Append to imported users' display name

Appends the name of the requestor to the name of each custom recipient created by directory synchronization. This allows you to immediately identify which custom recipients have been imported from the remote MS Mail system through directory synchronization.

Dirsync address

Selects by default the hidden system mailbox directory on the remote MS Mail directory server:

NETWORK/POSTOFFICE/$SYSTEM

Don't change this!

Address types

Besides MS Mail addresses, selects other types of addresses that the requestor will request.

Server

Lets you specify which server in your site will be the requestor.

Permissions

See the section "Permissions and Roles" at the beginning of this chapter.

Import Container

Lets you control which MS Mail addresses are imported from the connected MS Mail directory server and where they are imported to within your directory hierarchy. The import container contains addresses of MS Mail recipients imported from the MS Mail directory server using directory synchronization. Once an MS Mail address is imported, it becomes a recipient in the Exchange directory hierarchy. You need to specify:

Container

Lets you select a recipient container for receiving imported MS Mail addresses.

Trust Level

Lets you assign a *trust level* to recipients being imported. MS Mail systems do not use trust levels, but by importing recipients with trust levels assigned to them, you can control which Exchange recipients are exported to the MS Mail network when directory synchronization occurs. (See next item.)

Export Container

Lets you control which Exchange recipients are exported to the connected MS Mail directory server directory. Select the site where the recipient container resides, click Add to move the container into the Export list, and specify a trust level for that container. Trust levels are specified on the Advanced tab of a recipient's property sheet. If the recipient's trust level is less than or equal to the trust level specified here, it will be exported.

The checkbox lets you toggle whether to allow Custom Recipients to be exported.

Settings

Lets you configure various advanced directory synchronization settings, including:

Dirsync password

The password required to connect to the MS Mail dirsync server.

Participation

Whether to send only, receive only, or both send and receive addressing information between the Exchange server and the MS Mail dirsync server.

Template information

Whether to send only, receive only, or both send and receive template mapping. If you select one of these checkboxes, you must configure template mappings on the Directory Synchronization object. See "Directory Synchronization" in this chapter.

Dirsync information

Whether to send only, request only, or both send and request every available address the next time directory synchronization occurs. In other words, whether to do a full or partial synchronization. The default is unchecked (partial).

Schedule

Lets you schedule when the Dirsync Requestor will send directory updates to the dirsync server. This should normally happen only once a day, and it should coincide with the directory synchronization schedule of the remote MS mail dirsync server.

Notes

- Only one Dirsync Requestor should be created and configured for each remote MS Mail directory server.

- After the Dirsync Requestor has been created and configured, the Microsoft Exchange Directory Synchronization Service must be manually started using Services in the Control Panel. You should configure this service to start automatically on system startup.

- Dirsync Requestors can be used not just with Microsoft Mail networks, but with any mail system that supports the MS Mail 3.x directory synchronization protocol.

- You cannot create a Dirsync Requestor object on a server that already has a Dirsync Server object, and vice versa.

- After you have created and configured the Dirsync Requestor, you can further configure how directory replication occurs using the Directory Synchronization object for the server on which the requestor was created.

DirSync Server

Enables directory synchronization with remote MS Mail directory servers.

Type

Container

Path

`Organization\Site\Configuration\Connections\DirSync Server`

Can Contain

Remote Dirsync Requestor

Description

Dirsync stands for Directory Synchronization and refers to the sharing of addressing information between mail systems. While the MS Mail Connector can be used to enable messages to be transferred between an Exchange organization and a remote Microsoft Mail network, other components must be used for exchanging directory information between these systems.

Microsoft Mail makes use of the MS Mail directory synchronization protocol for exchanging address lists between MS Mail Postoffices. Two different components can be created on an Exchange server to enable the exchanging of addressing information between Exchange servers and MS Mail directory servers:

Dirsync Server
Receives updates from MS Mail requestors to update the Exchange recipients list and sends updates of new Exchange recipients to remote dirsync requestors. New MS Mail mailboxes are created as Custom Recipients on the Exchange dirsync server.

As far as MS Mail servers are concerned, an Exchange server with a Dirsync Server acts just like an MS Mail Directory Server Postoffice. For example, a possible scenario might be an Exchange server having a Dirsync Server installed replicating directory information with three MS Mail Directory Requestor Postoffices.

Dirsync Requestor
This component periodically polls the server it is installed on for any changes to the *Global Address List* (GAL). If changes are found, the Dirsync Requestor sends update messages to MS Mail directory servers at scheduled times and requests any updates the MS Mail server may have. See the entry "DirSync Requestor" for more information.

As far as MS Mail servers are concerned, an Exchange server with a Dirsync Requestor acts just like an MS Mail Directory Requestor Postoffice. For example, a possible scenario might be one MS Mail Directory Server Postoffice replicating directory information with two MS Mail Directory Requestor Postoffices and one Exchange server having a Dirsync Requestor installed.

The key thing to keep in mind is that requestors (which can be either Exchange or MS Mail servers) send their updates to dirsync servers (which can be either Exchange or MS Mail servers). The details of the MS Mail directory synchronization or *dirsync* process can be divided into four steps as follows:

Time 0 (T0)
> The MS Mail Postoffice administrator creates or modifies a MS Mail user or group participating in dirsync using the MS Mail Administrator program. This information must now be updated in the Global Address List of other MS Mail servers participating in dirsync.

Time 1 (T1)
> Dirsync Requestors create messages for the Dirsync Server containing updates of the Requestors' GALs. This is also called the Send Updates Time.

Time 2 (T2)
> The Dirsync Server receives the update messages from the Requestors, adds them to the master transaction list, and creates messages to send to the Requestor with updates for their GALs. This is also called the Process and Retransmit Updates Time.

Time 3 (T3)
> The Dirsync Requestors receive the updates from the Dirsync Server and incorporate them into their GALs. This is also called the Process Updates Time.

Note that you must create a Remote Dirsync Requestor directory object for each remote MS Mail dirsync requestor that will exchange address information with the Dirsync Server component. And you must also configure the MS Mail requestors to communicate with the Dirsync Server as well. For more information on setting up the MS Mail side of directory synchronization, refer to the documentation for MS Mail.

The Dirsync Server property sheet lets you:

- Specify a schedule for directory synchronization
- Configure other advanced parameters relating to directory synchronization

Properties

General
> Lets you specify settings for a Dirsync Administrator and an administrative note and select which Exchange server in your site will be the Dirsync Server. Also displays the display name, home site, date the object was installed, and date the object's configuration was last modified. In particular:

Dirsync Administrator
> The recipient who will receive directory synchronization error messages.

Other settings

The checkboxes enable the Dirsync Administrator to receive copies of all directory synchronization messages. Leave these settings unchecked unless you are trying to troubleshoot directory synchronization.

Permissions

See the section "Permissions and Roles" at the beginning of this chapter.

Schedule

Lets you schedule when the Dirsync Server will send directory updates to the remote dirsync requestors. This should normally happen only once a day, and it should happen shortly after the remote Dirsync Requestors send their updates to the Dirsync Server.

Notes

- Don't forget to create a Remote Dirsync Requestor object for each Dirsync Requestor in the Microsoft Mail network you are connecting to.

- Dirsync Servers can be used not just with Microsoft Mail networks, but with any mail system that supports the MS Mail 3.x directory synchronization protocol.

- You cannot create a Dirsync Server object on a server which already has a Dirsync Requestor object, and vice versa.

- After you have created and configured the Dirsync Server, you can further configure how directory replication occurs using the Directory Synchronization object for the server on which the Dirsync Server was created.

- There must be at least one instance of the MS Mail *dispatch.exe* program running on some machine in order for directory synchronization to occur. *dispatch.exe* runs the programs that transfer address list updates between MS Mail Postoffices.

Distribution List

A type of *recipient* representing a group of mailboxes or other recipients.

Type

Leaf object

Path

`Organization\Site\Recipients\Distribution List`

Description

Distribution Lists, or DLs, simplify the process of mass mailings. Sending a message to a Distribution List sends the message to all member of the list. Distribution Lists can contain mailboxes, custom recipients, and other Distribution Lists. Create Distribution Lists using the Exchange Administrator program (see Chapter 4).

The Distribution List property sheet lets you:

- Specify an owner for the list
- Specify an expansion server for the list
- Add or remove members from the list
- Add the list to other Distribution Lists (DLs)
- View and modify the list's email addresses
- Configure delivery restrictions for receiving messages
- Define custom attributes for the list

Properties

General

Lets you specify the display name, alias name, list owner, expansion server, list membership, descriptive note, home site to which the list belongs, date the list was created, and the most recent date the list's properties were modified. Also displays the list's home site, the date the list was created, and the most recent date the list properties were modified.

Some of the items on this tab bear explaining:

- The *alias* is used in the list's default email address, for example, *MarketingList@Toronto.SampleCorp.com* for SMTP.

- The *expansion server* is the Exchange server that will be used to resolve messages sent to the list into individual messages addressed to the list's member recipients. By default, this is any available server in your site.

- List members can include mailboxes, custom recipients, public folders, and other Distribution Lists.

- The list *owner* is the recipient designated for receiving *non-delivery reports* (NDRs) and other administrative notifications concerning the list. The owner also has the right to modify the membership of the Distribution List using the Outlook client program. A Distribution List can have only one owner.

Permissions

See the section "Permissions and Roles" at the beginning of this chapter.

Distribution Lists

Shows the Distribution Lists to which your list belongs and allows you to add your list to other lists.

E-mail Addresses

Displays the list's various email addresses and allows you to modify these addresses or add additional addresses. When a Distribution List is created, Exchange automatically creates four kinds of email addresses for the list. See the entry "Mailbox" in this chapter for more details.

Delivery Restrictions

Lets you control which recipients the list will accept messages from. If you specify another Distribution List, the members of the list are used (not the list itself) to restrict delivery.

Custom Attributes

Lets you specify the values for custom attributes defined using the DS Site Configuration object for your Exchange site.

Advanced

Miscellaneous settings including:

– Specify a *simple display name* for systems that cannot read special characters in normal *display names*.

– View the directory name (which is the first Alias Name assigned to the mailbox) and parent *Recipients* container of the mailbox object.

– Select a trust level when directory synchronization with MS Mail servers is performed using a MS Mail Connector.

– Specify that NDR and other administrative notifications are sent to the list owner specified on the General tab.

– Let users send messages to the list requesting delivery notifications from individual list members (checked) or from the list as a whole (cleared).

– Allow list members to reply with out-of-office notifications when a message is sent to the list.

– Hide the Distribution List and/or list members from the address book. Users can still send mail to a hidden DL if they know its email address, however.

– Provide a descriptive note.

Notes

• Use a dedicated Exchange server in your site as an expansion server if your site makes heavy use of Distribution Lists.

• Always assign an owner to a Distribution List. This will save you administrative work, as the owner of a list can change the list's name and membership using client software such as Microsoft Outlook. For most lists, the administrator can create the list with the owner as its only member and then email the list (i.e., the owner) a standard message explaining how they can add or remove members from their list using Outlook. This saves the administrator the task of creating list memberships.

- You can use the Permissions tab to give several people the capability of modifying a list's membership if you like.

- When you change the display name and alias of a Distribution List, the list's email addresses are not automatically updated. You will have to manually edit each email address to match the name of the list.

DS Site Configuration

Lets you configure various aspects of the directory services at the site level.

Type
Leaf object

Path
Organization\Site\Configuration\DS Site Configuration

Description
The DS (directory services) Site Configuration object is one of the directory objects that should be configured when you are implementing an Exchange site for your company. The DS Site Configuration object lets you globally configure certain aspects of the Exchange *directory services* for all servers in your site to ensure they maintain the directory database properly. This is important because the directory database acts as a kind of phone book for all mailboxes, custom recipients, and other recipients in your site, so if it functions poorly your whole messaging infrastructure will be affected.

In particular, the DS Site Configuration object lets you:

- Configure offline address books
- Define custom attributes
- Specify tombstone and garbage collection parameters

See the "Site" entry in this chapter for other directory objects that should be configured when setting up a new site.

Properties

General

Lets you configure the display name, tombstone lifetime, garbage collection interval, and anonymous account. Also displays directory name, home site, date the site was created, and most recent date the properties of this object were modified. Some of these bear further explanation:

Tombstone Lifetime

When you delete an object from the Exchange directory database, you are deleting it from the directory of the particular server you are connected to; other servers in your organization still have the object in their directories. To ensure that the object is eventually deleted from the directories of all Exchange servers in your organization, the object you deleted is replaced with a *tombstone marker*. This tombstone marker is then replicated to the directory database of other servers using automatic directory replication within a site or Directory Replication Connectors between sites, removing the object from those directories as well. When the specified lifetime of a tombstone marker expires, the tombstone is deleted from each directory.

Garbage Collection Interval

The scheduled interval in hours between times when the Exchange directory services looks for expired tombstones in the directory database and deletes them.

Anonymous Account

If you want untrusted users outside your organization to be able to access certain directory objects such as public folders or address lists, you need to specify or create a Windows NT account here that the directory services can use to impersonate these users and give them the desired access by assigning the appropriate permissions on that folder or address list to the account you created.

Permissions

See the section "Permissions and Roles" at the beginning of this chapter.

Offline Address Book Schedule

Offline address books are subsets of the Global Address List that a remote user can download and use for sending mail. An offline address book can be based on:

- The Global Address List if remote users need access to the entire Global Address List of all recipients in an Exchange organization.

- A recipients container or address book view if they only need access to a subset of all recipients (e.g., all recipients in the Toronto site or all Marketing Department recipients in the organization) or if the number of recipients in the organization makes download times for the entire address list impractical.

Use this tab to automatically schedule when Exchange servers in your site generate new versions of offline address books. Clients can then download the changes only from previous versions, ensuring that they always have up-to-date address book information.

Offline Address Book

Lets you specify:

- A specific server in your site for generating and storing offline address books.

- The Global Address List, recipients container, or address book view from which each offline address book will be generated.

- Generate All to immediately update all offline address books.

- Whether to support the offline address book formats for clients of earlier versions of Exchange (4.0 and 5.0). If you are using anything earlier than Outlook Version 8.03, you should enable this.

Offline address books are files stored in stored in hidden public folders, which clients such as Microsoft Outlook can connect to and download. To download offline address books using Outlook 98, select Tools → Synchronize → Download Address Book. Note that Outlook must first be configured to use offline folders.

You can also download offline address books to the Outlook Express client by enabling the LDAP protocol on the Exchange server and then using Outlook to connect to Exchange as an LDAP server. An alternative is to export the GAL from Exchange and then import it using Outlook Express.

Custom Attributes

Lets you create new attributes for grouping recipients and tracking messages. Examples could be creating Employee ID, Gender, or Social Security Number fields for recipient objects. These attributes appear on the Custom Attributes tab of recipient property sheets and can be used as a basis for address book views.

Attributes

Lets you specify which recipient attributes should be:

- Accessible to authenticated users from within your organization

- Accessible to anonymous users from outside your organization

- Replicated to other sites in your organization

for a given type of recipient. To access personal attributes of Exchange recipients, the client must support Lightweight Directory Access Protocol (LDAP). Microsoft Outlook and Microsoft Outlook Express both support LDAP.

Notes

- Be sure to set the tombstone lifetime long enough that tombstones will replicate to all Exchange servers within your organization. Take into account the replication schedule between sites, how long a replication takes to be accomplished, how frequently you delete directory objects such as mailboxes or custom recipients, your backup schedule, and so on.

- Make sure the intervals between generating offline address books are far enough apart that one version of the offline address books is completed before the next begins to be generated. Only use the Always option if you designate a particular server for updating offline address books that can handle the extra processing load, especially if you have a lot of recipients in your site.

- Replicating only a subset of recipient attributes to other sites can save substantially on disk space and directory replication processing time and can also be useful when directory replication takes place over slow WAN links.

Dynamic RAS Connector

Lets you configure asynchronous dial-up connectivity with other sites in your organization.

Type

Leaf object

Path

```
Organization\Site\Configuration\Connections\Dynamic RAS
Connector
```

Description

The Dynamic RAS Connector lets you use the Windows NT Remote Access Service (RAS) to provide messaging connectivity between Exchange sites that do not have a permanent, dedicated network connection. This can be a simple, inexpensive way to connect sites in your organization if messaging traffic is fairly low. It can also be useful as a backup connection between two sites if the dedicated network link between them goes down.

One of the features that makes the RAS Connector useful is the ability to schedule RAS messaging transfers. At predetermined times, the RAS Connector can use Windows NT RAS to dial up and transfer messages between each of several connected sites.

Prior to installing the Dynamic RAS connector on a server in your site, you must:

1. Install a RAS-compatible network protocol, usually TCP/IP or NWLink IPX/ SPX Compatible Transport.

2. Install a modem, ISDN terminal adapter, or X.25 PAD and its associated software, depending on what telecommunications service you plan to use.

3. Install and configure the Windows NT Remote Access Service on the computer.

4. Create a phonebook entry for the Dynamic RAS Connector in the remote site you wish to connect to.

5. Create an MTA Transport Stack of type suitable for RAS. See "MTA Transport Stack" in this chapter.

The Dynamic RAS Connector is one of four Exchange connectors that can be used to provide messaging connectivity between sites in an Exchange organization, the others being the X.400 Connector, Site Connector, and Internet Mail Service. Some of the advantages of using the Dynamic RAS Connector include:

- The connector has the capability of scheduling when message transfer takes place.

- It is the only connector capable of functioning over non-dedicated, asynchronous connections.

On the negative side:

- Message traffic is generally slow and depends upon the modem speed.
- The server with the connector installed acts as a bridgehead server and may become a bottleneck.

Use the Dynamic RAS Connector with caution and only if you have no other alternative, as there have been reports that it is buggy and prone to failure. There have been many reports of problems with the connector breaking and not being able to repair it. Service Pack 4 for Windows NT 4.0 fixes some of the underlying causes of these problems, but reports seem to indicate that the fix is not yet complete and additional hotfixes may be necessary. In any case, using a dial-up RAS connection to join two Exchange sites is probably a useless idea in most enterprise environments; you're better off paying the extra money for a dedicated 56Kbps or ISDN link and using the X.400 Connector instead since reliable messaging is the lifeblood of the modern corporation.

The Dynamic RAS Connector property sheet lets you:

- Specify Windows NT account information for logging on to the remote site's RAS server
- Schedule RAS sessions with remote sites for message transfer
- Override the MTA Site Configuration parameters
- Specify connected sites to enable directory replication through RAS
- Specify address spaces for load-balancing of connection paths
- Set delivery restrictions on outbound messages

Properties

General

Lets you specify the display name, remote server name, MTA Transport Stack, phone-book entry, maximum message site, and an administrative note. Also displays the directory name, the server's home site, date the connector was installed, and date the Dynamic RAS Connector configuration was last modified. Of interest are:

Remote server name

This is the name of the server in the remote site that has the other Dynamic RAS Connector installed. Remember that connectors must always be configured in pairs to provide connectivity for both ends of the communications link.

MTA Transport Stack

This must be a transport stack of type RAS. See the entry "MTA Transport Stack" in this chapter.

Phone Book Entry

Lets you specify the phone book entry for the remote server.

Message Size

Lets you specify a maximum size for outgoing and incoming messages being routed through this connector.

Permissions

See the section "Permissions and Roles" at the beginning of this chapter.

Schedule

Lets you schedule when the Dynamic RAS Connector will attempt to connect to remote sites for message transfer. There are four possible settings:

Always

The connector establishes a RAS session every time there is an outbound message in the local MTA queue. You probably don't want to use this setting unless your messaging traffic is very low.

Never

Disables the connector.

Selected times

Use the grid to assign times in 1-hour or 15-minute increments.

Remote initiated

The connector will never establish a RAS session, leaving this to the remote site's connector. Outbound messages in the local MTA queue are only sent when the remote site's connector establishes a RAS session.

RAS Override

Lets you specify the Windows NT account information used to log on to the remote site's RAS server. This account should have permissions to log on to the remote site's RAS server and access Exchange with Permissions Admin role. The Exchange *service account* for the remote site is the obvious choice here. The NT account specified here overrides the account associated with the RAS phone-book entry.

You can also specify a callback number and override the number in the selected phone-book entry on the General tab.

MTA Override

These settings override the local MTA Site Configuration settings only when messages are transferred using this connector. The settings here should match the Messaging Defaults tab of the MTA Site Configuration property sheet for the remote site. See the entry "MTA Site Configuration" for more information on these settings.

Connected Sites

Lets you view and modify the list of remote sites directly connected to your local site through Dynamic RAS Connectors. The remote sites must be listed here so that directory replication can take place with the local site. To specify a connected site, select the New button to open a dialog box for entering addressing and routing information, specifically:

Organization

The name of your organization.

Site

The name of the remote site you want to connect to. The Dynamic RAS Connector must be installed and configured on this site also, as connectors at both ends are needed to enable messaging between sites.

Routing Address

The X.400 address of the remote site. An example would be the following address for the site Winnipeg in the organization SampleCorp:

X.400:c=US;a= ;p=SampleCorp;o=Winnipeg;

For more information on X.400 addresses, see "X.400 Connector" in this chapter.

Cost

A value between 1 and 100 for routing purposes. Cost values are assigned to each routing address, and the one with the lowest cost is preferred. Routing addresses with similar costs are load-balanced in proportion to their cost.

You can also edit or delete existing connected sites.

The Dynamic RAS Connector is best used to connect to only a single remote site. If you use it to connect to two or more remote sites, you may find from time to time that the Message Transfer Agent (MTA) stops unexpectedly. This is another example of the problems with this connector I mentioned earlier. Microsoft has a hotfix for this problem available on their web site; see *support.microsoft.com/ support/supportnet.*

Address Space

Lets you specify address spaces for the Dynamic RAS Connector. An *address space* represents a messaging path through the connector to the remote site. When an MTA in your local site attempts to route a message through the local Dynamic RAS Connector, it checks the list of address spaces to determine whether the connector can route the message and load-balances using the connector based on the cost. An X.400 address space for the remote site is automatically entered into the list when the Dynamic RAS Connector is created.

The listbox on this property page displays four parameters for each address space created:

Type

SMTP, X.400, MS Mail, or Other type of address space.

Address

The addresses that the connector is responsible for routing messages to. Wildcards can be used:

- Asterisk (*) represents any number of characters

- Percent sign (%) represents any single character

Cost

Routing cost, defined earlier.

Scope

Restrictions on who can use this address space for sending messages through the connector. You can specify users at your location only, your local site only, or users throughout the entire organization.

For example, if the remote site is Winnipeg in the organization SampleCorp, the X.400 address space entered in the list when the Dynamic RAS Connector is created would be:

c=US;a= ;p=SampleCorp;o=Winnipeg

Note that an address space contains only a partial address, enough to uniquely identify messages to be routed to the remote site. That is actually why it is called an *address space*, because it represents a space of possible recipients having the same partial address fragment in their addresses.

To route messages of other types (e.g., SMTP or MS Mail) through this connector, you should add an address space for these types. See the entry "Internet Mail Service" for more information about creating new address spaces.

Delivery Restrictions

Lets you accept or reject outgoing messages, that is, messages from recipients in your organization that are attempting to use the connector as a path to another site, organization, or mail system. Incoming messages are not affected by these settings.

Notes

- Specify a maximum message size to prevent the Dynamic RAS Connector from becoming a bottleneck.

- If the Windows NT account specified on the Override tab is not the remote site's Exchange service account, make sure it has at least the User role on the Permissions property page of the Configuration and Servers containers for the remote site.

- The Connected Sites tab displays only those sites directly adjacent to the local site and connected using the Dynamic RAS Connector, unlike the similar tab on the Internet Mail Service property sheet.

- If connected sites are specified (and they should be!), additional messaging traffic can be expected through the connector in the form of directory replication messages. Make sure you plan for this in determining the bandwidth and scheduling of your connector.

EFORMS Registry

A hidden public folder that contains the organization form libraries created for an organization.

Type

Container

Path

Organization\Folders\System Folders\EFORMS Registry

Can Contain

Organization Forms Library

Description

The EFORMS Registry object contains the Organization Forms Library objects that have been created in an Exchange organization.

Properties

None

Notes

See the entry "Organization Forms Library" for more information.

E-Mail Address Generators

Automatically generates email addresses for new Exchange recipients.

Type

Container or leaf object

Path

Organization\Site\Configuration\Addressing\E-Mail Address Generators

Can Contain

E-Mail Address Generators

Description

E-Mail Address Generators are *.DLLs* that generate X.400, SMTP, MS Mail, and other types of addresses for new Exchange recipients. There are two types of directory objects to consider here:

E-Mail Address Generators container
This container holds the actual E-Mail Address Generators and has a General and Permissions tab with the usual attributes.

E-Mail Address Generators leaf objects

These are the actual E-Mail Address Generators and also have General and Permissions tabs with the usual attributes.

Properties

About the only thing of interest here is that you can view the name of the generator *.DLL* and its version number on the General tab.

Notes

If you install a new generator *.DLL* you should specify the name of the file, which should be located in the following directory:

%SystemRoot%\exchsrvr\address\MS

EventConfig_SERVER

A hidden public folder that contains event configuration information of Exchange servers.

Type

Leaf object

Path

```
Organization\Folders\System Folders\Events Root\
EventConfig_SERVER
```

Description

Contains configuration information for the Exchange Event service, which supports custom-developed workflow applications based on Exchange public folders.

Properties

The properties for this object are the same as for the Public Folders object.

Notes

There is nothing for administrators to configure here. This object is only useful to developers and is beyond this book's scope.

Events Root

A hidden public folder that contains objects for event configuration information of Exchange servers.

Type

Container

Path

```
Organization\Folders\System Folders\Events Root
```

Can Contain

EventConfig_SERVER

Description

The Events Root folder contains one EventConfig_SERVER object for each Exchange server in your organization.

Properties

None

Notes

See the entry "EventConfig_SERVER" for more information.

Extension

Separately purchased services that extend the capabilities of Exchange.

Type

Leaf object

Path

Organization\Site\Configuration\Add-Ins\Extension

Description

Extensions are *.DLLs* that provide new services for Exchange servers. Extensions add new tabs to property sheets of Exchange directory objects to allow these services to be configured.

An example of an extension *.DLL* is the Exchange Server Scripting Agent included with Microsoft Outlook, which installs a Scripting Agent service that lets you create and run server-side scripts using VBScript or Jscript. These scripts can be used to build custom workflow applications based on Exchange public folders, such as automatic validation of purchase requisition forms. The Exchange Server Scripting Agent extension adds an Agents tab to the property sheet of Exchange public folders.

Properties

General
Shows the display name, directory name, an Administrative note up to 1,024 characters, home site to which the container belongs, date that home site was created, and most recent date a new Exchange server was added to the site.

Permissions
See the section "Permissions and Roles" at the beginning of this chapter.

Notes

For developer information on the Exchange Server Scripting Agent, refer to the Microsoft Platform SDK.

Folders

Contains public and system folder objects for Exchange servers in your organization.

Type

Container

Path

`Organization\Folders`

Can Contain

Public Folders
System Folders

Description

The Folders container is used to logically group together public folders and system folders (hidden public folders) and forms the root of the Exchange directory hierarchy.

Properties

None

Notes

For more information, see the entries on "Public Folder" and "System Folders" in this chapter.

Gateway

Enables messaging connectivity with another mail system.

Type

Leaf object

Path

`Organization\Site\Configuration\Gateway`

Description

Gateways are custom third-party *.DLLs* implemented as Windows NT services that allow messages to be transferred and translated between Exchange and other mail systems.

Properties

Varies with the type of gateway installed but usually includes many settings that are similar to those of Dirsync Requestor objects.

Notes

The gateway object provides opportunity for third-party developers to enable connectivity between Exchange and foreign mail systems. Microsoft seems to have pretty well covered all the bases already in terms of connectivity, though.

Global Address List (GAL)

Displays all recipients and public folders defined in the organization.

Type

>   Container object

Path

>   Organization\Global Address List

Can Contain

>   Custom Recipient
>   Distribution List
>   Mailbox
>   Public Folder
>   Mailbox Agent

Description

The Global Address List (GAL) displays all recipients in your organization. By default, this list is available to all users in the organization through their client programs such as Microsoft Outlook.

Properties

None

Notes

- If you have several hundred or more recipients in your organization, the Global Address List becomes unwieldy for users to access with their client program. To make life easier for them, create Address Book Views to group recipients together according to departments or locations.

- If clients complain that they can't see the recipients in the GAL properly or that the appearance of the GAL in their client program has changed, you may have incorrectly applied the Search permission to your Address Book Views.

- When Outlook Web Access is enabled, anonymous (unauthenticated) users can be given access to the Global Address List if desired by assigning permissions to the anonymous account defined in the DS Site Configuration object.

HTTP (Web) Site Settings

Lets you configure Outlook Web Access to your site.

Type

Leaf object

Path

Organization\Site\Configuration\Protocols\HTTP (Web) Site
Settings

Description

Outlook Web Access is an optional feature of Exchange that allows users to log on
and securely access their mailboxes and public folders over the Internet from any
JavaScript-enabled web browser such as Microsoft Internet Explorer 3.0 or higher
or Netscape Navigator 3.0 or higher. Outlook Web Access uses Active Server Pages
(ASP) to translate Exchange Server's Messaging Application Programming Inter-
face (MAPI) data into Hypertext Transfer Protocol (HTTP) pages. Outlook Web
Access can also be used to grant anonymous users access to specified Public
Folders and the Global Address List on an Exchange site.

Before you install Outlook Web Access from the Exchange compact disk, you
must have Microsoft Internet Information Server (IIS) installed, either on an
Exchange server or on any Windows NT server on your network that has LAN
connectivity with your Exchange servers. You must also have ASP installed on the
IIS server and the WWW service must be running on the IIS server.

You must install both IIS with ASP and Outlook Web Access on your
Exchange server if you want HTTP users to be authenticated using
Windows NT Challenge/Response (NTLM) authentication. NTLM is a
secure way of authenticating HTTP users since their passwords are
not actually transmitted over the unsecured HTTP connection.
Instead, hashing is performed on the password and the results compared by the server and client. However, if your IIS server is a different machine than your Exchange server, NTLM authentication can't
work and Basic Authentication will be used instead. Basic Authentication is inherently insecure since it transmits user passwords over
the unsecured HTTP connection using clear text (Uuencoding).

Use the HTTP (Web) Site Settings property sheet to:

* Enable access to users' mailboxes
* Enable access by anonymous users to public folders and the Global Address
  List
* Configure specific public folders for anonymous access
* Set limits on downloading the Global Address List

Properties

General

Lets you specify the display name, enable HTTP, enable anonymous users access to public folders and the Global Address List, and specify an administrative note. Also lets you view the directory name, home site, date the object was created, and date it was last modified. In particular:

Enable protocol

Lets users in your Exchange organization access their mailboxes and public folders using Outlook Web Access.

Permissions

See the section "Permissions and Roles" at the beginning of this chapter. Note that a Custom role has been assigned to the Everyone group granting Search permissions so that anonymous users can access public folders and the Global Address List.

Folder Shortcuts

Lets you create Internet shortcuts for anonymous users to access public folders on Exchange.

Advanced

Lets you limit the number of entries in the Global Address Book that are returned at one time. The default value here is 50 entries. If the user's request returns more than 50 entries, a message asks the user to refine the search.

Notes

- If you give anonymous users access to public folders using this property sheet, you must also use the Client Permissions button on the property sheet for each Public Folder object to grant anonymous users the level of permission you want to give them.

- If you use the Folder Shortcuts property page and publish the "All Public Folders" folder, your anonymous users won't be able to view the list of published public folders. You must publish each public folder individually if you want them to have anonymous access to these folders using HTTP.

- To use Outlook Web Access to access their mail using a web browser, users will have to log on in the following way:

User
    `NT_Domain\NT_Alias\Mailbox_Alias`

Password
    `NT_Password`

IMAP4 (Mail) Settings

Lets you configure Internet Message Access Protocol, Version 4rev1 (IMAP4rev1) at the server level.

Type

Leaf object

Path

```
Organization\Site\Configuration\Servers\Server\Protocols\
IMAP4 (Mail) Settings
```

Description

See "IMAP4 (Mail) Site Defaults" in this chapter for a description of Internet Message Access Protocol, Version 4rev1 (IMAP4rev1).

Properties

Same as for the IMAP4 (Mail) Site Defaults object, except:

- You have the option on the General tab to inherit the properties of the site-level IMAP4 object.

- The additional tab Diagnostic Logging lets you specify the types and levels of IMAP4 service events that are logged to the Application Log. IMAP4 events are logged under the name IMAP4 in the Application Log and can be viewed using Event Viewer. See the related property under the "Server" entry for more information about diagnostic logging.

Notes

If you disable IMAP4 at the server level, it also disables IMAP4 for all Mailbox objects homed on the server.

IMAP4 (Mail) Site Defaults

Lets you configure Internet Message Access Protocol Version 4rev1 (IMAP4rev1) at the site level.

Type

Leaf object

Path

```
Organization\Site\Configuration\Protocols\IMAP4 (Mail) Site
Defaults
```

Description

Internet Message Access Protocol Version 4rev1 is a widely used Internet protocol that enables users of IMAP4 clients to retrieve their SMTP mail from an IMAP4 server. IMAP4 expands on the functionality of the POP3 protocol. As far as implementation on Exchange is concerned, users of IMAP4 clients can:

- Access messages in their Exchange mailbox

- Read the headers of messages without downloading the entire message from the server

- Select some mail for downloading from the server and other for leaving on the server

- Access other users' mailboxes (if they have permissions)
- Read and post messages to public folders

IMAP4 is not used for Internet mail transport; this is the job of the Simple Mail Transfer Protocol (SMTP), which is installed and configured using the Internet Mail Service on Exchange.

Microsoft Outlook Express is Microsoft's standard IMAP4 client, but any third-party IMAP4 client may be used as well to access Exchange when the Internet Mail Service is installed and configured.

IMAP4 can be configured at three different levels on Exchange:

- At the site level using the IMAP4 (Mail) Site Defaults object in the site Protocols container
- At the server level using the IMAP4 (Mail) Settings object in the server Protocols container
- At the recipient level using the property sheet of the Mailbox or Custom Recipient

The IMAP4 (Mail) Site Defaults property sheet lets you:

- Specify methods for IMAP4 clients to authenticate on Exchange
- Indicate the message format understood by the IMAP4 client
- Configure connection time-outs
- Allow anonymous access by IMAP4 clients to public folders

Properties

General

Lets you specify the display name, enable IMPA4 at the site level, enable fast message retrieval, configure access to public folders, and specify an administrative note. Worth further examination are:

Include all public folders when a folder list is requested

Clearing this checkbox disables listing of public folders for IMAP4 clients. This may improve performance on some clients.

Enable fast message retrieval

Fast message retrieval causes Exchange to estimate the size of messages instead of determining their exact size. This improves performance but causes difficulties for some IMPA4 clients. Enable or disable this setting as required by your client.

Permissions

See the section "Permissions and Roles" at the beginning of this chapter.

Authentication

Lets you select the authentication methods that are used when IMAP4 clients try to access the Exchange server. Supported authentication methods include:

Basic (Clear Text)

Sends username and password as clear text (unencrypted). Basic Authentication is supported by most IMAP4 clients and is commonly used in the Unix world. Because Basic Authentication transmits user credentials unencrypted over the network, it is not a secure authentication scheme. Anyone with a network packet sniffer who can capture authentication traffic can gain access to a user's credentials and access his mail.

Basic (Clear Text) using SSL

Uses Secure Sockets Layer (SSL) protocol to encrypt a Basic Authentication session. This makes Basic Authentication a secure authentication scheme. However, to use SSL you must have Internet Information Server (IIS) installed and obtain and install a key certificate from a Certificate Authority (CA). See the "Certificate Authority (CA)" entry in this chapter for more information.

Windows NT Challenge/Response (NTLM)

Uses the Windows NT network authentication method, in which the password is not actually transmitted over the network. This authentication scheme is supported only by the following IMAP4 clients:

– Microsoft Internet Mail and News Version 3 and higher

– Microsoft Outlook Express

Windows NT Challenge/Response (NTLM) using SSL

Uses Secure Sockets Layer protocol to encrypt an NTLM session.

MCIS Membership System

Uses the Windows NT network authentication method in conjunction with the Microsoft Commercial Internet Server (MCIS) Membership System.

MCIS Membership System using SSL

Uses Secure Sockets Layer protocol to encrypt a MCIS Membership System session.

You can select one or more authentication methods from this list, but you must ensure that your IMAP4 clients each support at least one of the authentication methods you have chosen.

Anonymous

Lets you specify a Windows NT account for anonymous access to Exchange by IMAP4 clients. Do this to make some of your public folders in your organization accessible to users on the Internet. You will also have to give anonymous users permissions on those public folders, using the Client Permissions button on the General property page of the Public Folder's property sheet. See the "Public Folder" entry in this chapter for more information.

Message Format

Lets you specify what format Exchange messages are converted to when an IMAP4 client accesses a mailbox. IMAP4 clients cannot read the native Exchange messaging format, so Exchange must convert messages from their native format to a format suitable for the particular IMAP4 client.

By default, Exchange converts messages from their native Exchange format to MIME-encoded messages to enable IMAP4 clients to access them. Additionally you can specify to provide the body of the message as plain text, HTML, or both in a MIME multi-part alternative message format. Most IMAP4 clients support all of these options.

You can also specify the Character set, which depends on the language used.

Idle Time-out

Lets you keep open or close idle IMAP4 connections after a time interval you specify. Connections that are open too long can tie up server resources and are subject to hijacking by hackers; connections that time out too quickly cause delays in messaging for the user and unexpected errors.

Notes

- If IMAP4 is disabled at the server level, it is also disabled for all mailboxes and custom recipients homed on the server.

- If you choose to enable or disable IMAP4, it may take several minutes before this takes effect.

- For Windows NT Challenge/Response (NTLM) to work with the Microsoft Outlook Express client, the user's mailbox alias name must be the same as the user's Windows NT user account.

- Messages sent by users on the Internet are *not* converted to other formats when IMAP4 clients access their Inbox on Exchange. For example, if a user on the Internet sends email with a Uuencoded attachment, then when the IMAP4 client retrieves the message from their Inbox on Exchange, it will still be Uuencoded. And since IMAP4 doesn't support Uuencoding, the attachment will be unintelligible to it.

- IMAP4 clients cannot access public folders that have a forward slash ("/") in their folder name.

- Do not use an anonymous Windows NT account that is the same as a mailbox alias, or IMAP4 clients on the Internet will be able to access the mailbox.

- Don't forget to configure the Routing property page of the Internet Mail Service object to support IMAP4 clients. This will automatically enable support for POP3 clients also.

- The IMAP4 email address of a user is the same as his SMTP address.

Information Store Site Configuration

Lets you configure various aspects of the information store at the site level.

Type

Leaf object

Path

```
Organization\Site\Configuration\Information Store Site
Configuration
```

Description

The Information Store Site Configuration object is one of the directory objects that should be configured when you are implementing an Exchange site for your company. This object lets you globally configure essential aspects of the Microsoft

Exchange Information Store service on all servers in your site. The information store service is a Windows NT service that maintains the *private information store* and *public information store* databases on an Exchange server. This is important because the information store is the central location where mail and public folders are stored on an Exchange server. See Appendix D for more on the Information Store service.

In particular, the Information Store Site Configuration property sheet lets you specify:

- The container for public folders
- Who can create top-level public folders
- Access for clients in your site to public folders in other sites
- Warnings for mailbox users exceeding their storage limits
- Message tracking for diagnostic troubleshooting

See the "Site" entry in this chapter for other directory objects that should be configured when setting up a new site. For more details on the information store, see "Private Information Store" and "Public Information Store" in this chapter.

Properties

General

Lets you configure the display name and public folder container and enable message tracking. Also displays directory name, home site, date the site was created, and most recent date the properties of this object were modified. In particular:

- Public folder objects are located by default in the site recipients container. Specifying a new recipients container for public folders here only affects new public folders, not existing ones, and simplifies administration by allowing related public folders to be grouped in related recipient containers.

- You can enable message tracking for messages processed by the information store service. Use the Message Tracking Center in Exchange Administrator to view message tracking events (see Chapter 4).

Permissions

See the section "Permissions and Roles" at the beginning of this chapter.

Top Level Folder Creation

Lets you specify who can create top-level public folders. Users that can create top-level public folders can give permissions to other users for creating sub-folders under the top-level folder. See the entry "Outlook 98" in Chapter 4 for details on how to create public folders using Microsoft Outlook.

Storage Warnings

Lets you specify when or how frequently users who exceed their mailbox storage limits will receive warning notifications. Notifications are also sent to a public folder's contact recipient when the folder becomes full.

Public Folder Affinity

Allows clients in your site to connect to public folders from other sites in your organization. If your users need to access public folders in other sites but you don't want to replicate those public folders to your site, use *public folder affinity* to specify which remote sites your users can connect to for accessing public folders. Each remote site can be assigned a *cost value* to determine the order in which connection attempts to public folders are made. This proceeds according to the following sequence:

1. A user tries to access a public folder.

2. If the user's home server has a replica of that folder (a copy of the folder's contents), a connection to this replica is attempted.

3. If this attempt fails or if the condition does not apply, connections are attempted one at a time with any replicas that are on servers in the user's location. (See the note concerning locations in Chapter 2.)

4. If these attempts fail or if the condition does not apply, connections are attempted one at a time with any replicas that are on servers in the same site but different locations.

5. If these attempts fail or if the condition does not apply, connections are attempted one at a time with replicas in remote sites that have public folder affinity configured. Sites with the lowest cost values are tried first.

Notes

- Remember that recipient objects such as mailboxes exist in two different databases on Exchange servers:

  – The directory database, which contains the properties of the recipient object

  – The information store database, which contains the actual personal or public folders and their messages and attachments

  Changing the location of the public folder container only affects the directory database; public folders are still located in the public information store.

- Message tracking creates a hit on server performance, so enable it only when necessary. Once you enable message tracking on a site's information store, you must stop and restart the Exchange information store service on all servers in your site before tracking will take effect. Use the Services utility in the Control Panel to do this.

The Exchange information store can stop responding when it tries to process a corrupted message. For example, if it receives a message with an encoded attachment that has no "END" section, it thinks it has to keep processing the message and appends more data until it finally hangs. Microsoft has a hotfix for this problem available on their web site. Go to *http://support.microsoft.com/support/supportnet.*

Internet Mail Service

Lets you configure the SMTP mail service on the server.

Type

Leaf object

Path

Organization\Site\Configuration\Connections\Internet Mail
Service

Description

The Internet Mail Service (IMS) is one of the core components of Exchange and is a Windows NT service that enables Exchange to send and receive SMTP mail. Although the main use for this service is to provide connectivity between Exchange servers and SMTP mail systems on the Internet, the service can also be used to:

- Connect together sites within your Exchange organization through an SMTP backbone such as the Internet
- Enable SMTP mail transfer between different Exchange organizations
- Provide connectivity with foreign mail systems that have SMTP gateways

> Note that although the Internet Mail Service is often abbreviated as IMS, it is referred to internally by Exchange as the IMC. For example, you can stop the Internet Mail Service from the command line by typing net stop MSExchangeIMC. The reason for this confusion is that in Exchange Server 4.0, this service was called the Internet Mail Connector, which of course is a more logical name since the service is represented in the directory hierarchy as a connector!

The Internet Mail Service can work with either dial-up or dedicated network connections. For details on how this service transfers SMTP messages and how it interacts with other Exchange components, see Chapter 2.

The Internet Mail Service is one of four Exchange connectors that can be used to provide messaging connectivity between sites in an Exchange organization, the others being the X.400 Connector, Site Connector, and Dynamic RAS Connector. Some of the advantages of using the Internet Mail Service include:

- The capability of setting limits to message size
- The capability of being configured to only send, only receive, or both send and receive messages

On the negative side:

- Conversion of the message format adds extra overhead to processing messages.
- The server with the connector installed acts as a bridgehead server and may become a bottleneck.

The Internet Mail Service property sheet lets you:

- Establish message size limits
- Specify address spaces and routing information
- Configure delivery restrictions on incoming mail
- View and modify message queues
- Configure encoding and character sets
- Enable message tracking for troubleshooting purposes
- Designate account information for authentication with other SMTP hosts
- Configure dial-up mail delivery using RAS
- Enable diagnostic logging and a whole lot more stuff

Additionally, some of these settings can be configured on a domain-by-domain basis with remote SMTP hosts.

In a heterogeneous networking environment, many administrators prefer to use Exchange for providing users with POP3/IMAP4 access to incoming SMTP mail and using Unix Sendmail for all outgoing SMTP mail. Clients are then configured with Exchange as their POP3/IMAP4 server and the Sendmail box as their SMTP server. Some feel that this is a more robust SMTP messaging solution than using Exchange alone; others simply prefer Sendmail because they have more experience with it.

Properties

General

Lets you specify message limits and an administrative note. Also displays the name of the server on which the Internet Mail Service is installed, the server's home site, date the server was installed, and date the Internet Mail Service configuration was last modified.

Note that the message size limit applies to both inbound and outbound messages. Messages exceeding the specified size are returned to sender along with a non-delivery report (NDR).

Permissions

See the section "Permissions and Roles" at the beginning of this chapter.

Connected Sites

Use this tab when using the Internet Mail Service to connect together sites within your Exchange organization to allow directory replication between the sites. You don't need to configure this tab when you are using the Internet Mail Service only to connect to SMTP mail servers on the Internet.

The main listbox shows all remote sites in your organization that are connected through the Internet Mail Service on this server. This includes sites that are indirectly connected through other connectors. For example, if your site A uses the Internet Mail Service to connect to site B, which uses the Site Connector to connect to site C, then both sites B and C will appear in the listbox here. You don't have to specify indirectly connected sites, as Exchange finds these using directory replication between sites.

To use the Internet Mail Service to connect your site to another Exchange site, select the New button to open a dialog box to specify addressing and routing information, specifically:

- The name of your organization (or some other organization you want to connect to).

- The name of the remote site you want to connect to. The Internet Mail Service must be installed and configured on this site also, as connectors at both ends are needed to enable messaging between sites.

- SMTP as the address type.

- The SMTP site address of the remote site as the address. Use the property sheet of the Site Addressing directory object for the other site to determine this address. An example is *@Winnipeg.SampleCorp.com* for the site Winnipeg in the organization SampleCorp.

- A cost value between 0 and 100 for routing purposes. *Cost values* are assigned to each connector in a site and are used to determine which connectors should be tried and in which order for routing messages. Table 3-5 explains the meaning of different cost values.

Table 3-5: Cost Values for Connectors and Their Meanings

Cost Value	Meaning
0	Try this connector first. If it fails, then try other connectors.
100	Only use this connector if all other connectors fail.
1 to 99	The lower the cost value, the more likely this connector will be used. Routes with equal costs are load-balanced.

Address Space

Lets you specify address spaces for the connector. These *address spaces* each represent a messaging path leading through the connector to another site, organization, or mail system. When the MTA attempts to route a message through the Internet Mail Service, it checks the list of address spaces to determine whether the connector can route the message.

The listbox displays four parameters for each address space created:

Type

SMTP, X.400, MS Mail, or Other type of address space.

Address

The addresses that the connector is responsible for routing messages to. Wildcards can be used:

- Asterisk (*) represents any number of characters.

- Percent sign (%) represents any single character.

Cost

Routing cost.

Scope

Restrictions on who can use this address space for sending messages through the connector. You can specify users at this location only, this site only, or throughout the entire organization.

An example of an address space for the Internet Mail Connector is shown in Table 3-6.

Table 3-6: A Sample Address Space Entry for SMTP

Parameter	Value	Meaning
Type	SMTP	This connector can route SMTP messages.
Address	*.com	This connector can route messages to any email sub-domain within the .com domain.
Cost	1	See Table 3-5.
Scope	Site	Only users whose home site is this site can route messages using this address space.

The key parameter is the address. For example, if you are using the Internet Mail Service to establish messaging connectivity with the Internet, specify the wildcard symbol—the asterisk (*)—as the address so *all* SMTP mail can be routed by the IMS to *any* SMTP domain. But if you are using the service to connect two sites in your organization, specify the DNS address of the other site (e.g., *site.organization.com*) as the address.

It's a common error to put your own domain name in the address space for the Internet Mail Service. Unfortunately this limits SMTP mail to your own organization! Most of the time you want to use the wildcard "*" to indicate that your recipients can send SMTP mail to anyone on the Internet. Specifying anything other than "*" will cause delivery of SMTP mail to be restricted to the specified domains only.

You can also use the Internet Mail Service as a connector for routing other types of messages to other sites, organizations, or mail systems such as X.400 or Microsoft Mail. To do this, you need to create an address space for these types of messages. To create a new address space, select the New button, choose the type (X.400, MS, SMTP, or Other) and specify:

– The destination addressing information

– The cost for this connection

– The scope restrictions

– The routing address

The routing address only needs to be specified when you create a non-SMTP address space for connecting to a foreign mail system. Specify the fully qualified domain name (FQDN) of the foreign system's SMTP server.

Actually, specifying the routing address only works when the foreign mail system is another Exchange server. This is because Exchange encapsulates outbound SMTP addresses so they look something like this:

IMCEASMTP-user+40domain+2Ecom@foreign.domain.com

Non-Exchange foreign hosts will have to strip off this encapsulation and deliver the message accordingly.

Delivery Restrictions

Lets you accept or reject outgoing messages, that is, messages from recipients in your organization that are attempting to use the connector as a path to another site, organization, or mail system. Incoming messages are not affected by these settings.

The Delivery Restrictions option can be useful if there are users in your organization to whom you want to enable internal Exchange-based messaging but deny SMTP-based Internet mail. For example, if a user violates your company's Acceptable use Policy for Internet Mail, you can temporarily deny him access to Internet mail as a reward.

Diagnostic Logging

Specify the types and levels of Internet Mail Service events that are logged to the Application Log. Internet Mail Service events are logged under the name MSExchangeIMC in the Application Log and can be viewed using Event Viewer. See the related property in the "Server" entry for more information about diagnostic logging.

If you find that the Internet Mail Service is filling up your hard drive by writing to the *\imcdata\in\archive* and *\imcdata\out\archive* directories, it's because you have diagnostic logging enabled on the service. Setting diagnostic logging for the Message Archival property to Medium or higher causes every incoming and outgoing SMTP message to be copied to these archive directories, which can quickly fill up all available disk space on your server unless you are well-prepared. You can free up disk space by deleting the contents of the archive directories, setting diagnostic logging for this property to None, and then stopping and restarting the Internet Mail Service. For more information on the *\imcdata* directories, see Appendix E, *Directories*.

Internet Mail

This tab, not the General tab, has the focus when you open the Internet Mail Service property sheet, probably because of the number of important settings you can configure here. These include specifying:

- An administrator's mailbox where postmaster and error notification messages will be sent by the Internet Mail Service. You can also specify which kinds of non-delivery events the administrator will be notified regarding.

- The default method for encoding attachments for outbound messages (MIME or Uuencode).

- The default character set for outbound MIME messages and in/outbound non-MIME messages.

- Whether users have client software that supports S/MIME.

- Whether to convert incoming messages to Courier font.

- Whether to enable message tracking for all messages routed through the Internet Mail Service. Use the Message Tracking Center to view message tracking events (see Chapter 4).

The Advanced Options button allows you to specify whether to:

- Always or never send outbound messages in rich-text format (RTF), or let users individually decide this. RTF messages can include bold, italics, color, and other features. This capability can also be enabled or disabled for each recipient individually using the Advanced tab of the recipient's property sheet. For example, you could specify Always here and then disable RTF for each Custom Recipient of mail systems not able to receive RTF messages.

- Prevent Out-of-Office and AutoReply notifications from being sent to users sending you SMTP mail from the Internet. (These might be considered a mild form of "spam"!) You may also want to disable this option to prevent messages from looping endlessly between an external SMTP mail host and the Internet Mail Service as described in the following tip.

You should make sure that Disable Automatic Replies/Out of Office Responses to the Internet are *selected* to avoid potential message loops. For example, say a user configures his Exchange account to auto-forward his office mail to his personal Internet SMTP account while on a trip. It may happen that his personal Internet mailbox may get full due to the large volume of additional messages. Then when Exchange tries to forward another message with a large attachment to his personal Internet mailbox, his Internet Service Provider's mail server rejects the message and returns the message with its attachment back to the Exchange server as an NDR, which receives the message and forwards it to the user's Internet mailbox again, which rejects it again, and so on until either the Exchange server crashes or the ISP intervenes and deactivates the user's Internet mailbox. Either way the outcome isn't pleasant for the user or the administrator.

- Prevent users' display name from being included in outbound SMTP messages.

- Enable or prevent message body text from word-wrapping, for remote clients that have trouble with this feature. This cannot be selected if MIME encoding is being used.

Note that you can also specify the message size limit (see General tab), encoding method, character set, and advanced options on a domain-by-domain basis for each recipient email domain. Select the Email Domain button to configure this. You could use this if your company has other SMTP mail systems throughout the enterprise, each with its own SMTP configuration settings. Listen to complaints from remote users within your enterprise concerning message lines being truncated, unreadable attachments, strange characters, or other problems and then try using this feature.

Spam

How you deny *unsolicited commercial email* (the polite term for spam) for your Exchange servers depends on which version of Exchange and which service packs you have installed. There is good information in the *readme* file on the Exchange Server 5.5 compact disc dealing with spam, as also on the Exchange Server 5.5 Service Pack 1 and 2 *readme* files.

You can also check out the following third-party solutions and resources:

- *http://www.mailshield.com*
- *http://www.junkmail.com*
- *http://www.blighty.com*

Also see *Stopping Spam*, by Alan Schwartz and Simson Garfinkel (O'Reilly).

Dial-Up Connections

The Internet Mail Service connector can be used together with Windows NT Remote Access Service (RAS) to periodically connect to another site or SMTP server and transfer messages. For example, if you are connecting sites using the Internet as your SMTP backbone, the Internet Mail Service in each site can periodically dial up your local Internet Service Provider's SMTP server. You must first add the RAS entries you want to dial up using the RAS phone book. See Eric Pearce's *Windows NT in a Nutshell* from O'Reilly for information on how to install and configure RAS on NT.

Use this property page to:

- Select which RAS phonebook entries should be available to the Internet Mail Service. At the scheduled time interval, the Internet Mail Service will use RAS to dial up each phone book entry, one at a time.

- Specify the amount of time RAS keeps the connection open after mail transfer with the remote SMTP server is complete. If you are using a dial-up RAS connection and mail arrives during the time-out period, a new transfer of inbound mail only is initiated and the timer resets to zero. Outbound mail is sent only when the RAS session is first established. You may want to set the time-out period to a lower number if messaging traffic is high; otherwise, your RAS connection may be always on due to the high volume of incoming messages. But if this is the case, you probably need to upgrade to a dedicated leased line anyway!

- Specify a Mail Retrieval notification method. This is a notification that the Internet Mail Service sends to the remote SMTP server after a network connection has been established, to identify itself to the remote SMTP server and indicate that it is ready to retrieve inbound messages. Depending on how the remote SMTP server is configured, you can select:

  - ETRN, an SMTP extension that causes a remote SMTP server to send mail to a specific domain. You will usually specify the domain by selecting Derive from Routing property page. If the remote network uses separate inbound and outbound SMTP servers, you can specify the DNS name of the server from which you retrieve your inbound mail.

  - TURN, an SMTP command.

  - A custom command that you specify, or an executable file such as ping.

  - No retrieval notification necessary.

- Specify logon information for your Internet Mail Service to be authenticated by the remote SMTP host.

- Configure a schedule for when the Internet Mail Service should initiate a RAS connection with the remote SMTP host.

Exchange Server can *not* function as a POP3 client! In other words, you can't just configure the Internet Mail Service to dial up your ISP and connect to your POP3 mailbox to download SMTP mail. In fact, before you try to use RAS to transfer SMTP mail between your Exchange organization and your ISP, check to see if they are even able to queue SMTP mail for an asynchronous dial-up connection (many ISPs can't or won't do this) and to find out how they want you to trigger SMTP mail retrieval.

Connections
Lets you configure message transfer mode and delivery options, retry intervals and time-outs, and miscellaneous security settings. Of interest are:

Transfer mode
Whether the Internet Mail Service will accept inbound, outbound, none, or both types of messages. The none option is used to flush Internet Mail Service message queues when planning scheduled maintenance of your server.

Advanced

Maximum numbers of concurrent inbound and outbound connections, max connections per remote SMTP host, and max number of messages sent using a single connection. Contact the administrators of your remote SMTP servers to find out if their systems have limits on simultaneous allowed connections.

Message Delivery

Specify whether to route outbound message by:

- Performing DNS lookups to a DNS server or the local *Hosts* file (the default). Select this if you want your users to be able to send mail to anyone on the Internet. If you want to send mail to an SMTP host that is not on the Internet and has no DNS name, select Email Domain and enter the IP address of the host. This is often· used behind a firewall as when internal email is sent to an SMTP relay agent on the firewall.

- Forwarding them to an SMTP smart host, which then routes the messages to their destinations. Enter the IP address or FQDN of the smart host.

If you use DNS for resolving domain names for the Internet Mail Service, names that are successfully resolved are cached by the IMS (up to a maximum of 1,000 cached entries). This is intended to improve DNS name resolution performance by the IMS, but it has the side effect of negating the possibility of using DNS's inherent load-balancing capability. Microsoft has a fix for this; see the *Microsoft Knowledge Base* article Q198021 for more info.

Accept Connections

Lets you accept or reject incoming SMTP connections to port 25 by individual IP address or subnet and by whether the incoming host uses authentication, encryption, or both. Exchange Server 5.5 Service Pack 1 adds messaging filters to this setting.

Service Message Queues

Specify retry intervals for connecting to remote SMTP hosts and time-out values for different message priority levels (see Figure 3-7). An NDR can also be sent when a time-out is exceeded.

Clients can submit only if homed on this server

The user's mailbox must be homed on this server (located in the server's information store) in order to use the Internet Mail Server. This is a security setting that requires that connections are only accepted from hosts using authentication, but it would be more useful if you could specify accounts homed in a site, not a server.

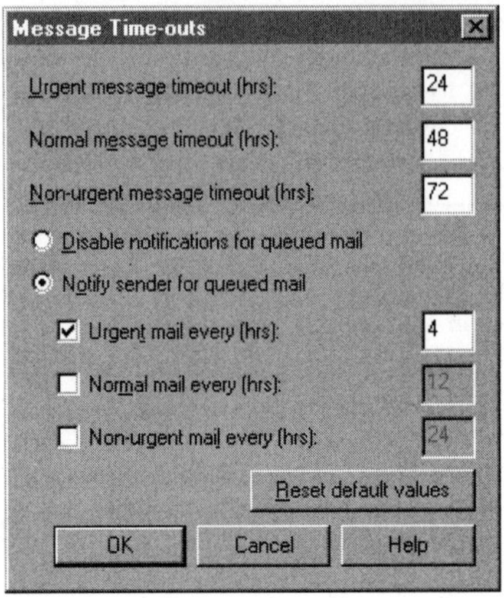

Figure 3-7: Configuring message time-outs for the Internet Mail Service

Clients can only submit if authentication account matches submission address
The client's From field in his SMTP messages must match his Windows NT account username, another security setting.

E-mail Domain
Lets you configure a number of the preceding properties on a domain-by-domain basis.

You can use the E-mail Domain button to specify the names of email domains to which your users frequently send SMTP mail. This will speed mail delivery since no DNS lookup will be required. Don't use this if you are using Forwarding to Host.

Queues
Displays the various message queues created by the Internet Mail Service and the number of messages in each queue awaiting delivery. There are four Internet Mail Service queues:

Outbound messages awaiting conversion
These messages have been delivered to the Internet Mail Service by the Message Transfer Agent (MTA) service but have not yet been converted into SMTP form. The messages are temporarily stored in the information store and cannot be opened and read. After they are converted to SMTP format, they are moved to the *Exchsrvr\Imcdata\Out* folder (see next item).

Outbound messages awaiting delivery

These messages have been converted for SMTP delivery and are waiting for the Internet Mail Service to deliver them. The message files are located in the *Exchsrvr\Imcdata\Out* directory, and you can open these files and read the messages using Notepad.

The other two queues relate to inbound messages and are similar in their name and operation.

Select a message in any queue and click Details to display the sender's address, message ID, destination host, time submitted, size, expiration time, and intended recipients. An error message may also be displayed indicating why the message is still in the queue. You can manually retry sending a frozen message or delete a message that is blocking the queue.

An inconsistency can sometimes appear with the IMS message queues: messages will be visible in the "Inbound Message Awaiting Delivery Queue," but when you select them and click the Message Details button, a dialog box says that the message has been deleted or delivered. Is it still in the queue or not? The inconsistency is due to the message pointer not being deleted from the *\imcdata\queue.dat* file, which is used to track the status of messages being processed by the IMS. To resolve this problem, stop the Internet Mail Service, delete the *queue.dat* file, and restart the service. For more information, see the *Microsoft Knowledge Base* article Q193862.

Routing

Lets you specify how incoming SMTP messages from POP3 and IMAP4 clients and from other SMTP hosts is routed by the Internet Mail Service. This includes:

Do not reroute incoming SMTP mail

If you select this, you can only send SMTP mail to recipients in the Global Address List. Anything else receives a non-delivery report!

Reroute incoming SMTP mail

This is a required setting if you are using POP3 or IMAP4 clients. In the default configuration, incoming SMTP mail addressed to your organization's domain name should be processed and forwarded to your recipients, while incoming mail not directed to your domain name should be rejected. In this case, there will be only one entry in the listbox on this page. For example, if the Internet Mail Service connector is configured on an Exchange server in the Vancouver site of SampleCorp, then the listbox should typically have the information shown in Table 3-7. This means that incoming mail addressed to *user@vancouver.samplecorp.com* will be accepted as inbound and all other incoming mail will be rejected.

Table 3-7: Typical Rerouting Setting for Incoming SMTP Mail

Sent to	Route to
Vancouver.SampleCorp.com	<inbound>

If you want, however, your Internet Mail Service can function as an SMTP smart host and reroute incoming mail addressed to other domains to other SMTP hosts. See Table 3-8 for an example.

Table 3-8: Using the Internet Mail Service as an SMTP Smart Host

Sent to	Route to
Vancouver.SampleCorp.com	<inbound>
OtherCorp.com	Big7.Dallas.OtherCorp.com
Denver.OtherCopr.com	High12.Denver.OtherCorp.com

In this case, messages sent to the following users would be processed as follows:

– *BobS@Vancouver.SampleCorp.com* would be processed by the Internet Mail Service and routed by exchange to mailbox BobS within the Vancouver site of SampleCorp.com.

– *JaneW@Seattle.OtherCorp.com* would be forwarded to the SMTP server Big7 in Dallas.

– *FrankB@Denver.OtherCorp.com* would be forwarded to High12 in Denver.

As a third example, consider a company with several domain names:

– *SampleCorp.com* for the current domain name of the company; by default all users have auto-generated primary SMTP addresses of the form *user@SampleCorp.com.*

– *OldCorp.com* for the previous domain name of the company; some users still receive the occasional email directed to *user@OldCorp.com.*

– *SampleCorpWeb.com* for the domain name of the company's Web services division; only a few special recipients need to be created for this domain, such as *info@SampleCorpWeb.com.*

By using the Reroute Incoming SMTP Mail feature you can correctly route incoming mail for these three domains by using the information shown in Table 3-9. Note the second line; this eliminates the need for recipients to maintain a second older SMTP address. In other words, a message sent to *BobS@oldcorp.com* will automatically be forwarded to *BobS@samplecorp.com.*

Table 3-9: Rerouting to Multiple Domain Names

Sent to	Route to
SampleCorp.com	<inbound>
OldCorp.com	SampleCorp.com
SampleCorpWeb.com	<inbound>

You can also use a custom routing *.DLL* for rerouting if you have one.

Rerouting all mail to another domain as shown in the second line of Table 3-9 may not always represent the best solution. For example, with the Routing property page configured as shown in Table 3-9, mail sent to *user@OldCorp.com* will *always* be forwarded to *user@SampleCorp.com*. In other words, no mail can be received by users who are strictly in the *OldCorp.com* domain. If you have a situation where two parts of your company (two different domain names) are being hosted on the same Exchange server, you could specify both domains as <inbound> on the Routing tab instead. Then if a user belongs to both parts of your company and needs to receive mail addressed to both domains, you can create a second SMTP address for that user's mailbox using the Email Addresses tab of his Mailbox property sheet.

Security

Lets you configure security for mail sent to outbound SMTP hosts that require it. For each remote email domain, you can specify:

– No authentication or encryption

– Simple Authentication and Security Layer (SASL) authentication

– Secure Sockets Layer (SSL) encryption

– Both SASL and SSL

– Windows NT Challenge/Response (NTLM) authentication and encryption

You can also provide one account and password for all domains or specify these on a domain-by-domain basis. Note that when using NT challenge/response you must specify the Windows NT domain of the account information.

There is a problem with trying to connect an Exchange 5.5 machine to an Exchange 5.0 one using Windows NT Challenge/Response (NTLM) authentication over SMTP connections: the Exchange 5.0 machine will reject the connection and return a "500 Command Not Recognized" message. This occurs because Exchange 5.5 uses the SMTP extension AUTH for establishing NTLM connections while Exchange 5.5 uses the SMTP extension XAUTH. Microsoft has a fix for this problem; see the *Microsoft Knowledge Base* article Q195201.

Notes

• After you modify any settings on the Internet Mail Service property sheet, use Services in the Control Panel to stop and then start the Internet Mail Service. This must be done in order for your modifications to take effect.

- If you are using the Internet Mail Service to connect sites together in your organization through an SMTP backbone such as the Internet, you need to perform the following steps:

  1. Create and configure one Internet Mail Service object at each site.

  2. Test messaging connectivity.

  3. Create a Directory Replication Connector at each site.

- Typically, you might use two Internet Mail Service connectors in a large site and have them configured either for the same SMTP address spaces for fault tolerance or for separate SMTP address spaces for load balancing.

- Another way to load-balance SMTP in an organization is to use one Internet Mail Service connector for outbound mail only and another for inbound mail. This is a common configuration in many enterprise-level implementations of Exchange.

- If you have several smart hosts for handling outgoing SMTP mail, you can specify their names separated by commas in the Forward all messages to host box on the Connections tab. The smart hosts will be used in a round-robin fashion.

- If you need to stop or disable the Internet Mail Service, you might think of using Services in the Control Panel, selecting the Exchange Internet Mail Service, and clicking Stop. *Don't do this!* Messages that users have sent that are currently in the queue will remain frozen. It's better to start by selecting None for Transfer Mode on the Connections property sheet. The service will then continue to operate and gradually flush its message queues. When the queues are finally empty, you can stop or disable the service using Services in the Control Panel.

- Don't set the dial-up RAS time-out period to zero or RAS may connect and timeout before a mail transfer is initiated!

- The maximum allowed connections should be fairly large if you are using POP3 or IMAP4 clients.

- If you are experiencing problems with SMTP mail, try checking the queues. If messages are piling up in a queue, examine the top message in the queue and compare its configuration with that of the destination SMTP server. Look at the submit times to determine messaging delays. If the delivery column shows "pending," delivery has not yet been attempted for the message; if it shows a time instead, this is the time of the intended next attempt.

- Message tracking creates a hit on server performance, so enable it only when necessary. Once you enable message tracking on the Internet Mail Service, you must stop and restart the Microsoft Exchange Internet Mail service on all servers where it is installed before tracking will take effect. Use the Services utility in the Control Panel to do this.

LDAP (Directory) Settings

Lets you configure Lightweight Directory Access Protocol (LDAP) at the server level.

Type

Leaf object

Path

Organization\Site\Configuration\Servers\Server\Protocols\LDAP
(Directory) Settings

Description

See the entry "LDAP (Directory) Site Defaults" in this chapter for a description of LDAP.

Properties

Same as for the LDAP (Directory) Site Defaults object, except you have the option on the General tab to inherit the properties of the site-level LDAP object.

Notes

Note that unlike other Internet protocol objects, the LDAP object has no diagnostic logging capability.

Directory

LDAP (Directory) Site Defaults

Lets you configure Lightweight Directory Access Protocol (LDAP) at the site level.

Type

Leaf object

Path

Organization\Site\Configuration\Protocols\LDAP (Directory)
Site Defaults

Description

Lightweight Directory Access Protocol (LDAP) is a widely used Internet protocol that specifies the structure and access methods for a directory service. Using an LDAP client, you can access an LDAP directory and create, view, edit, or delete attributes of objects in that directory. LDAP can also be used to provide "lightweight" access to any X.500 directory service such as the Microsoft Exchange directory service and database, since LDAP is a subset of the fuller X.500 directory service specification. Users with LDAP clients and appropriate permissions can view and even modify information in the Exchange directory database.

An example of a simple LDAP client is Microsoft Outlook Express, which can search the Exchange directory database for names or email addresses of recipients and display personal information about those recipients obtained from the directory attributes of the recipient objects in the directory. To configure Outlook Express to access your Exchange directory, do the following:

1. Select Tools → Accounts from the Outlook Express menu to open the Internet Accounts dialog box.

2. Select Add → Directory Service to start the Connection Wizard and specify the name of the Exchange server.

3. Select "My LDAP server requires me to log in" and click Next.

4. Choose "Log on using Secure Password Authentication (SPA)" and click Next.

5. Click Next twice and then Finish, and then close the Internet Accounts dialog box.

Now to use Outlook Express as an LDAP client for accessing the Exchange directory, select Edit → Find People from the Outlook Express menu, select the name of your Exchange server from the drop-down list, specify a recipient's name or email address, and click Find Now. You can select Properties to view more information about the selected recipient.

LDAP can be configured at two different levels on Exchange:

- At the site level using the LDAP (Directory) Site Defaults object in the site Protocols container

- At the server level using the LDAP (Directory) Settings object in the server Protocols container

The LDAP (Mail) Site Defaults property sheet lets you:

- Specify methods for LDAP clients to authenticate on Exchange

- Configure how LDAP clients use substrings to perform searches

- Configure connection time-outs

- Enable anonymous access to the Exchange directory

Properties

General
> Lets you specify the display name and port number, enable LDAP at the site level, and specify an administrative note. The default port number is port 389, but this may be changed for security reasons.

Permissions
> See the section "Permissions and Roles" at the beginning of this chapter.

Authentication
> Lets you select the authentication methods that are used when LDAP clients try to access the Exchange server. Supported authentication methods include:

> *Basic (Clear Text)*
>> Sends username and password as clear text (unencrypted). Basic Authentication is supported by most POP3 clients and is commonly used in the Unix world. Because Basic Authentication transmits user credentials unencrypted over the network, it is not a secure authentication scheme.

Anyone with a network packet sniffer who can capture authentication traffic can gain access to a user's credentials and access his mail.

Basic (Clear Text) using SSL

Uses Secure Sockets Layer (SSL) protocol to encrypt a Basic Authentication session. This makes Basic Authentication a secure authentication scheme. However, to use SSL you must have Internet Information Server (IIS) installed and obtain and install a key certificate from a Certificate Authority (CA). See "Certificate Authority (CA)" in this chapter for more information.

Windows NT Challenge/Response (NTLM)

Uses the Windows NT network authentication method, in which the password is not actually transmitted over the network. This authentication scheme is supported only by the following POP3 clients:

– Microsoft Internet Mail and News Version 3 and higher

– Microsoft Outlook Express

There is also an add-on available for Netscape Messenger to enable it to authenticate using NTLM.

Windows NT Challenge/Response (NTLM) using SSL

Uses Secure Sockets Layer protocol to encrypt an NTLM session.

MCIS Membership System

Uses the Windows NT network authentication method in conjunction with the Microsoft Commercial Internet Server (MCIS) Membership System.

MCIS Membership System using SSL

Uses SSL protocol to encrypt a MCIS Membership System session.

You can select one or more authentication methods from this list, but you must ensure that your LDAP clients each support at least one of the authentication methods you have chosen.

Anonymous

Lets you specify a Windows NT account for anonymous access to Exchange by LDAP clients. Do this to make your Exchange directory accessible to users on the Internet. You can also allow some directory attributes to be viewed by anonymous users and others to require authenticated users by using the Attributes property page for the DS Site Configuration object.

Search

Lets you configure how LDAP clients use substrings to search the Exchange directory. You can treat all substrings as the initial portion of the attribute or search for any occurrence of a substring within an attribute (which is much slower). You can also specify how many search results should be returned.

Referrals

Lets you configure Exchange to refer the LDAP client to other Exchange organizations if the desired directory object cannot be found in the first server's directory. In other words, when a LDAP client such as Outlook Express searches for information on a recipient on your LDAP-enabled Exchange server, this search can be extended to include LDAP-enabled servers in other Exchange organizations or non-Exchange LDAP servers. You can configure up to 350 different LDAP referral servers for Exchange. To configure a referral server, specify:

- The DNS name of the referral server (for example, *server7.othercorp.com*)

- The base X.500 directory name for the site where the referral server resides (for example, *ou=newyork,o=othercorp,c=us*)

- The LDAP port for the referral server (usually port 389)

For more information, see the *Microsoft Knowledge Base* article Q195104.

Idle Time-out

Lets you keep open or close idle LDAP connections after a time interval you specify. Connections that are open too long can tie up server resources and are subject to hijacking by hackers; connections that time out too quickly cause unexpected errors and delays in messaging for the user.

Notes

If you choose to enable or disable LDAP, it make take several minutes before this takes effect.

Link Monitor

Tests connections with other sites and mail systems using ping messages.

Type

Leaf object

Path

Organization\Site\Configuration\Monitors\Link Monitor

Description

Link monitors verify that messages are being routed properly within an organization and to foreign mail systems. At pre-specified polling intervals, special *ping messages* are sent to specified servers in remote sites and foreign mail systems, and the time for a *non-delivery report* (NDR) to arrive is determined. This round-trip time is called the *bounce time*. If the bounce time exceeds a specified threshold, alerts can be generated or messages sent to administrators indicating the link is down or not performing properly.

Once a link monitor has been created, it must be started using Tools → Start Monitor from the Exchange Administrator menu. A new monitor window opens showing the status of the various links being monitored. See Chapter 4 for more details on running link monitors.

The Link Monitor property sheet lets you:

- Specify polling intervals and expected bounce times

- Create a series of notifications

- Specify which servers in your organization you will monitor

- Specify a custom recipient for monitoring a link with a remote mail system

Properties

General

Lets you specify the display name, log file, and polling intervals. Also displays the directory name.

The log file is optional, since the monitor window displays real-time information about the state of message links in your system.

There are two polling intervals to configure:

Normal

Lets you specify how often a ping message should be sent when the link is functioning normally.

Critical sites

Lets you specify how often a ping message should be sent when the link is in a warning or alert state.

Permissions

See the section "Permissions and Roles" at the beginning of this chapter.

Notification

Lets you specify what should happen if a link goes into a warning or alert state. A link enters a warning or alert state when ping messages do not return in the expected bounce times. These bounce times are configured on the Bounce tab.

The symbols here are:

- Green triangle for normal operation

- Red exclamation point for warning state

- Red triangle for alert state

You can create a whole series of notifications, called an *escalation path*. A notification can:

- Launch a process on the server

- Send a message to an administrator

- Send a Windows NT administrative alert to a computer

For each notification created, you can also configure:

- Whether it is triggered by the link going into a warning or alert state

- How long after the state is entered the notification event occurs

Servers

Lets you specify which servers inside your Exchange organization you want to send ping messages to.

Recipients

Lets you specify a Custom Recipient for sending ping messages to remote mail systems outside your organization. You must specify a recipient that does not exist in the remote mail system so that it will generate an NDR that will be returned to you.

When an NDR from a remote mail system is received, the Link Monitor looks for the Subject field of the original ping message. If the remote mail system has auto-reply, add the Custom Recipient to the left list; otherwise, try the right list. Contact the administrator for the remote mail system to find out whether auto-reply is enabled on that system.

Bounce

Lets you specify maximum expected round-trip times for ping messages sent to servers in warning and alert states.

Notes

- You should hide from the Global Address List any Custom Recipients you create for sending ping messages to foreign mail systems.

- The bounce time for alert state should be greater than the bounce time for warning state. This way a link goes into a warning state before it escalates into an alert state.

Mailbox

A type of *recipient* that maps to a portion of the private information store database that contains all mail (messages and attachments) sent to the user who is associated with the mailbox.

Type

Leaf object

Path

`Organization\Site\Recipients\Mailbox`

Description

Mailboxes are the most common form of recipient object. (See the entry "Recipients" in this chapter.) Each mailbox is usually associated with a single Windows NT user account, called the *primary Windows NT account* of the mailbox, which is assigned Owner permission on the mailbox. (See "Permissions and Roles" at the beginning of this chapter.) Users access their mailboxes using client software such as Microsoft Outlook.

Mailboxes exist in two places on Exchange servers:

- Configuration settings for the mailbox are stored in the Exchange *directory database*, along with the properties of other directory objects. The directory database is automatically replicated to all other Exchange servers in the site, so the mailbox directory object exists within each server's directory database.

- Actual mail content (private folders, messages, and attachments) are stored in the *private information store* on the user's home server. Mail content is *not* replicated to other Exchange servers.

Mailboxes can be created using User Manager for Domains or Exchange Administrator or by importing mailboxes from other mail systems. See Chapter 4 for more details.

The Mailbox property sheet lets you:

- Specify personal information about the recipient
- Add the recipient to Distribution Lists (DLs)
- View and modify the recipient's email addresses
- Specify message store and message size limits
- Configure delivery restrictions for receiving messages
- Specify which Internet protocols the recipient can use
- Define custom attributes for the recipient

Properties

General

Lets you specify personal information for the user associated with the mailbox. This includes name, address, company, title, phone number, primary Windows NT account, display name, and an alias used in the user's email address. Also displays the mailbox's home site, the date the mailbox was created, and the most recent date when the mailbox properties were modified.

Organization

Lets you specify who the mailbox owner reports to and who reports to the mailbox owner.

Phone/Notes

Lets you specify various phone and fax numbers and any additional note concerning the mailbox owner.

Permissions

See the section "Permissions and Roles" at the beginning of this chapter. The significant setting here is the mailbox owner's NT account, which is assigned the User Role.

If you want to create a mailbox that will be shared by several users (for example, a shared resource mailbox for the Support Desk), you can either assign the User role on the Permissions property page to multiple Windows NT user accounts to the mailbox or to the Windows NT global group containing these users.

Distribution Lists

Shows the Distribution Lists (DLs) to which the mailbox owner belongs and allows you to add the user to other DLs.

Listservers

If users leave your company without unsubscribing from any external List-servers they were subscribed to and you go ahead and delete their mailboxes, the Listserver will continue to send messages to the deleted mailbox's address resulting in a lot of Inbound Failure notification messages being generated. Rather than recreate each ex-user's mailbox for sending a message to each list unsubscribing from them, someone who posted to the Usenet newsgroup *microsoft.public.exchange.admin* suggested that you:

- Create a single dummy mailbox.
- Assign the first ex-user's SMTP address as the dummy mailbox's primary SMTP address and collect some of the ex-user's Listserv messages.
- Send email to each list to which the ex-user was subscribed, unsub-scribing from the list.
- Assign the next ex-user's SMTP address as the mailbox's primary SMTP address and repeat the procedure.

The dummy mailbox will this way function as a dumping place for ex-users' Listserv messages until the Listserv program processes your request to unsubscribe from the lists. If worse comes to worst and certain lists can't be unsubscribed from, you can always deny access to their domain at your fire-wall (and then email the list administrator that you are doing this; maybe he'll finally get the message).

E-mail Addresses

Displays the user's various email addresses and allows you to modify these addresses or add additional addresses. Email addresses are the means by which Exchange recipients are known, both within your Exchange organiza-tion and by outside mail systems.

In order for a mailbox to receive messages from outside users, Exchange automatically creates four kinds of email addresses when the mailbox is created. These addresses are based on the directory names of the mailbox, its home site, and Exchange organization. For example, if Donna K. Smith has a mailbox called DonnaS created within the site Toronto in the organization SampleCorp, the email addresses shown in Table 3-10 are created (assuming the Lotus cc:Mail connector has been installed).

Table 3-10: Automatically Generated Email Addresses for the Mailbox of Donna Smith

Mail System	Address Type	Sample Email Address
Internet	SMTP	*DonnaS@Toronto.SampleCorp.com*
X.400	X.400	*c=US;a= ;p=SampleCorp;o=Toronto; s=Smith;g=Donna;I=K.;*
MS Mail	MS	*SAMPLECORP/TORONTO/DONNAS*
Lotus cc:Mail	CCMAIL	*Smith, Donna at Toronto*

These various address types are used as follows:

- Internet (SMTP) addresses are common in the Unix world and form the basis of email on the Internet.

- X.400 is a global address space for mail systems used worldwide and especially in Europe.

- MS Mail includes Microsoft Mail for PC Networks and Microsoft Mail for AppleTalk Networks (Quarterdeck Mail).

- Lotus cc:Mail forms the basis of messaging in Lotus workgroup mail systems. This address type is optional and is only available if the Connector for cc:Mail is installed at setup.

The formats used for each of these address types are shown in Table 3-11.

Table 3-11: Format of Each Email Address Type

Address Type	Format	Attribute
SMTP	**Example**: *DonnaS@Toronto.SampleCorp.com*	
	User (DonnaS)	The mailbox Alias name
	DNS Subdomain (Toronto)	The Exchange site (this is optional)
	DNS Domain (SampleCorp)	The Exchange organization
MS Mail	**Example**: *SAMPLECORP/TORONTO/DONNAS*	
	Mailbox Name (DONNAS)	The mailbox Alias name
	Postoffice Name (TORONTO)	The Exchange site
	Network Name (SAMPLECORP)	The Exchange organization
X.400	**Example**: *c=US;a= ;p=SampleCorp;o=Toronto;s=Smith;g=Donna;i=K.;*	
	c	Two-letter Country code (required)
	a	Administrative Management Domain (required—Exchange defaults to a space character)
	p	Private Management Domain (required—the Exchange organization)
	o	Organization
	ou1 – ou4	Organizational Units
	cn	Common Name
	q	Generation Qualifier
	i	Initials (Exchange uses the mailbox user's Initials)
	s	Surname (required—Exchange uses the mailbox user's Last Name)
	g	Given Name (Exchange uses the mailbox user's First Name)
cc:Mail	**Example**: *Smith, Donna at Toronto*	
	Username (Smith, Donna)	The mailbox Last Name followed by comma followed by First Name
	Siteproxy (Toronto)	The Exchange site

Each addressing scheme also has its own restrictions on allowed characters and field lengths. Other types of addresses may also be automatically generated by Exchange when mailboxes are created, depending on the installed connectors or gateway objects.

If a user requires more than one email address of a given type, you can create additional addresses for the user. Six different types of email addresses can be created for a user:

- Internet (SMTP)
- Lotus cc:Mail
- MS Mail
- MacMail
- X.400
- Custom

If more than one address of a given type is specified for the user, one of them must be selected as the Set As Reply Address.

Delivery Restrictions

Lets you control which recipients the mailbox will accept messages from. If you specify a Distribution List, the members of the list are used (not the list itself) to restrict delivery.

Delivery Options

Lets you redirect incoming mail to another recipient or allow a recipient to send messages on behalf of you in case you are on holidays or out of town.

The Alternate Recipient box lets you specify one additional recipient to which all incoming mail can be forwarded, but what if you need to forward incoming mail to *more* than one alternate recipient? The solution is to create a *Distribution List* with *custom recipients* for each forwarding address and specify this Distribution List in the mailbox's Alternate Recipient box.

If an employee frequently works from home and has an Internet email account such as a Hotmail account, you can forward all his company mail to his Hotmail account by creating a custom recipient with his Hotmail address and configuring this as his Alternate Recipient address on the Delivery Options property page. Make sure you hid the custom recipient in the Global Address List (GAL) so that the user doesn't have two entries in the GAL.

Protocols

Lets you specify which Internet protocols the mailbox can use when connecting to the Exchange server. Note that SMTP is not listed here since SMTP is enabled by installing the Internet Mail Service through File → New

Other → Internet Mail Service from the Exchange Administrator program menu (see Chapter 4). The configurable protocols include:

- HTTP: Hypertext Transfer Protocol (Web)

- POP3: Postoffice Protocol Version 3 (Mail)

- IMAP4rev1: Internet Message Access Protocol Version 4 rev 1 (Mail)

- NNTP: Internet News Transfer Protocol (News)

- LDAP: Lightweight Directory Access Protocol (Directory)

These protocols can be selectively enabled or disabled for individual mailboxes and can have their own configured properties or use the default properties of the Protocols container on their home server. Configurable properties for Internet protocols are shown in Table 3-12.

Table 3-12: Properties of Internet Protocols That Can Be Configured for Individual Mailboxes

Protocol Properties Configurable at Mailbox Level	Details for Each Protocol
Format server converts messages to when a POP3 client tries to retrieve them from server (applies only to messages from other mailboxes—messages from Internet users are not converted).	POP3 (MIME or Uuencode), IMAP4 (MIME), NNTP (MIME or Uuencode)
Support rich-text format in messages retrieved from server.	POP3, IMAP4
Specify character set to use when multiple character sets exist for the same code page.	POP3, IMAP4
Disable listing of public folders to improve performance for some clients.	IMAP4
Disable fast messaging to improve performance for some clients. Fast messaging allows Exchange to estimate size of message being retrieved instead of determining exact size.	IMAP4
Allow user to have delegate access to another user's personal mail folders.	IMAP4

Custom Attributes

Lets you specify the values for custom attributes defined using the DS Site Configuration object for your Exchange site.

Limits

Sets limits on the size of the user's message store and the size of outgoing or incoming messages. You can either issue a warning when the message store is full or prohibit any further sending or receiving of messages.

Also lets you set the retention period in days for deleted messages so users can recover items they have inadvertently deleted from their mailboxes.

These settings can be set globally for all mailboxes using the Private Information Store object's property sheet.

Advanced

Miscellaneous settings including:

- Specify a *simple display name* for systems that cannot read special characters in the normal *display name*.

- View the *directory name* (which is the first Alias Name assigned to the mailbox) and the parent Recipients container of the mailbox object. You cannot change the directory name.

- Select a *trust level* when directory synchronization with MS Mail servers is performed using a MS Mail Connector.

- View the *home server* for the mailbox or move the mailbox to another server in the same site.

- Specify an ILS server and account if your system uses Microsoft NetMeeting.

- Hide the mailbox from the address book. Users can still send mail to a hidden mailbox if they know its email address, however.

- Disable sending high priority X.400 messages if this is a performance issue.

- Provide a descriptive note.

Notes

- If you have to create a large number of mailboxes, it's best to create a mailbox template first. A *mailbox template* is a mailbox that has preconfigured settings for similar users, e.g., same department, phone number, manager, delivery restrictions, and so on. To create a mailbox template, do the following:

  1. Use the Exchange Administrator program to create a new mailbox. Give it a display name that identifies it as a template, such as SalesTemplate for employees in the Sales Department.

  2. Configure the properties of the template that will be common to all mailboxes based on the template.

  3. Hide the template from the address book using the Advanced tab so that no one will try to send messages to the template.

  4. Click OK to close the mailbox property sheet. When prompted for a primary Windows NT account, you can either choose to create a new account and give all your template accounts the same secure password so no one will be able to log on using these accounts, or you can create and assign accounts later. The second option is probably preferable.

  To create mailboxes based on your new template using Exchange Administrator, select View → Hidden Recipients to make the template visible in Exchange Administrator. (The mailbox is still hidden from the address book.) Select the template and choose File → Duplicate. Add the user's unique personal information and create his mailbox, either assigning it to an existing Windows NT account or creating a new account.

Unfortunately, if you use User Manager for Domains and try to copy the template account, the account properties will be copied but the mailbox properties won't! So you can use User Manager to create account templates for making similar accounts and Exchange Administrator to create mailbox templates for making similar mailboxes, but you can't do both at the same time!

You may also want to create a special Recipients container to group all your mailbox templates together.

Note that mailboxes created from templates are not linked in any way to the template. If you later change the template's properties, this has no effect on the properties of the mailboxes created from it. To simultaneously modify properties of a group of mailboxes, use Tools → Directory Export/Import from the Exchange Administrator menu (see Chapter 4).

Directory

- When you create a new mailbox, the display name and alias are auto-generated as follows:

    - Display name is first name, space, last name.

    - Alias is first name, first letter of last name.

    These auto-naming conventions can be configured using Tools → Options from the Exchange Administrator menu.

If your Exchange organization has multiple administrators who manage sites from different workstations running the Exchange Administrator, you should make sure that these options are configured the same for each copy of Exchange Administrator used.

- To move a mailbox from the private information store of one server to another, you can:

    - Use Tools → Move Mailbox from the Exchange Administrator menu. This only works if you want to move a mailbox from one server to another in the same site.

    - Use the Advanced tab on the Mailbox object's property sheet. Again, this only works if you want to move a mailbox from one server to another in the same site.

    - Use Tools → Directory Export to export the properties of a mailbox or set of mailboxes to a *.csv file, and then use Tools → Directory Import to import the properties into another server. You can use this method to move mailboxes from one site to another. You can also use this method to move mailboxes from one recipients container to another on the same server, provided you modify the recipients container field of the *.csv file before importing it. Note that the user will temporarily have two mailboxes; use Inbox Assistant in Microsoft Outlook to configure mail forwarding from the old mailbox to the new one. After the user has sent out notifications of his new email address, you can delete the old mailbox. See Chapter 4 for more information on Directory Import and Export.

You should be aware that if you move mailboxes between servers, any rules, delegates, and Distribution List memberships are lost and will have to be recreated.

- If you need to modify a property or group of properties simultaneously on a large number of mailboxes, you can use the following hack:

  1. Export the properties of the mailboxes to a *.csv file.

  2. Open the *.csv file using a text editor such as Notepad, or better, using a spreadsheet program such as Microsoft Excel.

  3. Modify the necessary fields for each mailbox and save the changes.

  4. Import the *.csv file back into the same server.

- Mailboxes shared by several Windows NT user accounts should be given generic names such as Info, Customer Support, Conference Room 12, and the like. Create these in a separate Recipients container for convenience.

- Note that when you change a user's first name, last name, or alias, the user's email addresses are not automatically updated. You will have to manually edit each email address to match the new personal information for the user.

- Specifying a mailbox manager for a user automatically updates the manager's mailbox information by adding the user's mailbox to the manager's Direct Reports list.

- When using POP3 or IMAP4 messaging clients, select Prohibit Send And Receive instead of Prohibit Send, as these clients do not support the Prohibit Send option.

It may seem unnecessary for custom recipients to have X.400, MS Mail, and Lotus cc:Mail email addresses when you are only planning on implementing Internet (SMTP) mail services, so you may be tempted to delete these extra addresses for housecleaning purposes. *Don't do this!* Deleting the automatically generated email addresses for a list can cause directory replication to fail and cause other messaging problems. This is especially true of the X.400 address, which is used internally together with a recipient's distinguished name (DN) in order to route messages throughout an Exchange organization. Deleting X.400 addresses of recipients may prevent them from receiving mail, and deleting the X.400 of an Exchange service or connector may prevent that service or connector from functioning.

You use the Site Addressing object to disable generation of the address types you don't need for future recipients you create, but don't disable the generation of X.400 addresses!

Mailbox Agent

Configures the associated mailbox agent.

Type

Leaf object

Path

Organization\Site\Recipients\Mailbox Agent

Description

A mailbox agent is a custom *.DLL* that can send and receive messages and supply schedule and routing information to connectors and message transfer agents (MTAs). Mailbox agents are implemented as Windows NT services on Exchange. See the "Microsoft Schedule+ Free/Busy Connector" entry in this chapter for an example of a mailbox agent.

Properties

Varies with agent.

Notes

Agents are typically used to support connectivity with Microsoft Mail networks and related mail systems using the MS Mail 3.x directory synchronization protocol. See the "MS Mail Connector" and "Directory Synchronization" entries for more information.

Message Transfer Agent

Configures the Message Transfer Agent (MTA) for the server.

Type

Leaf object

Path

Organization\Site\Configuration\Servers\Server\Message
Transfer Agent

Description

The Microsoft Exchange Message Transfer Agent (MTA) service is one of the core components of Exchange and is a Windows NT service that provides the addressing and routing information necessary for delivering messages. Acting as the "mail carrier" for Exchange, the MTA can deliver messages to:

- Other Exchange servers in the same site
- Exchange servers in other sites
- A different Exchange organization

- Any foreign mail system for which a connector has been configured (see "Connections" in this chapter)

When the MTA must deliver a message, it uses the server's internal routing table to route the message to the appropriate object within the organization's directory space. This could be to another server's MTA, a private or public information store, a connector to another mail system, or a third-party mail gateway. For more information on Exchange message routing, see Chapter 2.

The Message Transfer Agent property sheet lets you:

- Manually force a recalculation of the internal message routing table
- View and modify MTA message queues for troubleshooting purposes
- Configure diagnostic logging for troubleshooting purposes

Properties

General

Lets you recalculate the routing table and specify the Local MTA name and password, maximum message size, other delivery options, and an administrative note. Also displays the server's home site, date the server was installed, and date the MTA configuration was last modified. Some of the more important settings include:

Local MTA name and password

Identifies the MTA to foreign mail systems. The default MTA name is the name of the Exchange server, and the default password is blank.

When trying to connect to a foreign X.400 MTA, you may need to make the name and password of the Exchange MTA match those of the foreign X.400 MTA. The password is case-sensitive.

Message Size

Lets you return messages above a certain size to sender as undeliverable.

Be careful in applying Message Size limits at the MTA level. If you decide to do this, you should make sure that each Exchange server in your organization has the same Message Size limit. Otherwise, one server may let a message be sent to another server that is greater than the second server's limit, resulting in an NDR being return to the first server (unless re-routing is configured which will delay the process but not alter its outcome). But the NDR cannot be delivered because the second server's MTA has to return the entire message in the NDR and this exceeds the message size limit for the first server, so the original message will be lost without any notification to its sender that this occurred. It is probably better to set message size limits only at the Mailbox level or for the Internet Mail Service alone. Also, any Message Size limit you set at the MTA level *cannot* be overridden at the Mailbox level.

Expand remote Distribution Lists locally

Remote Distribution Lists (DLs) are defined on a different site and replicated to your site by directory replication. You can:

- Clear the checkbox if the overhead of expanding the DL locally on your server would be too great.

- Check the checkbox to first expand the list on your server and then send the messages to the list's recipients.

Convert incoming messages to MS Exchange contents

Select this only if you are connected to a foreign X.400 mail system using IA5 German, Swedish, or Norwegian character sets. This will ensure character information is not lost during messaging. Do this only on the Exchange server that has the X.400 Connector to that foreign mail system.

Only use least cost routes

Checking this checkbox causes the lease-cost route only to be attempted for delivery. If that fails, no other route will be attempted, and a non-delivery report will be returned. Configure this setting on all Exchange server MTAs in your site if you decide to use it.

Recalculate Routing

Forces the internal message routing table to be rebuilt. The routing table contains information about the various sites, connectors, and gateways in your organization and is used by the MTA for delivering messages.

The routing table is normally recalculated once a day automatically and also when any new site, connector, or gateway is added to your organization. Using this button just does it a little faster, but it still takes a few minutes for the updated routing table to replicate to other servers in your site.

Permissions

See the section "Permissions and Roles" at the beginning of this chapter.

Queues

Shows the various message queues created by the MTA and the number of messages in each queue awaiting delivery. One MTA queue is created for:

- The Public or Private Information Store on your server

- Every other server in your site

- Each connector to other sites or mail systems

- Each configured gateway

If your server is a bridgehead server for directory replication, there will also be a queue for its directory.

Selecting a queue lets you view the messages in the queue, which are listed by the sender's alias, when the message was sent (submitted to the MTA for delivery), and message size. Select an individual message and click:

Details

Lets you view the *distinguished name* (DN) and *O/R address* of the sender and the Exchange message ID string or MTSID (see Figure 3-8). The message ID uniquely identifies the message and can be used to trace the message using the tracking log, event log, and message queues. For more on distinguished names, see the section "Common Properties" at the beginning of this chapter.

Priority

Lets you change the priority of the message. Changing the priority of a message changes its order in the queue, with high priority messages grouped at the top of the queue.

Delete

Lets you delete the message.

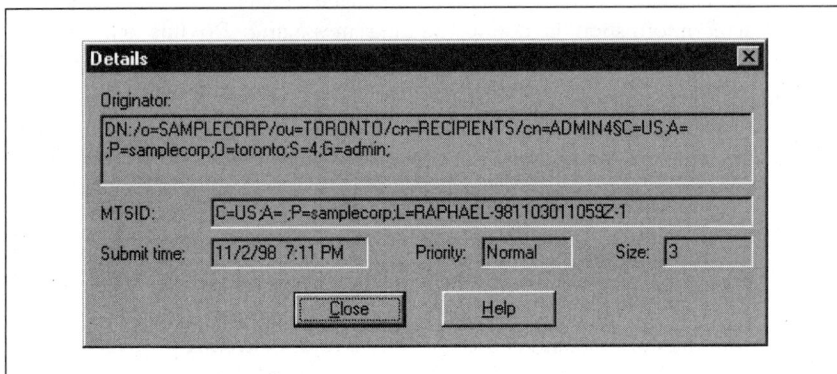

Figure 3-8: Details of a message in the MTA queue

Diagnostic Logging

Specify the types and levels of MTA events that are logged to the Application Log. MTA events are logged under the name MSExchangeMTA in the Application Log and can be viewed using Event Viewer. See the related property for the Server object for more information about diagnostic logging.

Specific to the MTA is the possibility of creating two kinds of advanced diagnostic logs:

–   Interoperability logs contain binary content of X.400 messages that can be used to diagnose MTA problems when communicating with foreign X.400 mail systems.

–   Application Protocol Data Unit (APDU) logs contain binary content of X.400 traffic between MTAs that can be used to diagnose MTA problems.

Both these logs can be used to diagnose MTA problems when using X.400 connectors between sites and with foreign mail systems, but this stuff is best left for those with deep familiarity with the X.400 protocol. Interoperability logging is enabled by setting the Interoperability and Interface categories to Medium or higher and produce logs in the *mtadata* directory of the form *Apx.log* where x = 1, 2, 3, and so on. APDU logging is enabled by setting the APDU and X.400 Service categories to Medium or higher and generated logs in the same directory of the form *Bfx.log*. Don't do this unless you know what you're doing, however, as these logs can quickly grow to be huge and can affect server performance.

Notes

- If you change the Local MTA name or password, you should notify administrators of foreign X.400 mail systems to update their connection information. Changing the name or password does not seem to have any effect on mail delivery within the organization itself, however.

- A growing MTA queue could indicate:

  - A physical connection or WAN link is down. Send some test messages and check the Application Log using Event Viewer. Check your Server Monitors and Link Monitors if configured.

  - An error in the configuration of the server, MTA or a connector. Check if the messages are originating from the same server.

  - Corrupt messages that are blocking the queue. Delete these, or lower their priority and investigate further.

- Instead of continually checking the MTA queue on the property sheet, try monitoring the following *object:counters* using Performance Monitor:

  - MSExchangeMTAConnections:QueueLength

  - MSExchangeMTAConnections:QueueBytes

- You can delete or change the priority of messages only for the following queues:

  - Local information stores

  - Other servers in your site

  - Site connector

  - X.400 connector

  - RAS connector

  You cannot delete or change the priority of messages in the Internet Mail Service or MS Mail Connector queues as these queues are not part of the MTA but instead interact with the MTA through its application programming interface. Note also that queues for the Internet Mail Service and MS Mail Connector are not displayed at all if there are no messages waiting in them.

Microsoft Schedule+ Free/Busy Connector

Configures sharing of free/busy information with Microsoft Mail networks.

Type

Leaf object

Path

```
Organization\Site\Recipients\Microsoft Schedule+ Free/Busy
Connector
```

Description

The Microsoft Schedule+ Free/Busy Connector is an example of a *mailbox agent*. Although it is called a connector, it is not found within a site's Connections container, but then not every object in the Connections container is called a connector either! These minor naming inconsistencies which appear so confusing at first are simply a result of the historical evolution of Exchange from earlier Microsoft Mail products and the concurrent evolution of terminology.

Free and busy times are times when the user's schedule indicate the user is either free or busy with an appointment. Microsoft Schedule+ is an earlier Microsoft Mail client that went through several versions and allowed a user to book meetings with other users and maintain a personal schedule. Schedule+ has now been replaced by Microsoft Outlook, which itself has already gone through several versions, but the mailbox agent that supports scheduling in Outlook is still called the Microsoft Schedule+ Free/Busy Connector.

The Microsoft Schedule+ Free/Busy Connector service is a Windows NT service that keeps track of a user's free and busy information by updating this information in the Schedule+ Free/Busy hidden public folder, which resides within the System Folders container. The connector also exchanges free/busy information with connected MS Mail Postoffices when the MS Mail Connector and Directory Synchronization objects are configured.

The Microsoft Schedule+ Free/Busy Connector property sheet lets you configure various settings for exchanging free/busy information with connected MS Mail Postoffices.

Properties

General
Lets you specify the display name, alias name, and an administrative note. Also displays the computer name, home site, date the object was installed, and date the object configuration was last modified. The default alias for the object is AdminSch and should not be changed.

Permissions
See the section "Permissions and Roles" at the beginning of this chapter.

Schedule+ Free/Busy Connector Options
Lets you configure how free/busy information is exchanged between Exchange and a connected MS Mail Postoffice. You don't need to configure this page if your organization is not connected to legacy Microsoft Mail networks. Settings of interest include:

Administrator Mailbox
Lets you specify a mailbox where non-delivery reports (NDRs) generated by the MS Schedule+ Free/Busy Connector Service will be sent.

Schedule+ Distribution List
The DL must contain all the connected Microsoft Mail Postoffices that will exchange free/busy information with Exchange.

Update Frequency
> Lets you schedule how frequently free/busy information will be exchanged with connected MS Mail Postoffices.

Send updates for this site only
> Limits the exchange of free/busy information to MS Mail Postoffices connected to the local Exchange site only.

Logging Level
> Lets you specify what types and levels of scheduling events are logged to the Application log.

Full Export
> Manually forces free/busy information to be exchanged with all connected MS Mail Postoffices.

Notes

- The Microsoft Schedule+ Free/Busy Connector supports MS Mail for PC but not MS Mail for AppleTalk.

- If you delete a recipient, the recipient's free/busy information will remain stored in the Schedule+ Free/Busy system folder. This information cannot be manually deleted, but will be automatically scavenged and removed after 100 days.

Monitors

Contains Server Monitors and Link Monitors for maintaining and troubleshooting your Exchange sites and servers.

Type

Container

Path

Organization\Site\Configuration\Monitors

Can Contain

Link Monitor
Server Monitor

Description

For more information, see the entries "Link Monitor" and "Server Monitor" in this chapter.

Properties

General
> Lets you specify the display name and an administrative note. Also displays the directory name, home site, date the server was installed, and date the object was last modified.

Permissions
> See the section "Permissions and Roles" at the beginning of this chapter.

MS Mail Connector

Lets you connect your organization to Microsoft Mail (MS Mail) systems.

Type

Leaf object

Path

Organization\Site\Configuration\Connections\MS Mail Connector

Description

The MS Mail Connector lets you transfer messages between your Exchange organization and a Microsoft Mail system. Microsoft Mail was the precursor to Microsoft Exchange and is a simple store-and-forward mail system using central postoffices. Unlike Exchange in which clients and servers communicate using *remote procedure calls* (RPCs), Microsoft Mail uses the file copy capability of the supporting network operating system to copy messages and attachments between clients and servers. Mail can be transferred between postoffices using the MS Mail External program, which functions as a message transfer agent (MTA).

The MS Mail Connector can connect to:

- Microsoft Mail for PC Networks
- Microsoft Mail for AppleTalk Networks (a.k.a. Quarterdeck Mail)

We will primarily consider connecting to PC networks here.

Creating a MS Mail Connector on an Exchange server installs the following three components on the server:

- Microsoft Mail Connector Interchange Service, a Windows NT service whose function is to route messages between the Exchange server and the temporary Microsoft Mail Connector Postoffice on that server
- Microsoft Mail Connector Postoffice, a temporary storage location on the Exchange server for processing messages in transit
- Microsoft Mail Connector Message Transfer Agent (MTA) Services or Connector MTAs, which are Windows NT services whose function is to route messages between the temporary postoffice and the remote MS Mail Postoffice

The configuration for using the MS Mail Connector varies with the type of network transport you are using:

LAN (TCP/IP or NWLink) connection
The MS Mail Connector can connect directly to any remote MS Mail Postoffice to transfer messages.

X.25 or asynchronous modem connections
The MS Mail External program must be installed and configured on the remote server hosting the MS Mail Postoffice.

In addition, the MS Mail Administrator program must be used to configure the remote postoffice for communication with the Exchange server. Refer to documentation on Microsoft Mail for further information on how to do this.

The MS Mail Connector property sheet lets you:

- Configure how messages are routed through the connector
- Display and edit the name of the temporary MS Mail Postoffice
- Connect to an MS Mail Postoffice using LAN, X.25, or asynchronous modem connections
- Create and configure a Connector MTA

Properties

Note first that you need to configure these property pages in a specific order, namely:

1. General
2. Interchange
3. Connections
4. Connector MTAs

Then configure the remaining property pages.

General

Specify message size limits and an administrative note. Also displays the server name, the server's home site, date the connector was installed, and date the connector's configuration was last modified. The message size limit applies to both inbound and outbound messages.

Address Space

Lets you specify address spaces for the MS Mail Connector. An *address space* represents a messaging path through the connector to the remote site. You can configure address spaces for routing messages:

- To specific MS Mail Postoffices
- To foreign mail systems (e.g., IBM SNADS) through an MS Mail gateway postoffice

Completing the configuration of the MS Mail Connector causes an address space for the configured remote MS Mail Postoffice to be automatically created. For example, if you connect to a MS Mail Postoffice called POST9 on a network called MYCORP, then the address space created would be:

Type
    MS

Address
    MYCORP/POST9

Cost
    Routing cost between 0 and 100 for load-balancing across multiple connectors. Default value is 1.

Scope

Restrictions on who can use this address space for sending messages through the connector. You can specify users at your location only, your local site only, or users throughout the entire organization. Default is Organization.

Note that an address space contains only a partial address of the form *NETWORK/POSTOFFICE* rather than a full address of the form *NETWORK/ POSTOFFICE/MAILBOX.*

This partial address is enough to uniquely identify which messages should be routed to the remote site. That is actually why it is called an *address space,* because it represents a space of possible recipients having the same partial address fragment in their addresses.

Diagnostic Logging

Specify the types and levels of MS Mail Connector events that are logged to the Application Log. MS Mail Connector events are logged under the following names in the Application Log:

— MSExchangeMSMI for connector interchange events (transfers between the Exchange server and the temporary Connector postoffice)

— MSExchangePCMTA for connector MTA events (transfers between the temporary Connector postoffice and the remote MS Mail Postoffice)

— MSExchangeATMTA for connector MTA events (transfers between the temporary Connector postoffice and a remote MS Mail [AppleTalk] Postoffice)

The Application log can be viewed using Event Viewer. See the related property for the Server object for more information about diagnostic logging.

Interchange

Lets you configure Microsoft Mail Connector Interchange Service, the Windows NT service that enables message transfer from the Exchange server to the MS Mail Connector. There are some differences here depending on what network transport you are using (LAN, asynchronous modem, or X.25). The important settings here are:

Administrator's mailbox

This is where messages will be forwarded along with their non-delivery reports (NDRs) if the connector cannot convert them. Create a special postmaster mailbox for your local MS Mail administrator and assign it here.

Primary language for clients

Lets you specify the primary language for messages routed through this connector. This setting may be required for interoperability with legacy MS Mail client software.

Maximize MS Mail 3.x Compatibility

Causes the MS Mail Connector to duplicate OLE information of embedded objects in messages, the copies using an earlier version of OLE acceptable to legacy MS Mail client software.

Enable message tracking

Lets you enable message tracking for both inbound and outbound messages routed through the connector. Use the Message Tracking Center to view message tracking events (see Chapter 4).

MS Mail Connector (AppleTalk) MTA

Lets you configure the MS Mail Connector for transferring messages to a Microsoft Mail for AppleTalk Networks system.

Local Postoffice

Lets you view and modify the identification information of the Microsoft Mail Connector Postoffice, a temporary postoffice on the Exchange server where the MS Mail Connector is installed. This information identifies the Exchange server to the remote MS Mail network and must be communicated to the postmaster of the remote Microsoft Mail network you are trying to connect to so that the postmaster can configure the other end of the connector using the MS Mail Administrator program's external postoffice list. Displayed here are:

Network

The name of the network where the temporary postoffice is located. By default this is the name of your Exchange organization or at most the first 10 characters of this name.

Postoffice

The name of the temporary postoffice. By default this is the name of the site where the MS Mail Connector is installed or at most the first 10 characters of this name.

Sign-on ID

The serial number for the shadow (temporary) MS Mail Postoffice, required by the remote MS Mail Postoffice. Note that all shadow postoffices have the same ID, which creates a conflict if you have two Exchange servers with shadow postoffices pointing to the same MS Mail Postoffice.

Password

A password for secure connectivity, at most eight characters, required by the remote MS Mail Postoffice. The default is PASSWORD.

If you change the network name or postoffice name on this page, then you should select the Regenerate button to update all MS Mail addresses for recipients in your organization.

Connections

Lets you configure network connections to remote MS Mail Postoffices. The Queue button lets you view, delete, and return messages queued for routing through the MS Mail Connector. What you do here depends on whether you have LAN (direct), asynchronous, or X.25 connectivity with the remote postoffice:

– LAN connection

This is the simplest method. If there is a direct network connection using TCP/IP or NWLink to the remote MS Mail Postoffice (shown as \\cafnto1\ maildata in Figure 3-9) the MS Mail Connector will automatically locate the remote postoffice and obtain the required network and postoffice names

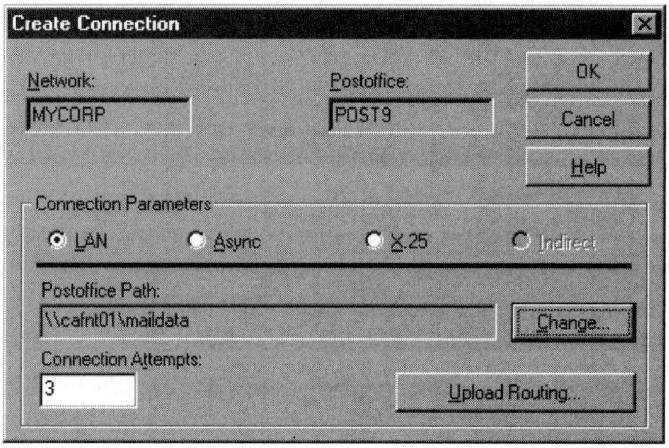

Figure 3-9: Configuring a LAN connection to a remote MS Mail Postoffice

Follow these steps to establish a connection with the remote MS Mail Postoffice:

1.Select LAN under Connection Parameters.

2.Select the Change button and enter the UNC path to the remote MS Mail Postoffice.

3.If the MS Mail Postoffice is in an untrusted Windows NT domain, specify the Logon ID in the Connect As box and enter the password. (See the Local Postoffice tab for these attributes.)

4.Click OK. The MS Mail Connector now will connect to the remote postoffice and if successful will automatically populate the Network and Postoffice fields on the dialog box.

5.Specify the number of allowed Connection Attempts before mail is returned to sender with a non-delivery report.

6.Select Upload Routing to show all MS Mail Postoffices indirectly connected to the MS Mail Postoffice you are connecting to, and choose which of these you want to include on the routing list for the MS Mail Connector.

7.You are now prompted to confirm the changes. (This can be prevented by clearing the checkbox on the Connections property page.)

– Async connection

This is a bit more complicated than using a direct LAN connection. You will have to manually enter the following information:

- Sign-on ID
- Password
- Connection attempts
- Phone number

Additional connection options can be specified, including:

- Message size limit
- Failed connection retry intervals
- Dialing frequency time interval
- Send and receive options
- Return receipts

- X.25 connection

  Same as Async connectivity, except you supply an X.121 address instead of a phone number for the remote postoffice.

- Indirect connection

  Lets you configure the MS Mail Connector to access remote MS Mail Post-offices that are not directly connected to your server. In other words, your Exchange server connects directly to remote postoffice A, which itself is connected directly to postoffice B, so your server is indirectly connected to postoffice B.

Connector MTAs

Lets you create and configure a Microsoft Mail Connector Message Transfer Agent (MTA) Service or Connector MTA (or PCMTA) that provides transport for delivering messages from the temporary MS Mail Connector Postoffice to the remote MS Mail Postoffice. Each Connector MTA you create is a new instance of a Windows NT service that can be started or stopped using Services in the Control Panel. What you do here again depends on whether you have LAN (direct), asynchronous, or X.25 connectivity with the remote postoffice:

- LAN connection

  Select the New button and specify the following information:

  Service Name
  Identifies the new Windows NT service for the Services utility in the Control Panel.

  Log Messages
  Lets you create logs for messages send and received.

  Polling Frequency
  Lets you schedule how often the new Connector MTA contacts the remote MS Mail Postoffice for messages and user information.

  Connection Parameters
  The type of network transport this Connector MTA is using.

  Options
  Lets you specify additional settings such as message size limits, critical disk space, startup configuration of service, and other advanced settings.

  Once a Connector MTA is created, you can specify which LAN post-offices it services by selecting the List button and adding Available LAN Postoffices to the list of Serviced LAN Postoffices. You can then select serviced postoffices from the list and select the Edit button to assign them a user account and password that has sufficient permissions for accessing the remote MS Mail Postoffice *maildata* directory.

A good rule of thumb is to use one Connector MTA for every seven MS Mail Postoffices being serviced by the MS Mail Connector.

– Async connection

Similar to LAN connection except that you must specify additional modem-specific parameters such as:

- Communication port
- Modem script
- Modem timeout

– X.25 connection

Similar to LAN connection except that you must specify additional X.25-specific parameters such as:

- X.121 address
- X.25 adapter port number
- X.25 listen user data and facilities

Note that the Log Status button can be used to force the writing of an event to the Application Log, describing the current status of the selected Connector MTA.

Notes

- After installing and configuring the MS Mail Connector on a server in your organization, you must manually start the MS Mail MTA service on that server using Services in the Control Panel. You also need to manually start any Connector MTAs you have created. You will probably want to configure these services to start automatically at system startup.

- Note that if you establish an indirect connection to a remote MS Mail Postoffice, you do not need to create a new Connector MTA for this connection.

- The MS Mail Connector is responsible for messaging connectivity with Microsoft Mail networks. To enable Exchange to replicate address lists with a Microsoft Mail network, use either a DirSync Requestor or DirSync Server object.

- Message tracking creates a hit on server performance, so enable it only when necessary. Once you enable message tracking on the MS Mail Connector, you must stop and restart the MS Mail Connector Interchange service on all servers where it is installed before tracking will take effect. Use the Services utility in the Control Panel to do this.

MTA Site Configuration

Lets you configure various aspects of the message transfer agent (MTA) at the site level.

Type

Leaf object

Path

Organization\Site\Configuration\MTA Site Configuration

Description

The MTA Site Configuration object is one of the directory objects that should be configured when you are implementing an Exchange site for your company. This object lets you globally configure essential aspects of the Microsoft Exchange Message Transfer Agent (MTA) service for all servers on your site. The MTA service is one of the core components of Exchange and is implemented as a Windows NT service. The MTA is responsible for routing messages between servers as described in Chapter 2.

In particular, the MTA Site Configuration property sheet lets you specify:

- Default settings for messaging
- Message tracking for diagnostic troubleshooting

See the "Site" entry in this chapter for other directory objects that should be configured when setting up a new site. For more details on the message transfer agent, see the entry "Message Transfer Agent."

Properties

General

Lets you configure the display name and enable message tracking for messages processed by MTAs in your site. Use the Message Tracking Center to view message tracking events (see Chapter 4). Also displays directory name, home site, date the site was created, and most recent date the properties of this object were modified.

Permissions

See the section "Permissions and Roles" at the beginning of this chapter.

Messaging Defaults

Lets you specify a variety of settings for messages processed within your site, including:

Reliable Transfer Service (RTS) values, specifically:

- Checkpoint size. The amount of messaging data transferred in KB before a checkpoint is inserted in the data stream. A connection error causes transmission to resume from the last checkpoint.

- Recovery timeout. The time in seconds that the MTA will wait for a connection error to be resolved before restarting the transmission from the beginning and resetting all checkpoint information.

- Window size. The minimum number of unacknowledged checkpoints before a connection error is generated.

Connection Retry values, specifically:

- Max open retries. The number of failed connection attempts that will trigger a non-delivery report (NDR).

- Max transfer retries. The number of attempts made to deliver messages across open connections.

- Open interval. How long the MTA waits before trying to reopen a connection after a connection error occurs.

- Transfer interval. How long the MTA waits before trying to resend a message over an open connection when the last attempt failed.

Association parameters, specifically:

- Lifetime. How long the MTA keeps an association open after messages are sent to remote sites. *Associations* are logical pathways to remote messaging systems.

- Disconnect. How long the MTA waits for a remote system to respond to a disconnect request before breaking the connection.

- Threshold. How many messages per association can be queued for a remote system.

Transfer timeout values, specifically

How long the MTA waits before issuing non-delivery reports for failed transfers. The higher the value, the longer the MTA waits. Transfer timeout values can be configured separately for:

- Urgent messages

- Normal messages

- Non-urgent messages

Notes

- Adjusting the messaging defaults can improve messaging performance with remote mail systems. Some things you can try include:

- Decreasing the checkpoint size over unreliable connections.

- Increasing the window size to increase the message transfer rate.

- Increasing association lifetimes to remote sites that messages are frequently sent to.

And if you mess things up, you can always click the Reset Default Values button—a nice touch!

- Message tracking creates a hit on server performance, so enable it only when necessary. Once you enable message tracking on the MTA, you must stop and restart the Microsoft Exchange Message Transfer Agent service on all servers where it is installed before tracking will take effect. Use the Services utility in the Control Panel to do this.

MTA Transport Stack

Configures the messaging transport protocol stack for either the Dynamic RAS Connector or the X.400 Connector.

Type

Leaf object

Path

```
Organization\Site\Configuration\Servers\Server\MTA Transport
Stack
```

Description

An MTA Transport Stack is a protocol stack that resides above and works together with the installed network protocol to enable message routing through a Dynamic RAS Connector or X.400 Connector. Prior to installing either of these two types of connector, you must install the appropriate transport stack for that connector. Exchange comes with four different types of transport stacks you can install, as shown in Table 3-13.

Table 3-13: Four Types of Transport Stacks for Exchange

Transport Stack	Supported Connector	Description
RAS	Dynamic RAS Connector	Use modem, ISDN, or X.25 to connect remote sites using RAS for Windows NT. Works with any network protocol (TCP/IP or NWLink).
TCP/IP	X.400 Connector	Use on any dedicated network connection using TCP/IP as the network protocol. The transport stack provides X.400 messaging connectivity over TCP/IP.
X.25	X.400 Connector	Use with Eicon X.25 port adapters over dedicated or dial-up connections.
TP4	X.400 Connector	Use on networks using connectionless Transport Class 4 (TP4) transport layer protocol.

Also, prior to installing any of these transport stacks, you may also need to install additional networking hardware or software, as shown in Table 3-14.

Table 3-14: Networking Hardware/Software Required for Different Transport Stacks

Transport Stack	Prerequisite Networking Hardware/Software
RAS	Windows NT Remote Access Service and a network protocol (TCP/IP or NWLink), ISDN terminal adapter and software or X.25 PAD and software.
TCP/IP	Windows NT TCP/IP network protocol on a TCP/IP internetwork.

Table 3-14: Networking Hardware/Software Required for Different Transport Stacks (continued)

Transport Stack	Prerequisite Networking Hardware/Software
X.25	Eicon X.25 port adapter and software, and an X.25 connection from a service provider.
TP4	A network adapter that supports TP4, a TP4 connection from a service provider, and the TP4 driver from the Windows NT compact disc. Configure the network Service Access Point (NSAP) address for TP4 using the Control Panel.

The default display names for each type of transport stack are shown in Table 3-15.

Table 3-15: Default Display Names for Different Transport Stacks

Type of Stack	Default Display Name
RAS	RAS (*<ServerName>*)
TCP/IP	TCP (*<ServerName>*)
X.25	Eicon X.25 (*<ServerName>*)
TP4	TP4 (*<ServerName>*)

The MTA Transport Stack property sheets let you:

- Specify general properties specific to each type of transport stack
- View and modify the list of connectors using the transport stack

Properties

General

The settings on this tab vary with the type of transport stack:

RAS

Display name and MTA callback number, the number used by the RAS server for callback (if enabled).

TCP/IP

Display name and server name where the stack is installed. If other applications are also using this transport stack, additional OSI address information needs to be specified. See your X.400 application documentation for more details.

X.25

Display name and various address information provided to you by your X.25 service provider. If other applications are also using this transport stack, additional OSI address information needs to be specified. See your X.25 application documentation or contact your X.25 service provider for more details.

TP4

> Display name. If other applications are also using this transport stack, additional OSI address information needs to be specified. See your TP4 application documentation for more details.

Permissions

> See the section "Permissions and Roles" at the beginning of this chapter.

Connectors

> Lets you view which connectors use this transport stack and access the property sheet for the connector.

Notes

If you delete a TCP/IP, X.25, or TP4 transport stack, this automatically deletes any X.400 connectors using the stack and all messages in that connector's queue.

Newsfeed

Lets you configure a Usenet newsfeed.

Type

> Leaf object

Path

> `Organization\Site\Configuration\Connections\Newsfeed`

Description

A newsfeed represents the flow of newsgroups and messages from one NNTP server to another. NNTP servers replicate newsfeeds between themselves to form a worldwide network of NNTP servers called Usenet. Replication of newsfeeds is controlled by a Windows NT service on Exchange called the Internet News Service, which is configured using the three different directory objects:

NNTP (News) Site Defaults

> Used to configure at the site level how Usenet newsfeeds are sent and received.

NNTP (News) Settings

> Used to configure at the server level how Usenet newsfeeds are sent and received.

Newsfeed

> Configures the Internet News Service and newsfeeds.

The Internet News Service is initially installed and configured by creating a new Newsfeed object using the Exchange Administrator program. See Chapter 4 for more details on how to do this. Besides replicating newsgroups with public Usenet hosts, you can also use this service to replicate newsgroups with Exchange servers running the Internet News Service in other Exchange organizations.

The Internet News Service also allows NNTP clients such as Microsoft Outlook Express to read and post messages to public Usenet newsgroups replicated with the Exchange server on which the service is installed. This Newsfeed directory object is used for configuring replication with Usenet newsfeeds.

Public Usenet newsgroups are stored in a public folder called Internet Newsgroups, which is homed on the Exchange server running the Internet News Service. Make sure you have sufficient disk space on this server to hold the portion of the public Usenet newsgroup hierarchy you plan to store, as this can run to several gigabytes.

If you want to enable your users to share information in *internal* Usenet-style newsgroups, use Outlook to create public folders within the Internet Newsgroups folder and then let them use Outlook to create public subfolders under these folders. For example, the administrator for company SampleCorp could create public newsgroup folders called *marketing, sales, support,* and so on. Then if a user creates a subfolder under *marketing* called *year2000,* this will appear in a newsreader such as Outlook Express as the newsgroup *marketing.year2000* in standard Usenet notation.

If you only need newsgroups that are accessible to users in your own Exchange organization, and do not need to be replicated as newsfeeds to the public Usenet system, it is simpler to create public folder hierarchies that simulate newsgroups on Exchange and then use Outlook Express to read and post messages to these newsgroups. To configure these *newsgroup public folders,* first use Microsoft Outlook 98 to create a public folder hierarchy on an Exchange server. Remember that public folders cannot be created using the Exchange Administrator program; see "Public Folder" in this chapter for more details.

Next select Tools → Newsgroup Hierarchies from the Exchange Administrator program menu, click Add, and specify the top folder of the public folder hierarchy you created. Wait a few minutes while Exchange does whatever it does.

Now configure your Outlook Express client by creating a new News account:

1. Select Tools → Accounts from the Outlook Express menu to open the Internet Accounts dialog box.
2. Select Add → News to start the Connection Wizard, and then specify your display name for posting messages and click Next.
3. Specify your return email address and click Next.
4. Enter the name of the Exchange server where the newsgroup public folders are homed, select "My server requires me to log on," and click Next.
5. Choose "Log on using Secure Password Authentication (SPA)" and click Next.
6. Specify a friendly name for your news account and click Next.
7. Specify a connection method and click Next.
8. Click Finish and then close the Internet Accounts dialog box. When prompted if you would like to download newsgroups from the News server, click OK. A

list of newsgroup public folders on the Exchange server appears (Figure 3-10). If this list doesn't appear, try resetting it using the Reset button. You can now subscribe to newsgroups and read and post messages in the usual way using Outlook Express or any third-party NNTP client.

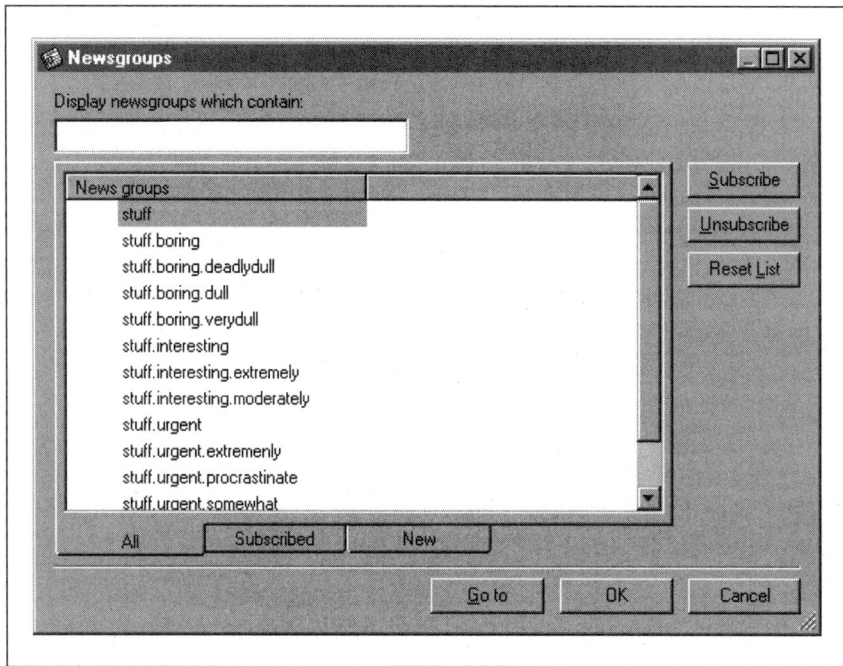

Figure 3-10: A listing of Exchange newsgroup public folders in Outlook Express

The Newsfeed property sheet lets you:

- Enable the newsfeed and specify an NNTP administrator
- Specify message size limits for both inbound and outbound feeds
- Specify the remote Usenet site and hosts
- Configure dedicated or dial-up connections to your Usenet service provider
- Specify accounts and passwords for secure feeds
- Select which newsgroups to send or receive in newsfeeds
- Schedule when feeds will occur
- Flush the newsgroup message queue

Properties

Note that not all of these tabs will be present on any given Newsfeed object. Some tabs are present for push feeds, others for pull feeds, and most for both types of feeds.

General

Lets you specify a display name, enable the newsfeed, specify an administrator's mailbox, and administrative note. Also displays the directory name, newsfeed type, date the object was created, home server, home site, and date the object was last modified. Here is some further explanation:

Enable newsfeed

Lets you allow the server to send or receive a newsfeed.

Administrator's mailbox

Lets you specify a recipient that will receive error notifications from the newsfeed.

Newsfeed type

Indicates whether the newsfeed is a push or pull feed.

A *push feed* is initiated by a remote Usenet host and is more suited for large newsfeeds over dedicated high-speed connections. The administrator of the remote Usenet host configures which newsgroups are sent in a push feed.

A *pull feed* is initiated by your Exchange server and is more suitable for small feeds over dial-up connections.

Note that most Usenet service providers do not support pull feeds without special arrangements being made with them.

Messages

Lets you specify separate message size limits for incoming and outgoing messages.

Hosts

Lets you specify the remote Usenet site and host names and configure additional inbound Usenet hosts. Contact your Usenet service provider for its Usenet site and host names. If your service provider has multiple Usenet hosts, add these to the list of inbound hosts.

An *inbound host* is one you pull a newsfeed from, while an *outbound host* is one you push a newsfeed to. When you create a newsfeed, you specify it as either inbound, outbound, or bi-directional.

Connection

Lets you specify the type of connection between your Exchange server and the remote Usenet host: dedicated or dial-up. Dial-up connections require the Windows NT Remote Access Service to be installed on the server and a phone-book entry configured for your Usenet service provider. You may need to specify an account name and password for the dial-up connection, if required by your service provider.

Security

Lets you specify credentials for your server to log on to the remote Usenet host, if required. By default no security is configured, but many Usenet service providers require authentication before they will send or receive newsfeeds. In particular you can specify:

- An account and password for outbound connections to your service provider's Usenet host, if needed. This option is enabled by default for outbound feeds and is not available for inbound feeds. The account and password are case-sensitive.

- A mailbox of custom recipient that your service provider's Usenet host must use for logging on to your Exchange server, if needed. This option is enabled by default for inbound feeds but cannot be configured for outbound feeds.

- Whether Secure Sockets Layer (SSL) protocol should be used to encrypt your newsfeed. This is not recommended as it creates an enormous hit on the server's performance.

Directory

If you want to practice creating a Newsfeed object, you can use the Microsoft public Usenet news host *msnews.microsoft.com,* which supports anonymous authentication.

Schedule

Lets you specify when the feed will occur. This should probably be every six hours or more, depending on the size of the feed.

Inbound

Lets you specify which inbound Usenet or Exchange newsgroup public folders you want to subscribe to, depending on whether you are connecting to a public Usenet host or an Exchange server running the Internet News Service in another organization. The options available on this page depend on whether your inbound feed is a push or pull feed.

For inbound push feeds:

Select trees of newsgroups or folders and click Accept to subscribe to them.

For inbound pull feeds:

Select trees of newsgroups or folders and click Include to subscribe to them.

You can also create public folders for storing Usenet newsgroups by importing an active file from a public Usenet host. An *active file* is a file listing the available newsgroups on a Usenet host. This is usually done when the newsfeed is created, but you can re-import the active file by using the Create Newsgroups Folder button and specifying either a direct connection to the remote Usenet host or a local path to where you have previously downloaded the active file.

Creating an Active File

The active file for your newsfeed can either be provided for you by your Usenet provider or you can generate one yourself using Telnet as follows:

1. Connect to your provider's NNTP host using Telnet; for example, click Start → Run and type:

   ```
   telnet FQDN_of_NNTP_host 119
   ```

2. If required, authenticate with the remote NNTP host, for example:

   ```
   authinfo user DomainName\UserName
   authinfo pass Password
   ```

3. In Telnet select Start Logging from the Terminal menu option and specify a filename. (The default is *telnet.log* but you can use any filename for the active file.)

4. Now type the following command to download a list of all newsgroups known to the remote host:

   ```
   list active
   ```

5. Finish by turning off logging in Telnet.

Outbound
  Lets you specify which inbound Usenet or Exchange newsgroup public folders you want to push to the remote Usenet host or Exchange server, depending on whether you are connecting to a public Usenet host or an Exchange server running the Internet News Service in another organization.

  Select trees of newsgroups or folders and click Include to include them in the outbound feed.

Advanced
  Lets you flush any newsgroup messages queued for delivery by marking all messages as delivered. This lets you catch up on newsgroup postings.

Notes

- Don't configure separate inbound and outbound feeds to the same remote Usenet server or it may not work properly. Configure a bi-directional feed instead.

- Usenet sites are not the same as Exchange sites. Contact your Usenet service provider for its Usenet site name.

- You can use either the IP address or the fully qualified domain name (FQDN) for your service provider's Usenet hostname.

- Make sure the Exchange Internet News Service is running if you try to connect to your Usenet service provider to obtain its active file. Use Services in the Control Panel to verify the service is running.

NNTP (News) Settings

Lets you configure Network News Transfer Protocol (NNTP) at the server level.

Type

Leaf object

Path

Organization\Site\Configuration\Servers\Server\Protocols\NNTP (News) Settings

Description

See the entry "NNTP (News) Site Defaults" in this chapter for a description of Network News Transfer Protocol.

Properties

Same as for the NNTP (News) Site Defaults object, except:

- You have the option on the General tab to inherit the properties of the site-level NNTP object or you can override the site default settings.

- The Newsfeeds tab also lets you:

    - Rename the Usenet site name for your site, in case you don't want your site name included in NNTP message headers for the world to see.

    - Create an active file for your site. An active file contains a list of the newsgroups available on your site and will be needed if you want to enable other Usenet hosts to download newsfeeds from your site.

- There is no Control Messages tab at the server level.

- The additional tab Diagnostic Logging lets you specify the types and levels of NNTP service events that are logged to the Application Log. NNTP events are logged under the name NNTP in the Application Log and can be viewed using Event Viewer. See the related property for the Server object for more information about diagnostic logging.

Notes

If you disable NNTP at the server level, it also disables NNTP for all Mailbox and Custom Recipient objects homed on that server.

NNTP (News) Site Defaults

Lets you configure Network News Transfer Protocol (NNTP) at the site level.

Type

Leaf object

Path

Organization\Site\Configuration\Protocols\NNTP (News) Site Defaults

Description

The Network News Transfer Protocol (NNTP) is a widely used Internet protocol that enables:

- NNTP clients to read and post messages to an NNTP server

- NNTP servers (often called NNTP hosts or Usenet hosts) to replicate newsgroups among themselves, forming a worldwide service called Usenet

Exchange supports Usenet through the Internet News Service, which is configured by using three different directory objects:

NNTP (News) Site Defaults
Used to configure at the site level how Usenet newsfeeds are sent and received

NNTP (News) Settings
Used to configure at the server level how Usenet newsfeeds are sent and received

Newsfeed
Configures the Internet News Service and newsfeeds

NNTP can also be configured at the Recipient level using the Protocols tab of the Mailbox or Custom Recipient property sheet.

The NNTP (News) Site Defaults property sheet lets you:

- Enable NNTP clients access Exchange

- View the properties of configured newsfeeds

- Accept or reject control messages from other NNTP servers

- Specify methods for NNTP clients to authenticate on Exchange

- Indicate the message format understood by the NNTP client

- Allow anonymous access by NNTP clients to public folders

- Configure connection time-outs

Properties

General
Lets you specify the display name, enable NNTP at the site level, enable client access, and specify an administrative note. You can also enable or disable NNTP on all servers within the site and allow or disallow NNTP clients access to newsgroup public folders.

Permissions
See the section "Permissions and Roles" at the beginning of this chapter.

Newsfeeds
Lets you view the properties of configured Newsfeed objects. See "Newsfeed" in this chapter for details.

Control Messages
Control messages are NNTP commands used by one NNTP server to communicate with another NNTP server. Control messages are used to create new

newsgroups, remove existing ones, cancel messages that have been posted, and perform other administrative functions. By default, Exchange queues NNTP control messages so that you can manually accept or decline them.

Authentication

Lets you select the authentication methods that are used when NNTP clients try to access the Exchange server. Supported authentication methods include:

Basic (Clear Text)

Sends username and password as clear text (unencrypted). Basic Authentication is supported by most POP3 clients and is commonly used in the Unix world. Because Basic Authentication transmits user credentials unencrypted over the network, it is not a secure authentication scheme. Anyone with a network packet sniffer who can capture authentication traffic can gain access to a user's credentials and access his mail.

Basic (Clear Text) using SSL

Uses Secure Sockets Layer (SSL) protocol to encrypt a Basic Authentication session. This makes Basic Authentication a secure authentication scheme. However, to use SSL you must have Internet Information Server (IIS) installed and obtain and install a key certificate from a Certificate Authority (CA). See "Certificate Authority (CA)" in this chapter for more information.

Windows NT Challenge/Response (NTLM)

Uses the Windows NT network authentication method, in which the password is not actually transmitted over the network. This authentication scheme is supported only by the following POP3 clients:

– Microsoft Internet Mail and News Version 3 and higher

– Microsoft Outlook Express

Windows NT Challenge/Response (NTLM) using SSL

Uses SSL protocol to encrypt an NTLM session.

MCIS Membership System

Uses the Windows NT network authentication method in conjunction with the Microsoft Commercial Internet Server (MCIS) Membership System.

MCIS Membership System using SSL

Uses SSL protocol to encrypt a MCIS Membership System session.

You can select one or more authentication methods from this list, but you must ensure that your NNTP clients each support at least one of the authentication methods you have chosen.

Message Format

Lets you specify what format Exchange messages are converted to when an NNTP client accesses a mailbox. NNTP clients cannot read the native Exchange messaging format, so Exchange must convert messages from their native format to a format suitable for the particular NNTP client. For example, some NNTP clients may prefer MIME encoding while older ones may prefer Uuencode or BinHex. Possible encoding options include:

MIME

> By default, Exchange converts messages from their native Exchange format to MIME-encoded messages for NNTP clients to access them. Additionally you can specify to provide the body of the message as plain text, HTML, or both in a MIME multi-part alternative message format. Most NNTP clients support all of these options.

Uuencode

> Lets you convert Exchange messages to the 8-bit encoding method common for older Unix clients. Additionally you can specify BinHex for encoding attachments for older Macintosh clients.

You can enable S/MIME to allow clients to access messages signed with S/MIME.

Idle Time-out

> Lets you keep open or close idle NNTP connections after a time interval you specify. Connections that are open too long can tie up server resources and are subject to hijacking by hackers; connections that time out too quickly cause unexpected errors and delays in messaging for the user.

Anonymous

> Lets you allow anonymous access to Exchange by NNTP clients. You also need to grant anonymous client permissions to the newsgroup public folders using the Public Folder property sheets.

Notes

- To enable anonymous access by NNTP clients, the Windows NT built-in Guest account is used, but strangely enough it does not need to be enabled. (It is disabled by default as a security measure.)

- If NNTP is disabled at the server level, it is also disabled for all Mailboxes and Custom recipients homed on the server.

- If you choose to enable or disable NNTP, it may take several minutes before this takes effect.

Offline Address Book

A hidden public folder that contains a subset of the Global Address List that remote users can download and use for addressing mail.

Type

> Container or leaf object

Path

> ```
> Organization\Folders\System Folders\Offline Address
> Book[\Offline Address Book]
> ```

Can Contain

Offline Address Book

Description

The Offline Address Book container object can contain one offline address book for each site, if they have been created, and has no configurable properties.

Offline Address Book leaf objects (or simply *offline address books*) have descriptive names assigned to them by users who create them and exist as a folder hierarchy within the Offline Address Book folder for the site in which they reside.

Offline address books can be downloaded by remote users who connect to Exchange remotely using laptops and contain convenient groupings for remote users of addresses of frequently used Exchange recipients. An offline address book can be based on:

- The Global Address List if remote users need access to the entire Global Address List of all recipients in an Exchange organization

- A recipients container or address book view if they only need access to a subset of all recipients (e.g., all recipients in the Toronto site, or all Marketing Department recipients in the organization) or if the number of recipients in the organization makes download times for the entire address list impractical

The name of the offline address book reflects the Exchange address of the site where the folder resides. For example, the offline address book folder for the site Toronto in the organization SampleCorp would have the following name in the Exchange Administrator windows:

EX:/o=samplecorp/ou=vancouver

Like other public folders, the contents of this folder reside in the Public Information Store of the server where the object was created and servers where other replicas exist.

Properties

The properties for this object are the same as for the Public Folders object.

Notes

Offline address books are generated using the DS Site Configuration object.

One-Off Address Templates

Lets you customize client-side dialog boxes for sending one-time messages to recipients *not* in the Global Address List.

Type

Container or leaf object

Path

```
Organization\Site\Configuration\Addressing\One-Off Address
Templates
```

Can Contain

Language
Language\One-Off Address Template

Description

When an Outlook client wants to send a one-time message to a recipient not in the Global Address Book, a dialog box opens allowing it to specify a one-off email address for the client. It is called a one-off email address because it is used once to send mail off and then forgotten rather than added to the address book.

The form of this dialog box depends on the type of email address (X.400, SMTP, MS Mail, and so on). Each type of dialog box is generated by a specific One-Off Address Template, which can be customized and configured using its property sheet.

The following example shows how to create an MS Mail one-off address in Microsoft Outlook 98:

1. Select File → New → Mail Message to open the Message window.

2. Click the To button to view the address book.

3. Select New to open the New Entry dialog box, and specify "Put this entry in this message only" to show the list of one-off address templates available (Figure 3-11).

4. Select Microsoft Mail Address and click OK to open the New Microsoft Mail Address Properties dialog box, which is generated by the Microsoft Mail one-off address template on the server (Figure 3-12).

The point here is that you can customize the appearance of these dialog boxes by modifying the properties of the associated One-Off Address Book directory objects.

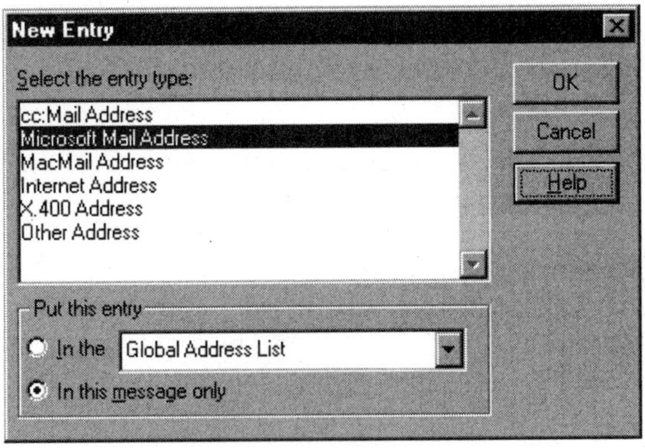

Figure 3-11: List of different one-off email address types in Microsoft Outlook

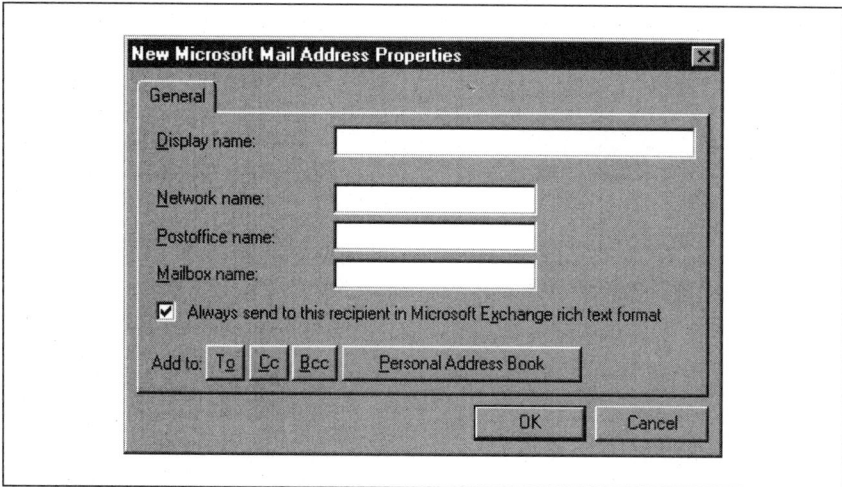

Figure 3-12: The Microsoft Outlook dialog box for a one-off MS Mail email address, generated by its associated One-Off Address Template

There are three levels of directory objects that we are dealing with here:

One-Off Address Template container
This container holds Language containers and has a General and Permissions tab with the usual attributes.

Language container
This container represents the installed language (e.g., English/USA) and has a General and Permissions tab with the usual attributes.

One-Off Address Template leaf objects
These are the objects of interest here. A collection of One-Off Templates is installed with Exchange, defining the appearance of the client-side one-off address dialog boxes for each of type of email address used by Exchange. These templates can be modified, for example, to add or remove a textbox or listbox or to rearrange the appearance of controls on a dialog box.

The One-Off Address Template property sheet lets you:

* Modify the type, position, and size of controls on the template

* Associate a Help file with the template

Properties

General
Lets you specify the display name, import a custom Help file, and specify an administrative note. Also displays the directory name, date the template was created, and date it was last modified.

The Help file is the file accessed when the client presses F1 while viewing the dialog box associated with the template. Microsoft has SDK tools for creating these Help files.

Permissions

See the section "Permissions and Roles" at the beginning of this chapter.

Templates

Lets you modify the type, position, and size of controls on the template. Controls include textboxes, listboxes, and other items. Click the Test button at any time to see what the dialog box created from the template looks like. Select Original to return to your default template and undo your changes.

MS-DOS Templates

Same as for Templates, except this is for the Microsoft MS-DOS Mail client.

Notes

• Importing a Help file overwrites the existing Help file for the template.

• Additional languages can be installed by importing the *.csv files from the Outlook compact disk.

Organization

The root container that directly or indirectly contains all other directory objects in your company's Exchange directory hierarchy.

Type

Container

Path

Organization

Can Contain

Address Book Views
Folders
Global Address List
Sites

Description

The Exchange *organization* is the top-level administrative unit of a company's Microsoft Exchange implementation. An organization is a collection of one or more *sites*, each site containing one of more Exchange *servers*, together with a *Global Address List, address book views,* and *public folders.* Together these components form the infrastructure that supports a company's messaging and collaboration needs.

The name of your Exchange organization should usually be the legal name of your company or the DNS domain name of your company on the Internet. This is because your organization name is used in addressing messages sent by users in your company. For example, if a user DonnaS belongs to a site Toronto within an organization SampleCorp, then her SMTP address would be the following: *DonnaS@Toronto.SampleCorp.com.*

Properties

General

Shows the display name, directory name, date the organization was created, and most recent date a new site was added to the organization.

Permissions

See the section "Permissions and Roles" at the beginning of this chapter. Granting permissions on this container only gives the users the right to change the display name, and new permissions assigned to this container are not inherited by other objects in the organization.

Notes

- When implementing Exchange for your company, choose your organization's name carefully, as it cannot be changed afterwards without re-installing Exchange on all your servers. An organization name must be specified during the installation of the first Exchange server in your company and is used in specifying the *distinguished name* (DN) of every directory object within your organization's Exchange directory database.

- Note that it is your organization's directory name that is used in addressing messages, not the display name. You cannot change your organization's directory name once Exchange is installed.

- You can now move an Exchange server from one site or organization to another without re-installing Exchange by using the Move Server Wizard included in Exchange Server 5.5 Service Pack 2. See the sidebar titled "The Move Server Wizard" in the "Server" entry in this chapter for more information on running the Move Server Wizard.

Directory

Organization Forms Library

A hidden public folder that contains forms commonly used by all users in your organization.

Type

Leaf object

Path

```
Organization\Folders\System Folders\EFORMS Registry\
Organization Forms Library
```

Description

Forms allow users to structure information for public posting or viewing. An example could be a supply request or expense report for a workgroup application or a special form used for posting to a public folder.

Form libraries are public folders containing collections of forms for public or personal use. Forms can be stored in three different libraries:

Organization forms library

Forms available to all users in your organization.

Public folder library
> Forms used with a specific public folder.

Personal forms library
> Forms used only by one user.

Like other public folders, the contents of an organization forms library reside in the Public Information Store of the server where the object was created and on servers where replicas of the folder exist.

Forms can be created and customized using Microsoft Outlook, but this is a developer issue and is beyond the scope of this book.

Properties

The properties are the same as for the Public Folders object.

Notes

Remember that users can connect to public folders in other sites only if:

- Public folder affinities are configured.

- Synchronous remote procedure calls (RPCs) are supported between the sites.

POP3 (Mail) Settings

Lets you configure Postoffice Protocol Version 3 (POP3) at the server level.

Type

> Leaf object

Path

```
Organization\Site\Configuration\Servers\Server\Protocols\
POP3 (Mail) Settings
```

Description

See the entry "POP3 (Mail) Site Defaults" in this chapter for a description of Postoffice Protocol Version 3 (POP3).

Properties

Same as for the POP3 (Mail) Site Defaults object, except:

- You have the option on the General tab to inherit the properties of the site-level POP3 object.

- The additional tab Diagnostic Logging lets you specify the types and levels of POP3 service events that are logged to the Application Log. POP3 events are logged under the name POP3 in the Application Log and can be viewed using Event Viewer. See the related property for the Server object for more information about diagnostic logging.

Notes

If you disable POP3 at the server level, it also disables POP3 for all Mailbox objects homed on the server.

POP3 (Mail) Site Defaults

Lets you configure Postoffice Protocol Version 3 (POP3) at the site level.

Type

Leaf object

Path

```
Organization\Site\Configuration\Protocols\POP3 (Mail) Site
Defaults
```

Description

Postoffice Protocol Version 3 (POP3) is a widely used Internet protocol that enables storage of incoming email. Using any POP3-enabled client, users can gain access to their personal Inbox on their Exchange home server and read their mail. To send mail, POP3 clients use the Simple Mail Transfer Protocol (SMTP). This is because POP3 does not handle the transfer of outgoing messages, since this is the job of SMTP. Since POP3 functionality is directly integrated into the information store, POP3 clients can directly access Exchange servers, but if you want POP3 access to Exchange over the Internet you must install the Internet Mail Service.

Microsoft Outlook and Microsoft Outlook Express are two Microsoft incarnations of POP3 clients, but any POP3 client such as Eudora Light can be used with Exchange.

POP3 can be configured at three different levels in Exchange:

- At the site level using the POP3 (Mail) Site Defaults object in the site Protocols container
- At the server level using the POP3 (Mail) Settings object in the server Protocols container
- At the recipient level using the property sheet of the Mailbox or Custom Recipient

The POP3 (Mail) Site Defaults property sheet lets you:

- Specify methods for POP3 clients to authenticate on Exchange
- Indicate the message format understood by the POP client
- Configure connection time-outs

Properties

General

Lets you specify the display name and an administrative note and enable or disable the protocol at the site level.

You must check the checkbox to allow POP3 clients to access their mailboxes.

Permissions

See the section "Permissions and Roles" at the beginning of this chapter.

Authentication

Lets you select the authentication methods that are used when POP3 clients try to access the Exchange server. Supported authentication methods include:

Basic (Clear Text)

Sends username and password as clear text (unencrypted). Basic Authentication is supported by most POP3 clients and is commonly used in the Unix world. Because Basic Authentication transmits user credentials unencrypted over the network, it is not a secure authentication scheme. Anyone with a network packet sniffer who can capture authentication traffic can gain access to a user's credentials and access his mail.

Basic (Clear Text) using SSL

Uses Secure Sockets Layer (SSL) protocol to encrypt a Basic Authentication session. This makes Basic Authentication a secure authentication scheme. However, to use SSL you must have Internet Information Server (IIS) installed and obtain and install a key certificate from a Certificate Authority (CA). See "Certificate Authority (CA)" in this chapter for more information.

Windows NT Challenge/Response (NTLM)

Uses the Windows NT network authentication method, in which the password is not actually transmitted over the network. This authentication scheme is supported only by the following POP3 clients:

–   Microsoft Internet Mail and News Version 3 and higher

–   Microsoft Outlook Express

Windows NT Challenge/Response (NTLM) using SSL

Uses Secure Sockets Layer protocol to encrypt an NTLM session.

MCIS Membership System

Uses the Windows NT network authentication method in conjunction with the Microsoft Commercial Internet Server (MCIS) Membership System.

MCIS Membership System using SSL

Uses Secure Sockets Layer protocol to encrypt a MCIS Membership System session.

You can select one or more authentication methods from this list, but you must ensure that your POP3 clients each support at least one of the authentication methods you have chosen.

Message Format

Lets you specify what format Exchange messages are converted to when a POP3 client accesses a mailbox. POP3 clients cannot read the native Exchange messaging format, so Exchange must convert messages from their native format to a format suitable for the particular POP3 client. For example, some POP3 clients may prefer MIME encoding while older ones may prefer Uuencode or BinHex. Possible encoding options include:

MIME

> By default, Exchange converts messages from their native Exchange format to MIME-encoded messages for POP3 clients to access them. Additionally you can specify to provide the body of the message as plain text, HTML, or both in a MIME multi-part alternative message format. Most POP3 clients support all of these options.

Uuencode

> Lets you convert Exchange messages to the 8-bit encoding method common for older Unix clients. Additionally you can specify BinHex for encoding attachments for older Macintosh clients.

Besides choosing one, you can also specify:

Character set

> Depends on the language used.

Use Rich Text Format (RTF)

> Converts RTF formatting of the native Exchange message format into an attachment for POP3 clients that can understand RTF, typically Microsoft clients.

Idle Time-out

Lets you keep open or close idle POP3 connections after a time interval you specify. Connections that are open too long can tie up server resources and are subject to hijacking by hackers; connections that time out too quickly cause unexpected errors and delays in messaging for the user.

Notes

- If POP3 is disabled at the server level, it is also disabled for all Mailboxes and Custom recipients homed on the server.

- If you choose to enable or disable POP3, it make take several minutes before this takes effect.

- For Windows NT Challenge/Response (NTLM) to work with Microsoft Internet Mail and News client, the user's mailbox alias name must be the same as the user's Windows NT user account.

- Messages sent by users on the Internet are *not* converted to other formats when POP3 clients access their Inbox on Exchange. For example, if a user on the Internet sends email with a Uuencoded attachment, then when the POP3 client retrieves the message from their Inbox on Exchange, it still uses Uuencoding, regardless of whether or not Uuencoding is selected on the Message Format property page.

- Don't forget to configure the Routing property page of the Internet Mail Service object to support POP3 clients.

- A user's POP3 email address is the same as his SMTP address.

Private Information Store

Configures the private information store on the server.

Type

Leaf object

Path

Organization\Site\Configuration\Servers\Server\Private
Information Store

Description

The *private information store* is the central storage location on the server for storing users' mail folders and messages. The private information store is a database structure based upon the Microsoft Joint Engine Technology (JET) database technology and by default is located in the *mdbdata* directory. This database is managed by the Microsoft Exchange Information Store service, a core component of Exchange Server that is implemented as a Windows NT service. The structure of the database files for the private information store follow the pattern of the Exchange directory database files located in the *dsadata* directory. See the beginning of this chapter for a description of these database files.

An Exchange server may have one private information store, one *public information store*, or one of each type. For example, one server in your site could be dedicated to hosting public folders and would have a public information store but not a private one. Other servers in the site would have private information stores but not public ones. By default, Exchange servers when installed have both private and public stores. You can delete either the private or public store using the delete button on the Exchange Administrator toolbar.

The Private Information Store property sheet lets you:

- Set mailbox size limits and deleted message retention time
- View mailbox resources used for each mailbox
- Display currently logged-on users and Exchange services
- Configure diagnostic logging for troubleshooting

In addition to configuring these settings on the property sheet, the mailbox resources used and users or services logged on can be viewed directly in the Contents pane of the Exchange Administrator program by selecting the Logons and Mailbox Resources objects in the Container pane (see Figure 3-13).

This is a bit confusing, since the Logons and Mailbox Resources objects, located under the Private Information Store object, are not true directory objects. Instead they are simply alternate representations of the information displayed on the Logons and Mailbox Resources tabs of the Private Information Store property sheet. The advantage of using these alternate representations, however, is that you can double-click on a specific logged-on user or service in the Contents pane and access the property sheet of that mailbox or service directly; it provides a kind of link to the associated property sheet.

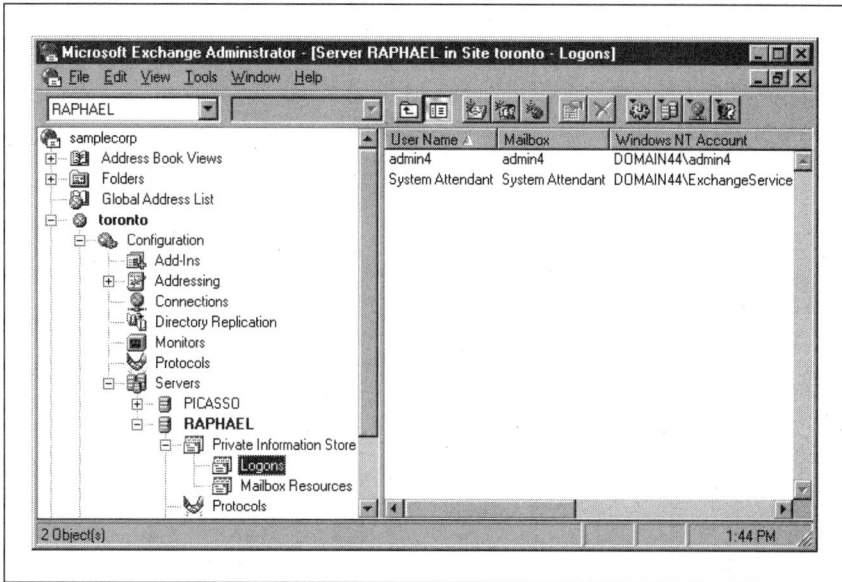

Figure 3-13: Double-click on a logged-on user or service to display its property sheet

Properties

General

Lets you specify deleted message retention time, mailbox disk space limits and warnings, and the public folder server associated with users with mailboxes on this server. Also displays the server's home site, the information store's home server, date the server was installed, and date the information store configuration was last modified. Some of the more important settings include:

Item Recovery

Lets you specify how long items are retained before being permanently deleted. You can also specify that no items are permanently deleted until the information store is backed up. Microsoft Outlook users can recover deleted items using the Recover Deleted Items menu command.

Storage Limits

Lets you specify mailbox size limits on the server. Once a limit is reached you can have a warning message issued, prohibit sending but allow receiving, or prohibit both sending and receiving. It's a good idea to specify some kind of value for Prohibit Send and Receive if only to ensure that a user's mailbox doesn't consume all of the server's free disk space. One GB or so should do!

Public Folder Server

Lets you specify the server where top-level public folders will be created by users whose *home server* is your server.

Permissions

See the section "Permissions and Roles" at the beginning of this chapter.

Logons

Displays the users logged on to the information store. This includes Exchange services also, which log on using the Exchange *service account*. Select the Columns button to customize the information visible for each user.

> If you check the Logons property page, you may see multiple entries for users or services logged on the server. This is because clients log on once for the private information store and once for the public store. Clients also log on once for each mailbox they open as a delegate. Services form multiple connections for similar reasons.

Mailbox Resources

Displays the number of messages stored, amount of disk spaced used, and other parameters for each mailbox in the information store on this server. Select the Columns button to customize the information visible for each mailbox.

Diagnostic Logging

Specify the types and levels of Exchange server events that are logged to the Application Log. Exchange server events are logged under the name MSExchangeS in the Application Log and can be viewed using Event Viewer. See the related property for the Server object for more information about diagnostic logging.

Notes

- The item retention and size limits set here are global settings for all mailboxes on the server and can be overridden for individual mailboxes using the property sheet for each Mailbox object.

- When using POP3 or IMAP4 messaging clients, select Prohibit Send And Receive instead of Prohibit Send, as these clients do not support the Prohibit Send option.

Protocols

Contains directory objects for configuring Internet protocols.

Type

Containers (two of them)

Path

```
Organization\Site\Protocols
Organization\Site\Configuration\Servers\Server\Protocols
```

Can Contain

For the Site-level container:

> HTTP (Web) Site Settings
> IMAP4 (Mail) Site Defaults
> LDAP (Directory) Site Defaults
> NNTP (News) Site Defaults
> POP3 (Mail) Site Defaults

For the Server-level container:

> IMAP4 (Mail) Settings
> LDAP (Directory) Settings
> NNTP (News) Settings
> POP3 (Mail) Settings

Description

There are two kinds of Protocols containers, one for each site and one for each Exchange server within a site. These containers let you configure general properties for standard Internet protocols supported by Exchange:

Hypertext Transfer Protocol (HTTP)
> An Internet protocol that allows web browsers such as Internet Explorer and Netscape Communicator to access mailboxes and public folders on an Exchange site where Outlook Web Access is enabled.

Internet Message Access Protocol Version 4 rev1 (IMAP4rev1)
> An Internet protocol that allows IMAP4rev1 clients access their mailboxes and public folders on Exchange when the Internet Mail Service is installed and configured.

Lightweight Directory Access Protocol (LDAP)
> An Internet protocol that allows LDAP clients to access information from the directory on an Exchange server.

Network News Transfer Protocol (NNTP)
> An Internet protocol that allows NNTP clients to read and post to NNTP newsgroups on an Exchange server and allows replication of newsgroups between NNTP servers.

Postoffice Protocol Version 3 (POP3)
> An Internet protocol that allows POP3 clients to access their Inbox on Exchange when the Internet Mail Services is installed and configured.

You can configure how Exchange implements these protocols by:

- Modifying the properties of the Protocols containers at either the site or the server level. Note that server-level settings override site-level settings.

- Modifying the properties of the individual protocol objects within these containers. Note that unlike the other four protocols, the HTTP protocol can only be configured at the site-level.

Additionally, you may need to create and configure the following two objects, located within the Connections container:

- The Newsfeed object is used to configure Usenet newsfeeds and NNTP connections.

- The Internet Mail Service is used to configure the Simple Mail Transport Protocol (SMTP) messaging service.

To confuse things further (or perhaps to give you the widest range of configuration options), you can also enable, disable, and configure Internet protocols for individual Mailbox and Custom Recipient objects using their property sheets. However, disabling protocols at the server-level also disables them for all recipients as well.

For more information on configuring Internet protocols on Exchange, see the topics on the previously mentioned directory objects elsewhere in this chapter.

The Protocols property sheet lets you:

- Accept or reject connections to a site or server

- Configure MIME mappings to file extensions for attachments

Properties

General

Lets you specify the display name and an administrative note. Also displays the directory name, the object's home site, date the object was installed, and date it was last modified.

On the server-level Protocols property sheet, you have two additional settings:

Use site defaults for all properties
Inherits the settings of the site-level Protocols container.

Outlook Web Access server name
Displays the name of the server running Internet Information Server (IIS) and Active Server Pages (ASP) to support access to users' mailboxes via a standard web browser.

Permissions
See the section "Permissions and Roles" at the beginning of this chapter.

Connections
Lets you accept or reject connections to your Exchange server based on the IP address of the remote client for POP3, NNTP, and LDAP clients. This is a security feature that can be useful if you want to:

- Grant access to a specific group of remote users on the basis of IP address and deny access to all others. For example, you might want to grant access to your travelling salespeople who access Exchange remotely using their laptops.

- Deny access to a specific IP address if the user of that address has been probing your network's security perimeter.

You do this by creating a series of rules that are applied in order from top to bottom when a remote client attempts a connection to your server. A rule consists of an IP address, a subnet mask, and an include/exclude setting. Rules can be specified for accepting or rejecting connections from:

Individual remote clients.
> For example, to include/exclude the remote host 209.33.155.9 use:

> IP = 209.33.155.9
> Mask = 255.255.255.0

Groups of remote clients comprising a remote subnet.
> For example, to include/exclude the group of hosts 173.44.48.1 through 173.44.63.254 use:

> IP = 173.44.48.0
> Mask = 255.255.240.0

For more information on subnetting, refer to *Windows NT TCP/IP Network Administration* by Craig Hunt and Robert Bruce Thompson, also available from O'Reilly & Associates.

Directory

MIME Types
> For inbound mail, specifies which file extensions Exchange assigns to attachments that are encoded using the Multipurpose Internet Mail Extensions (MIME) method. For outbound mail, specifies which MIME type will be used to encode attachments, based on their file extensions. You can create, edit, rearrange, and delete MIME mappings from this list.

Notes

- If you decide to use Secure Sockets Layer (SSL) protocol to encrypt Internet messaging traffic, you must make the Exchange service account a member of the Administrators local group, on the Exchange server.

- The settings on the Connections page apply to all Internet protocols except HTTP. Use the Internet Service Manager administrative tool for Internet Information Server (IIS) to configure HTTP connection restrictions for web access to Exchange mailboxes and public folders.

- Since rules on the Connections page are processed from top to bottom, move the most specific rules to the top and put the more general rules at the bottom of the list.

- If there are two or more MIME mappings for the same content type or same file extension, the one listed first is used.

- You should probably create a new MIME mapping for text/html → .htm since Microsoft applications often save web pages with the extension *.htm* instead of *.html*.

- If you want to control access by users to Exchange via HTTP using Outlook Web Access, you must use the Internet Service Manager of IIS to accept or reject IP addresses of remote clients.

Public Folder

A type of *recipient* that maps to a portion of the *public information store* and contains shared information for groups of recipients; also the name of a container for these recipient objects.

Type

Container or leaf object

Path

```
Organization\Folders\Public Folders[\Public Folder[\Public
Folder...]]
```

Can Contain

Public Folders

Description

Public folders have a variety of uses, including letting groups of users:

- Publish information for other users to see (e.g., notices, policies, and procedures)
- Participate in discussions through discussion forums and bulletin boards
- Collaborate on workgroup projects with other users
- Submit information through forms (e.g., invoices, requisitions, and timesheets)
- Establish support through online help systems and FAQs

and just about anything else you could think of.

The Public Folders container object contains all public folders created by users and has no configurable properties. Public folder leaf objects (or simply *public folders*) have descriptive names assigned to them by users who create them and exist as a folder hierarchy within the Public Folders container.

Like *mailboxes*, public folders exist in two places on Exchange servers:

- Configuration settings for all public folders are stored in the Exchange *directory database*, along with the properties of other directory objects. The directory database is automatically replicated to all other Exchange servers in the site, so the public folder hierarchy exists within each Exchange server's directory database.
- Actual public folder contents (other public folders, forms, posted messages, and attachments) are stored in the *public information store* on Exchange servers. Unlike mail content, public folder content need not be located on a single server. Instead, public folder content can be:
  - Located on one specific Exchange server in your organization that is dedicated to storing all public folders.
  - Distributed among several Exchange servers (e.g., bulletin board folders on Server A, project folders on Server B, and so on).

- Replicated among a number of Exchange servers to create multiple identical replicas of the public folder content. Changes made to one replica are copied to all other replicas, keeping them all up to date.

These techniques provide some flexibility for locating public folders and allow load-balancing when demand for access to public folders is heavy. From the point of view of the client, however, the entire public folder hierarchy appears to be a single entity. When a client tries to access a public folder, the client doesn't need to worry about which server or servers the folder's content actually resides on; Exchange takes care of that part.

Creating public folders is about the only administrative task you *can't* perform using the Exchange Administrator program. Client software such as Microsoft Outlook must be used to create public folders (see the entry "Outlook 98" in Chapter 4). Once created, however, public folders can be configured using either Exchange Administrator or the client software.

Access to public folders can be controlled using permissions by assigning recipients various *roles*. These roles are discussed in detail later.

One additional point is that public folder hierarchies can be created on Exchange that emulate Usenet-style newsgroups. These *newsgroup public folders* can then be accessed by any NNTP client such as Microsoft Outlook Express and messages can be read and posted to a newsgroup public folder by any user in the organization. The Exchange Internet News Service does not need to be running on the server hosting the public folders for NNTP clients to connect to these public folders. An alternative is to configure a *newsfeed* on the Exchange so that Exchange can participate in the full public Usenet network. For more information on newsgroup public folders and Usenet, see "Newsfeed" in this chapter.

Monitoring Public Folders

Sometimes you would like specific users notified when the contents of a public folder changes. The following procedure was suggested in a posting to the *microsoft.public.exchange.admin* Usenet newsgroup:

1. Enable the Microsoft Exchange Event Service on your Exchange server.

2. Make sure you have Folder Owner client permissions on the public folder.

3. In Outlook 98 select Tools → Options → Other → Advanced Options → Add-In Manager and install Server Scripting if it is not already installed.

4. Use Outlook to open the property sheet for the folder and select the Agents tab.

5. Create an agent (server-side script) as desired for monitoring changes that are made to the public folder.

Note: do not let users do this, as these agents run in the context of the Exchange *service account* and have unlimited privileges.

The Public Folder property sheet lets you:

- Configure public folder replicas
- Schedule replication of public folders
- View public folder replication status
- Add the folder to Distribution Lists (DLs)
- View and modify the folder's email addresses
- Configure delivery restrictions for receiving messages
- Specify storage limits and retention time
- Define custom attributes for the recipient

Properties

General

Lets you specify the public folder name, address book display name, alias, client permissions, propagation of properties to subfolders, limiting administrative access to home site, and a descriptive note. Also displays the folder's path, home site, home server, the date the folder was created, and the most recent date the folder properties were modified. Some of these bear further explanation:

Folder name

Name given to the folder when it was created.

Address book display name

Name of folder as it appears when clients access the global address book.

Alias

Name used in the email address for posting messages to the folder (e.g., *Bulletins@Vancouver.SampleCorp.com*).

Propagate these properties to all subfolders

Lets you apply various properties of the selected public folder to all its subfolders within the public folder hierarchy. Select this checkbox and click OK to open the Subfolder Properties dialog box (see Figure 3-14) and choose the properties you want to propagate down the folder hierarchy. Note that this option is only available if there are subfolders of the selected folder. Be careful using this as you will overwrite folder permissions.

Limit administrative access to home site

Lets you prevent public folders from being re-homed to other Exchange sites except by administrators in the folder's home site.

Folder Path

Shows the hierarchical address of the public folder starting from its top-level folder (e.g., *BulletinBoards\Marketing\WestCoast*).

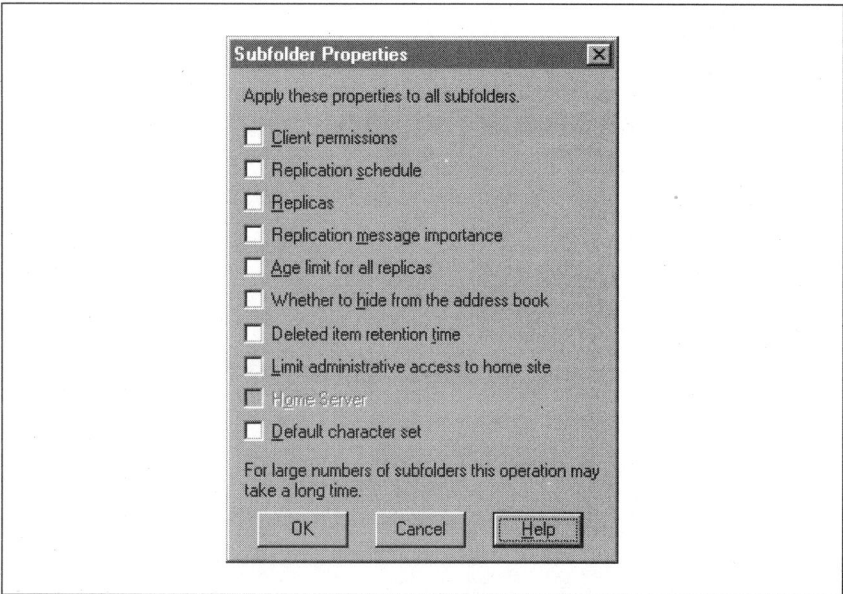

Figure 3-14: The Subfolder Properties dialog box

Client Permissions

Opens the Client Permissions dialog box (Figure 3-15), allowing you to grant permissions on the folder to recipients by assigning them various roles.

Public folder roles are predefined sets of client permissions that simplify the administrator's task of controlling access to public folders. Note that the roles and client permissions for public folders are different from the roles and permissions for administrative access to directory objects discussed at the start of this chapter.

Using this dialog box you can:

– Grant or deny a recipient access to the public folder by assigning a role

– Customize a recipient's role by assigning or removing specific permissions

– View a subset of the recipient's properties

Table 3-16 shows the *client permissions* that can be used to control access to public folders by clients.

The client permissions in Table 3-16 are combined together into the *roles* shown in Table 3-17. These roles can then be assigned to users and groups to control access to specific public folders.

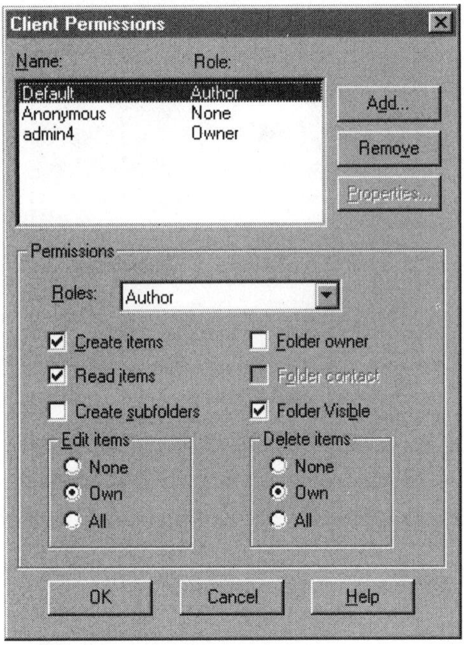

Figure 3-15: The Client Permissions dialog box

Table 3-16: Client Permissions for Accessing Public Folders

Client Permission	Allows Users to...
Create items	Create items in the folder
Create subfolders	Create new subfolders in the folder
Folder owner	Be the folder's owner
Folder contact	Be the recipient contacted when notification messages are generated for the folder by the information store
Folder visible	View the folder in the folder hierarchy
Read items	Read items in the folder
Edit items	Edit items in the folder (either All items or the user's Own items)
Delete items	Delete items in the folder (either All items or the user's Own items)

Table 3-17: Roles for Controlling Access to Public Folders

	CLIENT PERMISSIONS							
ROLE	Create items	Create subfolders	Folder owner	Folder contact	Folder visible	Read items	Edit items	Delete items
Owner	✓	✓	✓	✓	✓	✓	All	All
Publishing Editor	✓	✓			✓	✓	All	All
Editor	✓				✓	✓	All	All
Publishing Author	✓	✓			✓	✓	Own	Own
Author	✓				✓	✓	Own	Own
Non-Editing Author	✓				✓	✓		Own
Reviewer					✓	✓		
Contributor	✓				✓			
None					✓			

To assign a Custom role, assign them any of the preceding roles and then use the checkboxes and option buttons to grant or deny each kind of client permission.

Replicas

Lets you add replicas of public folders on your server to other servers in your site. To do this perform the following steps:

1. Select a site from the drop-down listbox at the bottom.

2. Select servers in that site where you would like to create replicas or your public folder.

3. Click the Add button.

Public folder directory objects are automatically replicated to all Exchange servers in a site; public folder contents are not, however. A *replica* is an exact copy of the contents of a public folder's contents and exists in the public information store of an Exchange server. All replicas of public folders have the same importance; there is no master replica of a public folder.

A public folder can have many replicas throughout an Exchange organization. When a client attempts to access a public folder, the client first connects to a server to access the directory. The directory service informs the client of the location of the public folder's replicas, and the client attempts access in the following order:

- If the user's home server hosts a replica of the public folder, the client attempts to connect to that replica.

- If that fails, the client tries one by one to connect to replicas in the user's site.

- If that fails, and *public folder affinities* are configured, the client tries replicas in different sites.

Moving Public Folders

To move a public folder from one server to another server in the same site, use the following procedure:

1. Use Exchange Administrator to open the property sheet of the public folder you want to move.

2. Select the Replicas property page.

3. Highlight the name of the server you want to move the folder to in the Servers box and click Add.

4. Highlight the name of the server you want to remove the folder from in the Replicate Folders To box and click Remove.

Note that the original folder will still be available until directory synchronization occurs within your site.

For information on configuring public folder affinities, see "Information Store Site Configuration" in this chapter.

Note that there are two ways of creating and managing public folder replicas:

— Use the Public Information Store object's property sheet to configure replicas on a global basis for a selected server.

— Use the property sheet of a particular Public Folder object to configure replicas for that folder alone. These settings override those configured, using the Public Information Store object.

Replication Status
   Displays all servers on which a replica of the folder exists, showing you when each replica was last updated and the replication status, which may be either:

In Sync
   The replicas are up to date.

Local Modified
   Changes have been made to some replicas that have not yet propagated to all other replicas.

Replication Schedule
   Lets you specify how often the selected public folder will be replicated. This setting can be globally specified for all public folders on a server using the server's Public Information Store directory object.

Permissions
   See the section "Permissions and Roles" at the beginning of this chapter.

Distribution Lists

Shows the *Distribution Lists* to which the public folder belongs and allows you to add the public folder to other Distribution Lists.

E-mail Addresses

Displays the public folder's various email addresses and allows you to modify these addresses or add additional addresses. Email addresses are the means by which Exchange recipients are known, both within your Exchange organization and by outside mail systems. See the "Mailbox" entry in this chapter for more details.

NNTP

This tab is only present when the Exchange Internet News service has been installed and the public folder has been configured as a *newsgroup public folder*. See the entries "NNTP (News) Site Defaults" and "Newsfeed" for more information.

Custom Attributes

Lets you specify the values for custom attributes defined using the DS Site Configuration object for your Exchange site.

Limits

Lets you specify how long messages deleted from the public folder are retained to enable clients to recover deleted messages, how much space the folder can utilize in the public information store before a warning notification is issued, and the period in days a message is allowed to remain in the folder until it is deleted.

Advanced

Miscellaneous settings including:

- Specify a simple display name for systems that cannot read special characters in the normal display name.

- View the directory name and the parent Recipients container of the public folder.

- Select a trust level when directory synchronization with MS Mail servers is performed using a MS Mail Connector.

- Specify the home server for the public folder.

- Hide the public folder from the address book. Users can still send mail to a hidden recipient if they know its email address, however.

- Specify the priority level for replication messages that are sent by this public folder replica to other replicas.

- Provide a descriptive note.

Notes

- When you create a subfolder of a public folder, it automatically inherits the client permissions of the parent folder. You can then use the Client Permissions dialog box to customize permissions for the subfolder.

- You can't use the Exchange Administrator program to completely remove the last replica of a public folder from its home site; you have to use Microsoft Outlook to do this!

- After you create a new replica of a public folder in your organization, some users may temporarily be unable to access the contents of the public folder. This occurs because the Public Folder directory object has a higher replication value or priority than the contents of the folder. Depending on how public folder affinity is configured for clients, some clients will see the new replica (folder object) in their client program but will be unable to access its contents until they have also replicated. Wait a bit and depending on the amount of content to be replicated, users should soon be able to access the folder's contents.

- Make use of the scheduling aspects of public folders to conserve network bandwidth. Some public folders such as those containing FAQs or company policies may need to be replicated only once a week; others such as those containing customer tracking information and invoices should be replicated more frequently.

- Users can connect to public folders in other sites only if:

    - Public folder affinities are configured.

    - Synchronous remote procedure calls (RPCs) are supported between the sites.

Public Information Store

Configures the public information store on the server.

Type
Leaf object

Path
Organization\Site\Configuration\Servers\Server\Public Information Store

Description

The *public information store* is the central storage location on the server for storing the contents of public folders. The public information store is a database structure based upon the Microsoft Joint Engine Technology (JET) database technology and by default is located in the *mdbdata* directory. This database is managed by the Microsoft Exchange Information Store service, a core component of Exchange Server that is implemented as a Windows NT service. The structure of the database files for the public information store follow the pattern of the Exchange directory database files located in the *dsadata* directory. See the beginning of this chapter for a description of these database files.

An Exchange server may have one *private information store*, one public information store, or one of each type. For example, one server in your site could be dedicated to hosting public folders and would have a public information store but

Re-Homing Public Folders

If you delete a Directory Replication Connector between two Exchange sites, you will be prompted to run the DS/IS Consistency Adjuster to clear up any inconsistencies in public folder directory information. If you never plan to re-establish directory replication again between your two sites, then go ahead and run the Consistency Adjuster, but if you anticipate trying to re-establish replication again between the sites, then *don't run the Consistency Adjuster!* Running this process causes public folders to be homed to each of your sites, to enable recipients in each site to continue to access public folder contents. Then when you try to re-establish replication between the sites, your public folders appear to the directory service to be homed in two different locations and re-homes each folder to the site that most recently modified the public folder's properties. This usually results in the owner and users of the re-homed folder no longer having their expected permissions on the folder.

The way to fix this is to move the contents of the public folder to a personal folder *.pst* file, delete the public folder and wait for its tombstone to replicate throughout your organization, recreate the public folder on its original home server, and move the contents of the *.pst* file back to the public folder. There is also a procedure using a utility from the Exchange Server Resource Kit called *pfadmin.exe* (Version 3.0) that can correct this problem. Refer to the *Microsoft Knowledge Base* article Q185010 for more information.

not a private one. Other servers in the site would have private information stores but not public ones. By default, Exchange servers when installed have both private and public stores. You can delete either the private or public store using the Delete button on the Exchange Administrator toolbar.

The Public Information Store property sheet lets you:

- Set mailbox size limits and deleted item retention time
- Configure public folder replicas and replication parameters
- Set age limits for items stored in public folders
- View disk resources used for each public folder
- Display users and Exchange services currently accessing public folders
- Configure diagnostic logging for troubleshooting

In addition to configuring these settings on the property sheet, the public folder resources used, replication status, and users or services logged on can be viewed directly in the Contents pane of the Exchange Administrator program by selecting each of the following objects in the container pane (see Figure 3-16):

- Folder Replication Status
- Logons

- Public Folder Resources
- Server Replication Status

This is a bit confusing, since these four objects, located under the Public Information Store object, are not true directory objects. Instead they are simply alternate representations of the information displayed on the associated tabs of the Public Information Store property sheet. The advantage of using these alternate representations, however, is that you can double-click on a specific logged-on user or service in the Contents pane and access the property sheet of that mailbox or service directly; it provides a kind of link to the associated property sheet.

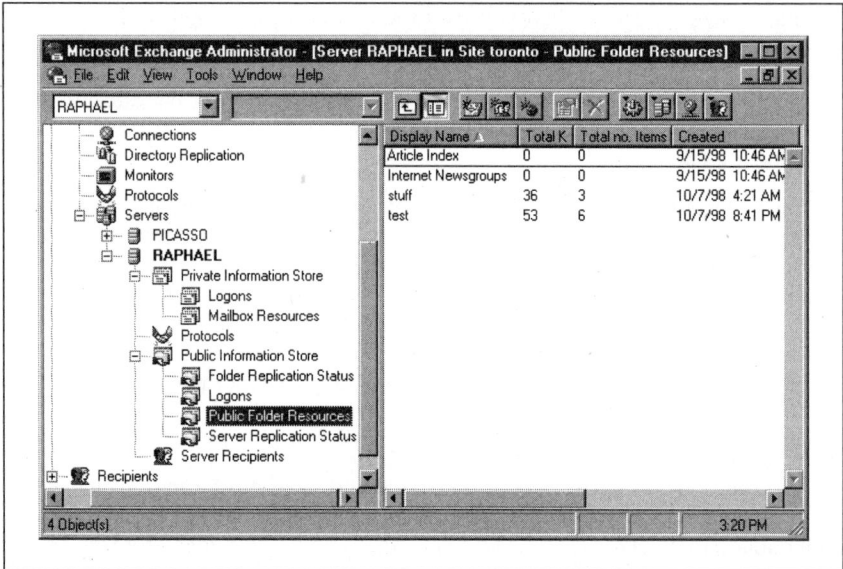

Figure 3-16: Double-click on a logged-on user or service to display its property sheet

Properties

General

Lets you specify deleted message retention time and public folder disk space warnings. Also displays the server's home site, the information store's home server, date the server was installed, and date the information store configuration was last modified. Some of the more important settings include:

Item Recovery

Lets you specify how long items are retained before being permanently deleted. You can also specify that no items are permanently deleted until the information store is backed up. Microsoft Outlook users can recover deleted items using the Recover Deleted Items menu command.

Storage Limits

Lets you specify a size limit for public folders on the server. Once the limit is reached, a warning message issued to all public folder contact recipients.

Instances

Lets you create replicas on your server of public folders on other servers in your organization. For more information on replicas, see the "Public Folder" entry in this chapter.

The left listbox shows those public folders in the selected site that do not have replicas on your server, while the right listbox shows those public folders that exist as replicas within your server's public information store. Click Add or Remove to move folders from one listbox to another.

Replication Schedule

Lets you globally specify how often public folders on your server are replicated. You can also configure this individually for each public folder using the property sheet for that Public Folder object.

Permissions

See the section "Permissions and Roles" at the beginning of this chapter.

Age Limits

Lets you set time limits for how long items can remain in public folders before being deleted. You can specify a default age limit for all new public folders on your server or select any listed public folder and click Modify to specify age limits for either:

–   The replica of the public folder stored in your information store

–   All replicas of your public folder throughout the organization

E-mail Addresses

Displays the various email addresses by which the Public Information Store is known on your server. These email addresses are used by the Directory Replication Connector object for addressing and routing directory replication messages between sites in your organization. You can modify these addresses or add additional ones if necessary. See the "Mailbox" entry in this chapter for more information about email addresses.

Logons

Displays the users logged on to the information store. This includes Exchange services also, which logs on using the Exchange *service account*. Select the Columns button to customize the information visible for each user.

Public Folder Resources

Displays the number of items stored, amount of disk spaced used, and other parameters for each public folder replica in the information store on this server. Select the Columns button to customize the information visible for each public folder.

Server Replication Status

Lets you determine whether public folders replicas in your organization are up to date. Each server hosting public folders in your organization is listed, along with status information indicating:

In Sync

No changes have been made to replicas on this server since updates were last sent to other servers.

Local Modified
> Changes have been made to replicas on this server that have not been sent to other servers.

Folder Replication Status
> Lets you view the replication status (In Sync or Local Modified), number of replicas, and other information for individual public folder replicas on your server.

Advanced
> Lets you specify:

> – The time interval at which public folder replication occurs when Always is selected on the Replication Schedule tab. The default is every 15 minutes.

> – The maximum size of a replication message. The default is 300KB.

Diagnostic Logging
> Specify the types and levels of Exchange server events that are logged to the Application Log. Exchange server events are logged under the name MSExchangeS in the Application Log and can be viewed using Event Viewer. See the related property for the Server object for more information about diagnostic logging.

Notes

- The Server Replication Status tab allows you to view the replication status for public folder replicas on all servers in your organization. You can also:

  - Use the property sheet of each Server object to view the replication status of all public folder replicas on that server alone.

  - Use the property sheet of each Public Folder object to view the replication status of all replicas of that folder.

- Try reducing the size of replication messages (Advanced tab) if your WAN connections are unreliable.

Recipients

Contains mailboxes and other recipient objects for a site.

Type
> Container

Path
> `Organization\Site\Recipients`

Can Contain
> Custom Recipient
> Distribution List
> Mailbox
> Public Folder
> Mailbox Agent

Description

Much of the work of administering an Exchange organization has to do with creating and managing recipients. A *recipient* is a directory object that can receive messages. The most common example is a *mailbox*, which is owned by a user and receives messages and attachments sent to the user by others or by Exchange services.

The Recipients container for a site groups together all the recipient objects in the site. You can use the Exchange Administrator to create additional recipients containers or subcontainers for your site. For example, you could create one recipient container for mailboxes, another for *Distribution Lists* (DLs), another for *custom recipients*, and so on. This can ease the management of recipient objects.

The contents of all your recipient containers are automatically merged into the *Global Address List* (GAL).

Properties

General

Shows the display name, directory name, an Administrative note up to 1,024 characters, home site to which the container belongs, date that home site was created, and most recent date a new Exchange server was added to the site.

Permissions

See the section "Permissions and Roles" at the beginning of this chapter.

Notes

If you use Exchange Administrator to move a mailbox from one server to another within the same site, it still resides in the same Recipients container; only its home server changes. This is because Recipient containers are directory objects and are properties of sites, not servers.

Plan your additional Recipient containers *carefully!* If you create a mailbox in one Recipient container, it can only be moved to another container by exporting the mailbox information, deleting the original mailbox, and importing the information into the new Recipients container. Note that this applies to all types of *recipients*, not just mailboxes.

So it's usually *not* a good idea to create Recipient containers based on geographical location or job function, as people tend to move about a lot, and you would have to create a new mailbox for them each time. In fact, it's generally much better to use Address Book Views to organize your recipients instead of placing them in separate Recipient containers.

Remote DirSync Requestor

An internal representation in the Exchange directory for a dirsync requestor on a Microsoft Mail network.

Type

Leaf object

Path

```
Organization\Site\Configuration\Connections\Dirsync Server\
Remote Dirsync Requestor
```

Description

When you create a Dirsync Server on an Exchange server for synchronizing your Global Address List with a Microsoft Mail directory server, you must also create one Remote Dirsync Requestor object for each dirsync requestor on the Microsoft Mail network. These Remote Dirsync Requestor objects assist in directory synchronization with the MS Mail directory servers. See the entry "DirSync Server" in this chapter for more information.

The Remote Dirsync Requestor property sheet lets you:

- Configure import and export containers for directory synchronization with dirsync servers
- Configure other advanced parameters relating to directory synchronization

Properties

General

Lets you specify the Dirsync Address, password, requestor type, language, and other settings related to directory synchronization with remote MS Mail dirsync requestors. Also displays the display name, home site, date the requestor was installed, and date the requestor's configuration was last modified. Of interest are:

Append to imported users' display name

Appends the name of the requestor to the name of each custom recipient created by directory synchronization. This allows you to immediately identify which custom recipients have been imported from the remote MS Mail system through directory synchronization.

Dirsync Address

Selects by default the hidden system mailbox directory on the remote MS Mail directory server:

NETWORK/POSTOFFICE/$SYSTEM

Don't change this!

Password

This should be the password of the remote MS Mail requestor.

Requestor address type

This can be MS for MS Mail (PC) or MSA for MS Mail (AppleTalk).

Export on next cycle

Force an export of all address information to the remote requestor when directory synchronization is scheduled to occur next.

Permissions

See the section "Permissions and Roles" at the beginning of this chapter.

Import Container

Lets you control which MS Mail addresses are imported from the connected MS Mail directory server and where they are imported to within your directory hierarchy. The import container contains addresses of MS Mail recipients imported from the MS Mail directory server using directory synchronization. Once an MS Mail address is imported, it becomes a recipient in the Exchange directory hierarchy. You need to specify:

Container

Lets you select a recipient container for receiving imported MS Mail addresses. To avoid possible address conflicts, you should probably create a special container for this using File → New Other → Recipients Container from the Exchange Administrator program menu.

Trust Level

Lets you assign a *trust level* to recipients being imported. MS Mail systems do not use trust levels, but by importing recipients with trust levels assigned to them, you can control which Exchange recipients are exported to the MS Mail network when directory synchronization occurs (see next item).

Export Containers

Lets you control which Exchange recipients are exported to the connected MS Mail directory server directory. Select the site where the recipient container resides, click Add to move the container into the Export list, and specify a *trust level* for that container. Trust levels are specified on the Advanced tab of a recipient's property sheet. If the recipient's trust level is equal to or lower than the trust level specified here, it will be exported.

The checkbox lets you toggle whether to allow Custom Recipients to be exported.

Notes

You can only create Remote Dirsync Requestors on a server that already has a Dirsync Server installed and configured on it.

Schedule+ Free Busy

A hidden public folder that contains objects for supporting the scheduling capabilities of Exchange clients.

Type

Container

Path

```
Organization\Folders\System Folders\Schedule+ Free Busy
```

Can Contain

Schedule+ Free Busy Information

Description

The Schedule+ Free Busy object contains one Schedule+ Free Busy Information object for each site in an Exchange organization.

Properties

None

Notes

See the entry "Schedule+ Free Busy Information" for more information.

Schedule+ Free Busy Information

A hidden public folder that supports the scheduling capability of Exchange clients like Microsoft Outlook. In the Exchange Administrator program window, each Schedule+ Free Busy Information object is identified by the Exchange address of the site it represents.

Type

Leaf object

Path

```
Organization\Folders\System Folders\Schedule+ Free Busy\
Schedule+ Free Busy Information
```

Description

Schedule+ Free Busy Information public folders support the group scheduling capabilities of Exchange clients such as Microsoft Outlook by keeping track of the free and busy time in users' calendars. When a user first logs on to Exchange using Outlook, the Schedule+ Free Busy Information folder for the user's site creates an entry for that user's mailbox. Whenever the user's calendar is modified, either directly by the user or by accepting an invitation to a meeting, the public folder entry for the user is updated to reflect the calendar change.

The name of the folder reflects the Exchange address of the site where the folder resides. For example, the Schedule+ Free Busy Information folder for the site Toronto in the organization SampleCorp would have the following name in the Exchange Administrator windows:

EX:/o=samplecorp/ou=toronto

Like other public folders, the contents of this folder reside in the Public Information tion Store of the server where the object was created and servers where other replicas exist.

Properties

The properties for this object are the same as for the Public Folders object.

You can allow users of other sites access to your schedule by using the Replicas tab to replicate the Schedule+ Free Busy Information folder for your site to servers in the other sites. Remember that users can connect to public folders in other sites only if:

- Public folder affinities are configured.

- Synchronous remote procedure calls (RPCs) are supported between the sites.

Server

Contains directory objects for configuring a specific Exchange server within your site. In the Exchange Administrator program window, each Server object is identified by the Windows NT name of the server.

Type

Container

Path

`Organization\Site\Configuration\Servers\Server`

Can Contain

Directory Service
Directory Synchronization
Message Transfer Agent
MTA Transport Stack
Private Information Store
Protocols
Public Information Store
Server Recipients
System Attendant

Description

A Server container represents a particular Exchange server within your site. Typical Exchange sites for medium to large companies will contain several Exchange servers, up to 50 or more servers per site, depending on your hardware configuration and network bandwidth.

Exchange servers may function as general purpose mail servers, or may be dedicated to one or more of the following server roles:

- Hosting mailboxes for users within a site (i.e., the *home server* for those users)

- Storing public folders on a dedicated server within your site

- Enabling directory replication between sites

- Enabling messaging connectivity with other sites in your organization, with foreign mail systems such as Lotus cc:Mail or with the Internet (SMTP)

- Enabling directory synchronization with foreign mail systems where this is applicable

- Providing key management services for the certificate authority (CA) server within your organization

Configuring an Exchange server usually means configuring both the properties of the Server object itself and the properties of the following directory objects contained within the Server object:

- Directory Service

- Message Transfer Agent

- Private Information Store

- Public Information Store

- System Attendant

Refer to the individual entries on these objects in this chapter for information on how to configure each of them.

Properties

General

Shows the directory name, an Administrative Note up to 1,024 characters, Location and Home Site to which the server belongs, date the home site was created, and most recent date the server's properties were modified. There is no option for modifying the display name, as this is the Windows NT name of the server itself.

The default location is <none>. Locations are a way of further grouping servers within a site to allow more efficient access to public folders within the site. See the note on locations in the "Multi-Site Scenario" section in Chapter 2 for more information.

Permissions

See the section "Permissions and Roles" at the beginning of this chapter.

Services

Specify which services on the Exchange server can be monitored using a Server Monitor. These services can be any of the services displayed by the Services utility in the Control Panel. Services monitored by default include:

- Microsoft Exchange Server directory service

- Microsoft Exchange Server information store service

- Microsoft Exchange Server MTA service

Locales

Let you specify date, time, and currency settings and format sorts and searches according to linguistic conventions.

Database Paths

Sets the local path to Exchange server database files. Server performance can be enhanced by distributing these files across multiple physical drives. Running the Performance Optimizer tool described in Chapter 4 is the preferred way of determining the optimal location for database files, but this tab offers you a way to configure these paths manually, if desired.

IS Maintenance

Lets you schedule when the public/private information store conducts automatic self-maintenance operations, such as cleaning out deleted messages. This slows down access to the information store, so leave it set to the default, which is to perform maintenance once a day late at night.

Advanced

Lets you configure circular logging and run the data consistency adjuster.

Circular logging reduces disk storage requirements by overwriting transaction logs after transactions have been committed to the databases.

Exchange ships with circular logging enabled by default, which is a poor choice. Enabling circular logging means that only normal (full) backups can be performed since differential or incremental backups need the transaction logs to be complete in order to work. Also, by overwriting your transaction logs between backups, circular logging can significantly reduce the value of your backup in the event of a disaster since you can't replay transaction logs that are no longer present. You should always disable circular logging; just make sure you have enough available disk space to hold the transaction logs that will accumulate.

The Consistency Adjuster (Figure 3-17) ensures that the information stored in the directory database and the information store match. Recipient objects such as mailboxes make use of both Exchange databases: the directory database stores the properties of the mailbox, while the information store holds the actual contents of the mailbox. The consistency adjuster is normally run after restoring one of the two databases from a backup, and allows you to:

- Create directory entries for mailboxes that don't have them

- Delete directory entries of public folders that don't exist in the information store

- Remove from the information store permissions of users that are no longer valid

The key thing to specify is the *latency period* in days. For example, if you create an item such as a public folder on a server, directory replication soon replicates this item to the directory database of every site in your organization. If one week later, you restore the information store on this server from a two-week old backup, the restored information store will not contain the public folder, since it didn't exist when the backup was run. Running the consistency adjuster on the server at this point will cause the directory entry for the public folder to be deleted also, and *voilà:* no more public folder! The solution is to specify a latency period of at least a week when you run the consistency adjuster; this preserves all directory entries older than the latency period, and the information store will be updated during the next directory replication, preserving the public folder from oblivion.

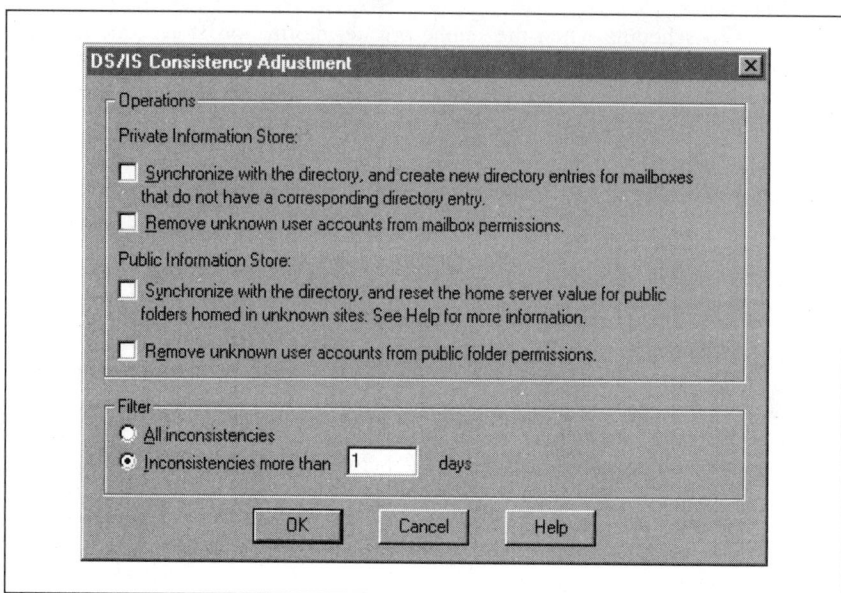

Figure 3-17: Consistency Adjuster

If you remove a directory replication connector between two sites, don't run the DS/IS Consistency Adjuster unless you never plan on connecting the sites again. If you reconnect the sites, directory inconsistencies can result. Refer to the sidebar titled "Re-Homing Public Folders" in the entry "Public Folder" in this chapter for more information about running the Consistency Adjuster.

Diagnostic Logging

Lets you specify which kinds of Exchange events are logged to the Windows NT Application Log so they can be viewed with Event Viewer. Select a service, choose a category, and then specify the desired logging level. You can select from four different logging levels for each event category:

None

This setting only logs critical events and application errors. This is the default setting for most categories and should only be changed when troubleshooting problems with your server.

Minimum

This setting logs high-level events, such as the completion of a major task like completion of a directory replication cycle.

Medium

This setting logs medium-level events, such as each individual step in the completion of a major task.

Maximum

This is the most verbose setting and can generate a large amount of information. Enabling this setting can adversely affect server performance and should be done only when troubleshooting problems with your server.

When an Exchange *event* occurs with a value less than or equal to the logging level you specified for the particular event category, that event is logged in the Application Log. Diagnostic logging can be enabled on the following services and connectors, depending on which optional components you have installed on your Exchange server:

MSExchangeCCMC (cc:Mail Connector)
MSExchangeDS (Directory service)
MSExchangeDX (Directory Synchronization service)
MSExchangeFB (Schedule+ Free/Busy Connector)
MSExchangeIMC (Internet Mail Service)
MSExchangeIS (Information Store)
Internet Protocols
IMAP4
NNTP
POP3
System
Public
Private
MSExchangeKM (KM Server)
MSExchangeMSMI (Microsoft Mail Connector)
MSExchangeMTA (Message Transfer Agent)

For full information on the various categories of events that can be logged for each of these services, refer to the Exchange Online Book "Microsoft Exchange Server Maintenance and Troubleshooting."

Notes

A few tips on implementing Exchange servers:

- Users and their home servers (the Exchange server within whose information store the user's mailbox is defined) should be on the same network segment for best performance. Of course, if your company network has 25 subnets that might not be possible!

- Create mailboxes so that Distribution Lists (DLs) don't span more than one server, if possible. Mailboxes and Distribution Lists for users in the same department or global group should be on the same Exchange server to optimize *single-instance message* storage.

- Use fault-tolerant hardware for servers hosting important public folders and mailboxes.

- Client/server bandwidth is more critical than server/server bandwidth.

- You can now move an Exchange server from one site or organization to another without re-installing Exchange by using the Move Server Wizard included in Exchange Server 5.5 Service Pack 2.

The Move Server Wizard

Before Microsoft released the Move Server Wizard as a freely downloadable extra to Exchange Server 5.5 Service Pack 1 (it is now included in Service Pack 2), the only way you could migrate an Exchange server from one site or organization to another was to completely re-install Exchange on the machine. The Move Server Wizard addresses this problem, but not very well as it doesn't always do what is expected. Here are a few tips on using the tool that are not included in its documentation:

- Make sure you make replicas of any public folders homed on your server prior to moving it. Otherwise the contents of these folders will be lost. Or back up the public folder contents on the server to a *.pst* file as an alternative.
- You should probably move any mailboxes on your server to another server in your site prior to attempting a server migration. The reason is that during the migration process, the wizard cleans up all its mailboxes, and if an error occurs so that the cleanup process can't be completed on a mailbox, annoying things can happen. For example, if the user has made heavy use of his calendaring feature in Outlook, his inbox will be flooded with overdue notices from past meetings when he first logs on to the migrated server. Furthermore, the user's free/busy information may no longer be available to other users after the server is migrated to the new site. The best way to prevent these problems is to move all mailboxes to another server prior to running the wizard, which sort of weakens the functionality of the tool.
- When you run the wizard and select the option Join an Existing Site, you are asked to specify an existing server in the destination site. Make sure you enter the NetBIOS name of the destination server, not its IP address; otherwise the migration will fail.
- You may find that you need to regenerate Offline Address Books after migrating your server. Use the DS Site Configuration object to do this.
- Don't modify the Windows NT permissions on the mailbox during the server migration process. The Move Server Wizard snapshots the directory settings prior to the move so any changes to these settings made during the move will be lost.
- The Move Server Wizard can take a lot of time to run in an enterprise-level Exchange implementation. For example, during the cleanup phase near the end of the wizard process, it takes about five seconds for each mailbox for this process to execute, which can add up to several hours or more.
- If you have any system folders homed on your server, replicate or re-home these to another server in your site before running the wizard. Also make sure your server is not configured as a routing calculation server, and be sure you remove all connectors from your server prior to migrating it. Otherwise migration will fail (unless your server is the last remaining server in your site).

—Continued—

- If you have the Microsoft Exchange Event Service installed on your server, you must remove it or the wizard will not be able to run. Re-run Exchange Server setup to do this and specify that this option be removed.
- If you run the wizard and the process fails, you may discover that you can no longer restart the directory service on your server. You need to restore the Registry on the server by going to the \mvsrvdata\archive folder where the temporary files were stored by the wizard and run *restore.reg*. See the *Microsoft Knowledge Base* article Q196159 for more information.
- There can be problems using the wizard if clients have encrypted mail stored in their mailboxes. See the *Microsoft Knowledge Base* article Q196688 for more information.
- The wizard automatically generates new SMTP proxy addresses in the form *@SiteName.OrgName.com* for all recipients on the moved server and sets these new addresses as the reply address, which may not be what you want to happen if, for example, all your recipients are using *@OrgName.com* instead. And it won't help afterwards if you just modify the Site Addressing object to *@OrgName.com* again since this proxy address already exists. You will have to export your recipients after running the wizard, specify the original SMTP proxy address as *@OrgName.com* again, and import the recipients back into your server.
- Finally, the wizard can lead to an unusual situation: a site with no private information store. For example, let's say you have two servers in your site: *ServerA* is a dedicated messaging server with a private store but no public one, while *ServerB* is a dedicated public folder server with a public store but no private one. If you use the wizard to move *ServerA* to another site or organization, you will be left with one server (*ServerB*) in your site and no private information store, a situation that normally can't happen. (You can use the Exchange Administrator program to delete an information store on a sever, but it won't let you delete the last private or public store in a site.) The result is that your site still has mailboxes (in the directory) but clients can't access them. To fix this situation, use Exchange Administrator to create a new private information store on your remaining server (or avoid the situation entirely with careful planning).

Server Monitor

Monitors services on an Exchange server in your organization.

Type

Leaf object

Path

```
Organization\Site\Configuration\Monitors\Server Monitor
```

Description

Server monitors verify that Windows NT services are running properly on Exchange servers in your organization. Server monitors can send notification messages and alerts if:

- A service stops unexpectedly
- The server is down or reboots
- The server cannot connect to the network

Server monitors can also:

- Attempt to restart services that have stopped
- Attempt to reboot servers that are in a problem state
- Reset a server's clock if it is off

Once a server monitor has been created, it must be started using Tools → Start Monitor from the Exchange Administrator menu. A new monitor window opens showing the status of the various servers being monitored. See Chapter 4 for more details on running server monitors.

The Server Monitor property sheet lets you:

- Specify polling intervals
- Create a series of notifications and actions
- Specify which remote servers in your organization you will monitor
- Specify whether to resynchronize the remote server's clock

Properties

General

Lets you specify the display name, log file, and polling intervals. Also displays the directory name.

The log file is optional, since the monitor window displays real-time information about the state of services on your servers.

There are two polling intervals to configure:

Normal

Lets you specify how often a service should be checked when the service is functioning normally.

Critical sites

Lets you specify how often a service should be checked when the service is in a warning or alert state.

Permissions

See the section "Permissions and Roles" at the beginning of this chapter.

Notification

Lets you specify what should happen if a service goes into a warning or alert state. A service enters a warning when the server's clock is off by a small amount. A service enters an alert state when the server's clock is off by a large amount, when the service is not functioning as expected, or when the server does not respond to the Server Monitor.

The symbols here are:

- Green triangle for normal operation

- Red exclamation point for warning state

- Red triangle for alert state

- Blue question mark for an undetermined state

You can create a whole series of notifications, called an *escalation path*. A notification can:

- Launch a process on the server

- Send a message to an administrator

- Send a Windows NT administrative alert to a computer

For each notification created, you can also configure:

- Whether it is triggered by the server going into a warning or alert state

- How long after the state is entered the notification event occurs

Servers

Lets you specify which servers inside your Exchange organization you want to monitor. You can also select a server and click the Services button to view or specify which Windows NT services on the Exchange server should be monitored.

Actions

Lets you specify a series of escalated actions when the Server monitor detects that a service is stopped. These actions include:

- Take no action

- Restart the service

- Restart the computer

You can also configure a restart message and a delay that can give users time to save their work and close their mail clients.

Clock

Specify how far out the server's clock must be off for the server to enter a warning or alert state and whether to force the server's clock to synchronize with the clock on the computer running the Server monitor.

Notes

- Server monitors can only monitor Exchange servers in remote sites if there is a dedicated LAN or WAN connection to the remote site running a network protocol that supports remote procedure calls (RPCs).

- Note that actions specified on the Actions tab and notifications specified on the Notification tab can be set independently of one another.

Server Recipients

Contains mailboxes and other recipient objects for the server.

Type

Container

Path

Organization\Site\Configuration\Servers\Server\Server
Recipients

Can Contain

Mailbox
Mailbox Agent

Description

See the "Recipients" entry for general information about Recipients containers.

Properties

See the "Recipients" entry in this chapter.

Notes

Recipients located on a server are said to be homed on the server. In other words, the server is their home server.

Servers

Contains an Exchange Server object for each Exchange server installed at your site.

Type

Container

Path

Organization\Site\Configuration\Servers

Can Contain

Server

Description

The Servers container is used to group all Exchange servers in a given site into a single directory object. For more information, see the "Server" entry in this chapter.

Properties

General
Shows the display name, directory name, an Administrative note up to 1,024 characters, home site to which the container belongs, date that home site was created, and most recent date a new Exchange server was added to the site.

Permissions
See the section "Permissions and Roles" at the beginning of this chapter.

Site

Contains the Configuration and Recipient containers for your Exchange site, which contain objects for configuring default site properties and users' mailboxes.

Type

Container

Path

Organization\Site

Can Contain

Configuration
Recipients

Description

A *site* is a group of Exchange servers connected together by high-speed permanent connections capable of supporting synchronous remote procedure calls (RPCs). This is usually satisfied by ensuring that all Exchange servers in a given site are attached to the same Local Area Network (LAN), although dedicated WAN links of 64Kbps or higher can also be used to connect Exchange servers in a site (depending on your messaging traffic needs). The point is a site is a logical entity, not necessarily a geographical one. All Exchange servers within a site automatically replicate directory information updates with each other every five minutes.

Sites are usually identified with geographical locations where your company has offices. The name of a site is usually the city, state, or country where your office is located, depending upon the scope and size of your business.

Configuring an Exchange site usually means configuring the following directory objects contained within the site:

- DS Site Configuration
- Information Store Site Configuration
- Public Folders
- MTA Site Configuration
- Site Addressing

Refer to the individual entries on these objects in this chapter for information on how to configure each of them.

Properties

General

Shows the display name, directory name, date the site was created, and most recent date a new Exchange server was added to the site.

Permissions

See "Permissions and Roles" at the beginning of this chapter. Additional permissions granted to this object are inherited by the Address Book View and Public Folder and Recipients containers but are *not* inherited by the site

Configuration container. To grant users permissions for configuring site-specific properties or a site, assign permissions to the site Configuration container.

Notes

- When implementing Exchange in your company, choose each site's name carefully, as they cannot be changed afterwards without re-installing Exchange on your servers. During installation of Exchange, a server can either join an existing site or establish a new site within your organization. The site name specified is used in specifying the *distinguished name* (DN) of every directory object within your organization's Exchange directory database.

  To join an existing site, you need the site's *service account*. Each Exchange site typically has a Windows NT account called a service account. This account is created prior to installing the first Exchange server within your site and must be specified when each additional server is added to your site. This account must configured to never expire, should be given a secure password, and should not be used by any user for logging on to the network. All Exchange servers within a given site must use the same service account. You may also choose to use one service account for your entire organization, depending upon the administrative structure of your company.

- You can now move an Exchange server from one site or organization to another without re-installing Exchange by using the Move Server Wizard included in Exchange Server 5.5 Service Pack 2. See the sidebar entitled "The Move Server Wizard" in the "Server" entry in this chapter for more information on running the Move Server Wizard.

- Exchange sites do not need to map one-to-one with your company's Windows NT domains if trusts between domains are properly configured (and understood!).

Site Addressing

Lets you view routing information and configure addressing and message routing at the site level.

Type

Leaf object

Path

Organization\Site\Configuration\Site Addressing

Description

The Site Addressing object is one of the directory objects that should be configured when you are implementing an Exchange site for your company. This object lets you configure essential aspects of addressing and message routing for your site.

In particular, the Site Addressing property sheet lets you specify:

- Default email addresses for the site
- A routing calculation server for the site

- How often routing tables are recalculated

See the "Site" entry in this chapter for other directory objects that should be configured when setting up a new site.

Properties

General

Lets you configure the display name and the routing calculation server and enable shared address space with other X.400 messaging systems. Also displays directory name, home site, date the site was created, and most recent date the properties of this object were modified.

- The *routing calculation server* is the Exchange server in your site responsible for building the routing table. The *routing table,* or GWART, contains information about how to route messages to remote mail systems using the various connectors and gateways installed in your organization. This table is automatically recalculated whenever a connector or gateway is added or deleted in your site and is propagated throughout the entire organization by directory replication. See the final sections of Chapter 2 for more information on routing and routing tables.

- If messages are received from an X.400 messaging system but the recipient cannot be found in your site, a non-delivery report (NDR) is generated. If you are migrating from an existing X.400 messaging system to Exchange, you can select Share Address Space to allow these incoming messages to be rerouted to your parallel X.400 system.

Permissions

See the section "Permissions and Roles" at the beginning of this chapter.

Site Addressing

Lets you edit or create the portion of your recipients' email addresses that are specific to your site. These site-specific partial addresses will be used when you create new recipients and when you modify them you can also specify that a background process be started for modifying all existing recipients as well.

Examples of site-specific address information for a site Toronto belonging to an organization SampleCorp are shown in Table 3-18.

Table 3-18: Examples of Site-Specific Portions of Different Kinds of Email Addresses

Mail System	Address Type	Sample Site-Specific Portion of Email Address
Internet	SMTP	*@Toronto.SampleCorp.com*
X.400	X.400	*c=US;a= ;p=SampleCorp;o=Toronto;*
MS Mail	MS	*SAMPLECORP/TORONTO*
Lotus cc:Mail	CCMAIL	*at Toronto*

Clear a checkbox here to disable automatic generation of the selected address type for new recipients. Note that this has no effect on the addresses of existing recipients.

Don't disable the generation of X.400 addresses, as these are used by Exchange for routing messages when the *distinguished name* (DN) of a recipient cannot be used. In general, it's a good idea not to disable the generation of any email address types that Exchange automatically generates, as this could lead to routing problems.

Routing Calculation Schedule
> Schedules how often the routing table should be recalculated. The routing table needs to be recalculated when:
> - Connectors are added or removed
> - Gateways are added or removed
> - Settings on the Connected Sites or Address Space tabs of connectors and gateways are reconfigured
>
> To recalculate the routing table after such a change you can:
> - Do nothing; the MTA will detect the change and perform the recalculation
> - Wait for scheduled recalculation to occur
> - Force a recalculation using the button on the Routing tab

Routing
> Displays the routing information for your site. See the final sections of Chapter 2 for more information on routing.

Notes

- Disabling automatic address generation for unnecessary address types can conserve server resources and reduce network traffic but should only be done understanding the implications of doing so. One reason for modifying the default site-specific address information would be if your organization or site name contained characters invalid in some of the address types. You can repair this using the Site Addressing object.

- To change the site-specific portion of MS Mail addresses, use the MS Mail Connector object.

- The rule with Exchange is often: *When in doubt—wait!* If the MTA detects a change in the configured connectors, it will initiate recalculating the routing table, but there may be an indeterminate time interval between when the table has been rebuilt and when the new information can be used by the MTA for message routing.

Site Connector

Lets you configure dedicated RPC connectivity with other sites in your organization.

Type

> Leaf object

Path

```
Organization\Site\Configuration\Connections\Site Connector
```

Description

The Site Connector is the simplest and most efficient way of connecting together Exchange sites in your organization. Site Connectors require dedicated, always-on connections between sites, so they can be used when sites are joined by LAN links or dedicated high-speed WAN links. To join sites together using dial-up connections, use the Dynamic RAS Connector.

To connect two sites together for messaging connectivity, one Site Connector must be configured in each site to establish the two ends of the link. An administrator having the Permissions Admin role for both sites can do this in a single step, or the administrator of each site can configure their Site Connectors separately.

You can specify which servers in the local and remote site are used for routing messages through the Site Connector by specifying:

- A *bridgehead server*, which is a server in one site dedicated to maintaining connectivity with the other site. The local bridgehead server in a site functions as a fixed endpoint for messaging connectivity with the remote site. You can specify a bridgehead server in one or both sites.

- A list of *target servers*, which are servers in the remote site that can receive messages routed through your local site's Site Connector. When messages need to be routed to the other site, each target server is successively tried until connectivity is achieved, which provides fault tolerance for messaging between sites. Additionally, each target server can be assigned a cost for load balancing purposes. Target servers with higher costs are used *less* frequently than lower cost servers, and target servers with a cost of 100 are only used when no other server is available. When a target server receives a message, it routes the message to the recipient's home server in the remote site.

The Site Connector is one of four Exchange connectors that can be used to provide messaging connectivity between sites in an Exchange organization, the others being the X.400 Connector, Dynamic RAS Connector, and Internet Mail Service. Some of the advantages of using the Site Connector include:

- Ease of configuration since both ends of the connector can be configured simultaneously

- Automatic fault-tolerance and load-balancing

On the negative side, message traffic over the Site Connector cannot be scheduled, so it is important that it be used only over network connections having sufficient bandwidth.

The Site Connector property sheet lets you:

- Configure bridgehead and target servers
- Create and view address spaces
- Assign routing costs
- Override the remote service account

Properties

General

Lets you specify the display name, directory name, cost value, local bridge-head server, and an administrative note. Also displays the name of the target site, the server's home site, date the server was installed, and date the Site Connector configuration was last modified. Of interest are:

Display Name

Note that the display name is of the form "Site Connector (*remote_site*)". You can change this if you like.

Target site

The site with the other end of the Site Connector messaging link. The target site is specified when the Site Connector is created and cannot be changed.

Cost

Assigns a routing cost to the connector. This is useful for load-balancing when there are other routes for sending messages to the remote site, either indirectly through a third site or directly using a different kind of connector such as the Internet Mail Service.

Messaging Bridgehead in the local site

Lets you either:

- Allow any server in your site to route messages to the remote site

- Specify one server in your site as the dedicated bridgehead server for routing messages to the remote site

Permissions

See the section "Permissions and Roles" at the beginning of this chapter.

Target Servers

Lets you specify which servers in the remote site are to be target servers. Assign a *cost* to the target server to balance the messaging load between them. Cost values range from 0 to 100 with the meaning shown in Table 3-19.

Table 3-19: Cost Values for Target Servers and Their Meanings

Cost Value	Meaning
0	Try this target server first. If it fails, then try other target servers in the remote site.
100	Only use this target server if all other target servers are unavailable.
1 to 99	The lower the cost value, the more likely this target server will be used. Routes to target servers with equal costs are load-balanced.

Address Space

Lets you specify address spaces for the Site Connector. An *address space* represents a messaging path leading through the connector to the remote site. When the MTA on a server in your local site attempts to route a message through the local Site Connector, it checks the list of address spaces to determine whether the Site Connector can route the message.

The listbox on this property page displays four parameters for each address space created:

Type
> SMTP, X.400, MS Mail, or Other type of address space.

Address
> The addresses that the connector is responsible for routing messages to. Wildcards can be used:
>
> – Asterisk (*) represents any number of characters.
>
> – Percent sign (%) represents any single character.

Cost
> Routing cost.

Scope
> Restrictions on who can use this address space for sending messages through the connector. You can specify users at your location only, your local site only, or users throughout the entire organization.

By default, an X.400 address space is created representing the remote site. For example, if the remote site is Toronto in the organization SampleCorp, the X.400 address space created and its interpretation would be as shown in Table 3-20.

Table 3-20: Sample X.400 Address Space for a Site Connector

Parameter	Value	Meaning
Type	X.400	This connector can route X.400 messages (includes native Exchange format messages).
Address	c=US;a= ;p=SampleCorp;o=Toronto	This connector can route messages to any recipient in the site Toronto.
Cost	1	See Table 3-5.
Scope	Organization	Any users in the organization can route messages using this connector.

Note that an address space contains only a partial address, enough to uniquely identify messages to be routed to the remote site. That is actually why it is called an *address space*, because it represents a space of possible recipients having the same partial address fragment in their addresses.

To route messages of other types (e.g., SMTP or MS Mail) through this connector, you need to add an address space for these types. See "Internet Mail Service" in this chapter for more information about creating new address spaces.

Override
> Avoids the messaging problems that can occur if the two connected sites are in two different Windows NT domains that do not have trust relationships

configured between them. Specify the account information for the Exchange *service account* in the remote site.

Notes

- Using the Site Connector requires a dedicated network connection and a network protocol capable of using RPCs, which includes TCP/IP or NWLink IPX/ SPX Compatible Transport.

- Resources on a bridgehead server can be dedicated to inter-site connectivity by not homing mailboxes or public folders on them.

Site Encryption Configuration

Lets you configure advanced security for your site.

Type
Leaf object

Path
Organization\Site\Configuration\Site Encryption Configuration

Description

The Site Encryption Configuration object is used together with the CA object to configure advanced security such as digital certificates and SSL encryption on your site. You need to configure the CA object first; refer to the entry in this chapter on the CA object.

Installing KM Server on Exchange adds an additional tab called Security to Mailbox property sheets. You can use this new tab to view and configure advanced security on individual mailboxes, which is the final step that needs to be done in order for users to use digital certificates or encryption.

The Site Encryption Configuration property sheet lets you:

- Select the KM Server you want to use to manage advanced security
- Assign Windows NT accounts permissions for the KM Server
- Specify an encryption algorithm

Properties

General
Lets you specify the display name and select a KM Server in another site to administer it. Also lets you view the location of your site's KM Server, the home site, date the KM Server was installed, and date the object was last modified.

Permissions
See the section "Permissions and Roles" at the beginning of this chapter.

Algorithms
> Lets you specify which encryption algorithms and methods you want to use:

> *Exchange 4.0 and 5.0 encryption algorithms*
>> Lets you specify CAST-40, CAST-64, or DES.

> *Preferred S/MIME encryption algorithms*
>> Lets you specify DES, 3DES, RC2-40, RC2-64, and RC2-128.

> *Preferred security message format*
>> Lets you select Exchange 4.0/5.0 or S/MIME (i.e., one of the two items listed earlier).

Notes

- Microsoft recommends that you only use one KM Server in your organization. Otherwise non-recoverable keys may result if things are not done exactly right.

- Security algorithms and rules governing where they may be used are constantly evolving. Expect changes to the algorithms listed in each Exchange service pack.

System Attendant

Configures the properties of the Exchange System Attendant service for the server.

Type
Leaf object

Path
```
Organization\Site\Configuration\Servers\Server\System
Attendant
```

Description

The System Attendant (SA) is one of the core components of Exchange and is implemented as a Windows NT service called the Microsoft Exchange System Attendant service. The System Attendant manages and coordinates the functions of all other Exchange services. In particular, the System Attendant:

- Collects information about Exchange servers in a site
- Monitors connections between sites
- Ensures directory replication works properly
- Generates email addresses for new recipients
- Builds internal message routing tables
- Maintains the message tracking log

The System Attendant property sheet lets you:

- Configure the message tracking log
- View and modify email addresses for this directory object

Properties

General

Lets you specify whether to maintain or overwrite old message tracking logs and specify an administrative note. Also displays the display name and Alias Name of the object, the server's home site, date the server was installed, and date the System Attendant configuration was last modified.

Messages can be tracked by different Exchange components as they flow throughout your organization and through connectors to foreign mail systems. Each component plays a different part in the messaging process, as was described in Chapter 2.

Enabling message tracking on any of the components shown in Table 3-21 causes the Exchange System Attendant service to generate logs with routing information about all messages that are processed by the information store. These logs are created daily and are stored in the \exchsrvr\tracking.log folder (or elsewhere, depending upon the results of running the Exchange Performance Optimizer program). Each component also has its own log created by the system attendant when message tracking is enabled. Message tracking is a useful diagnostic tool to locate:

- Lost mail
- Slow messaging routes
- Faulty connectors between sites
- The source of unauthorized messages

Once message tracking is enabled, select Tools → Track Message from the Exchange Administrator program menu to use the Message Tracking Center to trace the route of messages through your messaging system.

Table 3-21: Exchange Components for Which You Can Enable Message Tracking

Exchange Component	Enable Tracking Using This Directory Object
Information store	Information Store Site Configuration
MTA	MTA Site Configuration
Internet Mail Service	Internet Mail
MS Mail connector	MS Mail Connector

Permissions

See the section "Permissions and Roles" at the beginning of this chapter.

E-mail Addresses

Displays the various email addresses by which the System Attendant is known on your server. These email addresses are used by the Directory Replication Connector object for addressing and routing directory replication messages between sites in your organization. You can modify these addresses or add additional ones if necessary. See the entry "Mailbox" in this chapter for more information about email addresses.

- If disk space is at a premium, you could select to remove old log files instead of maintaining them indefinitely.

- Message tracking logs can also be imported into third-party reporting tools such as Crystal Reports for analyzing mail usage.

System Folders

Contains various hidden public folders for supporting capabilities of Exchange clients.

Type

Container

Path

Organization\Folders\System Folders

Can Contain

EFORMS Registry
Events Root
Offline Address Book
Schedule+ Free Busy

Description

The System Folder contains items that support scheduling and other capabilities of Exchange clients such as Microsoft Outlook.

Properties

None

Notes

See each item contained in the System Folders container for more information.

X.400 Connector

Lets you configure connectivity with other sites or foreign X.400 mail systems using TCP/IP, X.25, or TP4 network transports.

Type

Leaf object

Path

Organization\Site\Configuration\Connections\X.400 Connector

Description

The X.400 connector can be used to:

- Connect two sites in your organization over a TCP/IP internetwork
- Connect two sites in your organization using a public or private X.400 network as a messaging backbone
- Connect your organization with a foreign X.400 messaging system

One possible use for the X.400 Connector is as an alternative to the Site Connector for joining sites over low-bandwidth (64Kbps to 128Kbps) dedicated WAN connections where the Site Connector is not as efficient. This is because the X.400 Connector uses roughly one third of the bandwidth used by the Site Connector and involves less processing load on the server. The X.400 Connector is one of four Exchange connectors that can be used to provide messaging connectivity between sites in an Exchange organization, the others being the Dynamic RAS Connector, Site Connector, and Internet Mail Service.

Some of the advantages of using the X.400 Connector include:

- The capability of scheduling when message transfer takes place and controlling message size
- The capability of passing Exchange messages in their native format, which increases the efficiency of message transfer

On the negative side:

- It only supports the TCP/IP network protocol, TP4 transport protocol, and X.25
- The server with the connector installed acts as a bridgehead server and may become a bottleneck unless other bridgehead servers are created

When an X.400 Connector is installed on an Exchange server, that server is known as a *messaging bridgehead server*. You may have several messaging bridgehead servers in a site for load-balancing purposes.

Prior to installing the X.400 Connector on a server in your site, you must:

1. Find out what kind of MTA Transport Stack the foreign X.400 system uses: TP4, X.25, or TCP/IP.
2. Install a suitable network protocol that supports the MTA Transport Stack.
3. Create the appropriate MTA Transport Stack. See the entry "MTA Transport Stack" in this chapter.

For more information on the architecture and operation of an X.400 messaging system, see Appendix A, *X.400*. All that we will cover here is the issue of X.400 addressing, which is considerably more complicated (and more flexible) than SMTP, MS Mail, or any other forms of addressing. X.400 addresses are referred to as *Originator/Recipient* (O/R) *addresses* and are used to route messages in an X.400 mail system. This address consists of a large number of fields, not all of which need to be specified for a message to be routed to its destination. In fact, all that is necessary is enough of an address that the recipient is uniquely identified in the global hierarchical X.400 address space. To complicate things further, some address fields that may be mandatory in some X.400 systems are optional in other systems!

Table 3-22 shows the complete set of attributes (fields) available for X.400 addressing (see also Figure 3-18).

Table 3-22: The Attributes of an O/R Address

Field Name	Abbreviation	Label	Max Length
Given Name	Given Name	G	16
Initials	Initials	I	5
Surname	Surname	S	40
Generation Qualifier	Generation	Q	3
Common Name	Common Name	CN	32
X.121 Address	X.121	X.121	15
UA Numeric ID	N-ID	N-ID	32
Terminal Type	T-TY	T-TY	3
Terminal Identifier	T-ID	T-ID	24
Organization	Organization	O	64
Organizational Unit 1	Org.Unit.1	OU1	32
Organizational Unit 2	Org.Unit.2	OU2	32
Organizational Unit 3	Org.Unit.3	OU3	32
Organizational Unit 4	Org.Unit.4	OU4	32
PRMD Name	PRMD	P	16
ADMD Name	ADMD	A	16
Country	Country	C	2
Domain Defined Attribute	DDA	DDA	8,128

Only the DDA attribute in Table 3-22 is case-sensitive.

X.400 addresses are composed by combining selected attributes from Table 3-22 with their values, separated by an equals sign and followed by a semicolon such as:

```
attribute=value;
```

The following attributes are *required* in an X.400 address:

ADMD
Country

If no ADMD (Administrative Management Domain) need be specified, use a single blank character instead.

Additionally, at least one of the following attributes must be included in an X.400 address:

Surname
Common name
Organization
Organizational unit
PRMD

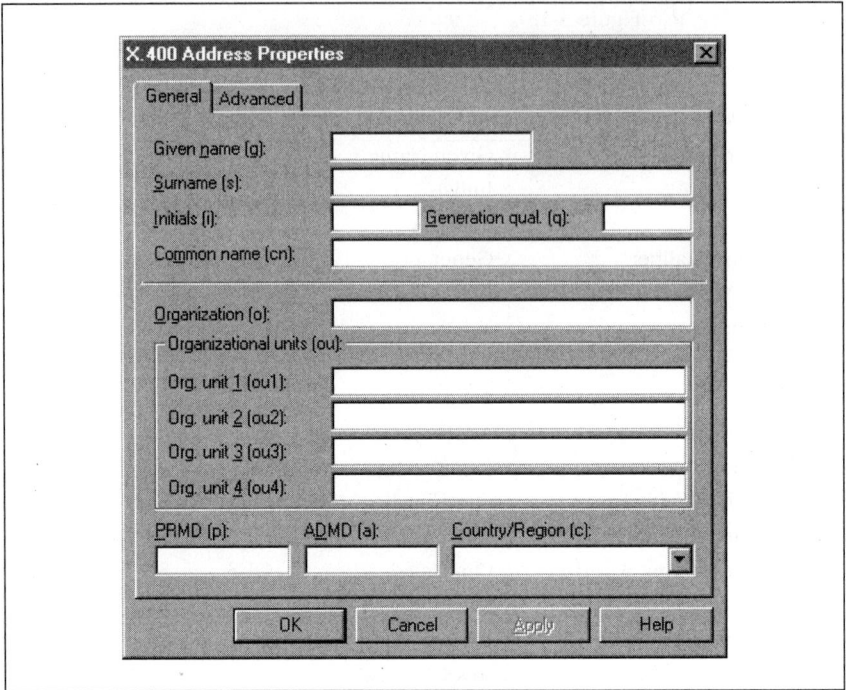

Figure 3-18: Creating a new X.400 email address for a Mailbox object

A typical X.400 address for connecting to a foreign mail system might be some-thing like this:

C=US;A=SPRINT;P=OTHERCORP;O=MARKETING;S=SMITH;G=MARY;

Table 3-23 analyzes the various fields in this sample O/R address.

Table 3-23: Analysis of a Sample X.400 Address

Attribute=Value;	Meaning
C=US;	The country (C) is the United States, US being the standard two-letter country code.
A=SPRINT;	The ADMD represents the public telecommunications provider needed for transmitting the message.
P=OTHERCORP;	The Private Management Domain (PRMD) represents the network owned by the destination company and is often some form of the company's name.
O=MARKETING;	The Organization (O) is the name of the network, repre-senting the department or branch within the company.
S=SMITH;	Mary Smith's surname (S).
G=MARY;	Mary Smith's given name (G).

As far as interoperability with Exchange is concerned, the main things to note are:

- The X.400 PDMD (P) is equivalent to the Exchange *organization*.

- The X.400 Organization (O) is equivalent to the Exchange *site*.

For example, a user Bob Jones whose mailbox is homed in the site Toronto of the organization SampleCorp in Canada would have the X.400 address:

C=US;A= ;P=SAMPLECORP;O=TORONTO;S=JONES;G=BOB;

Note that Exchange defaults to *C=US* for X.400 addressing; there seems to be no simple way to override this during setup, so you can either change it later to *C=CA* on all connected sites or perhaps better just leave it as it is. (We'll probably get absorbed some day anyway by our neighbor to the south.) Note also the blank character for the ADMD attribute, which is what Exchange generates by default.

Properties

General

Lets you specify the display name, remote MTA name and password, word-wrap for messages, MAPI support, and an administrative note. Also displays the directory name, the server's home site, date the connector was installed, and date the X.400 Connector configuration was last modified. Of interest are:

Remote MTA name and password

Lets you specify the name and password of the remote X.400 Message Transfer Agent (MTA).

If you are connecting to a remote site in your organization, this information can be found on the general tab of the Message Transfer Agent object on the remote server that has the other X.400 Connector, where they are referred to as the *local* MTA name and password.

If you are connecting to an MTA of a foreign X.400 messaging system, contact the administrator of the foreign system for this information.

MTA Transport Stack

This must be an MTA Transport Stack of type X.25, TP4, or TCP/IP. The transport stack does not have to be installed on the same server as the X.400 Connector. If the transport stack is on a different server in your site, X.400 messages will still be routed by the X.400 Connector through the transport stack to the remote system.

If no MTA transport stack appears in the drop-down list, then either you haven't installed one in your site or directory synchronization has not yet informed the server with the X.400 Connector of the existence of the stack. See "MTA Transport Stack" in this chapter for information on how to install and configure a transport stack.

Message text word-wrap

Lets you specify at which column a carriage return should be inserted in message lines for mail clients that require this.

Remote clients support MAPI

Select this checkbox to allow your mail clients to send rich-text-format (RTF) messages through the connector. Select this only if you are sure the recipient clients support RTF.

Permissions

See the section "Permissions and Roles" at the beginning of this chapter.

Schedule

Lets you schedule when the X.400 Connector will attempt to connect to the remote MTA for message transfer. There are four possible settings:

Always

The connector sends any outbound message in the local MTA queue. Use this setting if you have a permanent, dedicated connection to the remote site or foreign X.400 mail system.

Never

Disables the connector.

Selected times

Use the grid to assign times in 1-hour or 15-minute increments. At these times the X.400 Connector will create a connection with the remote site or foreign X.400 mail system and initiate mail transfer.

Remote initiated

The connector will never initiate a connection with the remote site or foreign X.400 mail system, leaving this instead to the remote site's MTA. Outbound messages in the local MTA queue are only sent when the remote site's connector establishes a connection. For this option to work, you must select the Two Way Alternate option on the Advanced tab.

Stack

Lets you specify transport address information for the remote MTA you are connecting to. This information must be correctly specified or the connector will not work. If you are trying to connect to a foreign X.400 mail system, you may have to obtain some of this information from the administrator of the foreign system.

This property page varies with the type of MTA Transport Stack your X.400 Connector is using, as shown in Table 3-24.

Table 3-24: Configurable Settings for Different Transport Stacks

Type of Stack	Property Page Settings
TCP/IP	IP address or DNS host name, plus additional OSI addressing information for foreign MTAs
X.25	Call user data, facilities data, X.121 address, plus additional OSI addressing information for foreign MTAs
TP4	Network service access point (NSAP) address, plus additional OSI addressing information for foreign MTAs

Override

These settings override the local MTA Site Configuration settings only when messages are transferred using this connector. If you are connecting to a remote site in your organization, the settings here should match the Messaging Defaults tab of the MTA Site Configuration property sheet for the remote site. If you are connecting to a foreign X.400 mail system, contact the administrator of the foreign system for this information. See "MTA Site Configuration" in this chapter for more information on these settings.

Note that you can override the name and password of your local MTA on this page also. This applies only to messaging through the X.400 connector you are configuring, not to any other connector in your site. You may need to override the name of your local MTA if it is too long or has special characters that are unacceptable to the foreign MTA.

Connected Sites

Lets you view and modify the list of remote sites directly connected to your local site through X.400 Connectors. These remote sites must be listed here so that directory replication can take place with the local site.

Note that this property page is used *only* when you are connecting to a remote site in your organization and does not need to be configured if you are connecting to a foreign X.400 mail system; it is used only for ensuring that directory replication takes place with the remote site.

To specify a connected site, select the New button to open a dialog box for entering addressing and routing information, specifically:

Organization

The name of your organization.

Site

The name of the remote site you want to connect to. The X.400 Connector must be installed and configured on this site also, as connectors at both ends are needed to enable messaging between sites.

Routing Address

The X.400 address of the remote site.

Cost

A value between 1 and 100 for routing purposes. The *cost* of your connector determines which messaging bridgehead server is used, if there are more than one in your site. The messaging bridgehead server with the lowest cost is preferred. Routing addresses with similar costs are load-balanced in proportion to their cost.

You can also edit or delete existing connected sites.

Address Space

Lets you specify address spaces for the X.400 Connector. An *address space* represents a messaging path through the connector to the remote site. When an MTA in your local site attempts to route a message through the local X.400 Connector, it checks the list of address spaces to determine whether the connector can route the message and load-balances using the connector based on the cost. An X.400 address space for the remote site must be specified when the X.400 Connector is created.

The listbox on this property page displays four parameters for each address space created:

Type
> SMTP, X.400, MS Mail, or Other type of address space.

Address
> The addresses that the connector is responsible for routing messages to. Wildcards can be used:
>
> – Asterisk (*) represents any number of characters.
>
> – Percent sign (%) represents any single character.

Cost
> Routing cost.

Scope
> Restrictions on who can use this address space for sending messages through the connector. You can specify users at your location only, your local site only, or users throughout the entire organization.

For example, if you are connecting to a remote site Winnipeg in your organization SampleCorp in country Canada, the X.400 address space you should specify when the X.400 Connector is created would be:

c=CA;a= ;p=SampleCorp;o=Winnipeg

Note that an address space contains only a partial address, enough to uniquely identify messages to be routed to the remote site. That is actually why it is called an *address space*, because it represents a space of possible recipients having the same partial address fragment in their addresses.

To route messages of other types (e.g., SMTP or MS Mail) through this connector, you should add an address space for these types. See "Internet Mail Service" in this chapter for more information about creating new address spaces.

Delivery Restrictions
> Lets you accept or reject outgoing messages, that is, messages from recipients in your organization that are attempting to use the connector as a path to another site, organization, or mail system. Incoming messages are not affected by these settings.

Advanced
> Lets you configure advanced settings for connecting to foreign X.400 mail systems. Explanation of these advanced settings is beyond the scope of this book, and there's not much point discussing them unless one has a deep understanding of how X.400 works. Bottom line is, if you need to establish connectivity with a foreign X.400 mail system, contact the administrator of the foreign system to configure the settings on this property page. And of course, the foreign mail system's MTA will need to be configured to connect to your organization, too!

Notes

- If you use an X.400 Connector to provide messaging connectivity between two sites in your organization, you should test the connector once it is set up. Try something like this:

  1. Send a plain-text message from one site to the other, and check to make sure it arrives and is readable. If the message doesn't arrive, check the Application log in Event Viewer for ExchangeMTA events.

  2. Then reply to the message and check to make sure the reply arrives and is readable.

  3. Then try sending an RTF message and include an attachment. If this fails, check the configuration of your connectors to make sure they match.

- Sending a message with an empty subject field to certain foreign X.400 messaging systems such as France's ATLAS system can generate NDR messages. Microsoft has a hotfix for this problem available on its web site. Go to *support.microsoft.com/support/supportnet.*

CHAPTER 4

GUI Tools

Administrators of Microsoft Exchange organizations require tools to administer the servers and sites within their organization; this chapter introduces the main GUI-based tools for administering the Microsoft Exchange directory hierarchy introduced in Chapter 3, *Directory*. Command-line tools and utilities are covered in Chapter 5, *Command-Line Tools*.

You should understand from the start that if you plan to administer an Exchange organization, you *must* use the GUI. About 98 percent of the common administrative tasks you perform from the GUI have no equivalent from the command line. This can be frustrating at times, since it often makes repetitive tasks such as configuring mailboxes tedious and time-consuming, and there are few shortcuts for allowing a series of similar tasks to be performed easily.

The main tool for administering Exchange is the Microsoft Exchange Administrator program *admin.exe*. This is the only tool for viewing and configuring the properties of the Exchange directory objects covered in Chapter 3 and is the primary tool for performing the most common administrative tasks, such as creating and configuring mailboxes, public folders, address book views, site connectors, custom recipients, and so on. The main point of this chapter is to give you the big picture on how to use Exchange Administrator to create and manage the Exchange directory hierarchy. The remaining GUI tools presented in this chapter are much narrower in scope, having limited but specific usefulness for administering Exchange.

The six tools covered here are ordered alphabetically according to their command-line equivalents (executable filenames), namely:

admin.exe
    Exchange Administrator

mailmig.exe
    Migration Wizard

ntbackup.exe
> Windows NT Backup

outlook.exe
> Outlook 98

perfwiz.exe
> Performance Optimizer

usrmgr.exe
> User Manager for Domains

Exchange Administrator

Lets you create and delete objects within the directory space of your Exchange organization and view or modify their properties. Also lets you run wizards and tools for various administrative purposes.

Path

```
\exchsrvr\bin\admin.exe
```

To Launch

Start → Programs → Microsoft Exchange → Microsoft Exchange Administrator
Start → Run → \exchsrvr\bin\admin.exe

Note that the first time you start Exchange Administrator, you are prompted to specify an Exchange server within your organization to which you wish to connect. You also have the option of selecting this as your default server. Once you are connected to an Exchange server, Exchange Administrator obtains the necessary information about your organization's directory hierarchy from the server's Exchange directory services database.

Description

The Exchange Administrator program displays a window with two panes, similar to Windows Explorer (see Figure 4-1):

Container pane
> The left pane gives a hierarchical view of the Exchange directory namespace, showing all *container objects* within the Exchange organization.

Contents pane
> The right pane shows all directory objects within the container object selected in the left pane. These objects are either containers themselves or are *leaf objects* (end nodes).

Exchange Administrator has the standard functionality (menus, customizable toolbar, status bar, resizable panes, and columns) of any software designed by Microsoft, with one strange omission: right-clicking on a directory object does not bring up the expected shortcut menu! This means that when you want to open the property sheet of an object, you must use the menu, toolbar, or the keyboard shortcut ALT-ENTER. You can also try double-clicking on an object in the Contents pane to bring up its property sheet, but this doesn't work if the object is a container: it expands the container instead. ALT-ENTER is simplest.

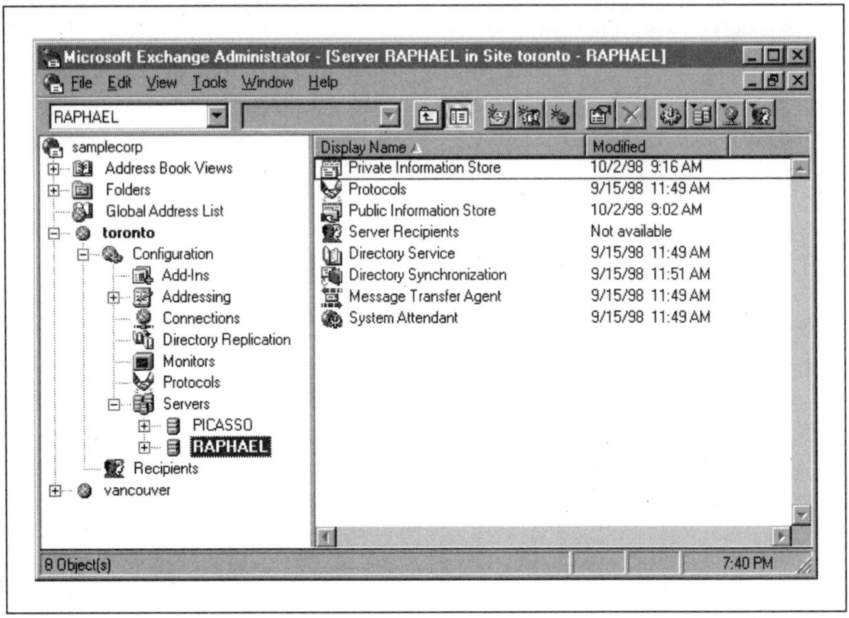

Figure 4-1: Microsoft Exchange Administrator program (admin.exe)

There are a few Exchange-specific keyboard accelerators for menu items that are easy to remember and are well worth knowing:

CTRL-M
: Create a new *mailbox*

CTRL-D
: Create a new *distribution list* (DL)

CTRL-R
: Create a new *custom recipient*

ALT-ENTER
: Access the property sheet for the selected directory object

Additional keyboard accelerators are available for certain toolbar buttons; these are summarized in Table 4-4 later in this chapter.

Exchange Administrator is a typical MDI (multiple document interface) windows application: you can open multiple windows, tile and cascade them, and so on. Each window can show a different view of the Exchange directory namespace. Note that if different multiple child windows are opened in Exchange Administrator, with each connected to a different Exchange server to obtain its namespace information, then when directory replication is out of sync the views in the various child windows may be different.

Exchange Administrator can also be installed separately (through the Custom setup option) on any Windows NT 4.0 Server or Windows NT 4.0 Workstation in the domain and thus be used to remotely administer Exchange servers within your site. It's a good idea to have at least one instance of Exchange Administrator installed on a non-Exchange server within your site for fault tolerance. Note that Exchange Administrator cannot be installed on Windows 95/98.

Of course, there is a way you can administer an Exchange organization from a Windows 95/98 machine: install remote-control software such as *PC Anywhere* on both your Windows 95/98 machine and an Exchange server (or perhaps more safely, on a Windows NT Workstation that has the Exchange Administrator program installed).

To administer an Exchange server remotely using Exchange Administrator, you must have a connection to that server that supports remote procedure calls (RPCs). In practice what this means is that you must have a LAN or WAN connection configured with TCP/IP, NWLink, or NetBEUI.

Being a member of the Windows NT Domain Admins group is not sufficient to allow you to run Exchange Administrator. You also need to be assigned the Permissions Admin role on the Exchange site you want to administer. (The administrator account used to install Exchange on a server automatically has this role assigned to it during installation.) To grant an administrator account the Permissions Admin role for your Exchange site, open the property sheet of the Site Container for your site and configure the Permissions tab as appropriate. (If the Permissions tab is hidden, use the menu first to select Tools → Options → Permissions → Show Permissions.)

It is possible to use the Exchange Administrator program running on a Windows NT Workstation in one domain to administer Exchange servers in a remote *untrusted* domain. To do this, you must create an account in the local Workstation's domain that has the same username and password as one in the remote domain and assign this account the Permissions Admin role on the remote server's Organization, Site, and Configuration containers. Then when you try to connect to the remote server with Exchange Administrator, you must do so by explicitly typing its NetBIOS name. (You cannot use the Browse function to attempt to locate it.) Finally, the remote Exchange server must be either a PDC or a BDC; you cannot perform remote administration from an untrusted domain on an Exchange server configured as a member server.

Menus

Exchange Administrator has an extensive set of menus that are used to create and configure directory objects, run wizards, and perform other administrative tasks. This section provides an overview of the menu options, focusing on what is complex or significant and omitting what is obvious.

First we'll take a summary look at the top-level menu options:

File menu

> Lets you connect to a particular Exchange server to retrieve directory informa-
> tion, create and configure new directory objects, access the properties of
> existing objects, duplicate directory objects, export the Exchange Adminis-
> trator view to a text file, and exit the program.

Edit menu

> Standard editing options (e.g., cut, copy, paste, select all, delete, and undo).
> The main thing to note here is that you can't copy and paste directory objects;
> use File → Duplicate instead.

View menu

> Mainly used to configure views of Recipients Containers but also used to sort
> objects, change the display font, toggle the toolbar and status bar, and adjust
> the split bar.

Tools menu

> A variety of useful tools are lumped together here, some of them dealing with
> moving selected mailbox information between different mail systems, others
> dealing with tracking messages and monitoring sites and servers. Also lets you
> customize the toolbar, configure general options, and create newsgroups and
> forms.

Window

> Standard options for configuring windows (e.g., new window, cascade, tile,
> refresh, and arrange icons).

Help menu

> Lets you access Online Help and a set of manuals called Books Online.

Now let's look deeper into the Exchange menu system and what you can do with
it. Some menu options will be covered in detail, but those options from the File
menu that create new objects in the Exchange directory hierarchy will be covered
only briefly; refer to the articles in Chapter 3 for full treatment on how to
configure these objects. I will also omit covering the Edit, Windows, and Help
menus since these have the standard functionality of any Microsoft program.

File Menu

File → Connect to Server

> Opens the Connect to Server dialog box, which lets you connect to an
> Exchange server to download information about your Exchange organiza-
> tion's directory space from the server's directory services. This information is
> used to construct the directory hierarchy that Exchange Administrator displays
> in its window. Click Browse to open the Server Browser dialog box
> (Figure 4-2) or simply type in the name of the server you want to connect to.

> Things to note:

>   —   When you connect to a server, you are really connecting to a site. Once
>   connected, you can view the directory information for all sites in your
>   organization, but you can only modify directory objects in the connected
>   site; directory information for other sites is read-only. However, since

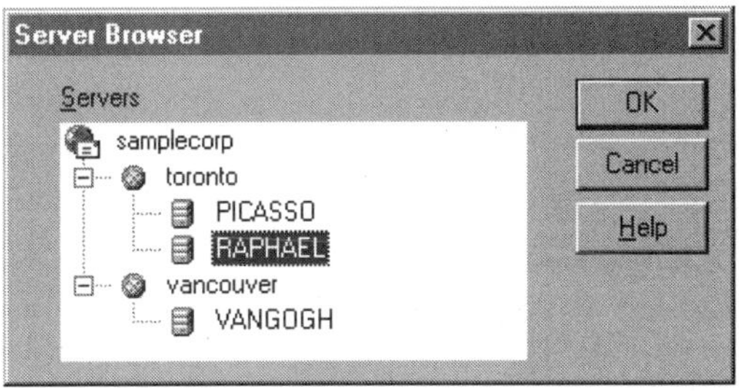

Figure 4-2: Connecting to a server

Exchange Administrator is an MDI application, you can connect to one server in each site to open a child window for administering each site.

- If the server you connect to is out of sync with parts of your Exchange organization, the information it displays may be incomplete or incorrect.

File → Close
Closes the active Exchange Administrator window.

File → New Mailbox (CTRL-M)
Creates a new *mailbox*, a type of *recipient*. The way it works is like this:

- First, if your connected site's Recipients container or a subcontainer thereof is *not* currently selected in the left (container) pane, you will be prompted to switch to it. This happens with most File menu selections: if you haven't selected the proper container in the container pane, you are prompted to switch to it first.

- Next the property sheet for the mailbox is displayed, allowing you to configure the mailbox settings (Figure 4-3). The only required items are Display Name (which appears in the Exchange Administrator windows and in the Address Book) and Alias. These fields are filled automatically when you enter information into the First and Last Name fields. See the entry "Mailbox" in Chapter 3 for more information about the various tabs of this property sheet.

- After you configure the mailbox and click OK, the Primary Windows NT Account dialog box appears, asking you to identify the NT user account that should have owner permissions on the mailbox. You can either select an existing account to associate with the mailbox or create a new account on the fly.

- If you choose to create a new account, the name of the account will be the Alias you defined previously. The new account will be assigned a blank password, and the user will be required to change the password the first time he logs on.

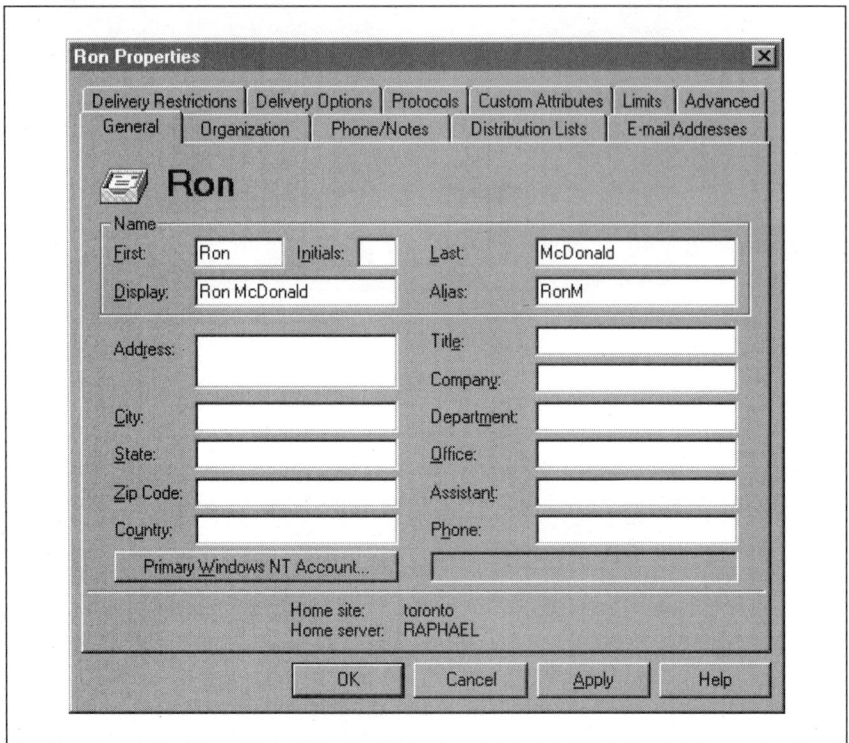

Figure 4-3: Creating a new mailbox

> Note that you cannot create a Mailbox on an Exchange server from which the private information store has been removed!

File → New Distribution List (CTRL-D)

Creates a new *distribution list* (DL), another type of recipient. The procedure is similar to creating a new mailbox. After switching to your site's Recipients container, the property sheet for the DL is displayed. The only required items are Display Name and Alias, but you will also want to configure the list membership, the list's Owner, and other settings. See the entry "Distribution List" in Chapter 3 for more information.

File → New Custom Recipient (CTRL-R)

Creates a new *custom recipient*. The way it works is:

1. First specify the type of email address your custom recipient will have, such as an SMTP Internet address (Figure 4-4).

2. Next a property sheet will be displayed, asking you to specify the new email address and possibly some additional information, depending on

the type of address being created. For example, the Advanced tab of the New Internet Address Properties sheet (Figure 4-5) deals with overriding the default message format settings for the Internet Mail Service. For example, the Internet Mail Service within your Exchange organization might be configured to use MIME for encoding messages with attachments; you could then override this so that your particular custom recipient uses Uuencode, if that is what the destination user's SMTP server requires.

3. Finally, a property sheet appears for you to configure the Display Name, Alias, and other settings. See the entry "Custom Recipient" in Chapter 3 for more details.

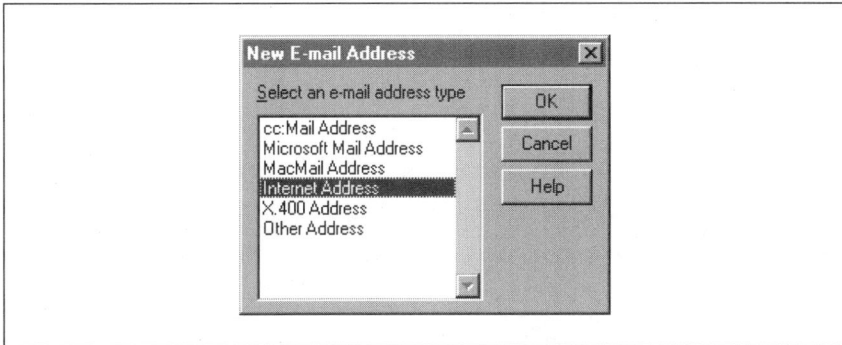

Figure 4-4: Select an email address type for your new custom recipient

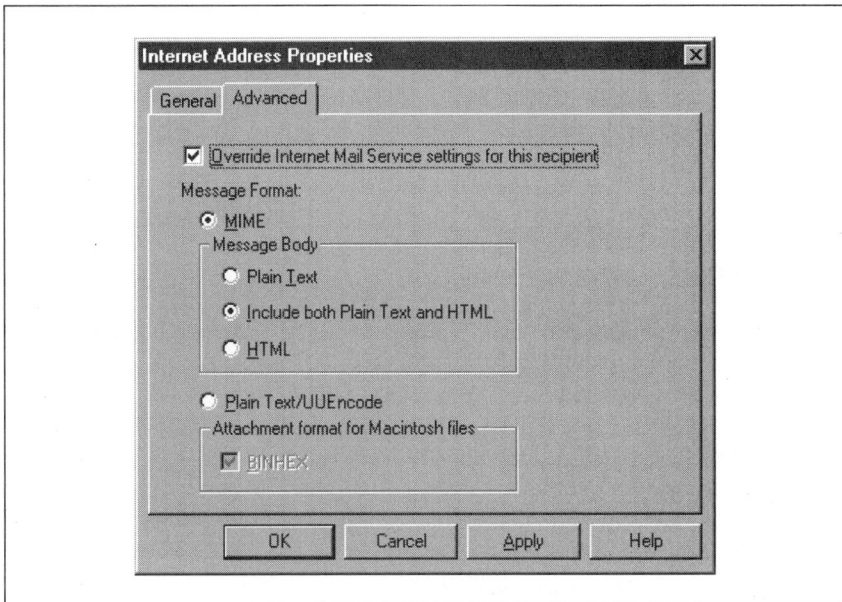

Figure 4-5: Configure the email address for the new custom recipient

File → New Other

    This menu selection leads to a submenu for creating a variety of different directory objects. The submenu items are grouped using separators, but the grouping is not always logical. Table 4-1 shows a summary of the groupings, after which the items will be considered one-by-one. Most of the menu selections open property sheets for the new object, though sometimes other dialog boxes appear also.

    Remember, for more information on configuring the property sheets for directory objects you create using the File menu, see their associated articles in Chapter 3.

Table 4-1: Submenus of File → New Other and the Various Directory Objects They Create

Type of Object Being Created	Submenu Items
Monitors	Server Monitor Link Monitor
Stuff related to the Address Book	Recipients Container Address Book View Address Book View Container
Various Connectors and Directory Replication	MTA Transport Stack X.400 Connector Dynamic RAS Connector Site Connector Directory Replication Connector
MS-Mail Directory Connectors	Dirsync Requestor Dirsync Server Remote Dirsync Requestor
Public or Private Information Store	Information Store
Usenet Newsfeed	Newsfeed
SMTP Mail	Internet Mail Service

File → New Other → Server Monitor

    Creates a new Server Monitor object and lets you configure the property sheet for the new monitor. The only required items are Display Name (appears in Exchange Administrator windows) and Directory Name (the name used internally for the object in the directory services database). However, the monitor must be further configured if it is to monitor anything! After configuring your monitor, you can start it using the Tools menu.

File → New Other → Link Monitor

    Creates a new Link Monitor object. Similar procedure to creating a Server Monitor.

File → New Other → Recipients Container

    Creates a new Recipients container for your site or a subcontainer for your existing Recipients container.

Note that if you create additional Recipients containers, you can only move recipients from one container to another by exporting their information, deleting the old recipient, and importing the information into the new Recipients container. For this reason it's a good idea to limit the number of Recipients containers you create.

One thing you might do is create one Recipients container for *mailboxes*, one for *custom recipients*, one for *distribution lists*, and so on. This would work because a mailbox never becomes a distribution list so there is no point trying to move it to the distribution list container. Additional Recipients containers can also be created for special recipients such as shared resource mailboxes and *mailbox templates*.

File → New Other → Address Book View

Creates a new *address book view* for grouping together recipients. Display Name, Directory Name, and at least one Group By attribute must be configured. After you click OK, a message will appear informing you that a process has been started to update the new address book view, which may take some time if there are a lot of recipients in your site.

File → New Other → Address Book View Container

Creates a subcontainer within an address book view for further grouping recipients. This option is dimmed out unless you select a specific address book view as the parent container.

File → New Other → MTA Transport Stack

Creates a new MTA Transport Stack, a step that must be performed prior to creating an X.400 connector or dynamic RAS connector. The underlying transport protocol and networking hardware must be installed and configured before the new MTA transport stack can be created (usually TCP/IP and a network card adapter). For example, if you wanted to create an X.25 MTA transport stack, you would first need to install and configure X.25 networking software and a host adapter on your server. If you wanted to create a RAS MTA transport stack, you would first need to install and configure the Remote Access Service for Windows NT. (For information on how to do this, see Eric Pearce's *Windows NT in a Nutshell* from O'Reilly.)

File → New Other → X.400 Connector

Creates a new X.400 Connector for message exchange with an X.400 mail system. You must create the appropriate MTA transport stack first using File → New Other → MTA Transport Stack.

This menu opens the New X.400 Connector dialog box (Figure 4-6), which lets you choose the type of X.400 Connector you want to create, based on the installed MTA transport stack. Exchange supports three types of X.400 Connectors:

- Eicon X.25
- TCP/IP
- TP4

The connector types visible in this dialog box depend on what underlying hardware and MTA stack you have installed. Unless you are configuring connectivity with some legacy packet-switching network, you will only see TCP/IP displayed here and should select it and click OK to open the X.400 Connector's property sheet.

The required fields are Display Name, Directory Name, Remote MTA Name, Remote Host Name/IP Address, and either Connected Sites (if you are connecting to another Exchange site) or Address Space (if you are connecting to a foreign X.400 mail system). See the entry "X.400 Connector" in Chapter 3 for further details on configuring the connector.

When you finish configuring your connector and click OK, you will be reminded that you have to configure a similar connector at the remote site before messaging will work between the sites.

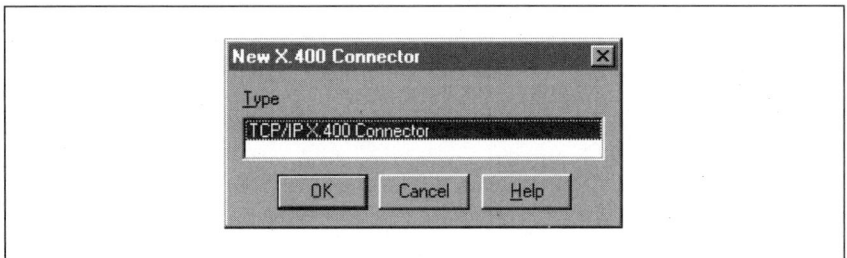

Figure 4-6: Creating a new X.400 Connector

File → New Other → Dynamic RAS Connector

Creates a new Dynamic RAS Connector for asynchronous messaging connectivity with a remote Exchange site via RAS. You must create a RAS MTA transport stack first using File → New Other → MTA Transport Stack.

The required fields are Display Name, Directory Name, Remote Server Name, Phone Book Entry, Windows NT domain and username to Connect As, and remote addressing information. See the entry "Dynamic RAS Connector" in Chapter 3 for more details. When you finish configuring your connector and click OK, you will again be reminded that you have to configure a similar connector at the remote site before messaging will work between the sites.

File → New Other → Site Connector

Creates a new Site Connector, the simplest way of connecting Exchange sites that have LAN or dedicated high-speed WAN network connectivity so that messages can be exchanged between them.

The menu opens the New Site Connector dialog box, where you specify the name of an available Exchange server in the remote site. (There is unfortunately no browse function for locating Exchange servers in remote sites; you must manually type in the name of the server.) You need administrative rights on the remote site to connect to it, and if the remote site is in a different Windows NT domain, you must be an administrator in that domain also.

Once a connection has been established with the server in the remote site, Exchange downloads information from the remote site's directory services and preconfigures some of the property sheet settings for you. When you configures the remaining settings and click OK, a dialog box appears offering to automatically create a complementary site connector in the remote site. Clicking Yes lets you configure the property sheet for the remote connector; click No if you want the administrator of the remote site to create the remote connector.

File → New Other → Directory Replication Connector

Creates a new Directory Replication Connector, allowing Exchange sites to share directory information. Without this connector, the directory database of each site only contains information about objects within that site. If you run Exchange Administrator on a server, the only site container will be the local site.

However, once directory replication has properly been established within an Exchange organization, all sites share their directory information so that each site's directory database contains info about all objects in the entire organization. If you run Exchange Administrator on any server in the organization, it will display all site containers in the organization and their contents. Remember, though, that directory objects for sites other than the one you are connected to are read-only: you can view their properties but not modify them. To connect to a different site and modify the properties of its directory objects, use File → Connect to Server as described earlier.

Prior to creating a Directory Replication Connector between two sites, make sure that you have established messaging connectivity between the sites using a site connector, X.400 connector, dynamic RAS connector, or some other messaging connector. Try sending a test message between sites to test connectivity and routing.

File → New Other → Dirsync Requestor

Creates a new Directory Synchronization (Dirsync) Requestor for sending and receiving updates of directory information with an MS Mail server postoffice. Name, Dirsync Address, and Import Container are required fields on the property sheet.

File → New Other → Dirsync Server

Creates a new Directory Synchronization (Dirsync) Server for processing directory updates from MS Mail requestors or Exchange dirsync requestors. The only required field is Name.

If you create a dirsync server, you must create a remote dirsync requestor for every dirsync requestor that uses your dirsync server. For more information see "DirSync Requestor" and "DirSync Server" in Chapter 3.

File → New Other → Remote Dirsync Requestor

Creates a new Remote Directory Synchronization (Dirsync) Requestor.

File → New Other → Information Store

Lets you create a *public information store* or *private information store* on a server if none exists. Information stores can be deleted and created like most other directory objects.

File → New Other → Newsfeed

Starts the Newsfeed Configuration Wizard, used to install the Internet News Service and to create and configure Usenet newsfeeds (Figure 4-7). The initial configuration is done using the wizard; afterwards the property sheet for the Newsfeed object can be opened and settings modified in the usual way.

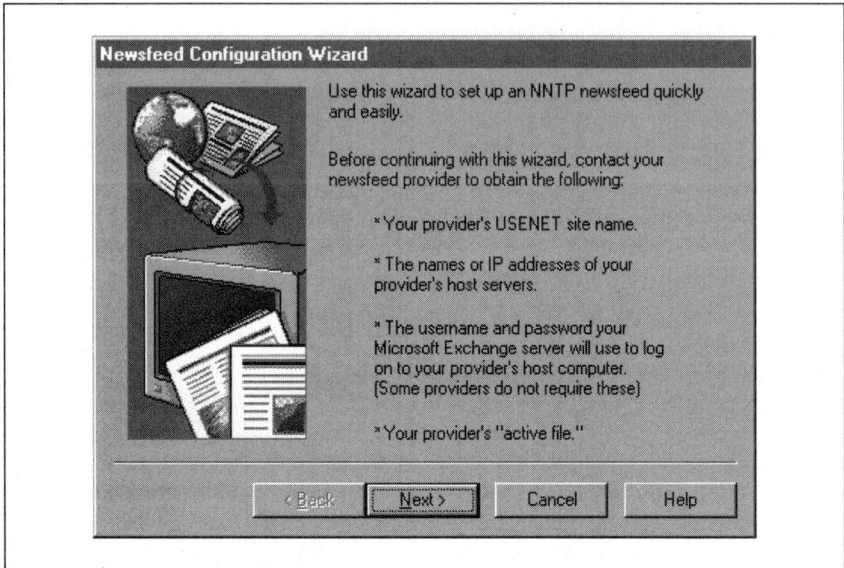

Figure 4-7: The Newsfeed Configuration Wizard

Prior to running the wizard, you should have TCP/IP installed and should contact your Usenet provider to obtain or provide the following information:

- The Fully Qualified Domain Names (FQDNs) or IP addresses of both your provider's Usenet host and the Exchange server in your organization on which the newsfeed will be created.

- The type of feed you will create: Inbound only, Outbound only, or Inbound and Outbound. An *inbound feed* only receives messages from a remote Usenet provider. An *outbound feed* only sends messages to a provider. If you want to import Usenet newsgroups from a Usenet provider, you must select Inbound and Outbound.

- The feed method for your server: push or pull. *Push feeds* are suitable for large newsfeeds that run over LAN or dedicated high-speed WAN connections. *Pull feeds* are preferable for smaller newsfeeds or over a dial-up connection. If you make the typical choice of creating an Inbound and Outbound newsfeed, your server will push newsgroup messages to your Usenet provider's host using the NNTP POST command. You can then choose whether to allow the remote Usenet host to push messages to your server using the NNTP IHAVE command, or have your server pull messages from the remote host using the NNTP NEWNEWS command.

- The provider's *active file*, the list of all available Usenet newsgroups. Obtain this from your Usenet provider.

- Any security information necessary, such as the inbound host account and password for your provider's Usenet host.

Here are the steps in the wizard, the settings you must configure for each step, and the default or suggested values for these settings:

- The name of the Exchange server in your organization on which the newsfeed will be created and its FQDN name.

- The type of newsfeed to create: Inbound only, Outbound only, or Inbound and Outbound (the default). For an inbound feed, choose whether it will receive messages from the remote Usenet host using push (the default) or pull.

- Whether a LAN (the default) or dial-up connection will be used.

- How often your server will connect to its Usenet provider (the default is every 15 minutes).

- The FQDN of your provider's Usenet host.

- The IP address of your provider's Usenet host. For an inbound feed, the names or IP addresses of additional inbound hosts may also be specified.

- For optional security in accessing your provider's Usenet host, a user account and password may be supplied for logging on to the remote host, and a mailbox recipient can be specified for the remote host to be authenticated by the Exchange server. You may also require that the Usenet host use Secure Sockets Layer (SSL) protocol for encrypted transmission, but this creates a significant performance hit.

- The password for the Exchange Service Account in your site.

- The Internet News Service is now created and started on the Exchange server. Once that is done, the wizard continues requesting that you specify information, namely:

  - An Exchange recipient designated for the job of Internet News Administrator, who will own the Internet News public folders.

  - For an inbound feed, import the active file supplied by your Usenet provider. Alternatively, you can download the file now from your provider or postpone that task until later. If you import or download the file, you can next decide which newsgroups from the file you want to include in your newsfeed. The default is all available newsgroups; make sure you have enough gigabytes of disk space to handle a full Usenet feed if you accept the default!

Once you finish the wizard, you can further configure your newsfeed by opening its property sheet. Additionally, you must configure the NNTP protocol properties at either the site or server level to enable sending and receiving of Usenet newsfeeds. See the entries "Newsfeed," "NNTP (News) Site Defaults," and "NNTP (News) Settings" in Chapter 3 for more details.

Note that you cannot create a newsfeed on an Exchange server from which the public information store has been removed!

File → New Other → Internet Mail Service

Starts the Internet Mail wizard, which lets you install and configure the Internet Mail Service so that your Exchange server can function as an SMTP server and connect to other SMTP servers on the Internet. Just as for the Internet News Service, the initial configuration is done using the wizard; afterwards the property sheet for the Internet Mail Service object can be opened and settings modified in the usual way.

Prior to running the wizard, you should have TCP/IP installed and have an A and MX record created for your Exchange server on your Internet Service Provider's DNS server (if you are using DNS).

Here are the steps in this wizard and the settings to configure at each step:

– The name of the Exchange server on which you will be installing the Internet Mail Service. Specify whether to use RAS to send mail to your ISP.

– Use DNS to locate the destination mail servers (the default) or route all SMTP mail through your ISP's mail server. The hostname or IP address of your provider's SMTP server must be specified if the second option is chosen.

– Whether to allow outbound mail to be sent to any Internet address (the default) or restrict outbound mail to certain SMTP domains. If you choose the second option, you must first finish the wizard and then configure the Address Space tab on the Internet Mail Service property sheet before you start the Internet Mail Service.

– The SMTP site address for your users (e.g., *@site_name.organization_name.com*).

– An Exchange recipient designated for the job of Internet Mail Administrator, who will receive non-delivery reports (NDRs).

– The password for the Exchange Service account for your site.

– The Internet Mail Service will be created and started, and a dialog box appears suggesting that you rerun Performance Optimizer on your server, which is always a good idea after creating new services or connectors on Exchange.

This finishes looking at the File → New Other submenus for Exchange Administrator. Now let's look at the remaining File menu options.

File → Save Window Contents

Basically, just saves the contents of the right-hand (Contents) pane as a plain text or comma-delimited text file. You can print it out or import it into Excel for documentation purposes. This is most useful for printing out information about recipient objects such as mailboxes. See View → Columns later in this entry for more details.

File → Properties (ALT-ENTER)

Opens the property sheet of the selected object. Try double-clicking or use ALT-ENTER instead.

File → Duplicate

Duplicates the selected directory object, allowing you to make copies of an object with the only settings unspecified being the essential identifying ones. For example, if you duplicate a mailbox object, the copy will have identical settings as the original, except that the First and Last Name, Display Name, and Alias are left blank and must be specified.

This is one of the more useful menu commands in Exchange Administrator, but it only duplicates recipient objects and is dimmed out if any other type of object is selected. It would have been nice if there were a proper keyboard accelerator for this menu command. I suppose ALT-F,U will just have to do!

View Menu

View → Mailboxes | Distribution Lists | Custom Recipients | Public Folders | All

Lets you toggle which types of recipient objects are displayed in the right-hand (Contents) pane when a Recipients container is selected in the left-hand (Containers) pane. These options are dimmed out unless you select a Recipients container.

View → Hidden Recipients

Displays or hides hidden recipients within a Recipients container selected in the Containers pane. Hidden objects are normally used for system configuration purposes, such as mailboxes for dirsync servers, offline address books, and other items. You will normally not need to configure these objects.

You may also want to deliberately hide some objects you create. For example, you could create and configure a mailbox and use it as a template to create other mailboxes, using the File → Duplicate menu command. You will probably want to hide your mailbox template to prevent it from appearing in the address book; otherwise, users may try to send mail to your template! To hide a mailbox, use the Advanced tab on the mailbox property sheet.

View → Columns

Lets you choose which directory object properties to display in the columns of the Contents pane (Figure 4-8). The available columns depend on the type of directory object selected in the Containers pane. This option is dimmed out unless you select one of the following objects:

- Address Book Views
- Global Address List
- Private Information Store objects
- Public Information Store objects
- Recipients or Server Recipients

Use this in conjunction with the File → Save Window Contents menu command to create a printed version of your address book.

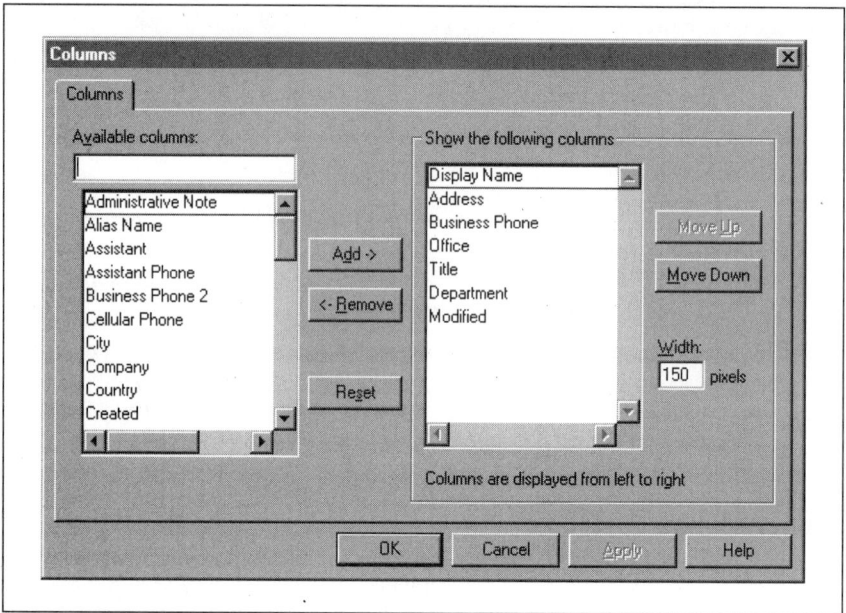

Figure 4-8: Modifying the columns displayed in the Contents pane

View → Sort By → Display Name | Last Modified Date

Sorts the directory objects visible in the Contents pane either alphabetically or by date they were last modified.

View → Font

Change the font used in the Exchange Administrator windows.

View → Move Splitbar

Sets the focus on the split bar between the two window panes—for the rodentially challenged, I guess, since you can also just point to it and drag!

View → Toolbar | Status Bar

Toggles the toolbar and status bar on and off as expected.

Tools Menu

Tools → Directory Import

Imports directory information when migrating from a foreign mail system. The information to import must be in a comma-delimited text file containing specific header fields. You can also use directory import to make global changes to the properties of recipient objects in your site. This is covered later under Tools → Directory Export.

Some of the more important configuration settings for Directory Import include (see Figure 4-9):

Windows NT domain

If you will be creating new Windows NT accounts from the imported information, this specifies the domain to which the accounts will belong.

MS Exchange server

The server on which you will run the import process.

Container

The Recipients container into which the directory information is imported.

Recipient Template

Usually a mailbox template used to configure default settings for the accounts you are creating.

Import File

Path to the *.csv file you wish to import.

Create Windows NT Account

Select this if you are importing recipient information when migrating from a foreign mail system to Exchange.

Note that you can also perform a directory import from the command line using admin /i. See Chapter 5 for more details.

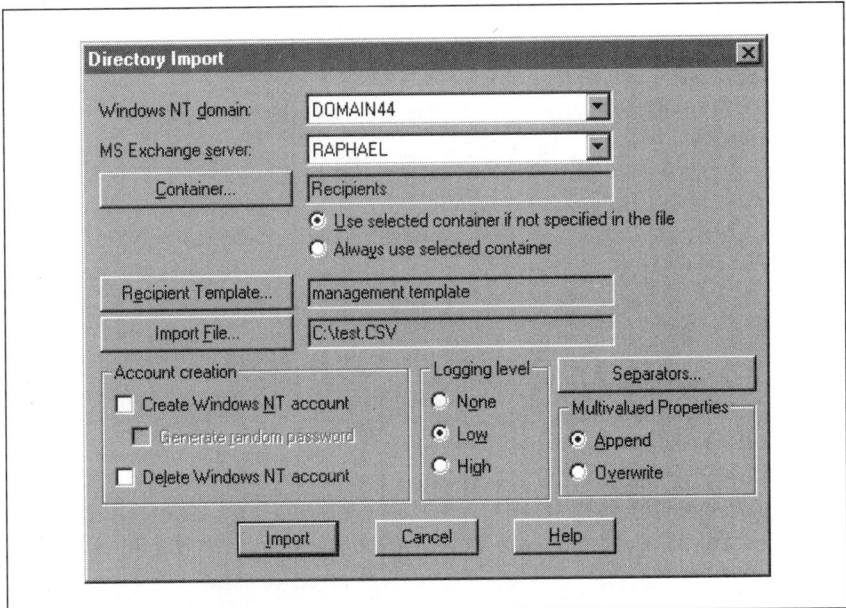

Figure 4-9: Configuring Directory Import

Tools → Directory Export

Exports directory information to a comma-delimited *.csv text file. This is especially useful when you need to make global changes to the properties of recipient objects. This is a simple way to quickly make thousands of changes to your recipients, but it seems a bit like a hack because Exchange should really have integrated tools for this purpose. We'll work through a simple example of exporting Exchange recipient information later.

Some of the more important configuration settings for Directory Export include (see Figure 4-10):

MS Exchange server
> The server on which you will run the export process.

Home server
> The server(s) containing the directory data to export. Remember that mailboxes and other recipients reside in the information store of their home server.

Export File
> Specify a name and location to store the exported information.

Container
> Select either a recipients container, the global address book, or an address book view as your source object.

Export objects
> Choose a type of recipient to export.

Other Settings
> Leave as defaults.

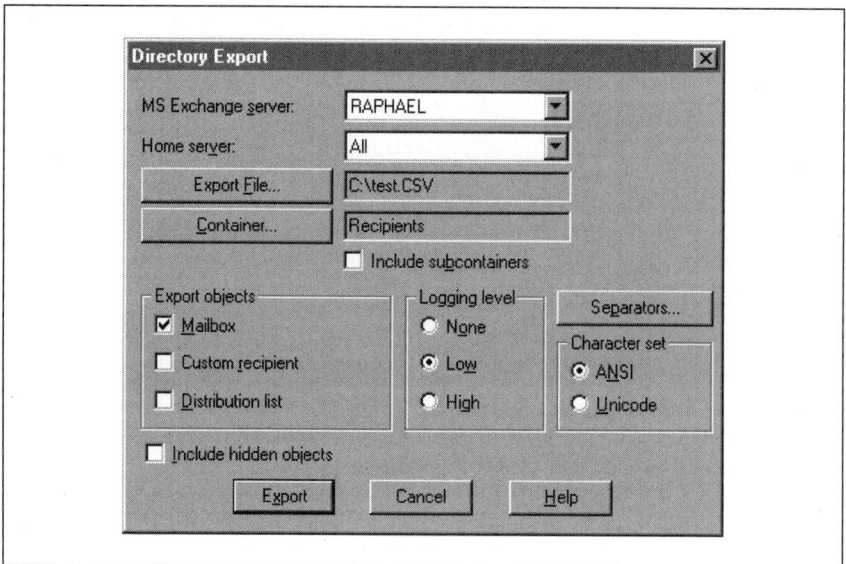

Figure 4-10: Configuring Directory Export

When directory export creates a *.csv* export file, the first record in the file contains header information indicating the recipient property for each field. Here is the default from an export file:

```
Obj-Class,First Name,Last name,Display Name,Alias Name,
Directory Name,Primary Windows NT Account,Home-Server,
E-mail address,E-mail Addresses,Members,Obj-Container,
Hide from AB
```

Table 4-2 shows each field from the header and a sample entry from some exported mailbox data. Most of the entries are self-explanatory.

Table 4-2: Sample Information from Exporting a Mailbox to a *.csv File

Header Field	Sample Entry
Obj-Class	`Mailbox`
First Name	`Donna`
Last name	`Lepkie`
Display Name	`Donna Lepkie`
Alias Name	`DonnaL`
Directory Name	`DonnaL`
Primary Windows NT Account	`DOMAIN44\DonnaL`
Home-Server	`RAPHAEL`
E-mail address	

E-mail Addresses	`"SMTP:DonnaL@toronto.samplecorp.com%`
	`MS:SAMPLECORP/TORONTO/DONNAL%`
	`X400:c=US;a=`
	`;p=samplecorp;o=toronto;s=Lepkie;g=Donna;%`
	`CCMAIL:Lepkie, Donna at toronto"`

Members	
Obj-Container	`Recipients`
Hide from AB	`0`

As an example of using Directory Export and Import to make bulk modifications to your recipients, say you wanted to change the main company phone number for all the mailboxes in your site at once. You might expect to accomplish this by doing the following:

- Export your mailboxes to a *.csv* file using Tools → Directory Export.

- Open the file with a spreadsheet program such as Microsoft Excel and make the necessary changes. If you are using Excel, use File → Open and choose Text Files in the Files As Type field to open the file. Then export the information as a new *.csv* file.

- Now import the mailbox information back into your Exchange directory using Tools → Directory Import.

Unfortunately this doesn't work, because directory export by default doesn't export the Phone property from the General tab of mailbox property sheets; it only exports the properties listed in Table 4-2. The way to work around this is to create a new *.csv* export file using Notepad and specify your own custom header record. Then when you run directory export, it exports the fields defined by the header you have created.

For example, create a new export file called *test.csv* with the following header record:

```
Obj-class,mode,Directory name,Phone number
```

Perform a directory export to the *test.csv* file. Your original file is renamed *test.c01* and a new *test.csv* file is created, which looks something like this:

```
Obj-Class,Mode,Directory name,Phone number
Mailbox,,BobT,204-555-1212
Mailbox,,DonB,204-555-1212
Mailbox,,DonnaL,204-555-1212
```

Open the file with Excel, change the phone numbers, and enter `modify` in the Mode field. Save the file as *test2.csv*, which now looks like this:

```
Obj-Class,Mode,Directory name,Phone number
Mailbox,modify,BobT,204-123-4567
Mailbox,modify,DonB,204-123-4567
Mailbox,modify,DonnaL,204-123-4567
```

Now perform a directory import with this file and the phone number will be changed on all your mailboxes.

The important thing is to know the exact syntax of the property you want to modify. For example, if you used this for your custom export file header:

```
Obj-class,mode,Directory name,PhoneNumber
```

and tried to run a directory export, you would get an error message in the Event Log, "The attribute PhoneNumber is unknown." There are three ways you can determine the syntax for attributes (property sheet settings) of recipient objects:

- Start Exchange Administrator in *raw mode* by using the /r switch at the command line (see Chapter 5). This enables access to the raw properties or schema attributes of every directory object in Exchange. You can then select a mailbox object and choose File → Raw Properties to open a property sheet showing the syntax of each attribute of the mailbox object (see Figure 4-11). This is a rather nerdy way of learning about header fields, though.

- Use the Import Header Tool *header.exe* utility from the Exchange Server Resource Kit to create an export *.csv* file with a header that allows you to export all attributes of your Exchange recipients. Export the file and have fun trying to figure out what each header field means. *header.exe* is actually a useful tool for creating custom header fields for *.csv* export files and should really have been included along with Exchange Server. It is almost worth purchasing the Resource Kit for this utility alone.

- Examine the sample *mailbox.csv*, *custom.csv*, and *dl.csv* files on the Exchange compact disk.

- Obtain a copy of the *Microsoft Exchange Server Programmer's Reference*, plus two toothpicks to hold your eyelids open.

Note that you can also perform a directory export from the command line using `admin /e`. See Chapter 5 for more details.

Tools → Extract Windows NT Account List

Lets you create mailboxes quickly for existing Windows NT accounts that lack them. Account information is extracted from a Windows NT domain controller

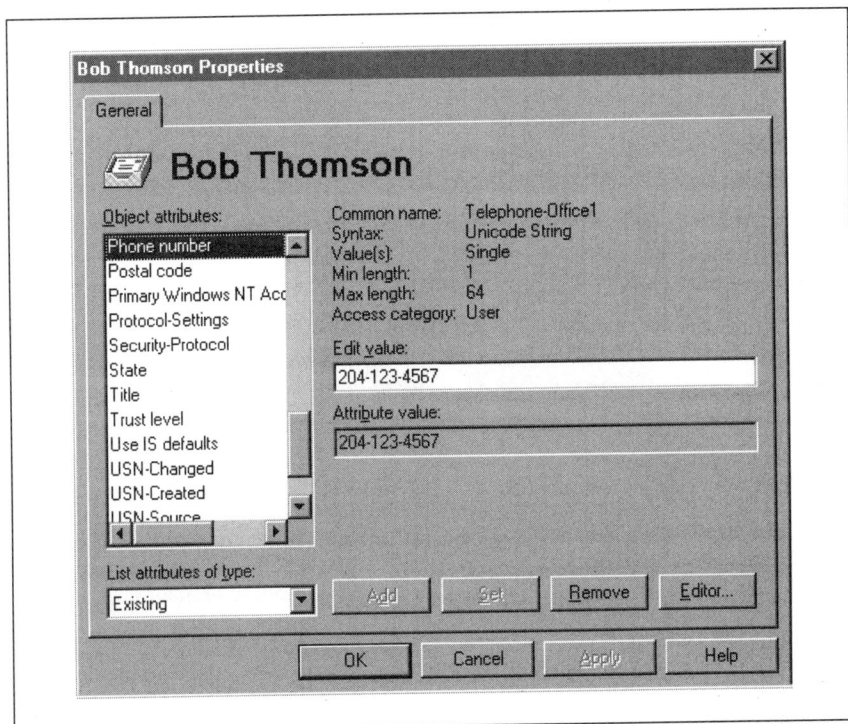

Figure 4-11: Schema attributes of a mailbox

and written to a *.csv file, which can then be used to create mailboxes for the accounts by using Tools → Directory Import.

The menu command opens the Windows NT User Extraction dialog box (Figure 4-12). Use this to specify:

– The Windows NT domain and domain controller from which you want to extract account information

– The path and filename of the *.csv export file to be created

For example, here is a sample file created by this process:

```
Obj-Class,Common-Name,Display-Name,Home-Server,Comment
Mailbox,AndyF,Andy Furgeson,~SERVER,
Mailbox,ArleneD,Arlene Davidson,~SERVER,
Mailbox,AxelD,Axel Decameron,~SERVER,
```

Using directory import on this file will automatically create mailboxes for the users in the list. If you specify a mailbox template for the process, the only settings you have to configure manually afterwards are First and Last Names. You can also import users from another NT domain by selecting the directory import option Create Windows NT Account.

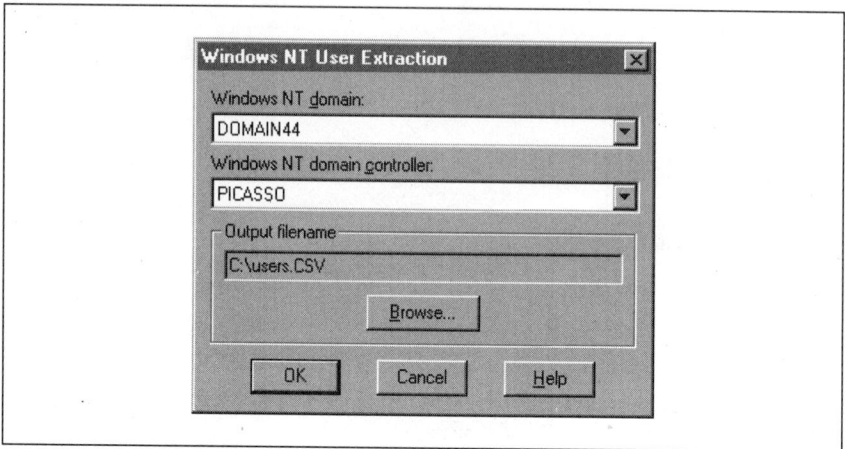

Figure 4-12: Extracting Windows NT account information

Tools → Extract NetWare Account List

Does the same thing as Tools → Extract Windows NT Account List, except for NetWare 3.x servers and 4.x servers running in bindery emulation mode. You require a supervisor account to perform this operation.

Tools → Find Recipients

Lets you search for recipients in your Exchange organization. The Find Recipients window opens (Figure 4-13), allowing you to specify a query and search for matching recipients in one of the these containers:

- Site Container
- Global Address Book
- Address Book View

Query parameters include any of the fields shown in Figure 4-13, or select Custom to search by custom attributes. Wildcards are unfortunately not supported, but partial strings may be used for query parameters. (The figure shows all Sales department people whose first names begin with R.)

Tools → Move Mailbox

Moves a mailbox to another server within the same Exchange site. This changes the home server of the mailbox.

This can have an unexpected effect on the size of the destination information store. This is because *single-instance messages* (messages sent to multiple mailboxes on one server) are stored as one instance to save space, but moving a mailbox creates copies of single instance messages it has received. As a result the destination information store may increase in size more than expected.

Tools → Add to Address Book View

Lets you change specific attributes of recipients.

For example, suppose you have an address book view called Departments, with subcontainers Sales and Management. Select your site's recipient

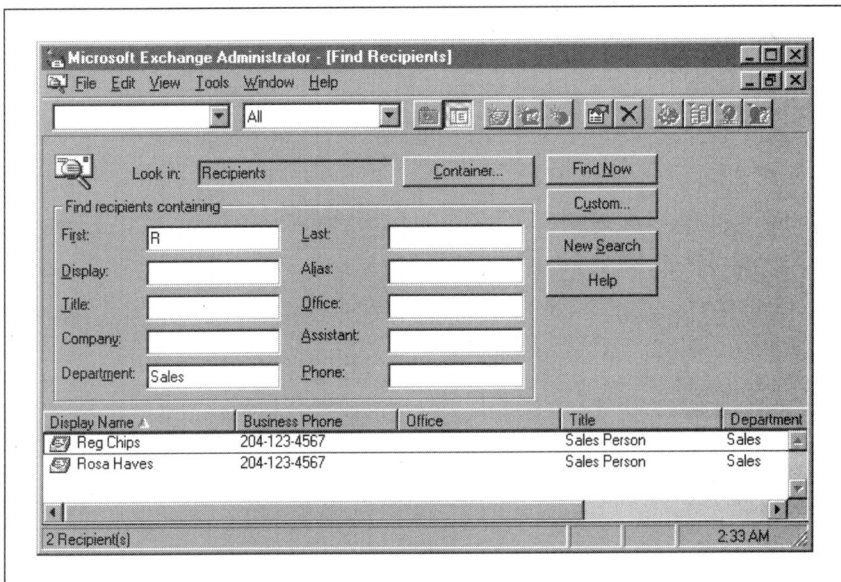

Figure 4-13: The Find Recipients window

container in the Containers pane, and then select a few mailboxes whose Department attribute is Sales. (Use CTRL-Click to make multiple selections in the Contents pane.) Now choose Tools → Add to Address Book View and add these accounts to the Management subcontainer of the Departments address book view. This automatically changes the Department attribute on the mailbox property sheets of these mailboxes to Management, leaving everything else the same.

It would be nicer, though, if you could just drag and drop recipients into an address book view!

Tools → Clean Mailbox

Lets you reclaim space for a user's mailbox from the server's private information store. You can delete messages according to the following criteria:

Age
  Delete messages older than a certain number of days.

Size
  Delete messages larger than a certain number of KB.

Sensitivity
  Delete messages that belong to any of four sensitivity levels: normal, personal, private, or confidential.

Read Status
  Deletes read messages, unread messages, or both (i.e., everything!).

Message Type
  Delete only mail messages or all types of messages, including contacts, tasks, and calendar entries.

Deferred Action Messages

Keep or delete commands queued in the deferred action folder. This includes message rules and copying or moving messages.

Action

Permanently delete messages or move them to the user's Deleted Items Folder.

Tools → Start Monitor

Starts a server or link monitor created using the File → New Other → {Server | Link} Monitor menu commands. Connects to a server you specify and starts a monitor on that server. A server or link monitor window opens to display the monitoring information. This menu item is dimmed out unless a monitor is selected in the Contents pane.

Figure 4-14 shows a typical server monitor window. The symbol in the first column indicates the condition of the server or link, as shown in Table 4-3.

Table 4-3: Symbols Indicating the State of a Server Monitor

Symbol	Description of State
Blue question mark	Unknown state
Green up arrow	Everything fine
Red exclamation point	Warning state
Red down arrow	Alert state

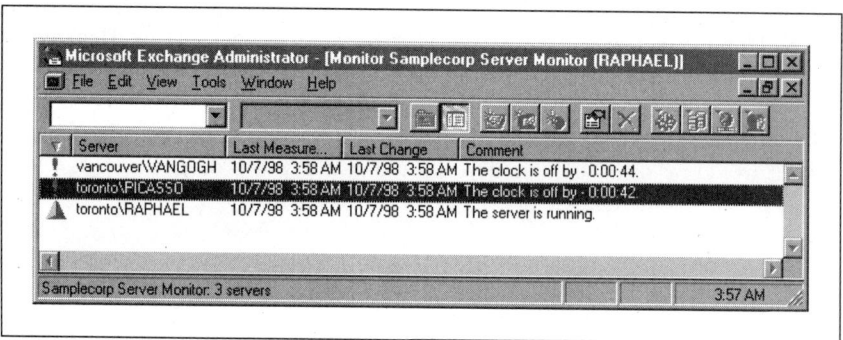

Figure 4-14: Typical server monitor window

Double-click on a server to open a modified property sheet for the monitor, displaying information such as:

- The status of Exchange services on the monitored server. You can also stop, pause, and resume Exchange services on the monitored server.

- A read-only view of the server's clock and time zone information.

- A list showing who has been notified concerning problems with the server and the form that this notification took.

- The server's current maintenance status. Lets you configure whether notifications or repairs are stopped during server maintenance.

Note that when the server monitor window is the active window in Exchange Administrator, the number of available menu options is reduced.

Figure 4-15 shows a typical link monitor window. Just as for a server monitor, double-clicking on a link will open a property sheet for the link, displaying information such as:

- Timing information for the last successful bounce message.

- A list showing who has been notified concerning problems with the link and the form that this notification took.

- The link's current maintenance status. Lets you configure whether notifications or repairs are stopped during link maintenance.

Server and link monitors can be started, stopped, and resumed from the command line using Exchange Administrator with the /m switch. Repairs and notifications started by monitors can be suspended using the /t switch. See Chapter 5 for details on the syntax of these commands.

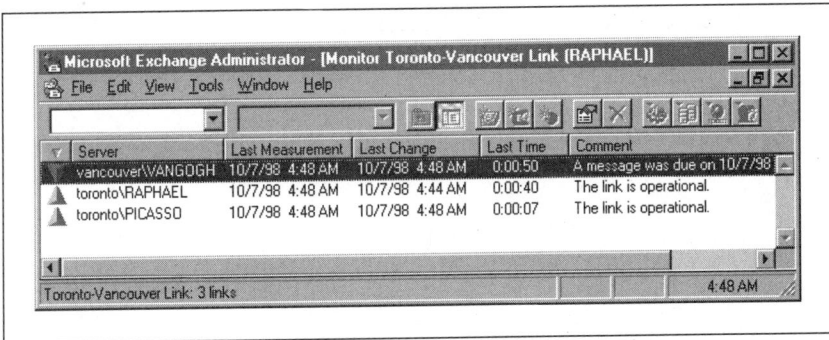

Figure 4-15: Typical link monitor window

Tools → Track Message

Opens the Exchange Message Tracking Center window (Figure 4-16) and prompts you to perform a search. With this tool you can:

- Search for messages coming from or going to a particular recipient within a specified number of days

- Perform an Advanced Search to search for a message by message ID, find all messages from external sites, or find messages generated by an Exchange service such as the system attendant

- View routing and delivery information for the messages your query finds

Note that message tracking must first be enabled on one or more Exchange components. See the entry "System Attendant" in Chapter 3 for more information.

Tools → Forms Administrator

Lets you create, modify, and assign permissions to Microsoft Exchange forms. Forms allow you to structure information for public posting or viewing. An example could be an invoice or expense report for a workgroup application

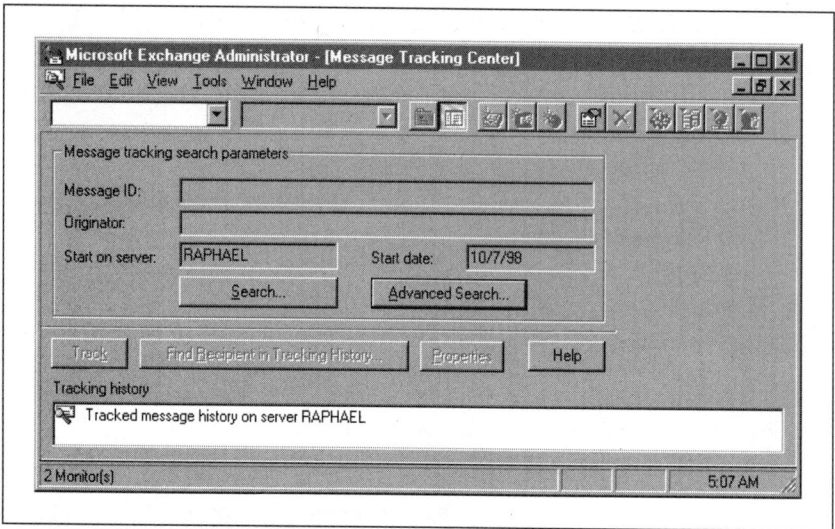

Figure 4-16: The Message Tracking Center window

or a special form used for posting to a public folder. The design and management of forms requires a treatment of its own and is beyond the scope of this book.

Tools → Newsgroup Hierarchies
Lets you turn a public folder tree into a newsgroup hierarchy.

Tools → Save Connections on Exit | Save Connections Now
Lets you configure Exchange Administrator so that the next time you start it, the same windows will open as you have now (or when you exit—it toggles between these two settings).

Tools → Customize Toolbar
Lets you add, remove, or change the position of buttons on your toolbar. The Exchange toolbar can be used instead of the menu for many common menu functions and can also be used to switch between various containers in the Container pane. The toolbar functions are summarized in Table 4-4 along with their menu bar equivalents and keyboard accelerators when available. Note that some toolbar functions are unavailable unless a specific container is selected first.

Table 4-4: Functions Available from the Exchange Toolbar and Their Menu Equivalents and Keyboard Accelerators

Function	Menu Bar Equivalent	Keyboard Accelerator
Server (select connected server)	Window → Server	
View filter (specify subset of recipients to view)	View → Mailboxes | ... | All	
Up one level		

Table 4-4: Functions Available from the Exchange Toolbar and Their Menu Equivalents and Keyboard Accelerators (continued)

Function	Menu Bar Equivalent	Keyboard Accelerator
Show/Hide Container View		
New Mailbox	File → New Mailbox	CTRL-M
New Distribution List	File → New Distribution List	CTRL-D
New Custom Recipient	File → New Custom Recipient	CTRL-R
Properties	File → Properties	ALT-ENTER
Delete	Edit → Delete	DEL
Configuration (switch to Configuration container of local site)		CTRL-SHIFT-C
Servers (switch to Servers container of local site)		CTRL-SHIFT-S
Connections (switch to Connections container of local site)		CTRL-SHIFT-N
Recipients (switch to Recipients container of local site)		CTRL-SHIFT-E
Connect to Server	File → Connect to Server	
Directory Import	Tools → Directory Import	
Directory Export	Tools → Directory Export	
Find Recipients	Tools → Find Recipients	
Move Mailbox	Tools → Move Mailbox	
Clean Mailbox	Tools → Clean Mailbox	
Start Monitor	Tools → Start Monitor	
Track Message		
Form Administrator		
Address Book Views (switch to Address Book Views container)		CTRL-SHIFT-A
Global Address List (switch to Global Address List container)		CTRL-SHIFT-G
Public Folders (switch to Public Folders container)		CTRL-SHIFT-P
Site (switch to Site container of local site)		CTRL-SHIFT-I
Monitors (switch to Monitors container of local site)		CTRL-SHIFT-T
Replication (switch to Directory Replication container of local site)		CTRL-SHIFT-R
Protocols (switch to Protocols container of local site)		CTRL-SHIFT-O
Refresh	Window → Refresh	F5

GUI Tools

Tools → Options

Lets you configure certain global settings for Exchange. These include:

- Auto Naming settings to configure the format in which display names and aliases are generated when you create new recipients. Choose from several default formats or customize your own.

- Toggling Permissions tabs on and off for directory objects and whether rights for roles should be displayed on the Permissions tab.

- Specifying the default Windows NT domain used when selecting user accounts for creating mailboxes and other operations.

- Indicating whether to try to locate a matching Windows NT account when creating a new mailbox and whether to automatically delete the associated NT account when deleting the mailbox.

- Specifying separators and character set to be used in creating *.csv* files using directory export.

> If your Exchange organization has multiple administrators who manage sites from different workstations running the Exchange Administrator, you should make sure that these options are configured the same for each copy of Exchange Administrator used.

Notes:

- Exchange Administrator can be started from the command prompt and has several useful command-line switches. These are described in the "admin" entry in Chapter 5.

Migration Wizard

Lets you migrate mailboxes, addresses, messages, and other information from third-party mail systems into Exchange.

Path

    \exchsrvr\bin\mailmig.exe

To Launch

Start → Programs → Microsoft Exchange → Microsoft Exchange Migration wizard

Start → Run → *exchsrvr\bin\mailmig.exe*

Description

The Migration Wizard, shown in Figure 4-17, is a tool for migrating mailboxes and their contents from third-party mail systems and importing them into Exchange. For MS Mail for PC Networks, Lotus cc:Mail, Novell GroupWise, and Collabra Share mail systems, the Migration Wizard can perform two functions:

- Using *source extractors* it can extract the directory, message, and (where applicable) schedule information and copy it into a set of *migration files* suitable for importing into Exchange.

- These migration files can then be imported into Exchange.

For third-party mail systems other than the ones listed earlier, a source extractor must be obtained from the vendor or custom-made for the occasion in order to generate the migration files that can then be imported using the wizard.

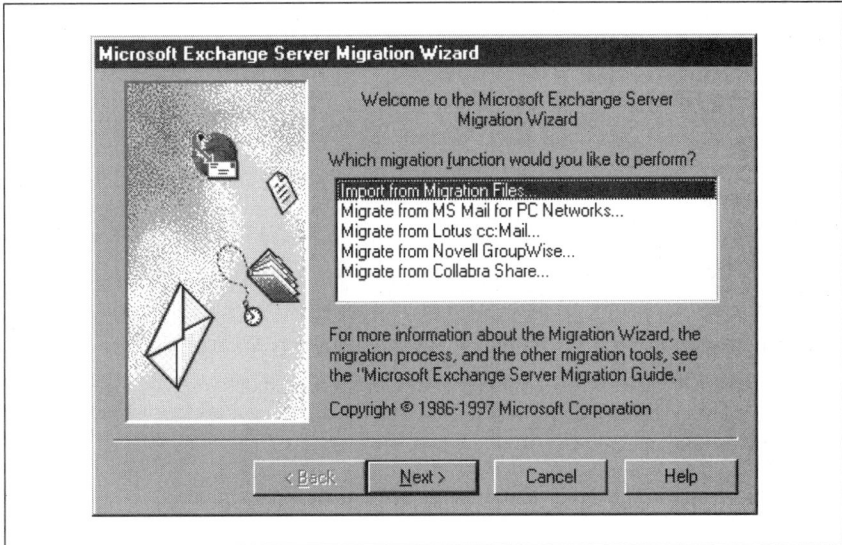

Figure 4-17: Initial screen of the Exchange Migration wizard

Generally, you can migrate your third-party mail system to Exchange in one of two ways:

Single-Phase Migration
> Moves everything at once. Use this method if you have only a small amount of information to migrate and if all the hardware and software necessary are already in place, such as connectors and gateways.

Multi-Phase Migration
> Moves information in stages, usually one group of users at a time. Use this method when a large amount of information needs to be migrated, and your administrative resources are insufficient to perform this migration all at once. In this case, both mail systems will need to coexist for a period of time until all users are successfully migrated. This requires more care and planning, including forwarding of mail from the old mail system.

Example: Migrating from MS Mail

Migration is a somewhat specialized aspect of Exchange administration, since it is likely to be performed only once or at most a few times by the administrator. Let's therefore briefly consider two examples of migration and how it works, starting with migrating from a legacy MS Mail 3.x network to Exchange. We won't look at all of the various issues involved in this migration process, such as the coexistence of mail systems and clients, migrating gateways to connectors, and so on; refer to the Exchange Books Online called "Migration" for detailed information on how to plan and implement the migration process. Instead we will focus on the role and operation of the Migration wizard in the migration process.

The Migration wizard offers three options for migrating from MS Mail to Exchange:

One-Step Approach
> The wizard extracts mailbox, message, address, and schedule information from the selected MS Mail Postoffice and imports it directly into Exchange.

Two-Step Approach
> The wizard extracts a User List file. You can then edit this file, for example, to modify the naming convention used for the migrated mailboxes or modify the associated Windows NT user account. The second step is then to import this file into Exchange.

Batch Approach
> The wizard can be run from the command line using various options. This is described in Chapter 5.

I'll briefly summarize the steps involved in the Two-Step Approach:

1. Map a drive letter or otherwise connect to the MS Mail server where the Postoffice you want to migrate resides.

2. Run the wizard and select "Migrate from MS Mail for PC Networks."

3. Enter the path to the MS Mail Postoffice you want to migrate, plus the Administrator account information for the Postoffice.

4. Select "Two-step migration" to extract a User List file from the MS Mail Postoffice.

5. Select whether to migrate the mailbox data to your Exchange server or to personal folder files (*.pst). If you don't have your Exchange server set up yet, migrate the mailbox data to *.pst files. Otherwise, migrate the data to the Exchange server.

6. Select "Step 1: Extract a User List file" and specify the path and name for the desired *.csv file.

7. Select the MS Mail accounts you wish to migrate from the list displayed.

The User List file is generated as a *.csv file. Make a backup copy of this file. Now open the *.csv file in a text editor, delete the first two lines that contain the Postoffice information, and save the changes. The resulting modified *.csv file contains the fields shown in Table 4-5. The first two fields should not be altered, and the first five fields must be kept in the same order.

Table 4-5: Fields in the MS Mail User List (.csv) File*

Field	Contents
SFS_UserName	The alias of the mailbox in the Postoffice. Do not change this field.
SFS_FullName	The display name of the mailbox in the Postoffice. Do not change this field.
MigrateUser	Y for migrate the mailbox; N for do not migrate the mailbox.
Obj-Class	Should be "mailbox". Other possible values are "remote" for custom recipient and "dl" for distribution list.
Mode	Determines what should be done with the object—create, modify, or delete. The default is create.
Common-Name	The directory name of the mailbox. Change this to match your Exchange naming convention. The default is the mailbox name.
Display-Name	The name as it is displayed in the Address Book.
Given-Name	The user's first name.
Surname	The user's last name.
Home-Server	The intended home server of the mailbox.
Comment	The comment that appears in the Address Book.
Assoc-NT-Account	The associated Windows NT account that has user access to the mailbox.

You can edit your modified *.csv* file using a spreadsheet or database program to make modifications such as changing the common name of mailboxes or associated Windows NT account. After making the desired modifications, export the information back into *.csv* format, copy the first two lines from the backup User List file to the top of your new *.csv* file, and save this file as your new User List file.

You are now ready to perform Step Two, namely to migrate the mailboxes specified in your new User List file into your Exchange server. This procedure does not delete the existing MS Mail mailboxes or their messages; it simply copies the information to your Exchange server. Here are the remaining steps involved in this Two-Step Approach to migrating MS Mail to Exchange:

8. Run the wizard and again select "Migrate from MS Mail for PC Networks."

9. Enter the path to the MS Mail Postoffice you want to migrate, plus the Administrator account information for the Postoffice.

10. Select "Two-step migration" to extract a User List file from the MS Mail Postoffice.

11. Select "Step 2: Use a User List file to do a migration" and specify the path and name for your new User List (*.csv*) file.

12. Select the information you want to import. This can include any or all of the following:

    – Information to create mailboxes

    – Personal email messages

- Shared folders
- Personal address books
- Schedule information

13. Select options for importing shared information into public folders (if specified).

14. Specify the name of the Exchange server you are importing the information into. You should normally run the Migration wizard on the destination Exchange server.

15. Specify the Recipients container on the destination server that will receive the imported mailboxes, plus an optional mailbox template if you have one.

16. Specify whether to create new Windows NT accounts for the imported users who do not have an existing Windows NT account in the Exchange server's domain.

The information will now be migrated from the MS Mail network into Exchange. This may take some time if you have a large amount of information to migrate and should be done during periods of low usage of your messaging system. Once the mailboxes and other information are imported into Exchange, you can delete the old MS Mail Postoffice or make it hidden, depending on your migration strategy.

Example: Migrating from cc:Mail

The migration process for cc:Mail is more generalized than that for Microsoft Mail and is similar to migrating from Novell GroupWise or Collabra Share. The main difference is in the format of the migration files: with MS Mail, the migration file consists of a single User List file in a *.csv format, while with cc:Mail and other mail systems, the migration files are more complex.

The Migration wizard offers two options for migrating from cc:Mail to Exchange:

One-Step Approach
> The wizard extracts mailbox, message, and address information from the selected cc:Mail server and imports it directly into Exchange.

Two-Step Approach
> The wizard extracts selected information into a set of migration files. You can then edit these migration files, for example, to modify the naming convention used for the migrated mailboxes or modify the associated Windows NT user account. The second step is then to import these migration files into Exchange.

I'll briefly summarize the steps involved in the Two-Step Approach:

1. Map a drive letter or otherwise connect to the cc:Mail server where the Postoffice you want to migrate resides.

2. Run the wizard and select "Migrate from Lotus cc:Mail."

3. Enter the path to the cc:Mail Post Office you want to migrate, the name of the Postoffice, and the password for accessing it.

4. Select "Extract Migration Files only" to extract the desired information from the cc:Mail Post Office, and specify a pathname for the migration files.

5. Select whether to migrate the mailbox data to your Exchange server or to personal folder files (*.pst). If you don't have your Exchange server set up yet, migrate the mailbox data to *.pst files. Otherwise, migrate the data to the Exchange server.

6. Specify what kinds of information you want to extract. You may select any or all of the following:

   – Information to create mailboxes

   – Personal email messages

   – Bulletin board information

7. Select the cc:Mail accounts you wish to migrate from the list displayed.

8. Specify a Windows NT account to be the owner of any public folders created during migration.

The migration files are now generated by the source extractor for cc:Mail, which is invoked using the Migration Wizard as described earlier. A source extractor is a program that can export directory information, mailboxes, addresses, distribution lists, messages, attachments, scheduling information, and public folder contents from a specific third-party mail system. A source extractor creates three types of migration files, namely:

Packing List File
> This is a *.csv file with the extension *.pkl that specifies the code-page used by other migration files and lists the various primary and secondary migration files produced during source extraction. It acts as a kind of table of contents of the various migration files produced by the source extractor.

Primary Files
> These are *.csv files with the extension *.pri that contain directory information, message headers, personal address book entries, and personal distribution lists. Primary files also contain pointers to secondary files.

Secondary Files
> These are binary files with the extension *.sec that contain actual migration data such as messages, attachments, and scheduling information, each saved in their native format. However, any header information in these files is stored in *.csv format.

Prior to continuing the migration process, you may want to edit the migration files. For example, you could edit the primary files in order to:

• Change the alias or common name of mailboxes

• Change the format of the display name

• Add additional fields to the directory, such as Phone Number or Department

• Delete messages prior to a specified date to speed the migration process

It is not recommended that you edit the secondary files in any way, as this will necessitate recalculating offsets and updating primary files.

You are now ready to perform Step Two, namely to migrate the mailboxes and other information specified in your migration files into your Exchange server. This procedure does not delete the existing cc:Mail mailboxes or their messages; it simply copies the information to your Exchange server. Here are the remaining steps involved in this Two-Step Approach to migrating cc:Mail to Exchange:

9. Run the wizard and again select "Import from Migration Files."

10. Enter the path to the packing list (*.pkl) file. All migration files should be located in the same directory and should be located on the destination Exchange server to speed migration.

11. Specify the name of the destination Exchange server.

12. Specify access options for shared data imported to public folders, if applicable.

13. Select a Recipients container as the destination for imported recipients. You can also specify a template mailbox if you have one.

14. Specify whether to create new Windows NT accounts for the imported users who do not have an existing Windows NT account in the Exchange server's domain.

The information will be migrated from the cc:Mail network into Exchange.

For detailed information on how to migrate third-party mail systems to Exchange, and how to design source extractors for unsupported mail systems, see the Exchange Books Online called "Migration."

Windows NT Backup

Lets you back up and restore critical system and user data on Exchange servers.

Path

```
%SystemRoot%\system32\ntbackup.exe
```

To Launch

Start → Programs → Administrative Tools (Common) → Backup
Start → Run → ntbackup

Description

Windows NT Backup is a standard Windows NT 4.0 administrative tool for backing up and restoring Windows NT servers. Installing Microsoft Exchange Administrator on a server installs an updated version of Windows NT Backup that facilitates backing up and restoring critical information on Exchange servers. This entry covers only the Exchange-specific features of the new Windows NT Backup tool; for general information about using Windows NT Backup, see Jody Leber's *Windows NT Backup and Restore* from O'Reilly.

Windows NT Backup (commonly just called Backup) lets you make backup copies of the Exchange directory database and information store. During a backup, users can still access their mail and public folders, but they can't during a restore. Backup can be run either locally on the Exchange servers or remotely from any Windows NT server on which Exchange Administrator is installed. To run Backup, you need to be logged on with an account that is a member of the Backup Operators local group on both the server running Backup and the Exchange servers being backed up.

If you are running Backup on a non-Exchange server, you must first connect to one Exchange server in your organization, after which you will be able to back up any Exchange server in your organization that you have network connectivity with. Choose Operations → Microsoft Exchange from the menu to open the Microsoft Exchange dialog box (Figure 4-18).

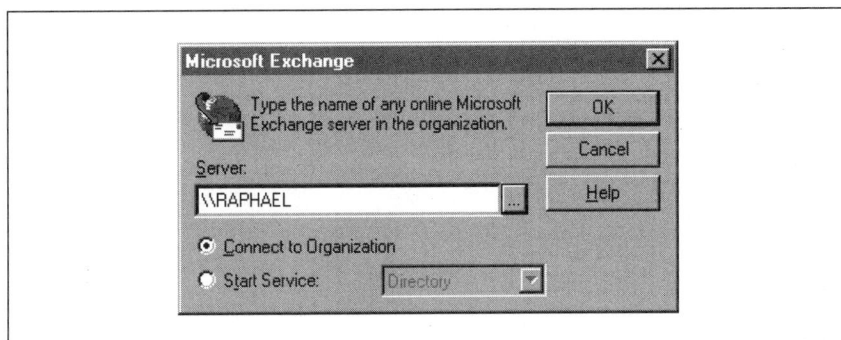

Figure 4-18: Starting Windows NT Backup

Specify or browse to an Exchange server in your organization and click OK. The Start Service option is only needed if you restored an Exchange server's components from tape and failed to select the Start Service After Restore option in the restore dialog boxes. (You may barely notice it, but the Start Service box is actually a listbox, not a textbox.)

The Microsoft Exchange window that appears shows all the available Exchange servers in your organization (Figure 4-19). Select the appropriate checkboxes in the left pane to back up:

- Your entire Exchange organization
- Selected Exchange sites
- Selected Exchange servers

Select each server separately in the left pane, and then select the appropriate checkboxes in the right pane to back up each server's:

- Directory database
- Information store

Note that a server's public and private information stores are both backed up together; during a restore, however, you have the option of restoring one or both of these components.

Select other items to back up such as drives or the Windows NT registry, configure the tape options, and start the backup in the usual way.

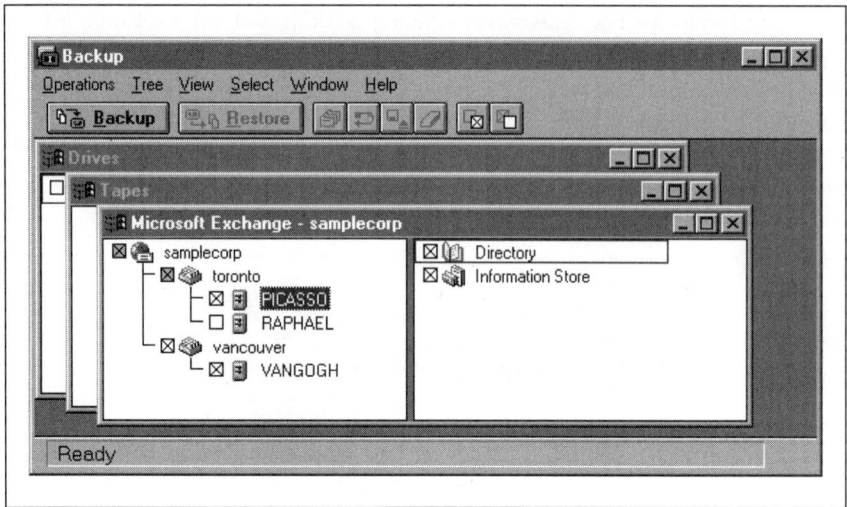

Figure 4-19: Selecting Exchange components to back up

Notes

- Exchange is able to allow users to continue sending and receiving mail during a backup because its directory database and information store are transaction-based. This means that directory changes are both logged in a transaction file and written to an instruction cache and are then asynchronously performed as necessary. This provides a measure of fault-tolerance for the directory database and information store but generates huge log files on busy servers.

  One way around this is to enable circular logging, where old transaction logs are overwritten once they have been committed to the directory. This will ensure log files don't grow beyond about 100MB, but unfortunately makes differential or incremental backups impossible; only normal (full) backups copy both the directory and those log files with uncommitted transactions. See the tip in the "Server" entry in Chapter 3 for more about enabling and disabling circular logging on Exchange servers.

- Be sure to regularly back up the directory on every Exchange server in your organization. Some of the information in a server's directory database is specific to that server and needed for performing restores.

- To restore an Exchange server that has failed completely:

  1. Remove the server's computer account from the domain.

  2. Reformat the hard drive and install Windows NT 4.0 with the same service pack level as was previously installed (NT SP3 or 4). Use the same server name as before.

  3. Run `setup /r` to install Exchange but prevent its services from starting. Make sure you use the same organization, site, and server names you had before. (Case matters here.)

4. Restore the directory from backup.

5. Restore the information store from backup.

6. Run the DS/IS Consistency Adjustment utility. This harmonizes the folder and mailbox information in the directory and information store and can be found on the Advanced tab of the Exchange server's property sheet.

There are many other possible restore scenarios, from partial restores to restoring to other servers. More information can be found in the "Maintenance and Troubleshooting" section of Exchange Books Online, but a much better resource is the "Disaster Recovery Whitepaper" which is available on the Microsoft web site or on the Microsoft TechNet compact disc.

- You can run Windows NT Backup from the command line or a batch file and schedule it using the at command. See Chapter 5 for details.

Outlook 98

Lets you create and manage public folders within a Microsoft Exchange organization.

Path

```
\Program Files\Microsoft Office\Office\outlook.exe
```

To Launch

Start → Programs → Microsoft Outlook
Start → Run → \Program Files\Microsoft Office\Office\outlook.exe

Description

Microsoft Outlook 98 is the newest version of the client-side component of Microsoft Exchange and lets users manage their mail, schedule, contacts, and tasks. Although the primary tool for administering Exchange servers is the Exchange Administrator program *admin.exe*, there is one aspect of the Exchange directory space that you must use Outlook to manage: *public folders*.

Surprisingly, the Exchange Administrator program can be used to manage public folders, but cannot be used to create them; client programs such as Microsoft Outlook must be used to create public folders. Basic configuration of the new folder can be done using Outlook, but for full control over all the folder's properties you must use Exchange Administrator. Probably the reason for this approach is to free administrators from the task by empowering users to create their own public folders for collaboration and workgroup sharing of information. Not every company's management appreciates this "empowerment," however, so as administrator you may often find yourself requested by management to create public folders for users with specific client permissions.

To create a new public folder, open Outlook and select File → New Folder to open the Create New Folder dialog box. Specify a name for the folder and the type of items it will contain, select All Public Folders within the folder hierarchy as the location to create the new folder, and click OK (see Figure 4-20).

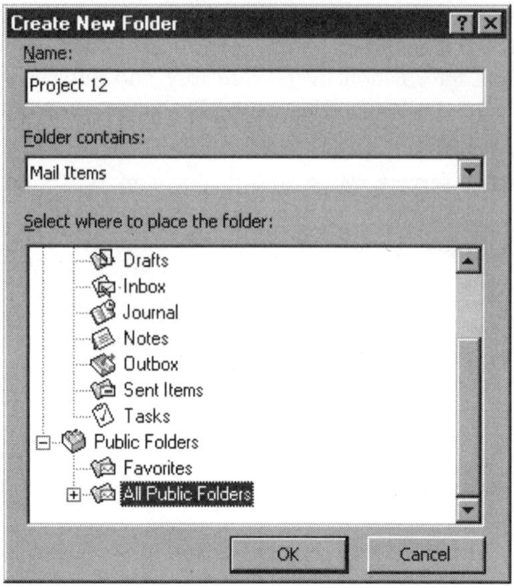

Figure 4-20: Creating a new public folder using Outlook 98

Once the new public folder has been created, its properties can be configured using either Outlook or Exchange Administrator. Outlook can only configure a limited selection of public folder properties; for full administration of the folder, use Exchange Administrator.

It's a good idea to restrict the creation of top-level public folders to administrators only and then give users permission to create subfolders only under these top-level folders. Otherwise, things get out of control fast and the folder list starts looking ugly in Outlook.

To configure public folder properties using Outlook, select View → Folder List to open the folder list pane, expand the folder hierarchy to locate the public folder, right-click on the new public folder, and select Properties from the shortcut menu. This opens the property sheet for the new public folder (Figure 4-21). Some of the more important settings that the owner (creator) of the folder can configure include:

- *Folder availability.* Leave as All Users With Access Permission unless you are going to edit the folder design.

- *Folder assistant.* Create or modify the rules for processing new postings to the folder. Rules trigger actions such as sending an automated reply when certain message conditions occur. For example, you could create a rule to reject any posting that has an attachment.

Outlook Tips

Although this book is about Exchange Server, administrators in smaller companies often find themselves not only maintaining the server-side but also providing client-side support to end users. Here are a few tips on situations you may have to deal with as an Exchange/Outlook administrator:

- Messages with attachments received over the Internet may often contain viruses, and unless you are really on top of things, your anti-virus configuration files may get out of date and be unable to trap and eradicate the little buggers, especially rapidly evolving strains of Word macro viruses. What happens if an employee receives a message with a virus and then forwards it to everyone in your company? Tell the employee immediately to open his Sent Items folder, select the forwarded message, and select Actions → Recall This Message.

- Outlook users cannot add recipients directly to the Global Address List (GAL), but sometimes you wish they could, as for example when users collect email addresses of business contacts and want to share them with the whole company. The solution is simply to create a new public contacts folder for these items and give users permissions that enable everyone to view and update items in the folder. You really don't want users messing up the GAL anyway!

- If a user has a few contacts in his address book that you *really* want to bring into the GAL, the user can use Outlook to export these users to a *.csv* file and then you can use Directory Import to import them into Exchange.

- You can use *profgen.exe* and *newprof.exe* from the BackOffice Resource Kit 2 together with logon scripts to set up roaming profiles for Exchange users. Another useful tool for this purpose is the third-party utility Profile-Maker from *http://www.profilemaker.com*.

- If your Outlook clients seem to take a long time to connect to your Exchange server, you may have to configure the RPC binding order. See Chapter 2, *Architecture and Operation*, for more information on this.

- *Moderated folder.* Items posted to the folder must be reviewed and accepted by the designated moderator before they can be made available.

- *Associated forms.* Add and delete forms for standardizing user postings to the folder.

- *Permissions.* Assign and modify permissions to control who can view, create, modify, or delete items in the folder.

To further configure the public folder, open its property sheet in Exchange Administrator. See the entry "Public Folder" in Chapter 3 for more details on configuring public folders.

Figure 4-21: Configuring a public folder using Outlook 98

Performance Optimizer

Lets you tune the performance of your Exchange server based on its role, configuration, and hardware components.

Path

```
\exchsrvr\bin\perfwiz.exe
```

To Launch

Start → Programs → Microsoft Exchange → Microsoft Exchange Optimizer
Start → Run → `\exchsrvr\bin\perfwiz.exe`

Description

Performance Optimizer is a wizard-based tool that analyzes your server's disk and memory resources and its role in your Exchange organization (e.g., bridgehead server, public folder server, etc.) and then recommends how to reconfigure your system for best performance. You are prompted to run the Optimizer at the end of installing Exchange and should run it whenever you modify your server's hardware or reconfigure its role.

For example, you should run Performance Optimizer when you:

- Add a new physical or logical drive

- Create a stripe set or mirror set

- Add more RAM

- Add, remove, or configure a connector or gateway

- Change the role of the server, for example, by deleting the private information store and making it a dedicated public folder server
- Change the anticipated load on the server, for example, if you planned to support 500 users and you are adding an additional 1,000 mailboxes

Based on its analysis, Performance Optimizer may make suggestions such as:

- Moving the transaction logs to the logical drive with fastest sequential access time
- Moving the information stores to the logical drive with fastest random access time
- Adding additional logical drives, stripe sets, or mirror sets
- Modifying the cache size for the directory and information store

The steps that the Optimizer wizard performs are:

1. All Exchange services are first stopped on the server you are optimizing.

2. You are prompted to provide the Optimizer with information about the expected number of mailboxes that will be homed on the server, the total number of mailboxes in your entire organization, and whether the server's role(s) will be to store users' mailboxes, store public folders, connect sites together, perform directory imports or exports, connect to other servers, or host Internet services such as POP3, IMAP4, or NNTP (see Figure 4-22). In particular, you can select any or all of the following server roles:

   Private Store
   This server will host users' mailboxes.

   Public Store
   This server will host public folder replicas.

   Connector/Directory Import
   This server will function as a backbone or bridgehead server for connecting sites together or for establishing messaging connectivity with foreign mail systems.

   Multiserver
   Clear this checkbox if you only have one Exchange server in your organization; otherwise, leave it checked.

   IMAP4/POP3/NNTP
   Check this if your server is being used for Internet mail or news only. Clear the checkbox if you are using MAPI clients such as Outlook or Outlook Web Access.

3. If your server is running other applications or services besides Exchange, you can also specify how much RAM Exchange will be allowed to use. The absolute minimum is 24MB, but 32MB is a more realistic minimum. Specifying 0MB allows Exchange to use as much RAM as it needs, but Exchange Version 5.5 now uses Dynamic Buffer Allocation (DBA) for allocating memory. The result is that Exchange uses as much memory as it needs and will release memory to other applications on the server as needed. So it's better just to leave the setting at 0MB and let Exchange manage memory on the server.

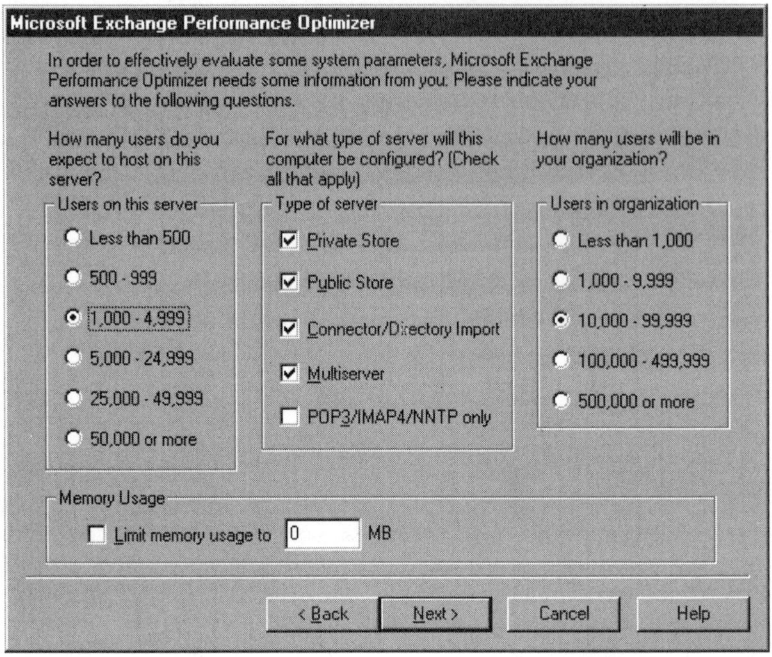

Figure 4-22: Running the Exchange Performance Optimizer wizard

4. At this point your server will be reconfigured if necessary, and the Exchange services that were previously stopped will be restarted. Entries are appended to the Performance Optimizer log file located in *%SystemRoot%\system32\perfopt.log*, documenting the configuration changes to your system. The sample log here is fairly easy to interpret:

```
----------------------------------------------------------------
Microsoft Exchange Server Performance Optimizer log file
opened.
----------------------------------------------------------------
Detected 1 processor(s)
Detected 133603328 bytes physical memory
Found fixed logical disk C:
The database file C:\exchsrvr\MDBDATA\PRIV.EDB is consistent.
The database file C:\exchsrvr\MDBDATA\PUB.EDB is consistent.
The database file C:\exchsrvr\DSADATA\dir.edb is consistent.
Set # of information store buffers from 1000 to 32618
Set # of directory buffers from 1000 to 32618
Set Minimum # of information store threads from 8 to 10
Set Maximum # of information store threads from 20 to 50
Set # of directory threads from 48 to 50
Set Maximum # of concurrent read threads from 0 to 10
Set # of background threads from 25 to 37
Set # of information store gateway in threads from 1 to 2
```

```
Set # of information store gateway out threads from 1 to 2
Set Buffer Threshold Low Percent from 5 to 3
Set Buffer Threshold High Percent from 15 to 3
Set Maximum # of pool threads from 10 to 50
Set # of dispatcher threads from 1 to 2
Set # of transfer threads from 1 to 2
Set # of kernel threads from 1 to 3
Set # of database data buffers per object from 3 to 6
Set # of RTS threads from 1 to 3
Set # of concurrent MDB/delivery queue clients from 3 to 10
Set # of concurrent XAPI sessions from 80 to 30
Set # of MT gateway clients from 8 to 10
Set # of retrieval queue clients from 2 to 10
------------------------------------------------------------
Microsoft Exchange Server Performance Optimizer log file
closed.
------------------------------------------------------------
```

How well should you trust Performance Optimizer? One school of thought is that you shouldn't trust wizards at all. Instead, experiment with providing Performance Optimizer with different information, subject your server to artificial loads using *Loadsim.exe,* and monitor your server's resulting performance using Windows NT Performance Monitor, Exchange server and link monitors, and other monitoring tools. Learn to navigate the Registry, tweak the Exchange settings, and observe the effect.

I think this is a poor approach for two reasons. Tweaking Registry settings to try to squeeze out additional performance advantages is a dangerous way to go. And who has the time these days to study their servers in a test tube? Instead, some good advice I heard from a friend of mine who is a network administrator was that his number-one priority when he has a new project is to lobby his boss for enough money to ensure hardware overkill. (If his boss doesn't agree, he yells.) In other words, always buy over-powered hardware and you'll never have to worry about optimizing performance; it will always run smoothly and you'll save yourself hours and hours of fiddling.

His recipe for the hardware needed to run an Exchange server for a medium-sized company (about 500 users) might be something like this:

- Pentium II 300MHz or faster, with motherboard option for a second processor
- 256MB RAM minimum; more preferred
- Separate physical disk for Windows NT operating system and pagefile
- Mirrored disk set for transaction log files
- RAID 5 stripe set with parity for other Exchange components such as the information stores and directory database
- One or more 100Mbps network cards

Configure the hardware as described here, install Exchange, run the Performance Optimizer, and you're all set. Just don't forget your backups!

Notes:

For the brave or adventurous, you can run Performance Optimizer from the command line and access more detailed configuration screens. See the entry "perfwiz" in Chapter 5 for details.

Speaking of hardware, there is an interesting problem that can occur on Exchange servers that have a lot of RAM (more than 1GB) and are heavily used: out of memory errors! The errors are caused by Exchange attempting to allocate more virtual memory than it has available within a process. Essentially, it is a problem with the way Performance Optimizer handles memory allocation for systems with large amounts of RAM. Microsoft has a fix for this; refer to *Microsoft Knowledge Base* article Q195006.

User Manager for Domains

Lets you create new users together with their Exchange mailboxes.

Path

```
%SystemRoot%\system32\usrmgr.exe
```

To Launch

Start → Programs → Administrative Tools (Common) → User Manager for Domains
Start → Run → usrmgr

Description

User Manager for Domains is a standard Windows NT 4.0 administrative tool for creating and configuring accounts for users and groups. Installing Microsoft Exchange Administrator on a server installs an extension for User Manager that allows you to create mailboxes for new users and access the property sheet of an existing user's mailbox. This article covers only the Exchange-specific features of the modified version of User Manager; for general information about using User Manager see *Windows NT User Administration*, by Ashley J. Meggitt and Timothy D. Ritchey (O'Reilly).

The extension for User Manager installed with the Exchange Administrator program has a new top-level menu called Exchange. The following are descriptions of the new menu options:

Exchange → Options
Lets you toggle whether to always:

– Create a new mailbox when a new user account is created.

– Delete the user's mailbox when their account is deleted.

–   Prompt the administrator to connect to an Exchange server in your organization each time a mailbox is created. This allows you to specify different home servers for different user accounts you create.

Lets you specify an Exchange server as the default home server for all user accounts you create.

Lets you specify a recipient container in your site for the mailboxes you create. If None is selected, the mailboxes are created in the Recipients container of the connected server.

Exchange → Properties
Opens the mailbox property sheet for the selected user account. You are prompted to browse to other servers in your organization if the mailbox is not on the connected server.

User Manager is most useful for creating new user accounts along with their associated mailboxes. To accomplish this, do the following:

1. Select File → New User.

2. Configure the property sheet for the user account and click Add.

3. Configure the mailbox property sheet and click OK.

4. Continue repeating steps 2 and 3 for additional new users.

CHAPTER 5

Command-Line Tools

This chapter covers the command-line tools that can be used for administering Exchange. As I indicated previously in Chapter 4, *GUI Tools*, probably 98 percent of Exchange administration must be performed using the GUI tools in that chapter. The command-line tools described here are used the other 2 percent of the time, and the kinds of tasks you can perform with them are limited and focus mainly on maintenance and troubleshooting. Some of them are simply GUI tools run from the command line with switches; others are command-line tools that are used only in an emergency and often in consultation with Microsoft Technical Support.

The eight tools covered here are ordered alphabetically according to their command-line equivalents (executable filenames), namely:

admin
Exchange Administrator (using command-line switches)

edbutil
Exchange Database Maintenance Utility (4.0/5.0 Version)

eseutil
Exchange Database Maintenance Utility (5.5 Version)

isinteg
Information Store Integrity Checker

mailmig
Exchange Migration Wizard (batch mode)

mtacheck
Message Transfer Agent Check Utility

ntbackup
Windows NT Backup (Exchange-aware Version)

perfwiz
Performance Optimizer (verbose mode)

admin

Lets you launch the Exchange Administrator program in special modes and perform various administrative tasks.

Path

```
\exchsrvr\bin\admin.exe
```

To Launch

```
admin /e ExportFile [/d DirectoryServerName /n /o OptionsFile]
admin /h
admin /i ImportFile [/d DirectoryServerName /n /o OptionsFile]
admin /m [SiteName\]MonitorName\ServerName]
admin /r
admin /s ServerName
admin /t [r | n | nr]
admin /?
```

Description

There are a number of options that can be used when running the Exchange Administrator program *admin.exe* from the command line. Some of these switches open the GUI window of the Administrator program, while others are used to perform some specific administrative task.

Command-Line Options

`<null>`
    Runs the Exchange Administrator program in normal GUI mode.

`/e ExportFile [/d DirectoryServerName /n /o OptionsFile]`
    Runs a command-line version of the Directory Export utility of Exchange Administrator that can be used to write information about mailboxes and other recipients to a text file. You can include this command in a batch file and schedule its execution using the Windows NT *at.exe* command.

The options in this command are:

`/e ExportFile`
    This is the only required option. *ExportFile* is the name of a text file to which the directory information will be written. This information is written in comma-delimited (*.csv*) format. If the file already exists, the old one is renamed with the extension *.A01*.

By default, Directory Export only exports the subset directory attributes shown in Table 5-1. These default attributes are relevant only if you are exporting recipient information (which is usually the case). When you export recipient information, the first line of the *ExportFile* is a header consisting of the various attributes listed in Table 5-1 separated by commas:

```
Obj-Class,First Name,Last Name,Display Name,
Alias Name,Directory Name,Primary Windows NT Account
Home-Server,Email Address,Email Addresses,Members,
Obj-Container,Hide from AB
```

Table 5-1: Attributes Exported by Default Using Directory Export

Attribute	Description
Obj-Class	Type of object
First Name	First name
Last Name	Last name
Display Name	Name of object in Exchange Administrator window
Alias Name	Alternate name of recipient
Directory Name	Internal name of object in directory database
Primary Windows NT Account	Windows NT domain\account associated with recipient
Home-Server	Server where recipient is homed
Email Address	Email address of custom recipient
Email Addresses	Multivalued string consisting of all email addresses belonging to recipient, separated by separator character ("%")
Members	Distribution lists to which the recipient belongs
Obj-Container	Container where recipient resides
Hide from AB	Whether recipient is hidden (1) or visible (0)

If you want to export different attributes—for example, if you wanted to export the attributes of all connectors in your site—you unfortunately need to preconfigure an *ExportFile* that contains a new header listing the various attributes you want to export, separated by commas. There are several ways to approach this:

- Manually create the header in your new *ExportFile* using a text editor. See the entry "Exchange Administrator" in Chapter 4 for an example of this. To determine the correct name for each attribute of the type of object you want to export, you can view the properties of the object when running Exchange Administrator in Raw Mode (see Appendix C, *Raw Mode*).

- Use the Import Header tool in the Microsoft Exchange Server Resource Kit.

/d DirectoryServerName

Lets you specify the name of the Exchange server from which the directory information will be obtained.

/n Suppresses the GUI bar showing the progress of the export process.

/o OptionsFile

Lets you specify which export options are selected. These options parallel those available in the Directory Export dialog box when Tools → Directory Export is selected in the Exchange Administrator window. The *OptionsFile* is a text file similar to an *.ini* file, which can contain any subset of the options shown in Table 5-2. Examples of using the *OptionsFile* are provided later in this section.

Table 5-2: Available Options in the Directory Export Options File

Line of OptionsFile	Description	Default
`[Export]`	First line of file (required)	
`DirectorySer-vice=ServerName`	Name of Exchange server from which the export process will be run	Local server
`HomeServer=ServerName`	Name of Exchange server on which recipients are homed	Local server
`Basepoint=DN_of_basepoint`	Distinguished Name of the basepoint of the directory hierarchy from which to export directory information	Local site
`Container=RDN_of_container`	Relative Distinguished Name of the container from which to export recipient information	Recipients container
`ExportObject=[Mailbox | Remote | DL | Recipients | All]`	Type(s) of directory objects to be exported. Remote exports Custom Recipients, Recipients exports all recipients, and All exports all object types	Mailbox
`InformationLevel=[None | Minimal | Full]`	Level of information to be exported for each directory object	Minimal
`BasepointOnly=[Yes | No]`	Whether to export only the directory information for the basepoint	No
`RawMode=[Yes, No]`	Whether to export information in raw mode	No
`Hiddenobjects=[Yes | No]`	Whether to export information for hidden objects	No
`Subcontainers=[Yes |No]`	Whether to export information for all subcontainers of selected container	No
`CodePage=[-1 | 0 | codepage-ID]`	Codepage for exported information	0
`ColumnSeparator=xx`	ASCII value of column separator character	44 (=comma)
`MVSeparator=xx`	ASCII value of multivalue separator character	37 (=percent)
`QuoteCharacter=xx`	ASCII value of quoted value delimiter	34 (=double-quote)

/h Opens the GUI window of Exchange Administrator and simultaneously opens a help window describing these command-line options.

/i `ImportFile` [/d `DirectoryServerName` /n /o `OptionsFile`]
Runs a command-line version of the Directory Import utility of Exchange Administrator that can be used to import information about mailboxes and other recipients from a text file.

The options in this command are similar to those of the /e switch described earlier. For more on Directory Export/Import, see the entry "Exchange Administrator" in Chapter 4.

/m[*SiteName*\]*MonitorName**ServerName*
> Opens the GUI window of Exchange Administrator and runs the specified Server Monitor or Link Monitor. *MonitorName* is the directory name of the Monitor, *ServerName* is the name of the server you want to connect to in order to run the Monitor, and *SiteName* is the directory name of the site in which the Monitor is defined. *SiteName* needs to be included only if the Monitor is not located within the site in which the server resides.

/r
> Opens the GUI window of Exchange Administrator in raw mode, exposing all directory attributes for each directory object selected. See Appendix C for more information.

/s *ServerName*
> Opens the GUI window of Exchange Administrator and connects to the specified server to obtain directory information.

/t [r | n | nr]
> Lets you suspend repairs and notifications that are initiated by Server Monitors and Link Monitors. Use this command when performing scheduled maintenance on a server being monitored. This prevents unnecessary alerts and email notifications from being generated and stops Monitors from initiating repairs on servers that have been deliberately taken offline.

If you have a Server Monitor running and fail to use admin /t on a server you want to perform maintenance on, an amusing thing may happen: you keep trying to shut down the Exchange services on your server, and they keep restarting again! Run admin /t nr and wait at least one polling interval for the Server Monitor before stopping the services on your server. When maintenance is complete and your server has been brought online again, run admin /t.

The four options available here are:

/t nr
> Suspends repairs and notifications from being initiated on the server by a Monitor.

/t n
> Suspends only notifications. If the Monitor detects a problem with the server, it will attempt repairs but will not send a notification. For example, if an essential service is stopped on the server, a Server Monitor may try to restart the service.

/t r
> Suspends only repairs. If the Monitor detects a problem with the server, it will send a notification but will not attempt to initiate repairs.

/t Resets the behavior of all Monitors with regard to the server.

/? Opens online help and displays information regarding the preceding switches.

Examples

To start a Server Monitor whose directory name is Watchman and run it on a server Raphael, use the following command from the *exchsrvr**bin* directory:

```
admin /mWatchman\Raphael
```

To export directory information about all recipients homed on server *Picasso* in the local site, first create an *<OptionsFile>* called *opts.ini* located in the *exchsrvr*\ *bin* directory and containing the following lines:

```
[Export]
HomeServer=Picasso
ExportObject=Recipients
```

Now run the following command from the *exchsrvr**bin* directory:

```
admin /e c:\testing /o opts.ini
```

To export directory information about all connectors in the site Toronto of organization SampleCorp, use the following options file:

```
[Export]
ExportObject=All
Subcontainers=Yes
Basepoint=/o=samplecorp/ou=toronto/cn=configuration
Container=connections
```

You will also need to create a new *ExportFile* that contains a header specifying which directory attributes you want to export for the connectors. Run the same command outlined earlier.

Notes

- You can configure a Server or Link Monitor to start automatically upon rebooting as follows:

  1. Create a new shortcut with the following command line:

     ```
     C:\exchsrvr\bin\admin.exe /mSiteName\MonitorName\ServerName
     ```

  2. Place the shortcut in the Startup program group. Configure your Exchange server to automatically log on using the administrator account when the server reboots by creating the AutoAdminLogon Registry entry. To do this, open the following Registry key:

     HKLM\SOFTWARE\Microsoft\Windows NT\CurrentVersion\Winlogon

  3. Specify the following values for the administrator account (create these values if any of them are not present):

     DefaultDomainName

     DefaultPassword

     DefaultUserName

  4. Create a new value called AutoAdminLogon of data type REG_SZ and assign it the value 1. Make sure your server's console is physically secure as it will automatically log on with the administrator's account whenever it is booted!

- Note the back slashes in the syntax for the /m switch. This is correct; the online documentation has forward slashes.

- You can start several monitors at once from the command line using multiple /m switches.

edbutil

Lets you defragment, repair, and check the integrity of the information store and directory databases (Exchange 4.0/5.0 only).

Path

```
\exchsrvr\bin\edbutil.exe
```

To Launch

```
edbutil /b BackupPath [options]
edbutil /c DatabaseName [options]
edbutil /d DatabaseName [options]
edbutil /mModeModifier FileName
edbutil /r [options]
edbutil /u DatabaseName /dPreviousDLL [options]
```

Description

Although this JET database maintenance utility is included with Exchange 5.5, you *must* use eseutil instead of edbutil when attempting to repair or defragment databases on Version 5.5 of Exchange Server since these databases are based on the newer JET97 database technology. eseutil replaces the earlier edbutil utility; use edbutil only for Exchange Versions 4.0 and 5.0. Because this book deals with Version 5.5 of Exchange, we will deal with the syntax of edbutil briefly here and will cover only those options that are different from the newer utility eseutil.

/b BackupPath [options]
    This switch is not documented by Microsoft but was intended to be used to back up Exchange databases to a temporary directory. Use *ntbackup.exe* instead.

/c DatabaseName [options]
    Use the /c switch to verify the consistency of a database. The *DatabaseName* parameter is the same as for the /d switch, while the possible options here are shown in Table 5-3.

Table 5-3: Explanation of Options Available for edbutil /c

Option for edbutil /c	Description
/a	Checks all nodes including deleted ones
/k	Generates key usage statistics
/p	Generates page usage statistics
/t *TableName*	Checks the specified table
/o	Suppresses the Exchange banner

/d *DatabaseName* [options]

The options are the same as for `eseutil` /d except:

- – The option r also repairs the database while defragmenting.
- – The option n dumps defragmentation information into the file *dfrginfo.txt*.

/m*ModeModifier FileName*

The options are the same as for `eseutil` /m except the "l" option is not supported.

/r [options]

The options are the same as for `eseutil` /r.

/u *DatabaseName* /d*PreviousDLL* [options]

The options are the same as for `eseutil` /u except the option n also dumps the upgrade information into the file *upgdinfo.txt*.

---

eseutil

Lets you defragment, repair, and check the integrity of the information store and directory databases (Exchange 5.5 only).

Path

    \%SystemRoot%\system32\eseutil.exe

To Launch

    eseutil /d DatabaseName [options]
    eseutil /g DatabaseName [options]
    eseutil /mModeModifier FileName
    eseutil /p DatabaseName [options]
    eseutil /r [options]
    eseutil /u DatabaseName /dPreviousDLL [options]

Description

`eseutil` is a JET97 database maintenance utility located in the system path and can be used to perform the following actions on an information store or directory database:

Check database integrity

Check the database for records that are damaged or unreadable

Defragment a database

Eliminate free space within a database and reduce its size and performance

Repair a corrupt database

Attempts to rebuild the database tables using only readable and undamaged records

`eseutil` is not considered a tool for regular maintenance of Exchange servers but rather a troubleshooting tool to be used in an emergency. (Microsoft recommends using `eseutil` only when in consultation with Microsoft Technical Support.) Be sure you have backed up your Exchange databases before running this utility.

Command-Line Options

<null>

Displays help information for `eseutil` at the command line. Press a key specified in Table 5-4 for further information on specific uses of `eseutil`.

Table 5-4: Help Keys and Switches for eseutil

Key for Help	Help Topic/eseutil Function	eseutil Switch
D	Defragmenting a database	/d
G	Checking the integrity of a database	/g
M	Performing a file dump of a database	/m
P	Attempting a repair of a database	/p
R	Attempting a recovery of a database	/r
U	Upgrading a database	/u

Pressing any other key returns you to the command prompt.

/d *DatabaseName* [options]

Lets you perform an offline compaction of an information store or directory database. Compacting a database frees up unused space in and reduces the size of the database, causing it to perform more efficiently. Since this process also makes database records contiguous, it is also referred to as *defragmentation*—hence the /d switch.

`eseutil /d` works by creating a new database and copying the records of the old database one at a time to the new database. (Make sure there is sufficient space for this to occur.) When this is finished, the old database is either deleted or moved to a new location, and the new database is renamed as the original one. If an unreadable record is encountered, the process stops with an error. Because the process makes a copy of the database, you must make sure that you have sufficient free space prior to running it.

Make *sure* you have free disk space equal to 110 percent of the size of the database you are compacting; otherwise, the process will fail. Also make sure you have scheduled sufficient maintenance time to run this utility. `eseutil /d` can defragment a database at a rate of approximately 10GB/hr.

Stop your Exchange Directory Service using the Services utility in the Control Panel before running `eseutil /d`. Because of service dependencies, this will also stop the Information Store and Message Transfer Agent services.

DatabaseName

This can be either the actual name (full path) of the database to be compacted or a switch representing that database. The filenames, their usual path, and the switches representing them are listed in Table 5-5.

Table 5-5: Exchange Databases, Their Default Paths, and the eseutil Switch Representing Them

Exchange Database	Default Path	eseutil DatabaseName Switch
Private information store	\exchsrvr\mdbdata\priv.edb	/ispriv
Public information store	\exchsrvr\mdbdata\pub.edb	/ispub
Directory	\exchsrvr\dsadata\dir.edb	/ds

[Options]

Specify zero or more of the options shown in Table 5-6, each separated by a space. If a path is not specified, the default path is the current directory.

Table 5-6: Explanation of Options Available for eseutil /d

Option for eseutil /d	Description
/l path	Specifies the location of transaction log files for the database
/s path	Specifies the location of checkpoint file and other database system files
/b path	Creates a backup copy of the original uncompacted database in the specified location
/t filename	Renames the new compacted database
/p	Keeps the original uncompacted database in the default location and locates the new compacted database in the current directory with the name *Tempdfrg.edb*
/o	Hides the Exchange banner

> Running eseutil /d with the /p option is useful if you just want to test the defragmentation process before actually running it live using the /b option.

/g *DatabaseName* [options]

Verifies the integrity of an information store or directory database by searching for damaged or unreadable records. No attempt is made to repair damaged records. This command is also known as the *eseutil consistency checker.*

Stop your Exchange Directory Service using the Services utility in the Control Panel before running eseutil /g.

DatabaseName

The actual name (full path) of the database to be compacted or a switch representing that database. (See Table 5-5.)

[Options]

Specify zero or more of the options shown in Table 5-7, each separated by a space. If a path is not specified, the default path is the current directory.

Table 5-7: Explanation of Options Available for eseutil /g

Option for eseutil /g	Description
/t filename	Specifies the temporary database name (the default is *Integ.edb*)
/v	Switches to verbose mode
/x	Gives detailed error messages when errors occur
/o	Hides the Exchange banner

/mModeModifier FileName

Lets you perform a file dump of selected database information. You can dump either database header information or checkpoint file information using this option. The output of the dump can be redirected to a text file, which is not obvious from the command-line help screen; just append `> path\filename.txt` to the command where `path\filename.txt` represents the full path to the desired dump file. An alternative could be to pipe the output of the command to the **more** command by appending `| more` to the **eseutil /m** command.

Note that the 1 *ModeModifier* shown in Table 5-8 is available only if you have Exchange 5.5 Service Pack 1 or higher installed.

Stop your Exchange Directory Service using the Services utility in the Control Panel before running **eseutil /m**.

ModeModifier

Specifies the type of database information to dump.

FileName

Specifies the name of the database or checkpoint file to be dumped. This must match the type of information dumped (see Table 5-8).

Table 5-8: File Type to Dump for a Given ModeModifier

ModeModifier	Action	File Type
h	Dump database header	*.edb
k	Dump checkpoint file	*.chk
1	Dump transaction log file	*.log

/p DatabaseName [options]

Verifies the integrity of an information store or directory database and attempts to perform a repair by reconstructing the database tables using only readable and uncorrupted records. This is known as a hard repair, in contrast to **eseutil /r**, which is called a soft repair. Perform a hard repair only as a last resort, as any bad pages that are encountered are removed and data may be lost.

Run this command *only* on a database that is damaged or corrupted. This is because **eseutil /p** does not attempt to apply information in the transaction logs to the database file, so information could be lost. After running this utility, you must delete the transaction log files for the database you repaired and should perform a full backup of the database.

You must also run the `isinteg` command in fix mode after repairing a database. Failing to do this could result in corrupt user mailboxes. (For example, users may have messages that they cannot open.)

Note that if you attempt a repair of either *priv.edb* or *pub.edb*, you must either repair the other database file or delete it. Otherwise, your information store will be inconsistent and will fail to start.

Stop your Exchange Directory Service using the Services utility in the Control Panel before running `eseutil /p`.

DatabaseName
  The actual name (full path) of the database to be compacted or a switch representing that database. (See Table 5-5.)

[Options]
  Specify zero or more of the options shown in Table 5-9, each separated by a space. If a path is not specified, the default path is the current directory.

Table 5-9: Explanation of Options Available for eseutil /p

Option for eseutil /p	Description
/t filename	Specifies the temporary database name (the default is *Repair.edb*)
/d	Check the database for errors but do not attempt a repair (same as running `eseutil /g`)
/v	Switches to verbose mode
/x	Gives detailed error messages when errors occur
/o	Hides the Exchange banner

/r [Options]
  Performs a recovery on the database to bring all of its associated files to a consistent state. This is known as a soft repair, in contrast to `eseutil /p`, which is called a hard repair.

  Stop your Exchange Directory Service using the Services utility in the Control Panel before running `eseutil /r`.

[Options]
  Specify zero or more of the options shown in Table 5-10, each separated by a space. If a path is not specified, the default path is the current directory.

Table 5-10: Explanation of Options Available for eseutil /r

Option for eseutil /r	Description
/is or /ds	Select either an information store or directory on which to perform recovery
/l path	Specify location of transaction log files associated with database
/s path	Specify location of checkpoint file and other system files associated with database
/o	Hides the Exchange banner

/u *DatabaseName* **/d***PreviousDLL* **[options]**

Lets you manually upgrade an information store or directory database from a previous version of Exchange. The database files are normally upgraded automatically when servers are upgraded to a newer version of Exchange. This utility would be used only if the normal upgrade process failed, as for example when upgrading a bridgehead server from Exchange 4.0 with Service Pack 4 to Exchange 5.5, which can result in Dr. Watson errors. For a detailed look at this problem and how to use eseutil /u to resolve it, see article Q183105 in the *Microsoft Knowledge Base.*

Stop your Exchange Directory Service using the Services utility in the Control Panel before running eseutil /u.

DatabaseName

The actual name (full path) of the database to be compacted or a switch representing that database. (See Table 5-5.)

PreviousDLL

The full path to the *edb.dll* of the previous version of Exchange.

[Options]

Specify zero or more of the options shown in Table 5-11, each separated by a space. If a path is not specified, the default path is the current directory.

Table 5-11: Explanation of Options Available for eseutil /u

Option for eseutil /u	Description
/b path	Creates a backup copy of the original database in the specified location
/t filename	Specifies the name of the temporary database (default is *Tempupgd.edb*)
/p	Keeps the original database in default location and locates the new upgraded database in the current directory with the name *Tempupgd.edb*
/o	Hides the Exchange banner

Examples

To compact the private information store database and save the compacted version as *Test.edb* in the *C:\Temp* directory, run the following command from the *\exchsrvr\bin* directory:

```
eseutil /d /ispriv /tC:\Temp\Test.edb
```

Note the absence of a space after the /t switch.

To check the *dir.edb* database for consistency, run the following command from the *\exchsrvr\bin* directory:

```
eseutil /mh C:\exchsrvr\dsadata\dir.edb | more
```

Read the line labeled "State," which will say either "Consistent" or "Inconsistent."

To determine which transaction logs have been committed to the information store, display the checkpoint file information for the database by running the following command from the \exchsrvr\bin directory:

```
eseutil /mk C:\exchsrvr\mdbdata\edb.chk | more
```

Look for a line that looks like this:

```
Checkpoint (xx, yyyy, zzzz)
```

Convert the decimal number **xx** to hexadecimal. This hexadecimal number is in the filename of the first uncommitted transaction log file. For example, consider:

```
Checkpoint (23,yyyy,zzzz)
```

Convert 23 (decimal) to 17 (hex) and look for a file named *EDB00017.LOG*

Notes

- If you cannot perform an online backup of a database after performing a hard repair using `eseutil /p`, try defragmenting the database using `eseutil /d`.

- A database is consistent if it was shut down normally. If upon restart a database is found using the `eseutil /m` command to be inconsistent, Exchange automatically performs a soft recovery and either commits or backs out of transactions to try to bring the database to a consistent state. If it cannot be brought to a consistent state, it will not start and a soft repair using `eseutil /r` should be attempted. If this fails, a hard repair using `esesutil /p` may be necessary.

- You can copy *eseutil.exe* to a Windows NT 4.0 server that does not have Exchange Server installed and use it to defragment a database file from there as long as Windows NT 4.0 Service Pack 2 or higher is installed.

- If you delete a number of mailboxes from your server, the size of the private information store does not immediately decrease. This is because the mailboxes are marked for deletion in the *priv.edb* database, but the actual reclamation of space takes place using a background thread when the system is idle. To immediately reclaim the space, wait 10 minutes after deleting the mailboxes, stop the Information Store service, and run `eseutil /d`.

- Running `eseutil /p` on *priv.edb* can occasionally cause an error condition where all available disk space will be used until the repair fails. This problem has been corrected in Exchange 5.5 Service Pack 1.

isinteg

Lets you locate and resolve errors in the Exchange information store.

Path

```
\exchsrvr\bin\isinteg.exe
```

To Launch

```
isinteg -test Testname[[, Testname]...] -pri | -pub [-fix]
    [-detailed] [-verbose] [-l LogFilename] [-t RefDbLocation]
isinteg [-patch]
isinteg -pri | -pub -dump [-l LogFilename]
```

Description

The Information Store Integrity Checker `isinteg` can find and resolve errors that prevent the Information Store service from starting on an Exchange server or prevent users from accessing their mailboxes or opening mail. Specifically, `isinteg` can be used to:

- Test the information store for table errors, unreferenced database objects, incorrect reference counts, and other aspects of referential integrity (check mode)

- Attempt to fix any errors found after testing, if desired (check and fix mode)

- Patch the information store after it has been restored from offline backup (patch mode)

`isinteg` is not considered a tool for regular maintenance of Exchange servers but rather a troubleshooting tool to be used in an emergency. (Microsoft recommends using `isinteg` only when in consultation with Microsoft Technical Support.) Be sure you have backed up your Exchange databases before running this utility.

Command-Line Options

`<null>`
> Displays the command-line help for `isinteg`.

`-test Testname[[,Testname]...] -pri | -pub [Options]`
> Lets you test and optionally fix the private or public information store database. A temporary database is created during testing for storing reference counts generated. At the end of the test process, the reference counts in the temporary database are compared with those in the original information store database and the temporary database is deleted. Any errors encountered are displayed and recorded in a log file. If `-fix` is selected, the information store will be fixed and any repairs done written to a log file. The name of the log file is either *isinteg.pri* or *isinteg.pub*, depending on whether the private or public information store is tested.
>
> Stop your Exchange Information Store Service using the Services utility in the Control Panel before running `isinteg -test`.

`-test Testname[[,Testname]...]`
> Performs the specified test or series of tests on the selected information store. See Table 5-12 for a list of possible tests you can run.

Table 5-12: Names of Tests You Can Run Using isinteg

Testname	Description
aclitemref	Verifies all reference counts for access control list items.
acllist	Examines all folders and validates their access control lists.
acllistref	Verifies all access control list reference counts.
allacltests	Runs a combination of the *acllist, acllistref,* and *aclitemref* tests.
allfoldertests	Runs a combination of the *folder, fldsub,* and *search* tests.

Table 5-12: Names of Tests You Can Run Using isinteg (continued)

Testname	Description
alltests	Runs all `isinteg` tests. Use this test when running the `-fix` option.
artidx	Checks the consistency of the NNTP article index. This test can only be run on the public information store.
attach	Validates the properties of all message attachments.
attachref	Validates all attachment reference counts.
deleteextracolumns	Deletes cached indexes and some extra columns.
delfld	Checks deleted folders, validates properties, and accumulates reference counts.
dumpsterref	Runs a combination of the *msgref* and *msgsoftref* tests. Checks the item count and size of the recoverable items available for Deleted Item Recovery.
dumpsterprops	Runs the *dumpsterref* test and also validates the presence of required columns in the folder table.
fldrcv (private store only)	Validates the counts of system folders such as Restrictions, Categorization, Inbox, Outbox, SentMail, Deleted Items, Finder, Views, Common Views, Schedule, and ShortCuts.
fldsub	Validates the counts of child folders and the number of child folders available for Deleted Item Recovery.
folder	Checks folder tables and validates properties. Checks message tables, validates properties, and accumulates reference counts.
mailbox	Checks folders, deleted folders, and tables for each mailbox. Validates properties, system folders (Inbox, Outbox, Sent Items, Deleted Items, etc.) in the folder table and checks their respective sizes. This test can only be run on the private information store.
message	Checks message tables and validates message table properties.
morefld	Tests all search links. When running the `-fix` option, deletes all cached categorization and restriction tables.
msgref	Validates message reference counts in all messages.
msgsoftref	Validates message reference counts in messages marked for Deleted Item Recovery.
namedprop	Checks the folder, message, and attachment tables and validates the named properties.
newsfeed	Validates all newsfeed table properties, including permissions. This test can only be run on the public information store.
newsfeedref	Validates all newsfeed reference counts. This test can only be run on the public information store.
oofhist	Validates out-of-office history information for all users. This test can only be run on the private information store.
peruser	Validates per user read/unread information.

Table 5-12: Names of Tests You Can Run Using isinteg (continued)

Testname	Description
rcvfld	Cross-checks receive folders against the folder table. This test can only be run on the private information store.
rowcounts	Validates the number of rows for all database tables.
search	Validates all search links.
timedev	Counts all timed events (maintenance, periodic tasks, etc).

-pri

Tests the private information store database *mdbdata**priv.edb*.

-pub

Tests the public information store database *mdbdata**pub.edb*.

[Options]

Specify zero or more of the options shown in Table 5-13, each separated by a space. If a path is not specified, the default path is the current directory

Table 5-13: Explanation of Options Available for isinteg -test

Option for isinteg -test	Description
-fix	Attempts to fix any problems encountered with the selected information store during testing. If you select this option you must also specify *alltests* for the Testname.
-detailed	Performs additional detailed tests.
-verbose	Gives the results of each test performed.
-l *filename*	Lets you specify the name of the log file. The default is *Isinteg.pri* or *Isinteg.pub*.
-t *RefDbLocation*	Lets you specify a location for the temporary reference database that isinteg creates while it is running. Placing this file on a different disk than where the information store is located can speed the process of running isinteg.

-dump -pri | -pub [-l *LogFilename***]**

Lets you dump the properties of the Folder Table for the selected information store database. The screen displays the dumped information, and you can optionally write it as text to a log file using the -l switch. This information is extremely verbose; make sure you have sufficient disk space available for the log file before running it.

-patch

Enables you to restart the Information Store service after an offline restore of the information store databases has been performed. You should run isinteg -patch after you have restored *priv.edb* and *pub.edb* from an offline backup, but before you attempt to restart the Information Store service. isinteg -patch ensures that the globally unique identifier (GUID) in the information store matches a corresponding entry in the Registry, allowing the

Information Store service to start. A GUID is a 64-bit hexadecimal string that uniquely identifies the creation time and location of a directory object.

isinteg -patch does not perform an integrity test on the information store; it only patches the base GUID of the store. After running isinteg -patch, you should also run isinteg -test to check the integrity of the store.

If you only have one Exchange server in your organization, you do not need to run isinteg -patch after an offline restore of *priv.edb* and *pub.edb*.

Examples

To check the integrity of mailbox folders in the private information store, run the following command from the *exchsrvr**bin* directory:

```
isinteg -test mailbox -pri
```

To enable the Information Store service to restart after running eseutil /p on the private information store database, run the following command from the *exchsrvr**bin* directory:

```
isinteg -test alltests -fix -pri
```

Notes

- If you try to run isinteg -patch while the Directory service is stopped, a DS_COMMUMICATIONS_ERROR message is generated.

- The difference between isinteg -fix and eseutil /p is that isinteg -fix repairs only high-level objects in the selected database, while eseutil /p attempts to repair low-level corruption in the database tables. You should run isinteg -fix after running eseutil /p.

- If you try to run isinteg -patch and an error occurs indicating that the information store could not be updated, try stopping and restarting the Information Store service using the Services utility in the Control Panel and then run isinteg -patch again.

- isinteg -patch should be run on the Exchange Server machine you are attempting to restore, not from a Windows NT Workstation machine running the Exchange Administrator program.

---

mailmig

Lets you run the Exchange Migration Wizard from the command line or in batch mode.

Path

```
\exchsrvr\bin\mailmig.exe
```

To Launch

```
mailmig [/h] | [/C:ControlFile /A:AccountName /P:Password /S]
```

Description

The Exchange Migration Wizard is a tool for migrating mailboxes and their contents from third-party mail systems and importing them into Exchange. The function and usage of the Migration Wizard is described in Chapter 4.

Command-Line Options

<null>

Runs the Migration Wizard program in normal GUI mode

/h

Opens a second command prompt window and displays help information about these command-line options. Using the /? switch does the same thing.

/C:ControlFile [Options]

Runs mailmig in batch mode using the settings specified in the ControlFile. The nature of the ControlFile and the available options are as follows:

ControlFile

A text file containing information that governs what actions are performed by the mailmig. The following example illustrates a typical ControlFile, specifically one for performing a one-step migration from an MS Mail Postoffice to Exchange:

```
Mode,MSMAILPC
ImportDestination,SERVER
Postoffice,\\DEGAS\MAILDATA\
EmailStart,19960101000000
EmailEnd,19981231235959
Home-Server,PICASSO
Template,/o=SampleCorp/ou=Toronto/cn=Recipients/
cn=SalesTemplate
NTAccounts,RANDOM
NTDomain,DOMAIN44
```

Looking at this file line-by-line, the following actions are performed:

- The information to be migrated resides on an MS Mail for PC Networks server.

- SERVER indicates that the data will be migrated to the Exchange information store. (The alternative is to migrate the data to personal folder [*.pst] files and personal address books [*.pab]).

- \\DEGAS\MAILDATA\ is the full UNC path to the MS Mail Postoffice to be migrated.

- Messages are migrated only if their date stamp is between Midnight, January 1st, 1996 and 11:59:59 P.M., December 31st, 1998. All other messages are discarded.

- Mailboxes and their messages will be migrated to the Exchange server named *Picasso*.

- The new mailboxes will be created on *Picasso* using the mailbox template called SalesTemplate.

    — New Windows NT accounts in the DOMAIN44 domain will be created for the new mailboxes and will be assigned random passwords.

For more information on creating a ControlFile for mailmig, see Exchange Server Books Online.

[Options]

    See Table 5-14 for a description of additional options available for this command.

Table 5-14: Explanation of Options Available for mailmig

Option for mailmig	Description
/A:AccountName	Specifies the administrator account name when performing a migration from MS Mail for PC Networks or Novell GroupWise.
/P:Password	Specifies the administrator account password when performing a migration from MS Mail for PC Networks or Novell GroupWise.
/S	Runs mailmig in silent mode, suppressing progress and error information. Errors are logged in the Application Log.
/g:o	This is an undocumented switch that allows you to speed up the migration process by migrating messages but not their attachments (OLE objects).

Examples

To migrate an MS Mail Postoffice having the administrator account "Supermailer" and password "mail321," run the following command from the \exchsrvr\bin directory:

```
mailmig /C:Stuff.txt /A:Supermailer /P:mail321
```

Here *Stuff.txt* is a ControlFile specifying how the migration will be performed.

Notes

If you use a ControlFile to specify a User List file and attempt to migrate users and messages from an MS Mail (PC) Postoffice using mailmig, the migration process may fail. This is due to a bug which has been fixed in Exchange 5.5 Service Pack 1.

mtacheck

Lets you fix problems associated with the message transfer agent (MTA).

Path

    \exchsrvr\bin\mtacheck.exe

To Launch

    mtacheck [/f *Filename* /v /rd /rl/ rp]

Description

Sometimes problems can occur with the internal database of the Exchange MTA, the most common of which is corrupt messages blocking an MTA queue. The result can vary from messages that can't be delivered to a stopped Message Transfer Agent service that can't be restarted.

The mtacheck utility can be used to:

- Check the integrity of the MTA queues
- Remove corrupt messages from MTA queues
- Rebuild MTA queues to enable the MTA service to be restarted

Corrupt messages that are removed from MTA queues are placed in a *Db*.dat* file located in the *\mtadata\mtacheck.out* directory. You can examine this file to attempt to recover these corrupt messages.

The mtacheck utility can be run manually from the command line, but it is also automatically run upon attempting to restart the MTA whenever the MTA does not shut down normally. Any events that occur during the automatic running of mtacheck are logged to the file *mtacheck.log* located in the *\mtadata\mtacheck.out* directory.

Stop the Message Transfer Agent service using the Services utility in the Control Panel and delete the contents of the *\mtadata\mtacheck.out* directory before manually running *mtacheck*.

Command-Line Options

`<null>`
Runs mtacheck with standard logging detail and displays the results.

`mtacheck [Options]`
Specify zero or more of the options shown in Table 5-15, each separated by a space.

Table 5-15: Options for mtacheck Command

Options for mtacheck	Description
/f Filename	Uses standard logging detail and displays the results while also copying them to the specified text file.
/v	Uses verbose logging detail.
/rd	Removes directory replication and dirsync messages.
/rl	Removes unwanted Link Monitor messages.
/rp	Removes public folder replication messages.

Example

To run mtacheck with standard logging detail and write the results to the file *test.log* in the *C:\Temp* directory, run the following command from the *\exchsrvr\bin* directory:

```
mtacheck /f C:\Temp\test.log
```

The output displayed by the command and saved in the text file when no problems are encountered is:

```
Starting object integrity checks
Database clean, no errors detected.
```

If a problem is encountered with one of the MTA queues, the output displays the name of the queue, the error type, and how many messages were returned to the queue after it was rebuilt. The output also displays the message ID (MTS-ID) and other information about each corrupt message removed from the queue.

If directory replication stops working due to corrupt directory replication messages in the MTA queues, run the following command from the *exchsrvr**bin* directory of directory replication bridgehead servers in your organization:

mtacheck /rd

Notes

- If mtacheck reveals corrupt messages in an MTA queue and you have message tracking enabled, you may be able to use the message ID (MTS-ID) of the corrupt messages to determine where in your messaging path the corruption occurred. MTS-IDs are assigned to messages when they are created and remain with the message until delivery is completed. An MTS-ID consists of the *distinguished name* of the originating Exchange server, the date/time when the message was sent, and a unique hexadecimal identifier.

- The MTA may not be able to restart after stopping if there is an existing *mtacheck.log* file located in the *mtadata**mtacheck.out* directory. Delete or rename the existing *mtacheck.log* file and try restarting the MTA again.

- If you configure directory replication to occur too frequently, the MTA queues may become flooded with directory replication messages causing other messages to not be delivered. Use mtacheck /rd to correct this after increasing the replication interval, or wait for the backlog of replication messages to work their way through the queue. The negative side of using mtacheck /rd is that you may be deleting replication messages containing tombstones for deleted directory objects in other sites; this can result in orphaned directory objects (directory objects that exist in one site but not in another).

A similar situation with regard to public folder replication *cannot* easily be resolved by running mtacheck /rp as you might expect. This may be because deleting public folder replication messages from the MTA actually results in *more* replication traffic being generated over the already almost saturated network connection, possibly because the directory service initiates a backfill process to ensure public folder replication is up to date.

- mtacheck cannot be run from a remote console; it must be run on the server you want to check.

- Sometimes a message stuck in an MTA queue can be freed by simply stopping and restarting the Message Transfer Agent service on the Exchange server.

---

ntbackup

Lets you back up and restore critical system and user data on Exchange servers.

Path

```
%SystemRoot%\system32\ntbackup.exe
```

To Launch

```
ntbackup [options]
```

Description

The modified Windows NT Backup utility on an Exchange server is described in Chapter 4. Here we will consider only the Exchange-specific command-line options of the modified Windows NT Backup tool; for general information about using Windows NT Backup from the command-line, see Jody Leber's *Windows NT Backup and Restore* from O'Reilly.

Command-Line Options

DS *ServerName*
: Backs up the directory database *dir.edb* on Exchange server *ServerName*.

IS *Servername*
: Backs up the information store databases *priv.edb* and *pub.edb* on Exchange server *ServerName*.

All other options remain the same as for the original version of Windows NT Backup.

Examples

To perform a normal backup of the directory database on Exchange server *Picasso* and the information store on Exchange server *Raphael*, run the following command from any directory in the system path:

```
ntbackup DS \\Picasso IS \\Raphael \t:normal
```

Notes

- If you stop a backup before it is completed, `ntbackup` may hang. This behavior has been fixed with Exchange 5.5 Service Pack 1.
- You can back up an Exchange server remotely from a Windows NT Workstation machine by installing the Exchange Administrator program on the workstation. Windows NT 4.0 Service Pack 3 must be installed first.

perfwiz

Lets you tune the performance of your Exchange server based on its role, configuration, and hardware components.

Path

```
\exchsrvr\bin\perfwiz.exe
```

To Launch

```
perfwiz [-r] | [-v]
```

Description

Runs Performance Optimizer, a wizard-based tool that analyzes your server's disk and memory resources and recommends how to reconfigure your system for best performance. For more information on Performance Optimizer, see Chapter 4.

Command-Line Options

`<null>`
> Runs the GUI Performance Optimizer wizard in normal mode as described in Chapter 4.

`-r`
> Runs a read-only version of the verbose version of the GUI Performance Optimizer wizard. This mode lets you view Exchange Registry settings but does not allow you to view data locations such as where transaction logs are located. `perfwiz -r` also runs without shutting down any Exchange services.

`-v`
> Runs the verbose version of the GUI Performance Optimizer wizard. This mode gives you more control on how the wizard is run, including the option of skipping disk subsystem analysis. You might use this when, for example, you have added more RAM to your server but have not changed the disk configuration; this will allow you to run the wizard more quickly than it would run in normal mode.

Another advantage of verbose mode is that you can switch back and forth between screens of the wizard and observe the effects of different memory restrictions on Exchange resource settings.

Running `perfwiz -v` begins by stopping all Exchange services on your computer. Just as in normal mode, the initial screen after services are stopped and disk analysis is performed (refer back to Figure 4-22) lets you specify the number of users homed on your server, number of users in the entire organization, role(s) of your server within your organization, and amount of memory reserved for Exchange. See Chapter 4 for more information on these initial screen settings.

After this comes a series of verbose screens showing the values of different Exchange Registry settings. You can modify these settings directly or return to the initial screen, change your settings, and see the new recommendations on the verbose screens. If you manually modify these settings, follow these guidelines:

- Make incremental changes instead of large ones.

- Change one setting at a time and observe its effect.

- Make changes only to solve a specific problem, not to tweak your system for better performance.

- To improve performance of your server, upgrade your hardware instead of tweaking `perfwiz` parameters.

Table 5-16 shows a list of configurable parameters for each verbose screen, with additional comments added for those parameters that have been shown to have some useful effect in manual tuning of Exchange, albeit sometimes the results are minor. The screen numbers themselves have no significance; all screens have the same heading, and screens will not be present unless the Internet Mail Service is installed on your machine. Most settings have to do with buffers allocated for the JET97 database engine and other processes and the number of threads available for different processes.

Many of these parameters are dependent on each other, and changing one requires that others be changed by a similar amount. Even a small change in some parameters may result in services that fail to start. Be sure to record the initial configuration of these parameters for your machine before you start making alterations, and follow the guidelines described earlier.

Table 5-16: Configurable Parameters on Verbose Screens of Performance Optimizer

Parameter	Function
Screen 1 Parameters	
# of information store buffers	JET97 buffers 4KB in size allocated for the Information Store service. This number should be fairly large. Do not manually increase in size without adding more RAM or other process may become starved.
# of directory buffers	JET97 buffers 4KB in size allocated for the Directory service. This number should be fairly large. Do not manually increase in size without adding more RAM or other process may become starved.
Minimum # of information store threads	Minimum threads used by the Information Store service for MAPI client-to-server interaction.
Maximum # of information store threads	Maximum threads used by the Information Store service for MAPI client-to-server interaction. Increasing this value may improve performance when a large number of clients concurrently connect to the server.

Parameter	Function
# of directory threads	Number of threads used by the Directory service for directory replication and servicing client requests for address lookups. If this is increased, the "minimum # of information store threads" setting should be increased proportionally.
Maximum # of concurrent read threads	Number of threads used solely for directory replication. If this is increased, the "# of directory threads" setting should be increased proportionally.
# of background threads	Number of threads used for communication between information store and other Exchange components and for system maintenance tasks. This setting should not be changed or the Information Store service may not start.
# of heaps	Memory areas used for dynamic memory allocation.
Screen 2 Parameters	
# of private information store send threads	Number of threads used for communication between the information store and the message transfer agent. Should be greater than or equal to 2. Increase to 3 or 4 if MTA queues are frequently congested, and increase "# of background threads" and "# of submit/delivery threads" proportionally.
# of private information store delivery threads	Same as above.
# of public information store send threads	Same as above.
# of public information store delivery threads	Same as above.
# of information store gateway in threads	Number of threads used for communication between the information store and a connector or gateway. Should be greater than or equal to 2. Increase to 3 or 4 if MTA queues are frequently congested, and increase "# of background threads" and "# of submit/delivery threads" proportionally.
# of information store gateway out threads	Same as above.
Buffer Threshold Low Percent	Percentages of available buffers remaining before flushing to disk. The lower the value, the fewer disk writes.
Buffer Threshold High Percent	Percentage of available buffers that must be reached before flushing to disk stops. This should be equal to or slightly greater than the value above.

Command-Line Tools

Table 5-16: Configurable Parameters on Verbose Screens of Performance Optimizer (continued)

Parameter	Function
Maximum # of pool threads	These threads service connections with the information store using Internet protocols such as POP3, IMAP4, and NNTP. Try increasing this if the Internet Mail Service queues are frequently congested.
Screen 3 Parameters	
# of information store users	Corresponds to "Users on this server" in initial screen.
# of concurrent connections to LAN-MTAs	Minimum number of concurrent MTA associations using LAN connections.
# of concurrent connections to RAS LAN-MTAs	Minimum number of concurrent MTA associations using RAS connections.
# of LAN-MTAs	Minimum number of network MTAs support by the message transfer agent.
# of X.400 gateways	Maximum number of remote X.400 MTAs.
ds_read cache latency (secs)	Number of seconds the message transfer agent caches resolved directory entries to speed address resolving. This parameter can be edited to solve the "Move User Problem," namely, when you move a user to a different Exchange server, any messages sent to the user during the operation may become stuck in the MTA queue. To solve this, change this parameter to 0 and stop/restart the MTA, move the users, and then change the parameter back to 60 (the default) and stop/start the MTA again.
Screen 4 Parameters	
# of dispatcher threads	Total number of threads used for message routing.
# of transfer threads	Total number of threads used to transfer messages.
# of kernel threads	Used for OSI protocols such as TP4 only.
# of submit/delivery threads	These threads work together with the information store send/delivery threads. If you increase one, you should increase the other proportionally.
# of RAS LAN-MTAs	Maximum number of concurrent associations to remote MTAs using RAS connections.
# of database buffers per object	Number of 4KB buffers per cached database file for the message transfer agent.
# of RTS threads	Used for OSI protocols such as TP4 only.
Screen 5 Parameters	
# of concurrent MDB/delivery queue clients	Optimal value is 2 or slightly greater.
# of concurrent XAPI sessions	Maximum number of sessions to information store and XAPI clients.

Table 5-16: Configurable Parameters on Verbose Screens of Performance Optimizer (continued)

Parameter	Function
Max # of RPC calls outstanding	If there are RPC errors in the Application Log, try increasing this parameter but not beyond 50.
Min # of RPC threads	Minimum number of concurrent RPC threads.
# of MT gateway clients	Maximum number of gateways the message transfer agent can support.
# of retrieval queue clients	Maximum number of XAPI retrieval queue clients.
# of TCP/IP control blocks	The message transfer agent uses one control block for each association. (A control block specifies how an association processes messages.) This can be increased if you have slow or congested network connections to remote connectors or foreign X.400 mail systems. If this parameter is increased, the "# of TCP/IP threads" should be increased proportionally.
# of TCP/IP threads	See "# of TCP/IP control blocks."
Screen 6 Parameters	
# of TP4 control blocks	The message transfer agent uses one control block for each association (a control block specifies how an association processes messages). This can be increased if you have slow or congested network connections to remote X.400 connectors or foreign X.400 mail systems. If this parameter is increased, the "# of TP4 threads" should be increased proportionally.
# of TP4 threads	See "# of TP4 control blocks."
Screen 7 Parameters (Internet Mail Service Must Be Installed)	
# of inbound threads	Number of threads used for processing inbound SMTP mail. This includes moving the mail from the Internet Mail Service to the information store and performing content conversion. Try increasing this if the inbound IMS queue is frequently congested.
# of outbound threads	Number of threads used for processing outbound SMTP mail. This includes moving the mail to the Internet Mail Service from the information store and performing content conversion. Try increasing this if the outbound IMS queue is frequently congested.
# of InOut threads	Should be greater than or equal to the sum of the last two values above.
# of threads per processor	Available threads for processing messaging traffic between the Internet Mail Service and the Internet.

PART III

Appendixes

APPENDIX A

X.400

This appendix deals with:

- Background information relating to X.400 messaging standards
- X.400 versus SMTP messaging standards
- Architecture and operation of X.400 messaging systems

For information on X.400 addresses see the entry "X.400 Connector" in Chapter 3, *Directory*.

About X.400

X.400 is a series of recommended standards for interoperability between messaging systems, developed by the Comité Consultatif International Télégraphique et Téléphonic (CCITT), which is now the International Telecommunciations Union (ITU) and the Electronic Messaging Association (EMA). The X.400 standards are based on the Open Systems Interconnection (OSI) reference model, which was developed by the International Standards Organization (ISO).

X.400 defines:

- A layered architecture for a messaging system.
- The structure and parts of a message.
- A standard store-and-forward method for transferring messages.
- An integrated messaging architecture that supports interpersonal mail, voice, fax, telegraph, telex, and Electronic Data Interchange (EDI); though no single X.400-compliant product does all of these simultaneously!

X.400 is widely recognized by industry as a global standard for messaging interoperability and is widely implemented by Post, Telephone, and Telegraph (PTT) carriers throughout Europe and by many government agencies around the world.

An example of a major X.400 service provider in Europe is ATLAS, an X.400 provider servicing France.

The Message Transfer Agent, or MTA in Exchange, is endorsed by Microsoft as conforming to X.400 standards. If you are involved in an enterprise rollout of Exchange for a government agency or a global enterprise with branch companies around the world, chances are you will probably have to incorporate X.400 connectivity into your Exchange implementation. On the other hand, because of the rapid worldwide growth in the Internet and SMTP messaging, you may be able to get by with SMTP connectivity instead using the Internet Mail Service connector.

X.400 messaging standards were first published in 1984 in the ITU "Red Book." These standards defined a hierarchical global messaging system similar to the Internet's DNS naming system, but with a much more complicated and flexible naming scheme. The 1984 standards were based on the OSI seven-layer networking protocol stack and were intended to cover all the necessary aspects of a comprehensive global messaging system. In 1988, the ITU revised and enlarged the X.400 standards in their "Blue Book." Together the 1984 and 1988 standards comprise the basic X.400 messaging standards, but in reality there is a whole family of related standards, including the X.420 Interpersonal Mail (IPM) recommendations, X.435 Electronic Data Interchange (EDI) recommendations, and so on.

X.400 Versus SMTP

At their defining level as standards, SMTP and X.400 are quite different. SMTP was developed by the Internet Engineering Task Force (IETF) and first published in 1982 as Request For Comment (RFC) 822. SMTP is as a simple, open, and elegant messaging standard that has undergone further revisions and enhancements in later RFCs. These RFCs are available for free at *http://www.ietf.org,* the IETF web site. As a result of this openness, SMTP messaging has become widely implemented in both commercial and free software and has spread rapidly around the world. Further RFCs have defined other messaging-related protocols such as POP3 and IMAP4, with the result that SMTP-based messaging systems are now powerful and flexible global communication tools.

In contrast, the X.400 standards must be purchased from the ITU and are much more complex to understand and implement. In addition, makers of X.400 software must pay to have it certified as X.400-compliant. These three factors have tended to slow the development of X.400 messaging products and have precluded anyone but large corporations from attempting to develop X.400 messaging software. Also, the European bias of the ITU (at least as far as Americans are concerned) has resulted in X.400 implementations being centered mainly in Europe, although as recently as 1996 this standard was officially adopted as the messaging standard for the Federal Government of Canada.

In general, X.400 appeals more to bureaucrats; the ITU itself reminds one of that massive hierarchical civil service bureaucracy which has existed in much of Europe since the 17th century, and the whole X.400 project has a kind of "build it and they will come" philosophy to it. In fact, some of the ITU members involved in developing these standards were large European companies that had a significant stake in who had the power to implement them as actual messaging software. In contrast, SMTP attracts the freedom-loving wild-West geek type with its lack of centralized authority, freedom for anyone to democratically propose a de-facto standard, and agreement by consensus approach.

Another important contrast between these two systems is that SMTP was designed from the start as a text-only messaging system. Later protocols and mechanisms were devised for encoding and sending binary attachments with SMTP mail, but the messages themselves remain text-based in their basic format. X.400, however, uses a native binary messaging format called ASN.1, which means that it is fundamentally language-independent. This seems to be the main reason why the Federal Government of Canada, for example, adopted X.400 as its messaging standard: it is natively multilingual and supports French-language diacritics. Of course, most Canadians send mail to their government using SMTP; it's just intergovernmental messaging that uses costly X.400 leased-line networks!

The positive side of SMTP messages being text-based is that SMTP messaging systems are relatively simple to troubleshoot; just open the message with a text editor and read the headers to find out the route it traveled and how it was processed, or Telnet to port 25 and type in a few text commands from the keyboard to see how an SMTP host responds. The negative side of this is that other methods such as Uuencode and MIME had to be developed to send binary content in SMTP messages, which is unnecessary with X.400. The down side of the ASN.1 binary encoding of X.400 messages, however, is the additional processing overhead involved in converting text messages to binary and then back to text and the wasted bandwidth due to the fact that these ASN.1 encoded messages are generally significantly larger than their SMTP equivalents. And since the vast majority of interpersonal messages are in fact text, X.400 seems quite wasteful of bandwidth and processing power compared to SMTP. Furthermore, special tools are needed to decode failed mail in an X.400 system and interpret the message headers.

Another obvious difference between the two systems is in addressing. A typical email address might look something like this:

marys@toronto.samplecorp.com

The first portion of an SMTP address is the username or alias, while the portion after @ is the DNS name of the user's receiving network or SMTP host. DNS names are hierarchical and simple to understand; most school children today understand the difference between a *.com* and a *.org* top-level domain, for example.

X.400 addresses can be much more complex. A typical Originator/Recipient (O/R) address (the name given to an X.400 address) might look something like this:

c=ca;admd=govmt.canada;prmd=gc+nlc.bcn;g=mary;s=smith;

Addresses like this are not likely to be seen in the average Canadian student's textbook, at least not in my lifetime!

In terms of messaging reliability, X.400 probably has the edge. This is because each message transfer agent in a typical X.400 system maintains a list of its local users, and when a message is routed through the MTA it is stored in the destination user's message spool in the Message Store (MS). As a result, mechanisms like delivery notification and read receipts are native to an X.400 messaging system. In contrast, when an SMTP host sends a message to another host, it connects to port 25, transfers the message, and disconnects; the message is not stored in any intermediate location. As far as the sending host is concerned, the message has reached its destination once the receiving host accepts it, regardless of whether the destination recipient even exists.

Another difference is the underlying network protocols used by the systems. SMTP is part of the TCP/IP suite of Internet protocols and runs only on TCP/IP internetworks. X.400, being designed on the seven-layer OSI protocol model, was originally designed to work with TP0/TP4/X.25 leased-line networks but is now frequently implemented on TCP/IP also.

Finally, X.400 security was defined in the recommendations in only broad and general ways. As a result, many different encryption algorithms have been implemented on different X.400 systems, making it difficult at times for different X.400 service providers to communicate across gateways. SMTP did not have any security defined for it at all, but since then a number of different standards have emerged, including PGP and S/MIME. These standards continue to evolve as the Internet moves ahead.

How X.400 Works

I will briefly describe an X.400 Message Handling System (MHS) by considering its:

- Management domains
- Components
- Protocols
- Message types

See the entry "X.400 Connector" in Chapter 3 for more information about X.400 addresses.

Management domains

A management domain is a collection of X.400 components that includes at least one Message Transfer Agent. Note that X.400 management domains are not the same thing as Internet DNS domains. There are two types of management domains:

Administrative Management Domain (ADMD)
This is an MHS that is managed by a registered private operating agency. ADMDs are top-level management domains and represent X.400 services provided by major international telecommunications carriers such as AT&T or MCI or by a local telephone company.

Private Management Domain (PRMD)
This is an MHS that belongs to a private corporate network and is analogous to an individual subscription to an ADMD. In other words, PRMDs are like end nodes on a mesh of interconnected ADMDs (see Figure A-1). PRMDs are not supposed to communicate directly with each other, but in practice they often do so.

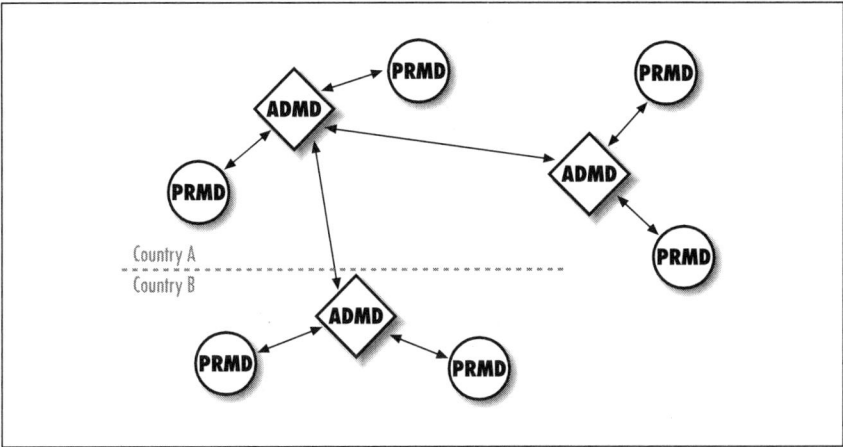

Figure A-1: ADMDs and PRMDs

MHS Components

For simplicity, we will focus here on the main components of an X.400 Message Handling System (see Figure A-2).

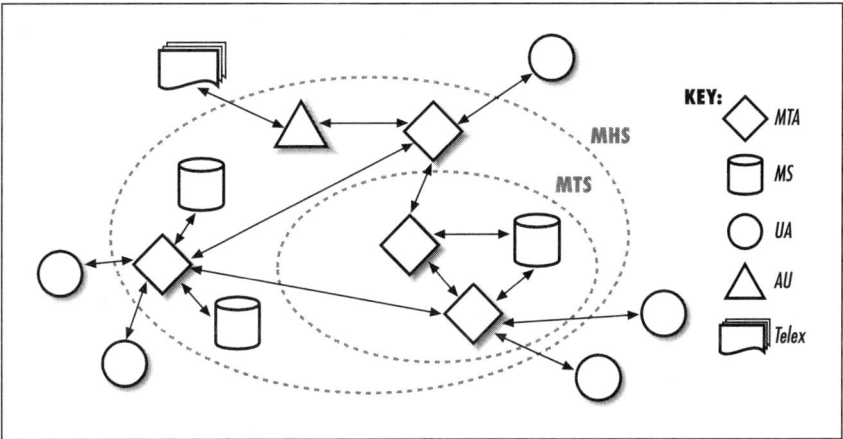

Figure A-2: An X.400 Message Handling System

User Agent (UA)

    This is the component that the user directly interacts with. In other words, a UA is an X.400 client program installed on a computer or terminal that a user can use to send or receive an X.400 email message. UAs are typically tailored to support one or more different kinds of message contents, including interpersonal mail, voice, EDI, and so on. The UA maintains the user's personal folders, messages, and address books. When a user creates a message, the UA converts it to ASN.1 format and moves it to a spool on the Remote User Agent

(RUA). The RUA is another component in the UA's domain that provides messaging capabilities when the user is not permanently connected to the MTA. In other words, the RUA provides "offline mail" support for dial-up messaging. When the user wants to send or receive mail, the RUA establishes a connection with the MTA and transfers the mail.

Message Transfer Agent (MTA)

This component is responsible for routing messages and returning delivery notifications. Each MTA has:

– A database where all UAs in its local domain are registered

– Routing information about how to transfer mail to other domains

Messages that arrive for a UA can either be delivered directly to the UA (if it is connected) or moved to the MS for pickup later.

Message Store (MS)

This component is responsible for temporarily storing messages received by the MTA until they can be processed and delivered to a UA. The MS makes possible the "store and forward" messaging architecture of an X.400 messaging system.

Access Unit (AU)

This component provides a link between an X.400 MHS and some other communications system such as telex, fax, or snail-mail.

Message Transfer System (MTS)

This signifies a collection of MTAs and MSs working together to transfer messages.

Protocols

There are many different X.400 protocols, but we will only consider a few here.

P1 Protocol

Also called the Message Transfer Protocol, this is the OSI protocol used for UA-to-MTA and MTA-to-MTA communications. P1 is the protocol used for the "envelope" of a message and contains the routing information necessary for the MTAs in a MHS to deliver the message. The P1 envelope also contains message trace information added during transit.

P2 Protocol

This is used for UA-to-UA communication via message headers. P2 is defined within the X.420 recommendations that describes the contents of an Interpersonal Mail (IPM) or email message. The 1988 version is called P22 (which stands for P2 Version 2).

P3 Protocol

Also called the MTS Access Protocol, this is used for MTA-to-MS communication.

P7 Protocol

Also called the MS Access Protocol, this is used for UA-to-MS communication for permanently connected UAs only.

Message types

As mentioned previously, X.400 provides supporting message transport for much more than just email; it also supports voice, telex, fax, EDI, and other forms of "messaging." As far as email messaging is concerned, however, there are three message types:

Interpersonal Message (IPM)
> These are email messages created by a user using a UA. These can contain multiple binary body parts.

Interpersonal Notification (IPN)
> This refers to Delivery Notifications (DN), Non-Delivery Notifications (NDN), Receipt Notifications (RN), and so on.

Probe Messages
> These messages are used for configuring and troubleshooting MTS components.

X.400

APPENDIX B

X.500

This appendix deals briefly with:

- Background information relating to X.500 directory standards
- How X.500 and X.400 standards interrelate
- X.500 and the Exchange directory hierarchy

About X.500

X.500 is a series of recommended standards for a global, hierarchical, distributed directory, developed by the Comité Consultatif International Télégraphique et Téléphonic (CCITT), which is now the International Telecommunciations Union (ITU) and the Electronic Messaging Association (EMA). The X.500 standards are based on the Open Systems Interconnection (OSI) reference model, which was developed by the International Standards Organization (ISO).

X.500 defines:

- A global, hierarchical, distributed directory database
- The architecture of a directory service for maintaining this database
- The protocols for accessing, updating, and searching for information in this database

X.500 is an attempt by the ITU in 1988 and 1993 to define how a global directory of information should operate. In other words, it describes the architecture and operation of a "Directory of Directories," which can successfully and uniquely store, access, search, and identify information about any user, component, or service on any network in the world. This is a big goal, and the X.500 recommendations are correspondingly complex to try to achieve this goal. However, the complexity of the original X.500 recommendations means that there are few "pure X.500" directories in the world today.

Nevertheless, many universities have implemented X.500-based directories for storing personnel and other information, and Internet white pages such as Four11 and Bigfoot have X.500-based directories that can be accessed either through a web interface or using an LDAP client such as Microsoft Outlook Express. X.500 is also the basis for Microsoft's Active Directory for the upcoming Windows 2000 network operating system.

How X.500 Works

I will briefly describe an X.500 directory by considering its:

- Directory management domains
- Components
- Protocols

If you have read Appendix A, *X.400*, you will immediately see some similarities with the following exposition.

Directory management domains

A Directory Management Domain (DMD) is a collection of X.500 components that includes at least one Directory System Agent (DSA) managed by an organization called the Domain Management Organization (DMO). The DMO is responsible for both managing the equipment and maintaining the information in the DMD. Note that DMDs are not the same thing as Internet DNS domains. There are two types of DMDs:

Administrative Directory Management Domain (ADDMD)
 This is a DMD that provides public directory access such as Four11 or Bigfoot.

Private Directory Management Domain (PRDMD)
 This is a DMD that provides private directory access, such as an Active Directory server on a corporate Windows 2000 network.

Directory components

For simplicity, we will focus here on the main components of an X.500 directory (see Figure B-1).

Directory User Agent (DUA)
 This is the component that the user directly interacts with. In other words, a DUA is an X.500 client program installed on a computer or terminal that can access, update, and search an X.500 directory. DUA functionality can be provided by a variety of interfaces, including web clients, email programs, or dedicated directory access software.

Directory Information Base (DIB)
 This is the hierarchical database of information stored by the directory. The DIB is not located in any single location; it is distributed across multiple servers and locations. From the point of view of a DUA, however, the entire directory appears to be locally accessible, provided the user has appropriate access permissions. The DIB contains *entries* and each entry describes an *object* (user, group, file, printer, server, system—whatever). Each object can

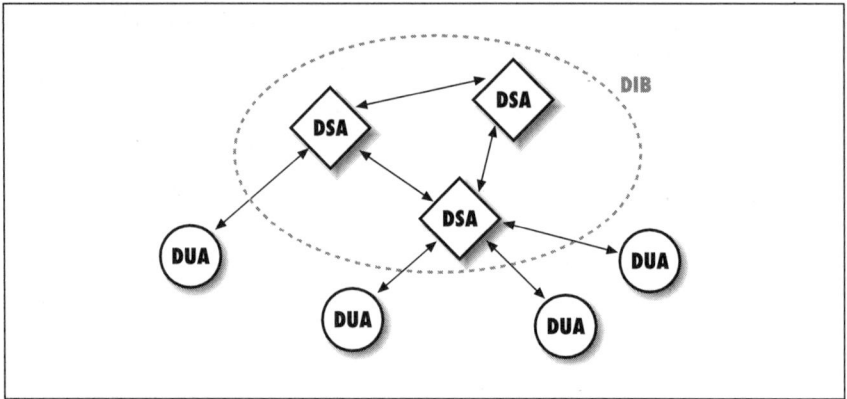

Figure B-1: An X.500 directory system

have several entries, but only one entry (the *object entry*) fully represents the object within the DIB. Directory *schema* are a necessary set of rules defining things such as classes of objects that are used to enforce consistency between objects so that no object exists more than once in the directory. Every object in the DIB must also have at least one unique name so that it can be located and accessed when desired. This is accomplished by arranging the objects in the DIB in a naming hierarchy called a *Directory Information Tree* (DIT).

Directory System Agent (DSA)

This is a server that maintains and provides access to the DIB. From a purely functional point of view, an X.500 directory consists of a set of interconnected DSAs. Each DSA contains and is responsible for a portion of the DIB. This portion consists of a group of *naming contexts*, each of which consists of objects close to each other in the DIT. Each local DSA is also aware of what portions of the DIB other remote DSAs are responsible for. A local DSA is responsible for providing access by DUAs to the DIB and for communicating with remote DSAs for directory replication and management. The local DSA can either provide access to the portion of the DIB information it contains, or it can route the DUA's request to the remote DSA responsible for the desired information. This routing can take place either as an iterative forwarded request (called *chaining*) or the local DSA can refer the DUA to contact the remote DSA directly.

Protocols

The important X.500 protocols are as follows:

Directory System Protocol (DSP)

This is the protocol used in DSA-to-DSA communication. Administration of the directory and directory replication are handled using the DSP.

Directory Access Protocol (DAP)

This is the protocol used in DUA-to-DSA communication. DAP defines the rules and procedures by which DUAs can locate, access, and update information in the DIB. Unfortunately this protocol is quite complex to implement because of its broad generality, and hence LDAP was developed.

Lightweight Directory Access Protocol (LDAP)

This is a simplified version of DAP developed for TCP/IP networks by the University of Michigan for Internet users. Its initial implementation was similar to DAP but without support for security, data replication, and non-ASCII character sets. However, LDAP has been evolving and many of these features have been re-introduced with the result that LDAP may soon become as complex as DAP.

X.500 and Exchange

How much of this is important for the Exchange administrator to know? Not very much at this point. Microsoft claims that the Exchange Directory Service is based upon the X.500 recommendations, but with one significant difference: the *entire* directory database is contained on *each* Exchange server instead of distributing it in portions among different servers.

X.500 may become an issue when the Platinum version of Exchange is released for the Windows 2000 network operating system, whose Active Directory service is based more closely on X.500 concepts. Until then, this material can safely be left where it is right now—as an appendix.

X.500

APPENDIX C

Raw Mode

This appendix deals with running the Exchange Administrator program in raw mode.

By running the GUI window of the Exchange Administrator program from the command line using the /r switch:

```
C:\exchsrvr\bin\>admin /r
```

you can run the program in *raw mode*, a version that exposes the schema attributes of each object in the Exchange directory hierarchy.

When the window opens and you have connected to a server, select View → Raw Directory to provide a view of the directory hierarchy that exposes all the schema attributes of each object. (See Figure C-1 and note that for simplicity the organization has only one server called *Picasso*.) The *schema* for a directory is the set of rules that defines the structure of the directory and its allowable content. The *schema attributes* of a directory object are the attributes that the directory object possesses. With Exchange, only a portion of an object's schema attributes are exposed on the property sheet for the object; there are other hidden attributes that administrators usually don't have to know about but which govern things such as how directory replication occurs between servers.

Note that the directory hierarchy shown in Figure C-1 looks a little different from normal view, specifically:

- There are no Folders or Global Address List containers. Exchange considers these *virtual containers* and they are not implemented in the directory in the same way other objects are.

- The Directory Service leaf object of server *Picasso* is now a container object and contains a new leaf object called SUPREF.

- There is a new leaf object called Schema within the Site (Toronto) container, which is selected in Figure C-1.

346

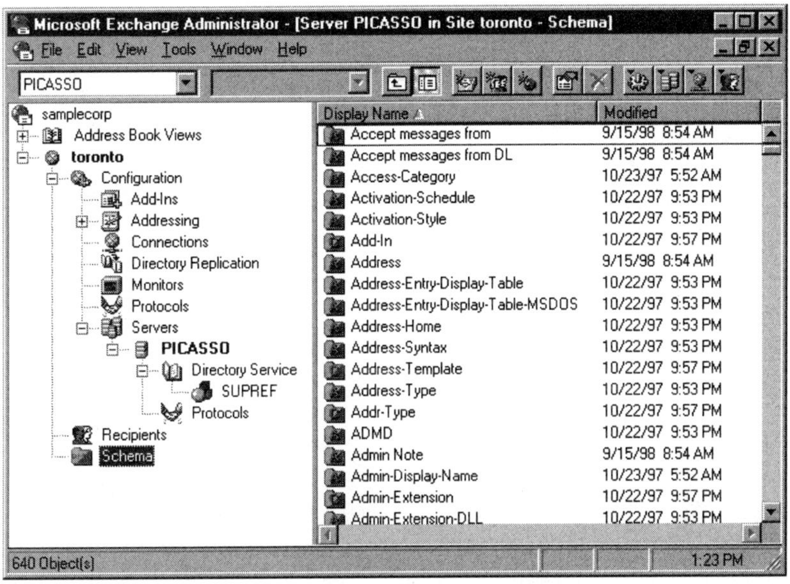

Figure C-1: Exchange directory schema exposed in raw view

The Schema container contains special directory objects representing all possible schema attributes of Exchange directory objects ("little fleas have littler fleas and so on ad infinitum"). For example, if you scroll down the right-hand pane and select the schema attribute called "Display Name," you can expose the schema attributes of this schema attribute by choosing File → Raw Properties. This opens the property sheet called "Display Name Properties" shown in Figure C-2.

From the property sheet, you can examine each of the schema attributes (here called "Object attributes") of the selected directory object "Display Name." Using the "List attributes of type" drop-down box, you can view different subsets and supersets of the existing schema attributes for the object.

One schema attribute is of particular interest as far as the directory itself is concerned: the Obj-Dist-Name attribute. This stands for "Object Distinguished Name" and represents the unique *distinguished name* (DN) of the object within the directory hierarchy. (See the note on Distinguished Names in the section "Single-Server MAPI Message Flow" in Chapter 2, *Architecture and Operation*, for information on distinguished names). By selecting this schema attribute in the listbox and selecting the Viewer button, you can view the full distinguished name of this directory object (see Figure C-3).

Note the field "Microsoft DMD" within the distinguished name of this object. This indicates that this Exchange directory falls under the Microsoft Directory Management Domain (Microsoft DMD) of the X.500 directory space. for more information on Directory Management Domains, see Appendix B, *X.500*.

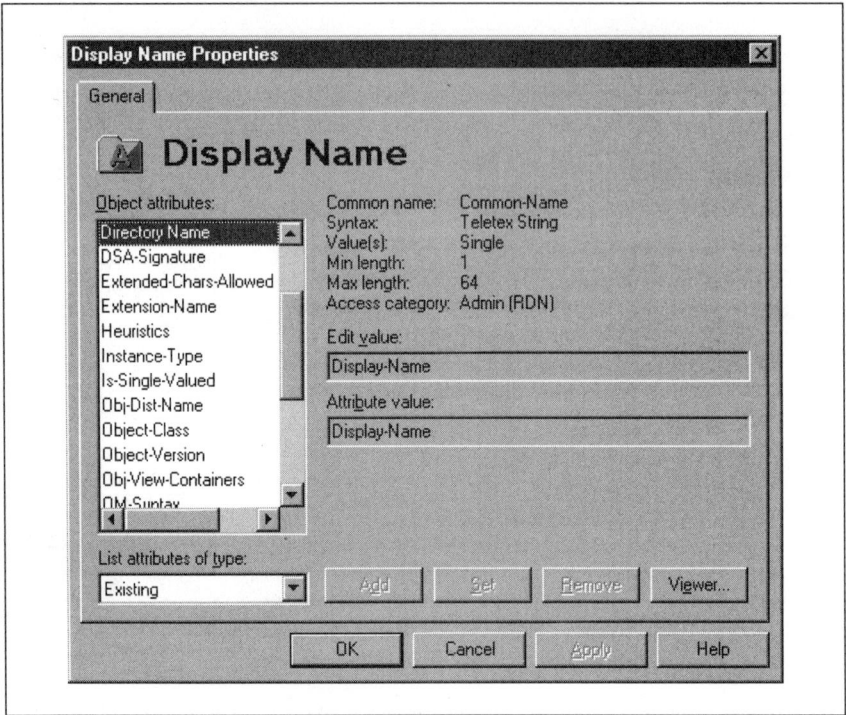

Figure C-2: Raw properties of the Display Name object

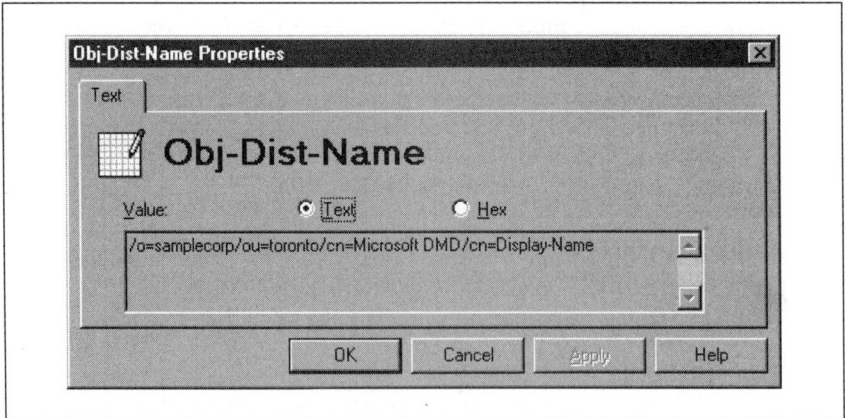

Figure C-3: Viewing the distinguished name of the Display Name object

You can also use the Add, Remove, and Set buttons in Figure C-2 to directly modify the schema attributes of the selected object or even create new attributes. You shouldn't do this unless directed to by Microsoft Technical Support or you could render your Exchange directory inconsistent.

You can use the same procedure to view the distinguished name (or any other attribute) of a mailbox or any other object in your directory. Just follow these steps:

- Open a command prompt and change to the \exchsrvr\bin directory.

- Type admin /r to run Exchange Administrator in raw mode.

- Select the mailbox or other object you want to examine. (It is not necessary to use View → Raw Properties unless you want to examine the attributes of the schema itself.)

- Select File → Raw Properties.

- Choose the Obj-Dist-Name or any other attribute you want to see and click the Viewer button.

You can find a complete list of directory schema for Mailbox and other objects in the last page of the "Migration" book of Exchange Server Books Online. You can use this table to identify the various possible header fields in the Directory Export process described in Chapter 4, *GUI Tools*.

APPENDIX D

Services

This appendix lists the various Exchange services and describes:

- Their dependencies (Table D-1)
- Their executables (Table D-2)
- Their command-line equivalents (Table D-3)
- Their Event Source identifiers for the Application Log (Table D-4)

If you want to start or stop Exchange services, you can use:

- The Services utility in the Control Panel
- The net start and net stop commands at the command prompt, followed by the command-line equivalent of the service

You can also view information about each running service by starting Task Manager with CTRL-ALT-DEL and finding the executable for the service on the Processes tab. Use *kill.exe* from the Microsoft Windows NT Server Resource Kit to kill any runaway services that can't be stopped in the usual fashion. (Data loss may result.)

Table D-1: Dependencies of Exchange Services

Exchange Service	Depends on
Connector for Lotus cc:Mail	Directory Service Information Store Event Log
Directory	System Attendant
Directory Synchronization	Message Transfer Agent
Event Service[1]	Information Store
Information Store	Directory Service

Table D-1: Dependencies of Exchange Services (continued)

Exchange Service	Depends on
Internet Mail Service	Information Store Also requires TCP/IP protocol
Internet News Service	Information Store Also requires TCP/IP protocol
Message Transfer Agent	Directory Service
MS Mail Connector Interchange	Directory Service Event Log
MS Schedule+ Free/Busy Connector	Directory Service Information Store Event Log
MS Mail Connector (PC) MTA	System Attendant Event Log
System Attendant	Event Log NT LM Security Support Provider Remote Procedure Call (RPC) Locator Remote Procedure Call (RPC) Server Server Workstation

[1] The Exchange Event Service can only run on Public Folder servers and runs the Exchange Scripting Agent (when installed).

Table D-2: Exchange Service Executables

Exchange Service	Path	File
Connector for Lotus cc:Mail	*exchsrvr\connect\ccmail\bin*	*ccmc.exe*
Directory	*exchsrvr\bin*	*dsamain.exe*
Directory Synchronization	*exchsrvr\bin*	*dxa.exe*
Event Service[1]	*exchsrvr\bin*	*events.exe*
Key Management Server	*security\bin*	*kmserver.exe*
Information Store	*exchsrvr\bin*	*store.exe*
Internet Mail Service	*exchsrvr\connect\msexcimc\bin*	*msexcimc.exe*
Internet News Service	*exchsrvr\bin*	*exchins.exe*
Message Transfer Agent	*exchsrvr\bin*	*emsmta.exe*
MS Mail Connector Interchange	*exchsrvr\connect\msmcon\bin*	*mt.exe*
MS Schedule+ Free/Busy Connector	*exchsrvr\connect\msfbconn*	*msfbconn.exe*
System Attendant	*exchsrvr\bin*	*mad.exe*

[1] The Exchange Event Service can only run on Public Folder servers and runs the Exchange Scripting Agent (when installed).

Table D-3: Command-Line Equivalents of Exchange Services

Exchange Service	Command-Line Equivalent
Connector for Lotus cc:Mail	MSExchangeCCMC
Directory	MSExchangeDS
Directory Synchronization	MSExchangeDX
Event Service[1]	MSExchangeES
Information Store	MSExchangeIS
Internet Mail Service	MSExchangeIMC
Internet News Service	MSExchangeINS
Key Management Server	MSExchangeKMS
Message Transfer Agent	MSExchangeMTA
MS Mail Connector Interchange	MSExchangeMSMI
MS Mail Connector (PC) MTA	MSExchangePCMTA
MS Mail Connector (AppleTalk) MTA	MSExchangeATMTA
MS Schedule+ Free/Busy Connector	MSExchangeFB
System Attendant	MSExchangeSA

[1] The Exchange Event Service can only run on Public Folder servers and runs the Exchange Scripting Agent (when installed).

Table D-4: Exchange Event Source Identifiers for Application Log

Exchange Service	Event Source
Connector for Lotus cc:Mail	MSExchangeCCMC
Directory	MSExchangeDS
Directory Synchronization	MSExchangeDX
Event Service[1]	MSExchangeES
Information Store	MSExchangeIS Private MSExchangeIS Public
Internet Mail Service	MSExchangeIMC
Internet News Service	MSExchangeNNTP
Message Transfer Agent	MSExchangeMTA
MS Mail Connector Interchange	MSExchangeMSMI
MS Mail Connector (PC) MTA	MSExchangePCMTA
MS Mail Connector (AppleTalk) MTA	MSExchangeATMTA
MS Schedule+ Free/Busy Connector	MSExchangeFB
System Attendant	MSExchangeSA

[1] The Exchange Event Service can only run on Public Folder servers and runs the Exchange Scripting Agent (when installed).

APPENDIX E

Directories

This appendix deals with the Exchange Server directory structure created during setup.

Table E-1 shows the names of the Exchange directories and subdirectories along with their path relative to the root folder *\exchsrvr*. Note that running Performance Optimizer on a multi-drive system may give some of these directories different paths.

Table E-1: Default Directory Structure for Exchange Server

Directories	Subdirectories	Contains
\Add-ins		Subdirectories with extensions (DLLs) for various connectors as described later
	\Ins	File listing SMTP addresses of newsgroup moderators
	\Ms\I386	Extension for MS Mail Connector
	\Msfb\I386	Extension for MS Schedule+ Free/Busy Connector
	\Smtp\I386	Extension for Internet Mail Service
\Address		Subdirectories for email address proxy generators
	\Ccmail\I386	Lotus cc:Mail address proxy generator
	\Ms\I386	MS Mail address proxy generator
	\Smtp\I386	SMTP address proxy generator
	\X400\I386	X.400 address proxy generator
\bin		Exchange Administrator, Performance Optimizer, Migration Wizard, and other executables; Exchange core services; supporting DLLs and miscellaneous files

Directories	Subdirectories	Contains
\ccmdata		Subdirectories used as temporary storage by the Connector for cc:Mail and the Lotus *import.exe* and *export.exe* files
\connect		Subdirectories for Exchange optional services (connectors) as described later
	\Ccmail\bin	Binaries and supporting files for Connector for cc:Mail
	\Msexcimc\bin	Binaries and supporting files for Internet Mail Service
	\Msfbconn	Binary for MS Schedule+ Free/Busy Connector
	\Msmcon\Bin	Binaries and supporting files for MS Mail Connectors for PC and AppleTalk networks
	\Msmcon\Bin	Shadow Postoffice directories and files for MS Mail Connector
\docs		HTML and other files for Exchange Server Books Online
\Dsadata		Directory service database file (*dir.edb*) and associated files and transaction logs
\Dxadata		MS Mail for PC Networks directory synchronization database (*xdir.edb*) and associated files
\imcdata		Working directories for Internet Mail Service and the *queue.dat* file, which tracks messages being processed in the Internet Mail Service in and out queues
	\in	Inbound messages queued and waiting to be processed by the Internet Mail Service
	\log	The *route.txt* file, which lists the routes for which the Internet Mail Service is responsible, and log files when diagnostic logging for the SMTP Protocol category is increased to Medium or higher
	\out	Outbound messages queued by the Internet Mail Service
	\Pickup	Properly formatted SMTP message files can be manually dropped here (or moved to here by a script or application) and they will immediately be picked up and delivered by the Internet Mail Service
	\work	Temporary files
	\in\Archive	Copies of all inbound SMTP messages when diagnostic logging for the Message Archival category is set to Medium or higher. Also saves copies of incoming messages with data conversion problems

Directories	Subdirectories	Contains
	\out\Archive	Copies of all outbound SMTP messages when diagnostic logging for the Message Archival category is set to Medium or higher
	\Pickup\archive	Copies of all outbound SMTP messages dropped into the Pickup directory
\insdata		Working directories for the Internet News Service and the *Ics.dat* checkpoint file that tracks successful postings
	\log	Logs generated when protocol logging is enabled for the Internet News Service
\kmsdata		Files for Key Management (KM) Server, when installed
\mdbdata		Information store database files (*priv.edb* and *pub.edb*) and associated files and transaction logs
\mtadata		MTA database files (*db*.dat*) for temporary message storage (queuing), event log files (*Ev*.log*) of events logged to Application Log, a text version of the current Gateway Routing Table (*gwart0.mta*), and other files essential to the operation of the Message Transfer Agent (MTA)
	\Mtacheck.out	Results of running mtacheck utility either manually or automatically when the MTA is restarted
\Res		Miscellaneous Exchange DLLs for Event Viewer and Performance Monitor
\tracking.log		Log files used for message tracking (when enabled)
\Webdata		Components for Outlook Web Access, when installed

APPENDIX F

Share Points

This appendix deals with the Exchange Server shares created during setup.

Table F-1 lists the various Exchange share points and their permissions. You can restrict access to these shares by modifying the permissions, but this should be done carefully because problems can result. Do not change any of the permissions granted to the Exchange service account or to the Administrators local group.

Table F-1: Permissions for Exchange Share Points

Directory	Share Name	Purpose	User/Group Account	Permissions
\exchsrvr\ Add-ins	Add-ins	Provides access to Exchange Development Kit objects	Administrators	Full Control
			service_ account	Full Control
			Everyone	Read
\exchsrvr\ Address	Address	Provides access to address objects	Administrators	Full Control
			service_ account	Full Control
			Everyone	Read
\exchsrvr\ Connect	connect$	Provides access to gateway connectors	Administrators	Full Control
			service_ account	Full Control

Table F-1: Permissions for Exchange Share Points (continued)

Directory	Share Name	Purpose	User/Group Account	Permissions
\exchsrvr\ Connect\ Msmcom\ Maildata	maildat$	Provides access to MS Mail Interchange shadow postoffice	Everyone	Read
			Administrators	Full Control
			service_ account	Full Control
\exchsrvr\ Res	Resources	Provides access to Event logging files	Everyone	Full Control
			Administrators	Full Control
			service_ account	Full Control
\exchsrvr\ Tracking.log	tracking.log	Provides access to message tracking logs	Everyone	Read
			Administrators	Full Control
			service_ account	Full Control
			Everyone	Read

It may seem like a security risk for the *maildat$* share to be shared with Full Control for Everyone (and it is!), but unfortunately this is necessary because MS Mail 3.x is a *shared-file mail system* and all users must be able to create, delete, and modify files in the \maildata directory. You could replace the Full Control permissions with (RWXD)(RWXD) for the Everyone group (make sure you assign Full Control to CREATOR OWNER), but this really doesn't help since a user who knows the location of this hidden share can still instigate a denial-of-service attack by filling up the \maildata directory with junk files. The best you can really do is to configure auditing on the \maildata directory and regularly check your Event logs.

APPENDIX G

Ports

This appendix lists the various well-known TCP port numbers for Internet protocols on Exchange.

Table G-1 lists the TCP port for each Internet protocol, depending on the authentication method. When configuring a firewall between an Exchange server and the Internet, you may have to selectively enable these ports to provide remote users with access to the server. For example, for a POP3 client such as Outlook Express or Eudora to be able to connect to an Exchange server using Basic Authentication, the firewall must be configured to allow communication over port 110.

One important port number that is not listed in the table is port 135, which represents the Windows NT Remote Procedure Call (RPC) End-Point Mapper. Exchange servers listen on port 135 for MAPI clients such as Outlook that request a connection using RPCs. Once a connection is accepted, Exchange allocates two randomly chosen port numbers for the client to connect to the directory service and information store on the server. Similarly, if two Exchange servers are in the same site, they must be able to connect to each other using RPCs. Once a connection is accepted, the two servers allocate two randomly chosen port numbers for their directory services and MTAs to communicate with each other. If allocation of these random ports conflicts with the security configuration of your firewall, you can manually specify which ports will be allocated by Exchange for RPC access to the directory service, information store, and MTA. See *Microsoft Knowledge Base* articles Q155831, Q161931, and Q180795 for information on how to successfully accomplish this.

Finally, if two Exchange servers in different sites are connected to each other using the Site Connector, port 135 must be open along with an additional randomly chosen port for the MTAs to communicate. (See *Microsoft Knowledge Base* article Q161931 for info on how to manually specify the MTA port.) However, if the servers are connected using the X.400 Connector, port 135 is not required since there is no RPC traffic; instead these servers require that port 102 be open for ISO over TCP/IP traffic between the two MTAs.

Table G-1: Well-known Port Numbers for Internet Protocols on Exchange

Protocol	Authentication Method	Port Number
SMTP	Any	25
POP3	Basic or NTLM	110
	With SSL added	995
IMAP4	Basic or NTLM	143
	With SSL added	993
LDAP	Basic	389
	With SSL added	636
NNTP	Any	119
DNS	N/A	53
X.400	Any	102

Ports

APPENDIX H

Service Packs

This appendix summarizes the results of applying Exchange Server 5.5 Service Pack 1 (SP1) and Service Pack 2 (SP2).

Besides bug fixes, Service Pack 1 for Exchange Server 5.5 includes a number of new enhancements both to Exchange Server and to the Outlook client program. Table H-1 lists general server enhancements, Table H-2 enhancements related to coexistence and migration of foreign mail systems, and Table H-3 enhancements related to clients and collaboration. You need to install SP1 on *all* Exchange 5.5 servers in your organization to take full advantage of these enhancements.

Service Pack 2 for Exchange Server 5.5 includes additional bug fixes, Y2K-related fixes, and the enhancements listed in Table H-4. SP2 fixes and enhancements are cumulative; you don't need to install SP1 before installing SP2.

Table H-1: Service Pack 1 General Enhancements

Enhancement	Description
Key Management (KM) Server	KM Server has been updated to use Microsoft Certificate Server from the Windows NT 4.0 Option Pack as its Certificate Authority (CA). Key Management Server can manage and distribute public/private key pairs and X.509v3 digital certificates to clients such as Outlook 98, enabling them to send mail encrypted and signed using S/MIME. The Key Management Server also supports secure messaging between Exchange organizations using Certificate Trust Lists (CTLs).
Prevention of Unsolicited Commercial Email (UCE)	"Message Turfing" allows mail from specific DNS domains to be deleted.
MTA enhancements	Lets you control message priority, limits, and timeouts through Registry settings. Also lets you filter incoming X.400 mail by Originator name.

Table H-1: Service Pack 1 General Enhancements (continued)

Enhancement	Description
Free Space Message	Application Log now has regular messages estimating the remaining free space in the private and public information store databases.
Message Journalling	Saves copies of all mail messages sent or received by Exchange users, enabling administrators to record all email when required by law. Message Journalling is enabled through the Registry. Copies of messages can be saved to a mailbox, public folder, or custom recipient.
Clean Mailbox feature updated	Using Tools → Clean Mailbox, which lets administrators remove unwanted mail from users' mailboxes, now works with Outlook's special Calendar, Contacts, and Tasks folders and can be configured to work on either Received Date or Last Modified Date.
GUI changes	Miscellaneous updates to certain property sheets and dialog boxes.

Table H-2: Service Pack 1 Coexistence and Migration Enhancements

Enhancement	Description
Lotus Notes Mailbox Migration Tool	Exchange Migration Wizard now includes support for migration of mailbox and calendar information from Lotus Notes and Domino servers (releases 3.x and 4.x).
New connectors for DEC Alpha platforms	Connectors for OfficeVision/VM (PROFS) and SNADS.
Support for X.25 Winsock	X.400 connectors now support Winsock 2.0 using the Cirel X.25 card.

Table H-3: Service Pack 1 Client and Collaboration Enhancements

Enhancement	Description
Microsoft Outlook 98	Includes latest version of Outlook.
Outlook for Macintosh	Includes version of Outlook compatible with Mac OS Version 8 and Mac 68K platforms.
Outlook Web Access updates	Updated Outlook Web Access includes a contacts module, ability when sending mail to check names against the Exchange directory, and facility for user to change his Windows NT password.
Outlook HTML Form Converter	Wizard-based tool for converting Outlook-based forms to HTML forms based on Active Server Pages.
Exchange Routing Objects	Adds functionality to Exchange Scripting Agent to facilitate development of routing and approval applications.
Exchange Chat Service updates	Updated Exchange Chat Service includes Channel Transcription and Profanity Filter extensions.
Collaboration Data Objects (CDO) 1.21 update	Updated CDO supports both server and client-based applications.

Table H-4: Service Pack 2 Additional Enhancements

Enhancement	Description
InterOrg Replication Utility	Lets you selectively replicate public folder content and free/busy scheduling information between separate Exchange organizations either in unidirectional or bi-directional fashion
Move Server Wizard	Lets you move Exchange servers between sites and organizations without the need to reinstall
Lotus Notes Connector	Replicates directories and enables messaging with Lotus Notes systems
Importer for cc:Mail Archives	Lets you import information from cc:Mail personal email folders
Outlook for Macintosh	Updated client now includes support for S/MIME, read-only access to Outlook 97/98 calendars, and support for Mac OS 8.5

APPENDIX I

Links

This appendix lists some useful web sites, Usenet newsgroups, listservers, and zines that may be of help to the Exchange administrator.

Web Sites

http://www.slipstick.com
Slipstick Systems, the terrific Exchange site of Sue Mosher (MVP). Sue currently lives in Moscow and runs her SOHO business via the Internet. Chris Scharff reports that she may also run most of the former Soviet Union from her kitchen table as well, but these reports can neither be confirmed nor denied.

http://www.amrein.com/EWORLD
A great site, recommended by Charles Festel.

http://www.swinc.com
Excellent info on connecting Exchange to your ISP through the Internet Mail Connector.

http://www.exchangestuff.com
A lot of great third-party add-ons for Exchange.

http://www.msexchange.org
Much useful stuff in the archives, when they work.

http://www.mail-resources.com
This site should be running by June 1999. Chris Scharff claims it will be the coolest spot ever, but he's biased.

http://www.ema.org
Home of the Electronic Messaging Association (EMA), a lot of useful info on general X.400 messaging.

http://www.eema.org
>European Electronic Messaging Association (EEMA); more general X.400 messaging info.

http://support.microsoft.com/support
>When all else fails, as it often does.

http://www.microsoft.com/exchange
>A lot of great white papers on implementing Exchange.

http://www.microsoft.com/outlook
>Another obvious choice for similar reasons.

Usenet Newsgroups

microsoft.public.exchange.*
>The *.admin* group is the busiest and the most useful, generally.

microsoft.public.outlook.*
>More of the same.

microsoft.public.mail
>This is for MS Mail only.

comp.mail.headers
>Useful for discussing general SMTP header issues.

comp.mail.sendmail
>If you are using the Internet Mail Service on Exchange, you are probably connecting to your ISP's Sendmail box. This is a good place to share tips and ask for advice.

Listservers

http://www.msexchange.org
>This may have moved to *http://www.swynk.com* by the time this book is published.

http://www.swynk.com
>See the previous note.

http://lists.lansoft.com/mailing_lists/ms-exchange-l
>This is a low-traffic list with perhaps several hundred admins participating.

http://lists.lansoft.com/mailing_lists/ms-mail-l
>This is almost dead but still useful if you're connecting Exchange to legacy MS Mail systems.

http://www.jskay-consulting.com/e-lists.htm
>Join the list *Adv-Exchng* via a web interface for discussion of advanced support issues regarding Exchange.

Zines

Windows NT Exchange Administrator
>From the editors of *Windows NT Magazine*, you can access NTEA at *http://winntmag.com/exchange*.

APPENDIX J

BORK

This appendix lists some of the more useful Exchange-specific utilities included in the Microsoft BackOffice Resource Kit 2 (BORK 2):

CleanSweep
> Lets you delete bad forms, views, or rules templates.

Crystal Reports
> Lets you create reports from message tracking logs, address lists, and other data sources.

Import Header tool
> Use *Header.exe* to obtain create-header fields for performing Directory Import/Export.

Mailbox Cleanup Agent
> Lets you delete and move outdated messages from mailboxes.

MAPIsend
> Lets you send a message to an Exchange user from the command line.

ONDL
> Lets you display the membership of an Exchange distribution list (DL) from the command line.

Profile Generator
> Used for generating profiles for roaming Exchange users.

Unix Mail Source Extractor tool
> Helps you extract user accounts, messages, and associated information from Unix-based SMTP mail systems so that they can be imported using the Exchange Migration Wizard. This tool is provided as C source code and must be compiled on the host computer before being used.

Another useful tool you can obtain directly from Microsoft Product Support Services is the Microsoft Exchange Mailbox Merge program, or *exmerge.exe*. You can use this utility to check the integrity of mailboxes and to copy the contents of Exchange mailboxes to *.pst files. This is useful if a user's mailbox becomes corrupted and he can't access some of the messages in it.

Glossary

This is a brief glossary of Exchange-specific terminology. It does not include information about specific directory objects; for example, you will find an entry for Connector but not for the Site Connector. Look up directory objects in Chapter 3, *Directory*, for an explanation of these items.

Address book view
A subset of the global address list created according to common properties of its recipients

Address list
Any collection of recipients

Address space
A path consisting of a partial email address that a connector uses to deliver messages outside your site or organization

Alias name
A shortened version of the name of a mailbox owner that is used for addressing messages

Backbone
Any network that provides messaging transport between sites in your organization

Bridgehead server
An Exchange server that functions as the endpoint of a messaging connection between two sites and routes messages through the connection

Client permissions
Permissions that govern the access of public folder contents by users

Connector
Any Exchange component that can route messages between sites and to foreign mail systems

Container
> Any directory object in Exchange Administrator that can contain other directory objects

Custom recipient
> A recipient from a foreign mail system that is listed in the Global Address List

Delegate
> A user who has been granted permissions to manage or send mail on behalf of another user

Directory
> The X.500-based database that contains all information about the recipients, connectors, services, and configuration of an Exchange organization

Directory database
> See *Directory*

Directory export
> The process of exporting recipient information from the directory

Directory hierarchy
> The visible hierarchy of directory objects in the Exchange Administrator program window

Directory import
> The process of importing recipient information into the directory

Directory name
> The name of an object as stored internally in the Exchange directory database

Directory replication
> The process of replicating directory updates within and between sites

Directory replication bridgehead server
> An Exchange server that functions as the endpoint of directory replication between two sites and makes requests for directory updates

Directory service
> The Exchange server responsible for maintaining and replicating the directory in an Exchange organization

Directory synchronization
> The process of replicating directory information between an Exchange server and a MS Mail 3.x directory server; also sometimes used to refer to directory replication within a site.

Dirsync
> The MS Mail 3.x directory synchronization protocol or process

Display name
> The name of a directory object as displayed in the Exchange Administrator window

Distinguished Name (DN)
> A form of address that uniquely identifies each directory object within the Exchange directory database and is used for routing messages within your organization

---

Distribution List (DL)
   A mailing list; that is, a group of recipients to which a message can be sent as a single entity

Foreign mail system
   A mail system external to your Exchange organization, such as a Lotus cc:Mail network

Form
   Any structure that simplifies posting, viewing, or searching for information in public folders

Gateway
   A component that enables messaging connectivity with a foreign mail system; a connector

Global Address List (GAL)
   The superset of all address lists containing all recipients in an organization

Home server
   The Exchange server where a user's mailbox was created and which contains his folders, messages, and attachments

Inbound host
   A Usenet host that provides a newsfeed

Information store
   The central database of mailbox and public folder content on an Exchange server

Inherited permissions
   Permissions assigned to a container object that automatically flow down the hierarchy of objects inside a container

Knowledge Consistency Checker (KCC)
   A component of Exchange that periodically checks for new servers in your site and new sites in your organization

Leaf object
   Any directory object that is not a container; a directory object at the endpoint of a branch in the directory hierarchy

Mailbox
   The delivery location for messages that are incoming to a user

Mailbox template
   A mailbox with properties specified that is used as a template for creating new mailboxes, not as a receptacle for receiving messages

Message Transfer Agent (MTA)
   The component of Exchange responsible for routing messages to other servers or connectors

Newsfeed
   A flow of newsgroups and their messages from one Usenet host to another

One-off address
> An email address that you manually enter into the To: field of your messaging client program; used to send mail to users not listed in the Global Address List

Organization
> A collection of Exchange sites that share messaging connectivity and directory information

Originator/Recipient (O/R) address
> An X.400 address

Outbound host
> A Usenet host that receives a newsfeed

Private information store
> The portion of the information store that stores mailbox content

Public folder
> A folder on an Exchange server that is used for sharing information with other users

Public folder affinity
> A feature of Exchange that enables users in one site to access public folders on servers in a different site

Public folder replica
> A copy of the contents of a public folder

Public folder replication
> The process of keeping public folder replicas up to date

Public information store
> The portion of the information store that stores public folder content

Raw mode
> A mode of running the Exchange Administrator program that exposes the full schema attributes of objects in the directory

Recipient
> Any directory object that can receive messages, including mailboxes, custom recipients, distribution lists, mailbox agents, and public folders

Remote procedure call (RPC)
> A network protocol for client/server communication that requires dedicated connectivity

Role
> A set of permissions grouped together for a specific function

Routing
> The process of delivering messages

Routing table
> The Gateway Routing Table, or GWART, contains information that enables the MTA to route messages

Service account
> A Windows NT user account that is used as a security context in which to run Exchange services in a site or organization

Single-instance message
A message sent to more than one mailbox on the same Exchange server, as in a distribution list. Exchange stores only one instance of this message in the private information store in order to reduce disk storage requirements.

Site
One or more Exchange servers that share directory information through directory synchronization

Target server
An Exchange server that acts as an endpoint of a connection between two sites

Transaction log
A file that provides fault tolerance for an Exchange directory or information store database

Update Sequence Number (USN)
A number assigned to an object in the Exchange directory database and used in directory replication to ensure that directory replication updates are properly processed. Replication partners request all changes that the last USN received for each object.

Index

A

ADE (Automatic Directory Exchange), 94

ADMD (Administrative Management Domain), 338

Admin. role, 81

admin.exe utility, 305–310
(see also Microsoft Exchange Administrator)

administration tools for Exchange Server, 258–303

Administrative Directory Management Domain (ADDMD), 343

Administrative Management Domain (ADMD), 338

Administrator Mailbox setting (Schedule+ Free/Busy Connector Options), 174

"Administrator's mailbox" setting
General tab (Newsfeed), 190
Interchange tab (MS Mail Connector), 178

Connector for cc:Mail, 94

administrator-level account, 81

Administrators (CA objects), 89

Advanced Options button (Internet Mail tab), 146

Advanced tab
Address Book View, 85
Connections tab, Internet Mail Service, 149
Custom Recipients, 100
Mailbox, 166
Newsfeed, 192
Public Folders, 219
Public Information Store, 224
Server, 231
X.400 Connector, 256

Age Limits tab (Public Information Store), 223

Algorithms tab (Site Encryption Configuration), 247

Alias setting (public folders), 214

aliases for distribution lists, 118

All (View menu; Exchange Administrator), 273

Always setting
Dirsync Schedule, 95
Dynamic RAS Connector schedule, 125
X.400 Connector schedule, 254

Anonymous Account (DS Site Configuration), 121

Anonymous tab
IMAP4 (Mail) Site Defaults, 137
LDAP (Directory) Site Defaults, 157
NNTP (News) Site Defaults, 196

"Append to imported users' display name" setting
Dirsync Requestor, 113
Remote Dirsync Requestor, 226

architecture of Exchange servers, 37–39

assigning permissions (see permissions)

associated forms, 297

association parameters (MTAs), 184

Async connections, configuring, 180, 182

AU (Access Unit), X.400 protocol, 340

authentication
IMAP4 clients, 136
LDAP (Directory) Site Defaults, 156
NNTP (News) Site Defaults, 195
POP3 (Mail) Site Defaults, 204

Automatic Directory Exchange (ADE), 94

auto-naming conventions, 167

B

backing up server data, 292–295, 326

BackOffice Resource Kit 2, 365

Backup (see Windows NT Backup)

"Basic (Clear Text)" authentication
IMAP4 protocol, 136
LDAP4 protocol, 156
NNTP protocol, 195
POP3 protocol, 204

"Basic (Clear Text) using SSL" authentication
IMAP4 protocol, 137
LDAP4 protocol, 157
NNTP protocol, 195
POP3 protocol, 204

L

LAN connections
  configuring, 179
  configuring MTA for, 181
Language container
  Details Templates, 102
  One-Off Address Templates, 199
Last Modified Date (Sort By menu;
    Exchange Administrator), 274
latency period, 231
LDAP (Lightweight Directory Access
    Protocol), 44, 45, 155–158, 345
  configuring, 209
leaf objects, 72
least-cost routing, 67, 126, 244
"Leave as All Users With Access
    Permission" setting, 296
lifetime (MTAs), 184
"Limit administrative access to home
    site" setting, 214
Limits tab (Mailbox), 165
link monitors, 158, 175
  creating with Exchange
    Administrator, 266
  starting with Exchange Administrator,
    282
listservers, 162
  Exchange-related, 364
local bridgehead servers, 105
Local Modified status (Server
    Replication), 224
"Local MTA name and password"
    setting, 170
Local Postoffice tab (MS Mail
    Connector), 179
Local Procedure Calls (LPCs), 33, 39
Locales tab (Server), 230
locations (subsites), 60
Log Messages setting (Connector MTAs
    tab, MS Mail Connector), 181
logging
  circular logging, 231
  diagnostic (see Diagnostic Logging
    tab)
  levels of, 232
Logging Level setting (Schedule+ Free/
    Busy Connector Options), 175
Logon Rights, 81

Logons tab
  Private Information Store, 208
  Public Information Store, 223
Lotus cc:Mail, 93
  migrating data into Exchange,
    290–292
  Postoffice, 94
Lotus cc:Mail-type addresses, 163
LPCs (Local Procedure Calls), 33, 39

M

Mail 3.x, 10, 20
mail addresses (see addresses)
mail clients, 43–45
  client permissions, 82
  client-side messaging products, 9–15
  interoperability among, 15–22
  server compatibility charts, 20–22
Mail for AppleTalk Networks, 6
Mail for PC Networks, 4–6
Mail for Windows 3.x, 10
Mail Remote Client, 10
Mail Retrieval notification methods, 148
mail routing (see routing)
mail servers
  backing up data, 292–295, 326
  client compatibility charts, 20–22
  event configuration information, 129
  messaging bridgehead server, 250
  Move Server Wizard, 234
  performance optimization, 298–302,
    327–331
  Server container, 229
  server monitors, 175, 235
  server recipients, 238
  server-side messaging products, 3–9
  Servers container, 238
  single-server operation, 39–42
mailbox agents, 169
Mailbox Owner right, 80
Mailbox Resources tab (Private
    Information Store), 208
mailboxes, 160–168
  creating new accounts, 302
  distribution lists, 99, 117
  mailbox templates, 166

one-off addresses, 105
templates for, 197
"Only use least cost routes" setting, 171
open interval (MTAs), 184
operation of Exchange servers, 39–67
Exchange Administrator (see
Exchange Administrator)
mail clients, 43–45
multiple-server single-site operation,
50–56
multiple-site operation, 56–67
single-server operation, 39–42
MAPI message flow, 46–47
SMTP message flow, 47–49
optimizing server performance,
298–302, 327–331
optional components of Exchange
servers (list), 38
Options menu item
Exchange menu (User Manager for
Domains), 302
Tools menu (Exchange
Administrator), 286
Options setting (Connector MTAs tab,
MS Mail Connector), 181
organization, 200
Organization address space restriction,
60
Organization container, 200
permission inheritance and, 79
Organization forms library, 128, 201
Organization setting (Connected Sites,
RAS Connector), 126
Organization tab
Mailbox, 161
Recipients, 99
Originator/Recipient (O/R) addresses,
52, 64, 251
Other Settings (Exchange Administrator
Directory Export), 276
"Out of Office Responses to the
Internet" setting (Internet Mail
Service), 146
outbound hosts (newsfeeds), 190
"Outbound messages awaiting
conversion" message queue, 150
"Outbound messages awaiting delivery"
message queue, 151
outbound newsfeeds, 270

outbound sites, 106
Outbound tab (Newsfeed), 192
Outgoing Templates (Directory
Synchronization), 111
Outlook 97, 14, 19–20
Outlook 98, 14, 19–20, 295–297
Outlook 2000, 15
Outlook Express, 13, 18–20
Outlook Web Access, 13, 16
configuring, 133
Override tab
Site Connector, 245
X.400 Connector, 255
owl icon (in this book), x
owners of distribution lists, 118

P

Participation (Dirsync Requestor), 114
Password setting
Local Postoffice tab (MS Mail
Connector), 179
Remote DirSync Requestor, 226
Passwords (CA objects), 89
path notation in this book, ix
Performance Optimizer, 298–302,
327–331
perfwiz.exe utility, 298–302, 327–331
permissions, 79–82, 297
Address Book View, 85
share points, 356
Permissions Admin. role, 81
Permissions tab (property sheets), 78
(see also specific directory object)
Permit ADE setting (cc:Mail), 94
Personal forms library, 202
Phone Book Entry tab (Dynamic RAS
Connector), 125
Phone/Notes tab
Mailbox, 161
Recipients, 99
ping messages, 158
Pocket Outlook, 15
Polling Frequency setting (Connector
MTAs tab, MS Mail Connector),
181
POP3 protocol, 43–45, 50
configuring, 202–205, 209
port numbers, 358

SMTP protocol, 31
  configuring, 141
  single-server operation, 47–49
  X.400 protocol, 336–338
SMTP-type addresses, 52, 163
Sort By (View menu; Exchange
    Administrator), 274
source extractors, 287
SP1 and SP2 (service packs), 360–362
spam, denying, 147
splitbar (Exchange Administrator), 274
Stack tab (X.400 Connector), 254
Start Monitor (Tools menu; Exchange
    Administrator), 282
status bar (Exchange Administrator),
    274
Storage Limits setting
  Private Information Store, 207
  Public Information Store, 222
Storage Warnings tab (Information
    Store Site Configuration), 139
store-and-forward mail systems, 4
subsites (see locations)
synchronization, directory (see
    directory synchronization)
System Attendant (SA), 38
  configuring, 247
  Directory Service (DS) and, 40
  Information Store (IS) and, 41
  MTA and, 41
system data, backing up, 292–295, 326
system folders, 249

T

tabs (see property sheets, directory
    objects)
Target Servers tab (Site Connector), 244
target site (Site Connector), 244
TCP/IP protocol
  port numbers, 358
  transport stack, 185, 186
Tech Support container (Address Book
    View), 84
temp.edb file, 76
Template information (Dirsync
    Requestor), 114

Templates tab
  Details Templates, 103
  One-Off Address Templates, 200
This Location address space restriction,
    60
This Site address space restriction, 60
threshold parameter (MTAs), 184
Tombstone Lifetime (DS Site
    Configuration), 121
tombstone markers, 121
toolbar for Exchange Administrator,
    274, 284
Tools menu (Exchange Administrator),
    262, 274–286
Top Level Folder Creation tab
    (Information Store Site
    Configuration), 139
TP4 transport stack, 185, 187
Track Message (Tools menu; Exchange
    Administrator), 283
traffic, routing cost values and, 59
transaction log file, 73
transfer interval (MTAs), 184
Transfer mode (Connections tab,
    Internet Mail Service), 148
transfer timeout values (MTAs), 184
transport stacks, 185
  configurable settings, 254
  creating with Exchange
    Administrator, 267
troubleshooting
  monitor for (see monitors)
  MTAs, 323–326
trust levels, recipients, 113, 227
tuning performance, 298–302, 327–331
turkey icon (in this book), x
TURN mail retrieval notification, 148
Type setting
  Internet Mail Service Address Space,
    143
  RAS Connector Address Space, 126

U

UA component, X.400, 339
Unix users, 16–18
unsolicited commercial email, 147

About the Author

Mitch Tulloch is an independent trainer, consultant, and author living in Winnipeg, Canada. He is a Microsoft Certified Trainer (MCT) and Microsoft Certified Systems Engineer (MCSE) with almost 20 years of experience in teaching scientific and technical subjects. His home page can be found at *http://www.mtit.com*.

Colophon

Our look is the result of reader comments, our own experimentation, and feedback from distribution channels. Distinctive covers complement our distinctive approach to technical topics, breathing personality and life into potentially dry subjects.

The animal on the cover of *Microsoft Exchange Server in a Nutshell* is a southern lesser bush baby (*Galago moholi*), so named for its baby-like cries. These chipmunk-sized, brownish-grey South African primates are characterized by foldable ears, elongation of the tarsus (or upper part of the feet), and pads of thick skin on fingers and toes; these pads help them climb trees, where they sleep in nests and hollows during the day. At night, adults forage for insects and acacia gum, then return to the small family groups; the males are very territorial and urinate to scent their territory.

Bush babies usually travel by climbing and swinging through the trees. On the ground, they sit upright and move by jumping around on their hind legs. Their habitat includes woodland, savannah, and scrub desert. They mate every 4–8 months, and after a gestation period of 120 days, females give birth to about two offspring, which mature around 10 months of age and live up to 16 years.

Like many species, the southern lesser bush babies' existence is thought to be threatened as a result of habitat loss.

Jane Ellin was the production editor and proofreader for *Microsoft Exchange Server in a Nutshell*, Sheryl Avruch was the production manager, Sarah Jane Shangraw and Mary Anne Weeks Mayo provided quality control, and Betty Hugh, Maureen Dempsey, and Trisha Manoni provided production support. Mike Sierra provided FrameMaker technical support. Seth Maislin wrote the index.

Hanna Dyer designed the cover of this book, based on a series design by Edie Freedman. The image is an original illustration by Lorrie LeJeune. The cover layout was produced by Kathleen Wilson using Quark XPress 3.3 and the ITC Garamond font. Whenever possible, our books use RepKover™, a durable and flexible lay-flat binding. If the page count exceeds RepKover's limit, perfect binding is used.

The inside layout was designed by Nancy Priest and implemented in FrameMaker 5.5.6 by Mike Sierra. The text and heading fonts are ITC Garamond Light and Garamond Book. The illustrations that appear in the book were produced by Robert Romano and Rhon Porter using Macromedia FreeHand 8 and Adobe Photoshop 5. This colophon was written by Nancy Kotary.

14/6/01

MAPI32.DLL

copied from SP4

to BIN

& connect / msexcimc / bin

(on c:/exchsrvr)

started internal mail service

More Titles from O'Reilly

In a Nutshell Quick References

VB & VBA in a Nutshell: The Languages

By Paul Lomax
1st Edition October 1998
656 pages, ISBN 1-56592-358-8

For Visual Basic and VBA programmers, this book boils down the essentials of the VB and VBA languages into a single volume, including undocumented and little documented areas essential to everyday programming. The convenient alphabetical reference to all functions, procedures, statements, and keywords allows VB and VBA programmers to use this book both as a standard reference guide to the language and as a tool for troubleshooting and identifying programming problems.

Windows 95 in a Nutshell

By Tim O'Reilly & Troy Mott
1st Edition June 1998
528 pages, ISBN 1-56592-316-2

A comprehensive, compact reference that systematically unveils what serious users of Windows 95 will find interesting and useful, capturing little known details of the operating system in a consistent reference format.

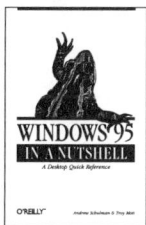

Windows NT in a Nutshell

By Eric Pearce
1st Edition June 1997
364 pages, ISBN 1-56592-251-4

Anyone who installs Windows NT, creates a user, or adds a printer is an NT system administrator (whether they realize it or not). This book features a new tagged callout approach to documenting the 4.0 GUI as well as real-life examples of command usage and strategies for problem solving, with an emphasis on networking. *Windows NT in a Nutshell* will be as useful to the single-system home user as it will be to the administrator of a 1,000-node corporate network.

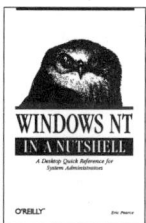

UML in a Nutshell

By Sinan Si Alhir
1st Edition September 1998
290 pages, ISBN 1-56592-448-7

The Unified Modeling Language (UML), for the first time in the history of systems engineering, gives practitioners a common language. This concise quick reference explains how to use each component of the language, including its extension mechanisms and the Object Constraint Language (OCL). A tutorial with realistic examples brings those new to the UML quickly up to speed.

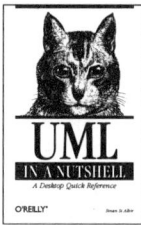

Year 2000 in a Nutshell

By Norman Shakespeare
1st Edition September 1998
330 pages, ISBN 1-56592-421-5

This reference guide addresses the awareness, the managerial aspect, and the technical issues of the Year 2000 computer dilemma, providing a compact compendium of solutions and reference information useful for addressing the problem.

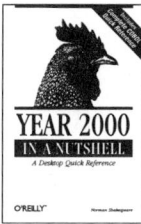

Windows 98 in a Nutshell

By Tim O'Reilly & Troy Mott
1st Edition August 1999 (est.)
600 pages (est.), ISBN 1-56592-486-X

From the authors of the bestselling Windows 95 in a Nutshell comes this easy-to-use quick reference for all serious users of Windows 98. It summarizes differences between Windows 95 and Windows 98, covers almost every Windows 98 command and utility available, gives advice for using the Registry, includes short-hand instructions on many important Win98 tasks, and much more.

In a Nutshell Quick References

Visual Basic Controls in a Nutshell

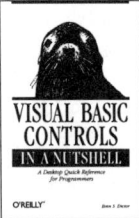

By Evan S. Dictor
1st Edition July 1999 (est.)
686 pages (est.), ISBN 1-56592-294-8

This quick reference covers one of the crucial elements of Visual Basic: its controls, and their numerous properties, events, and methods. It provides a step-by-step list of procedures for using each major control and contains a detailed reference to all properties, methods, and events. Written by an experienced Visual Basic programmer, it helps to make painless what can sometimes be an arduous job of programming Visual Basic.

MCSE

MCSE: The Electives in a Nutshell

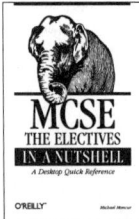

By Michael Moncur
1st Edition September 1998
372 pages, ISBN: 1-56592-482-7

A companion volume to *MCSE: The Core Exams in a Nutshell* (a five-star book per reader reviews at amazon.com), this comprehensive study guide covers the most important and popular elective exams for the MCSE, as well as the Internet requirements and electives for the MCSE+Internet. For sophisticated users who need a bridge between real-world experience and the MCSE exam requirements.

MCSE

MCSE: The Core Exams in a Nutshell

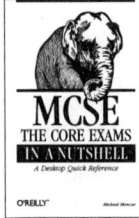

By Michael Moncur
1st Edition June 1998
416 pages, ISBN 1-56592-376-6

MCSE: The Core Exams in a Nutshell is a detailed quick reference for administrators with Windows NT experience or experience administering a different platform, such as UNIX, who want to learn what is necessary to pass the MCSE required exam portion of the MCSE certification. While no book is a substitute for real-world experience, this book will help you codify your knowledge and prepare for the exams.

Networking Essentials Flashcards

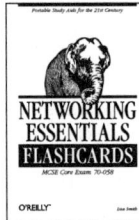

By Lisa Smith, Trident Data Systems
1st Edition March 1999
280 double-sided cards
ISBN 1-56592-568-8

You need to remember a lot of terminology, acronyms, and facts to pass the MCSE exams. An ideal complement to *MCSE: The Core Exams in a Nutshell*, these flashcards will help you memorize all the key facts you need for Exam #70-058, Networking Essentials. Convenient for quick study sessions on the subway or bus.

O'REILLY®

TO ORDER: **800-998-9938** • **order@oreilly.com** • **http://www.oreilly.com/**
OUR PRODUCTS ARE AVAILABLE AT A BOOKSTORE OR SOFTWARE STORE NEAR YOU.
FOR INFORMATION: **800-998-9938** • **707-829-0515** • **info@oreilly.com**

How to stay in touch with O'Reilly

1. Visit Our Award-Winning Site

http://www.oreilly.com/

★ "Top 100 Sites on the Web" —*PC Magazine*
★ "Top 5% Web sites" —*Point Communications*
★ "3-Star site" —*The McKinley Group*

Our web site contains a library of comprehensive product information (including book excerpts and tables of contents), downloadable software, background articles, interviews with technology leaders, links to relevant sites, book cover art, and more. File us in your Bookmarks or Hotlist!

2. Join Our Email Mailing Lists

New Product Releases

To receive automatic email with brief descriptions of all new O'Reilly products as they are released, send email to:
listproc@online.oreilly.com
Put the following information in the first line of your message (*not* in the Subject field):
subscribe oreilly-news

O'Reilly Events

If you'd also like us to send information about trade show events, special promotions, and other O'Reilly events, send email to:
listproc@online.oreilly.com
Put the following information in the first line of your message (*not* in the Subject field):
subscribe oreilly-events

3. Get Examples from Our Books via FTP

There are two ways to access an archive of example files from our books:

Regular FTP

- ftp to:
  ftp.oreilly.com
  (login: anonymous
  password: your email address)
- Point your web browser to:
  ftp://ftp.oreilly.com/

FTPMAIL

- Send an email message to:
  ftpmail@online.oreilly.com
  (Write "help" in the message body)

4. Contact Us via Email

order@oreilly.com
To place a book or software order online. Good for North American and international customers.

subscriptions@oreilly.com
To place an order for any of our newsletters or periodicals.

books@oreilly.com
General questions about any of our books.

software@oreilly.com
For general questions and product information about our software. Check out O'Reilly Software Online at **http://software.oreilly.com/** for software and technical support information. Registered O'Reilly software users send your questions to:
website-support@oreilly.com

cs@oreilly.com
For answers to problems regarding your order or our products.

booktech@oreilly.com
For book content technical questions or corrections.

proposals@oreilly.com
To submit new book or software proposals to our editors and product managers.

international@oreilly.com
For information about our international distributors or translation queries. For a list of our distributors outside of North America check out:
http://www.oreilly.com/www/order/country.html

O'Reilly & Associates, Inc.
101 Morris Street, Sebastopol, CA 95472 USA
TEL   707-829-0515 or 800-998-9938
          (6am to 5pm PST)
FAX   707-829-0104

O'REILLY®

International Distributors

UK, EUROPE, MIDDLE EAST AND AFRICA (EXCEPT FRANCE, GERMANY, AUSTRIA, SWITZERLAND, LUXEMBOURG, LIECHTENSTEIN, AND EASTERN EUROPE)

INQUIRIES
O'Reilly UK Limited
4 Castle Street
Farnham
Surrey, GU9 7HS
United Kingdom
Telephone: 44-1252-711776
Fax: 44-1252-734211
Email: josette@oreilly.com

ORDERS
Wiley Distribution Services Ltd.
1 Oldlands Way
Bognor Regis
West Sussex PO22 9SA
United Kingdom
Telephone: 44-1243-779777
Fax: 44-1243-820250
Email: cs-books@wiley.co.uk

FRANCE

ORDERS
GEODIF
61, Bd Saint-Germain
75240 Paris Cedex 05, France
Tel: 33-1-44-41-46-16 (French books)
Tel: 33-1-44-41-11-87 (English books)
Fax: 33-1-44-41-11-44
Email: distribution@eyrolles.com

INQUIRIES
Éditions O'Reilly
18 rue Séguier
75006 Paris, France
Tel: 33-1-40-51-52-30
Fax: 33-1-40-51-52-31
Email: france@editions-oreilly.fr

GERMANY, SWITZERLAND, AUSTRIA, EASTERN EUROPE, LUXEMBOURG, AND LIECHTENSTEIN

INQUIRIES & ORDERS
O'Reilly Verlag
Balthasarstr. 81
D-50670 Köln
Germany
Telephone: 49-221-973160-91
Fax: 49-221-973160-8
Email: anfragen@oreilly.de (inquiries)
Email: order@oreilly.de (orders)

CANADA (FRENCH LANGUAGE BOOKS)

Les Éditions Flammarion ltée
375, Avenue Laurier Ouest
Montréal (Québec) H2V 2K3
Tel: 00-1-514-277-8807
Fax: 00-1-514-278-2085
Email: info@flammarion.qc.ca

HONG KONG

City Discount Subscription Service, Ltd.
Unit D, 3rd Floor, Yan's Tower
27 Wong Chuk Hang Road
Aberdeen, Hong Kong
Tel: 852-2580-3539
Fax: 852-2580-6463
Email: citydis@ppn.com.hk

KOREA

Hanbit Media, Inc.
Sonyoung Bldg. 202
Yeksam-dong 736-36
Kangnam-ku
Seoul, Korea
Tel: 822-554-9610
Fax: 822-556-0363
Email: hant93@chollian.dacom.co.kr

PHILIPPINES

Mutual Books, Inc.
429-D Shaw Boulevard
Mandaluyong City, Metro
Manila, Philippines
Tel: 632-725-7538
Fax: 632-721-3056
Email: mbikikog@mnl.sequel.net

TAIWAN

O'Reilly Taiwan
No. 3, Lane 131
Hang-Chow South Road
Section 1, Taipei, Taiwan
Tel: 886-2-23968990
Fax: 886-2-23968916
Email: benh@oreilly.com

CHINA

O'Reilly Beijing
Room 2410
160, FuXingMenNeiDaJie
XiCheng District
Beijing
China PR 100031
Tel: 86-10-86631006
Fax: 86-10-86631007
Email: frederic@oreilly.com

INDIA

Computer Bookshop (India) Pvt. Ltd.
190 Dr. D.N. Road, Fort
Bombay 400 001 India
Tel: 91-22-207-0989
Fax: 91-22-262-3551
Email: cbsbom@giasbm01.vsnl.net.in

JAPAN

O'Reilly Japan, Inc.
Kiyoshige Building 2F
12-Bancho, Sanei-cho
Shinjuku-ku
Tokyo 160-0008 Japan
Tel: 81-3-3356-5227
Fax: 81-3-3356-5261
Email: japan@oreilly.com

ALL OTHER ASIAN COUNTRIES

O'Reilly & Associates, Inc.
101 Morris Street
Sebastopol, CA 95472 USA
Tel: 707-829-0515
Fax: 707-829-0104
Email: order@oreilly.com

AUSTRALIA

WoodsLane Pty., Ltd.
7/5 Vuko Place
Warriewood NSW 2102
Australia
Tel: 61-2-9970-5111
Fax: 61-2-9970-5002
Email: info@woodslane.com.au

NEW ZEALAND

Woodslane New Zealand, Ltd.
21 Cooks Street (P.O. Box 575)
Waganui, New Zealand
Tel: 64-6-347-6543
Fax: 64-6-345-4840
Email: info@woodslane.com.au

LATIN AMERICA

McGraw-Hill Interamericana
Editores, S.A. de C.V.
Cedro No. 512
Col. Atlampa
06450, Mexico, D.F.
Tel: 52-5-547-6777
Fax: 52-5-547-3336
Email: mcgraw-hill@infosel.net.mx

O'REILLY®

O'REILLY WOULD LIKE TO HEAR FROM YOU

Which book did this card come from?

_____

Where did you buy this book?
- ❏ Bookstore
- ❏ Direct from O'Reilly
- ❏ Bundled with hardware/software
- ❏ Other _____

What operating system do you use?
- ❏ UNIX
- ❏ Windows NT
- ❏ Macintosh
- ❏ PC(Windows/DOS)
- ❏ Other _____

- ❏ Computer Store
- ❏ Class/seminar

What is your job description?
- ❏ System Administrator
- ❏ Network Administrator
- ❏ Web Developer
- ❏ Other _____
- ❏ Programmer
- ❏ Educator/Teacher

- ❏ Please send me O'Reilly's catalog, containing a complete listing of O'Reilly books and software.

Name _____ Company/Organization _____

Address _____

City _____ State _____ Zip/Postal Code _____ Country _____

Telephone _____ Internet or other email address (specify network) _____

Nineteenth century wood engraving
of a bear from the O'Reilly &
Associates Nutshell Handbook®
Using & Managing UUCP.

POST CARD

‖‖‖

BUSINESS REPLY MAIL
FIRST CLASS MAIL   PERMIT NO. 80   SEBASTOPOL, CA

Postage will be paid by addressee

O'Reilly & Associates, Inc.
101 Morris Street
Sebastopol, CA 95472-9902